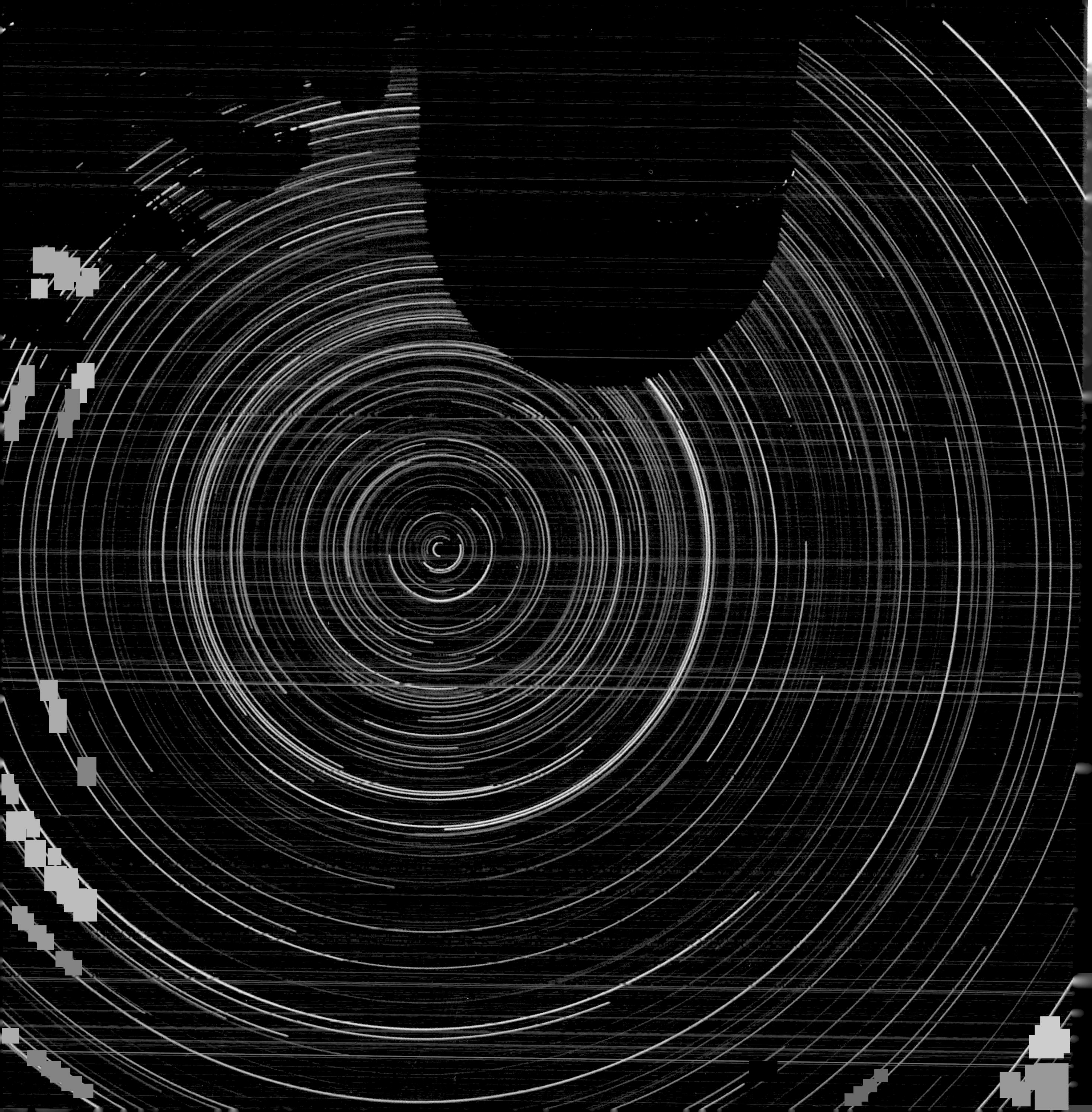

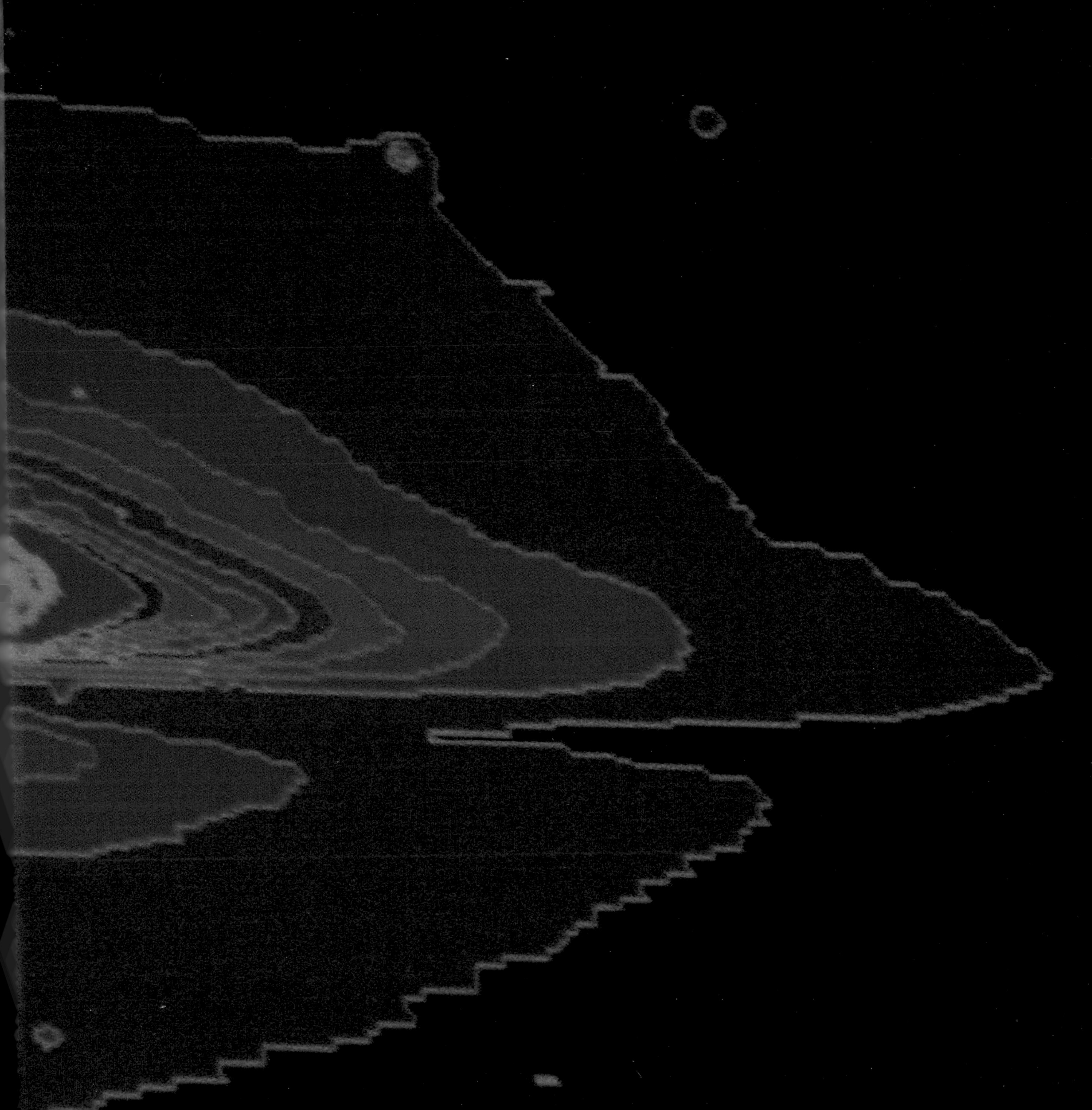

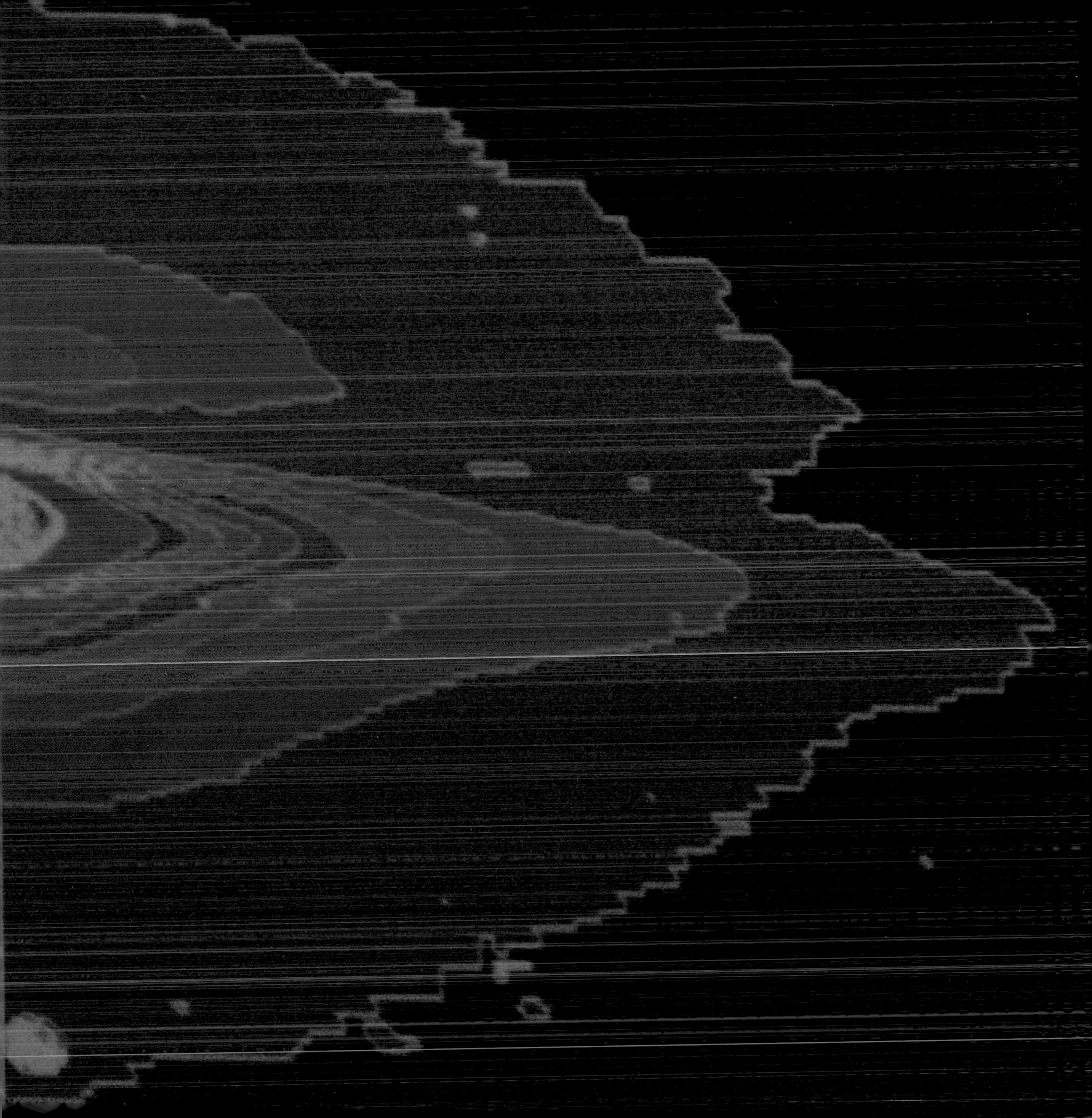

Also by James Trefil:

Physics as a Liberal Art

The Unexpected Vista

Living in Space

Are We Alone? (with Robert Rood)

From Atoms to Quarks

The Moment of Creation

A Scientist at the Seashore

SpaceTimeInfinity

James S. Trefil

The Smithsonian Views the Universe

Introductory Essays by Kenneth L. Franklin

Pantheon Books
New York

Smithsonian Books
Washington

Smithsonian Books
Editor-in-Chief Patricia Gallagher
Senior Editor Alexis Doster III
Project Editor Joe Goodwin
Editor Amy Donovan
Assistant Editor John F. Ross
Project Picture Editor Nancy Strader
Picture Editor Frances C. Rowsell
Picture Researchers R. Jenny Takacs, Bonnie Stutski
Production Consultant Irv Garfield
Production Editor Patricia Upchurch
Production Assistant June G. Armstrong
Business Manager Stephen J. Bergstrom
Marketing Consultant William H. Kelty
Marketing Manager Margaret Kei Mooney
Marketing Assistant Melanie Levenson

Design Phil Jordan
Mechanical Preparation Barbara Page, Mannie Tobie, Mary Gephart
Headline Type Julian Waters
Copy Editor Terence Winch
Separations Lehigh Press Colortronics
Typography Carver Photocomposition, Inc.
Printing W. A. Krueger Company

Manufactured in the United States of America

Library of Congress Cataloging-in-Publication Data

Trefil, James S., 1938–
Space, time, infinity.

Includes Index.
1. Astronomy—History. 2. Cosmology—History.
I. Smithsonian Institution. II. Title.
QB32.T74 1985 520 85-42940
ISBN 0-394-54843-4

First Edition
5 4 3

Dedication

Many of us have wondered how—as poets and songwriters suggest—to "hitch your wagon to a star," or "carry moonbeams home in a jar." Astronomers, both professional and the amateur, have learned how to manage both of these tricky maneuvers. We also note that the professionals almost invariably started out as amateurs, and that today's amateurs are often very professional in their methods and theoretical approach to this most ancient science. Yet, in another sense, astronomy is the newest of sciences now that astrophysics and cosmology have become an integral part of it. Whether experienced through planetarium shows or the eyepiece of one's own scope, astronomy is a mighty opener of horizons. Thus the author and the staff of Smithsonian Books dedicate *Space, Time, Infinity* to amateur stargazers. Most especially, though, we wish to recognize those amateurs who today raise a remarkable hobby to the level of fine art and splendid science. Truly, they are voyagers through space and time.

Contents

Page 1, wheeling around the South Celestial pole, stars silhouette a telescope dome of the Anglo-Australian Observatory; 2-3, Galaxy M 104 appears in a visually enhanced version that highlights changes in the shape from center to edge; 4-5, Comet West from the mid-seventies photographed by Ronald E. Royer and Steve Padilla. Woodcut above from the Nuremberg Chronicle *of 1493.*

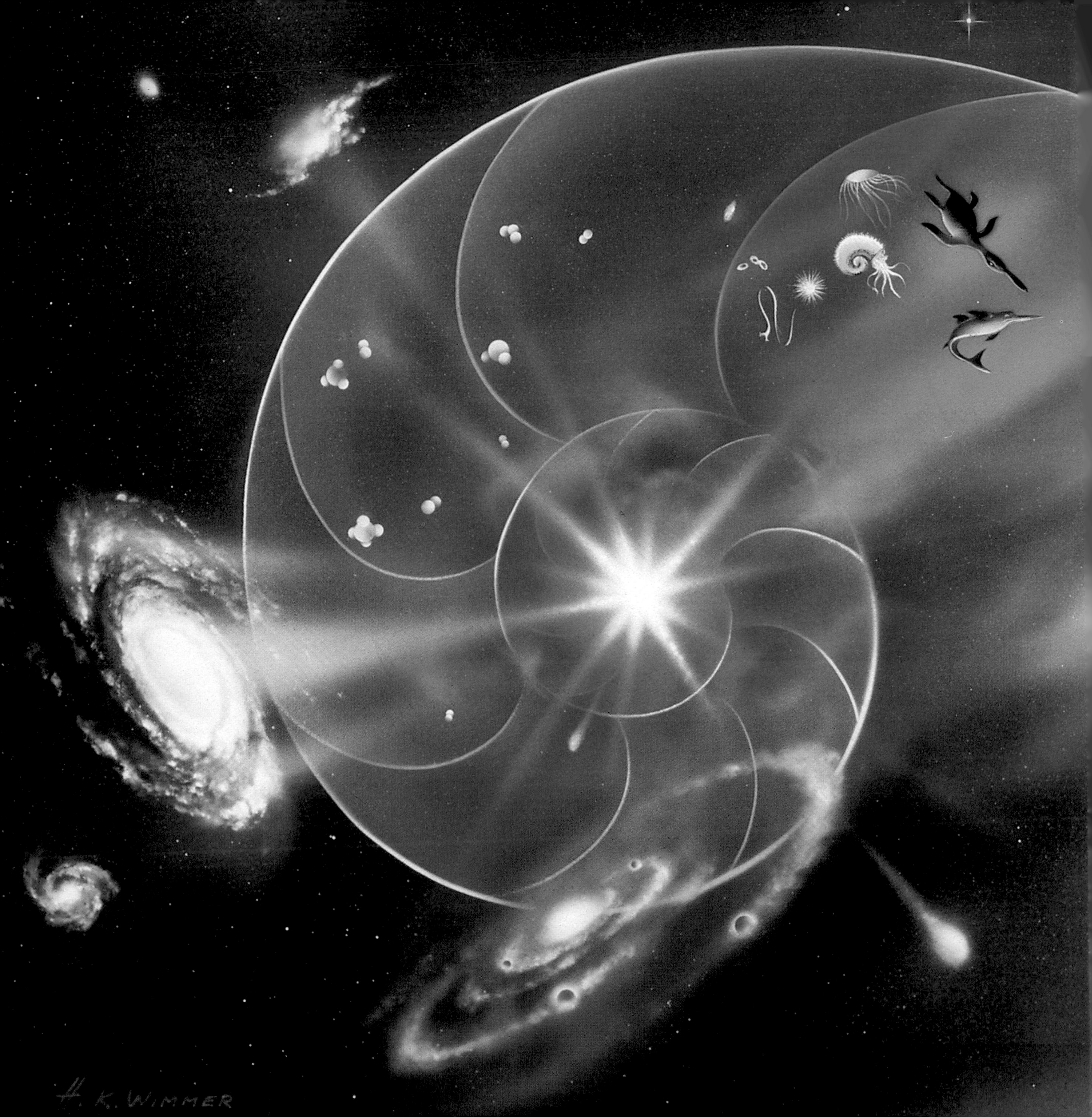
H. K. WIMMER

Prologue

The First Yesterday

Overleaf: In a specially commissioned panorama covering time since the Big Bang, Helmut Wimmer captures the drama of creation itself. Now, through the eyes of both scientists and artists, we can look back with confidence to recognize our kinship with the stars and the ages.

How it began, no one is quite sure. The evidence strongly suggests, however, that a tiny fraction of a second after the moment of its creation, our universe consisted of a dense, rapidly expanding collection of matter. It wasn't the familiar, homey kind of stuff that surrounds us now, sedately composed of atoms, but a swarm of strange and exotic particles with names like *gluon*, *quark*, and *boson*. Impossibly dense, impossibly hot, the universe expanded; and as it did so, it cooled. The cooling, in turn, wrought changes in the matter, something along the lines of water freezing into ice.

In the case of the universe, one such change followed another as what passed for matter cooled through the various phase changes. Before the first microsecond had elapsed, the universe had "frozen" three times, each time becoming relatively more familiar, as the exotic particles present at the beginning combined or decayed to produce matter in a more organized and potentially recognizable form.

After about 10 microseconds, the important fourth freezing occurred. Those particles we call quarks came together to form other, more familiar particles. These include the protons and neutrons that exist today in the nuclei of atoms.

But the temperature was still far too high, and the collisions of the particles too violent, for anything so complex as a nucleus to remain intact. After three minutes, the temperature had dropped to the point where nuclei of hydrogen and helium atoms swam in a sea consisting of loose electrons mixed with the hot radiation left over from the first seconds. All the building blocks of modern materials existed in their final forms. Time alone was needed for cooling until the electrons and the nuclei could come together to make atoms.

This required another half million years, during which the mixture of nuclei, electrons, and radiation continued to expand and cool. The outward pressure of radiation kept the particles spread out so that little or no clumping occurred. Once atoms were formed, however, the matter in the universe became transparent and the radiation could no longer exert as much pressure as before. From then on, the force of gravity began to dominate the behavior of the universe.

Here and there, scattered throughout the uniform distribution of atoms that filled space, we see small concentrations of matter. How they came about is still a subject of debate, but their effect is clear. Because the mass at these points was higher than normal, nearby atoms were pulled into the concentration zone by the force of gravity. The new atoms, in turn, added their contribution to the force of gravity and yet more material was attracted. In short order, the smeared-out collection of atoms that characterized the universe prior to the 500-million-year mark was transformed into a collection of large, discrete clouds of material. Inside these clouds, the same process of gravitational clumping went on, dividing the newly formed clouds into smaller clouds that would eventually become the clusters of galaxies. At the same time, the overall expansion that started with the Big Bang continued; the distances between groups of galaxies continued to increase.

Shifting our attention from the overall structure of the universe to a single protogalaxy, we see the gravitational forces continuing to segregate the gas cloud into small pieces. As these small bits of gas contracted, the pressure and temperature at their centers began to increase. It quickly became so hot that electrons were stripped from the atoms. Soon temperatures rose to the point where nuclear reactions were ignited and hydrogen fused into helium. The energy streaming out from the new fusion furnace created a pressure that balanced the inward force of gravity, and stars were born.

These early suns were made from a gas containing only the primordial atoms of hydrogen and helium that were created three minutes after the Big Bang; but the nuclear reactions that went on during the life and death of the early stars quickly produced other chemical elements. Explosions and other less dramatic star deaths dispersed metal-rich gases into the clouds of the newborn galaxies. Stars that emerged from such a polluted medium contained chemical elements heavier than helium and hydrogen. As they matured and died, these stars also manufactured new atoms of their own. In essence, they operated like the legendary alchemical crucible—transmuting one element into another. This slow process of star creation, element production, and star death went on for about 10 billion years in galaxies throughout the universe.

Then, about five billion years ago, a particular bit of enriched gas began to contract. It was located about a third of the way out in the arm of a spiral galaxy we call the Milky Way. It also began to spin faster and faster, much as ice skaters do by pulling their arms in closer to the body. The rotation became so fast that, while most of the gas in the clouds wound up in the newly forming star, some was left spread out in a thin disk. As the star was forming, this disk broke up and arranged itself (by a process whose details are poorly understood) into a series of relatively small bodies orbiting the hub. The center grew denser and hotter. When the star finally ignited, the resulting stream of outgoing particles blew the remaining gas from the system, leaving a sun with planets—nine at best count.

On the third planet, a series of rather extraordinary events started to unfold, beginning with the evolution of an atmosphere and—after a billion years—culminating with a series of simple one-celled organisms we would grace with the title "living creatures." They spread, became more complex, and, after billions of years, moved from the oceans to the land. Eventually the planet came to be dominated by huge reptiles. They, like other species before them, passed on and mammals moved to center stage, and for more than 60 million years the world teemed with their forms.

Finally, a few million years ago, the first of our lineage appeared upon the planet. The iron in their blood, the calcium in their bones, and the carbon in their tissues were all the stuff of stars. These new creatures gradually learned the use of primitive stone tools, then fire. Social groups developed agriculture and built powerful and long lasting civilizations based upon their accumulated wealth. Somewhere along the line—no one really knows when—some human being somewhere looked back up at the stars and wondered.

That's where our story begins.

The massive star eta Carinae shines from a dusty nebula called the Homunculus or "little man." This computer-enhanced image shows what may be a star very near to the end of its life and ready to blow itself apart in a supernova. The blast could stimulate the conception of new stars while the ashes feed their growth.

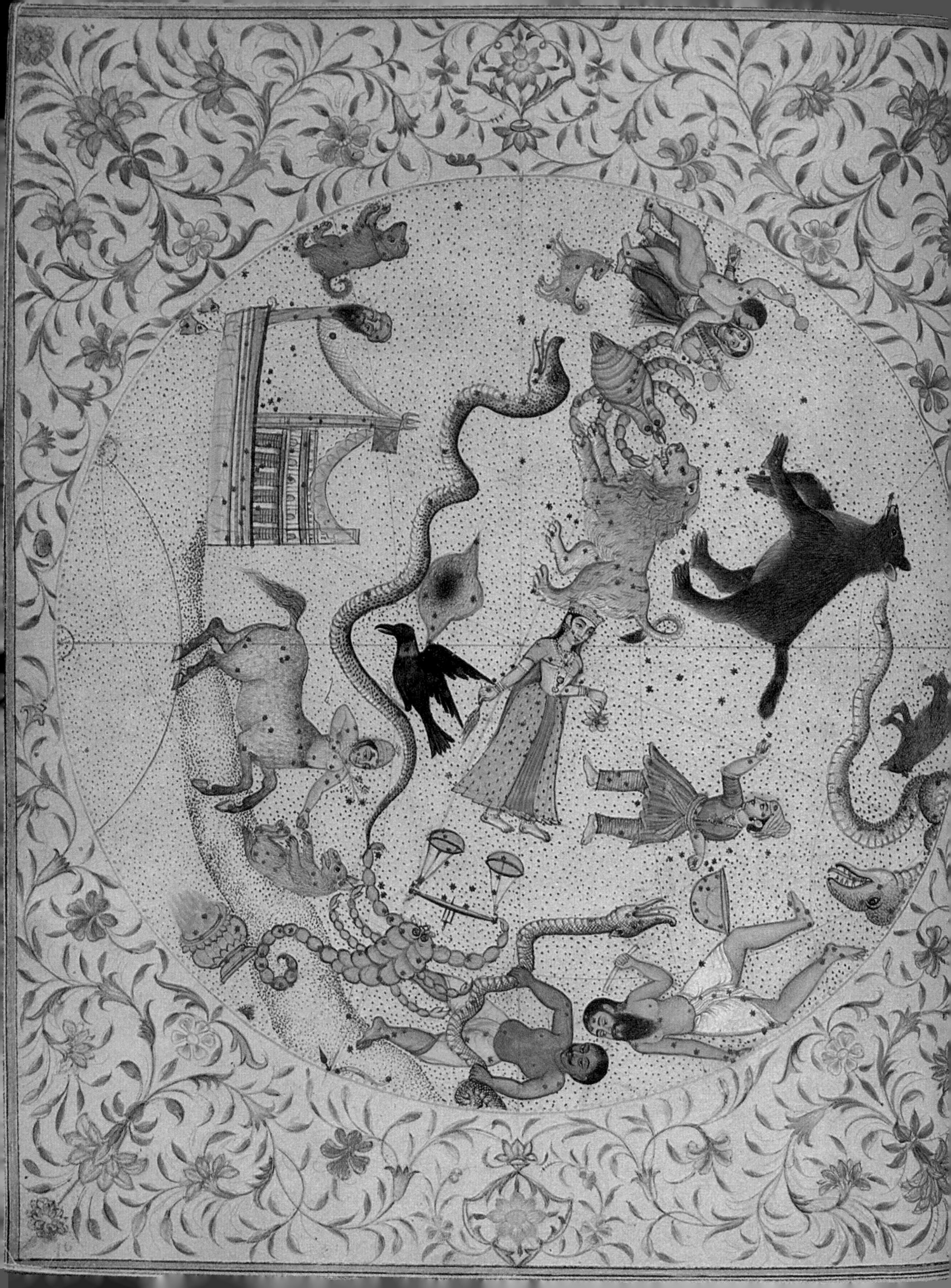

Part 1

The Oldest Science

Overleaf: Though draped in Eastern garb, the familiar figures of the Western constellations roam the sky with animals of the zodiac. They are part of a treatise from India called "Jewel of the essence of all sciences." Painted before 1840, this astrological work abounds with Greek and Islamic touches, including an elaborate floral border reminiscent of Persian textiles and mythical beasts of the Mediterranean. American Indian rock art from New Mexico displays a star and a spiral, among the oldest of all sky symbols, opposite.

In the many pages to follow, you will be led through a fine introduction into how astronomers and other celestial workers view our universe today. We must say "today" because tomorrow other researchers may have a significantly different picture to paint. But as you read, remember that people have not always known what we know today, and that people of the distant past would not have been able to understand what we would have to tell them.

The universe had to be discovered before it could be understood.

In your imagination, drift back a few thousand years to a time when people were beginning to emerge from their long existence as hunter-gatherers. Some developed the enterprise we know as agriculture. Others were concerned with animals that had to be moved from place to place to find the food they needed. These people became nomadic, as they herded their animals, season by season, following nature's varying supply of fodder.

The lives and cultures of people in these separate groups steadily diverged. Yet they shared the same sky. Farmer and herder—Cain and Abel—both got wet when it rained. And lightning and thunder were terrifying to all. And each night, people looked up to see the same star patterns wheel across the sky. Yet there were some brighter points of light that seemed to defy the laws of regularity that obviously ruled the vast majority of "sky folk." Yes, they rose and set like the others, but they wandered from place to place, sometimes going eastward among the sky folk, sometimes reversing, dancing their way through time.

People almost always attempt to figure out how some phenomenon can be explained. Today, we call the results of such an attempt a model. But in all ages, such stories and scenarios are only approximations of reality, aids to thinking. They can never be so complex (nor as simple) as the real thing—never as real. And a model must be constructed from the ideas that people or, at least, the model "builders," have in mind. It must be understandable in terms of whatever is known at the time.

The people of antiquity could conceive of nothing mechanical to explain the motions and behavior of the wandering stars. Since they obviously violated the rules for the common stars, the planets must be, or represent, the gods themselves. Thus we find that the first model of the planetary system—the known world of those days—was a supernatural model.

Even today, the names of the planets reflect that ancient first suggestion about the nature of the world. Elusive Mercury was the fleet messenger of the gods. And ruddy Mars, a wandering star, was named for the gory god of war. Usually every two years he would return to our view, seeming to come back from some mysterious campaign. But at times, he would return quietly, licking his wounds, not shining very brightly, just enough to be seen. Then in intervals varying between 15 and 17 years, he would return in a mighty triumph, even outshining omnipotent Jupiter.

The king of the gods, Father Zeus, Zeus Pater, Jupiter, as the Romans slurred the name, is still the planet that each thirteen months clearly dominates the sky for the entire night, outshining all but Venus—a goddess who retires early each evening—and the occasionally boastful Mars. Then there is Saturn, the god of Time, the slowest of these heavenly bodies, moving around the starry sky in a stately 30 years.

As the priests in charge of sky watching began to understand the rules governing planetary behavior, they could make accurate predictions of which gods would visit which, and where and when such meetings were to take place. The common folk of the earth must have held these priests in awe for the foreknowledge they possessed.

It is clearly in such a context that the venerable "science" of astrology was born.

It fell to an early Greek philosopher, one Eudoxus of Cnidus who flourished about 350 B.C., to find the first mechanical model of the universe (as the planetary system was known for millennia). He followed his senses. If one saw something move, then it moved! Thus it was obvious to him that the sky moved past our world. That meant the earth was fixed and, surely, no one ever felt the regular motion of it. The moon revolved about us and that was that! The sun also moved around the earth but much more slowly. It appeared to make sense to have everything—planets included—revolve around us. What could be more obvious: we live at the center of the universe.

We are still making models—or theories, according to the terminology popular in Einstein's day. By the time the reader reaches the last chapter of this introductory section, he or she will have gained a strong sense of all the varied work and workers that were required to make the first strong scientific theories. Here, too, the reader will witness the birth of cosmology, that apex of all the sciences—in which humans attempt to know space and time as gods must know them.

K.L.F.

The Beginnings

historians tell us that astronomy is the oldest of the physical sciences, and that one of the first tasks that faced the ancient astronomers was that of constructing a calendar. Fortunately, this work can be performed without knowledge of the true relationship of the Earth to the sun, moon, and stars. This can occur because the movements of the skies are cyclical and thus generally predictable.

Heavenly bodies all appear to revolve about us—in our sky. As we know now, our solar system works in a manner opposite to its appearance. It has taken mankind many a millennium to figure out that bit of scientific truth: though in no way did such ignorance keep the ancients from systematically codifying their observations.

In modern terms, we know that the Earth moves around the sun in a nearly circular orbit, and that the seasons change according to where the Earth is on that orbit. If it's winter now, then in six months from now the Earth will be on the opposite side of the orbit and it will be summer. If you want to know when to plant your crops, then, the most important piece of astronomical information you need is the location of the Earth in its orbit.

Unfortunately, it's not easy to determine this location by simple observation. On the average, such phenomena as the weather are known to follow the lead of the sun in its seasonal procession across the sky. But from day to day the weather is so changeable that

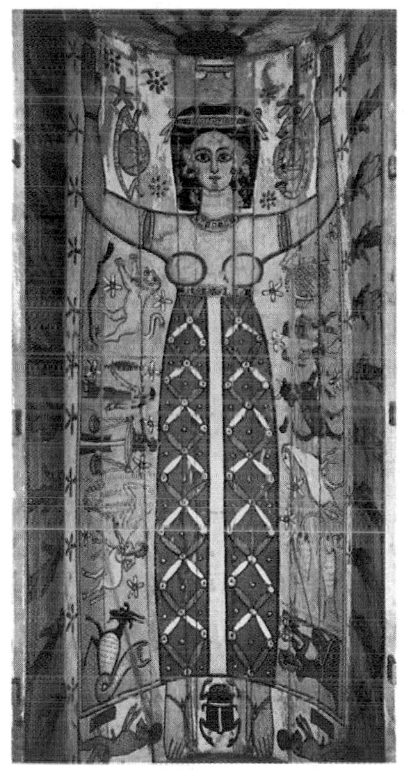

Building their stairway to the stars, as mentioned in Genesis, Mesopotamians raise a mighty tower—certainly the first great observatory, at least in intent. Oil by Pieter Bruegel the Elder, 1563. Nut, an Egyptian sky goddess, appears on a mummy case from second century A.D.

The Prophet Muhammad replaces the Black Stone of Mecca in the wall of the Ka'bah, an Islamic sanctuary. While scientists believe the stone to be a meteorite, Islamic tradition relates how once the stone was white, but has turned black from absorbing the sins of all who have touched and kissed it over the centuries.

it is difficult to make accurate predictions. Perhaps a personal example will bring this point home. My oldest daughter was born in the middle of February. On the day of her birth, our part of Virginia was in the grip of an unseasonal heat wave and the temperature was in the seventies. It *looked* like spring, but it snowed a month later. Had we planted our garden during the warm spell, we could have lost the entire crop. By the same token, at her third birthday party I spent a good part of the day digging our guests' cars out of two feet of snow.

Despite differences in the weather on these two particular birthdays, the Earth was in exactly the same place with relation to the sun—and with St. Patrick's day a month off, it was not a very good time for planting potatoes in Virginia.

Nobody relying on weather signs alone would have been able to figure this out. The task of the first calendar makers, then, was to produce something like our own calendar—a system by which the same day (e.g. March 17) falls when the Earth is in the same position in its orbit each year. Fortunately, the most primitive calendar of all—and an unpublished one—takes care of the above problem quite nicely. It is the horizon calendar of American Indians and others in which the "day counter" notes alignments of the rising or setting sun with permanent geographic features on the horizon. The sun moves back and forth with the season and precisely cuts the horizon line at a specific spot on particular days of the year.

In addition to going around the sun, the Earth also turns on its axis. The most obvious unit of time, the day, is simply the time it takes the Earth to turn once. Unfortunately, if we divide the time it takes the Earth to go around the sun by the length of the day, we don't get a whole number. There are a little less than 365 days and six hours in a year, and it's this extra fraction that causes trouble.

Suppose that your observations of the sky were good enough to tell you that the year was 365 days long, but not good enough to give you the extra fraction—not quite a quarter of a day. You could construct a calendar by counting days from a convenient point. One choice would be the summer solstice, when the sun is as high in the sky as it ever gets. You could then mark days on a stick until 365 had accumulated and then declare a New Year. But the Earth wouldn't be in exactly the same place on this "New Year's Day" as it was the last time around—it would be six hours behind. Four years into your new calendar you would be a day behind, and after 120 years you would have slipped back by a month. You would be telling people to plant their potatoes when the Earth was in the place we label February, because your calendar would be saying it was March.

Not too many such episodes are required to make farmers somewhat ill-tempered with the Astronomer Royal. In some old legends, in fact, we find that some wizards who failed to make correct predictions of celestial events were beheaded!

What was needed, then, was some way of marking the important events on a yearly basis. Until the mid-1960s, it was generally assumed that sophisticated astronomy was quite beyond the abilities of Neolithic people. After all, they didn't even have a written language. In the words of one eminent archeologist, they were little more advanced than "howling barbarians." In 1965, however, Gerald Hawkins, a naturalized American astronomer at Boston University, published a book about the mysterious monument called Stonehenge. A structure of giant stones on the plain near Salisbury, in southern England, this monument has been shrouded in mystery through most of recorded history. The medieval chronicler Geoffrey of Monmouth claimed the stones were transported to England from a location in Ireland by no less a personage than Merlin. Other writers have attributed the monuments to the Romans, the Danes, and the Druids. But it all happened long before any of these groups were around. How the early Britons managed the job, with only a few tools fashioned from bone and rock, is a fascinating story. Even more interesting, however, is the question of why they went through all that trouble to raise several concentric circles on a flat plain. All these rings are not of stone, as we shall discuss later, and the embankments and stone structures were built over many centuries.

Hawkins' astronomical expertise helped clarify an admittedly confused picture. Standing at the center of the stone rings, he noted that the giant arches actually defined narrow fields of view. The most famous of these lines of sight goes through the outer ring of stones to another stone 100 feet outside the circle—the so-called "Heelstone." (As with so much else at Stonehenge, the origin of the name is a mystery. Some claim that a depression on the side of the stone is the print of a heel, others say that the term derives from the Greek *helios*, for "sun.") Hawkins showed that this 35-ton stone had been placed in the ground so that the midsummer sun would rise over it.

Further investigations suggest that other significant astronomical events were marked by the stones. These include the midsummer sunset (in cloudy England, it paid to cover one's bets and mark both sunrise and sunset), midwinter sunrise and sunset, and the positions of the rising full moon nearest these events.

Hawkins also argued that Stonehenge functioned as a sort of megalithic computer, allowing the priest-astronomers to predict the times when eclipses of the sun and moon were most likely to happen. An eclipse of the sun requires that the moon be between the Earth and the sun, while an eclipse of the moon requires that the Earth be between the sun and the moon. Both of these are well-defined situations, and predicting eclipses was one of the earliest skills acquired by astronomers.

Carved figures of a magnificent zodiac caught the eye of French archeological artists who accompanied Napoleon to Egypt and created this engraving around 1800. The bas-relief originated at Dendera, a temple sacred to the Egyptian goddess of sky and fertility, Hathor. Created sometime during the Ptolemaic Period (305–30 B.C.) the disk contains all 12 zodiac signs in its center.

Hawkins noted that at the latitude of Stonehenge the appearance of the moon follows a cycle that repeats itself every 56 years. As it happens, there is a set of exactly 56 holes at the monument. Called the Aubrey Holes after John Aubrey, an English antiquary, they form an accurate circle 285 feet in diameter. It surrounds the inner edifice of tall megaliths. Sticks or poles may have been erected in the holes. It is always difficult, if not impossible, to know just what ancient people had in mind, yet it is clear that observers could keep track of the times when eclipses were likely to occur by moving stone markers around the Aubrey Holes. We have also discovered that the Aubrey Holes were in place perhaps a millennium before the great standing stones were raised.

Since Hawkins' work, hundreds of other ancient monuments around the world have been analyzed for their astronomical significance. Many seem to be aligned to significant celestial events, although none is as complex as Stonehenge.

Though we have discussed early astronomy in terms of the needs of agriculture, it was not only farming societies that marked the course of the sun and the stars. The North American Plains Indians, nomads who followed the buffalo herds, left behind dozens of large stone arrangements known as medicine wheels. John A. Eddy of the High Altitude Observatory of the National Center for Atmospheric Research studied a number of these wheels and concluded that they, like Stonehenge, represent attempts of early men to mark the movements of objects in the sky.

The best example of this sort of structure in the United States is located on Medicine Mountain, 9,000 feet above sea level in the Big Horn Range of the Rockies in Wyoming. The wheel was built by laying rocks

Precursors of Astronomical Science

	4000	3000	2000
Malta Temple Complexes			
Brittany Standing Stones			
Megalithic Chamber Tombs			
Mesopotamian Civilizations			
Egyptian Civilization			
British Stone Circles *Stonehenge I*			
Stonehenge II			
Stonehenge III			
Chinese Civilization			
Hindu Civilization			
Early Greece			
Mesoamerican Civilizations			
North American Civilizations			
Arab Civilization			

in patterns on the ground. At its hub lies a large cairn of rocks about 12 feet across. From this raised central point, 28 spokes reach outward, each line of rocks about 35 feet long. John Eddy has shown that other wheels scattered around the United States and Canada show similar alignments and, like the Medicine Mountain structure, were used most likely to mark important astronomical events.

As evidence has accumulated for the astronomical origins of places like Stonehenge, the medicine wheels, and other ancient sites, the "howling barbarian" school has gradually faded. It has come to be accepted that Neolithic men, even though illiterate, were capable observers and recorders of the movement of objects in the sky.

Resistance to this idea came, in part, from a reluctance on the part of archeologists to believe that illiterate peoples could be capable of the scientific knowledge necessary to build these sites. It also stems, I think, from the same urban background that separates a lot of twentieth-century humanity from nature. This facet of the problem is some-

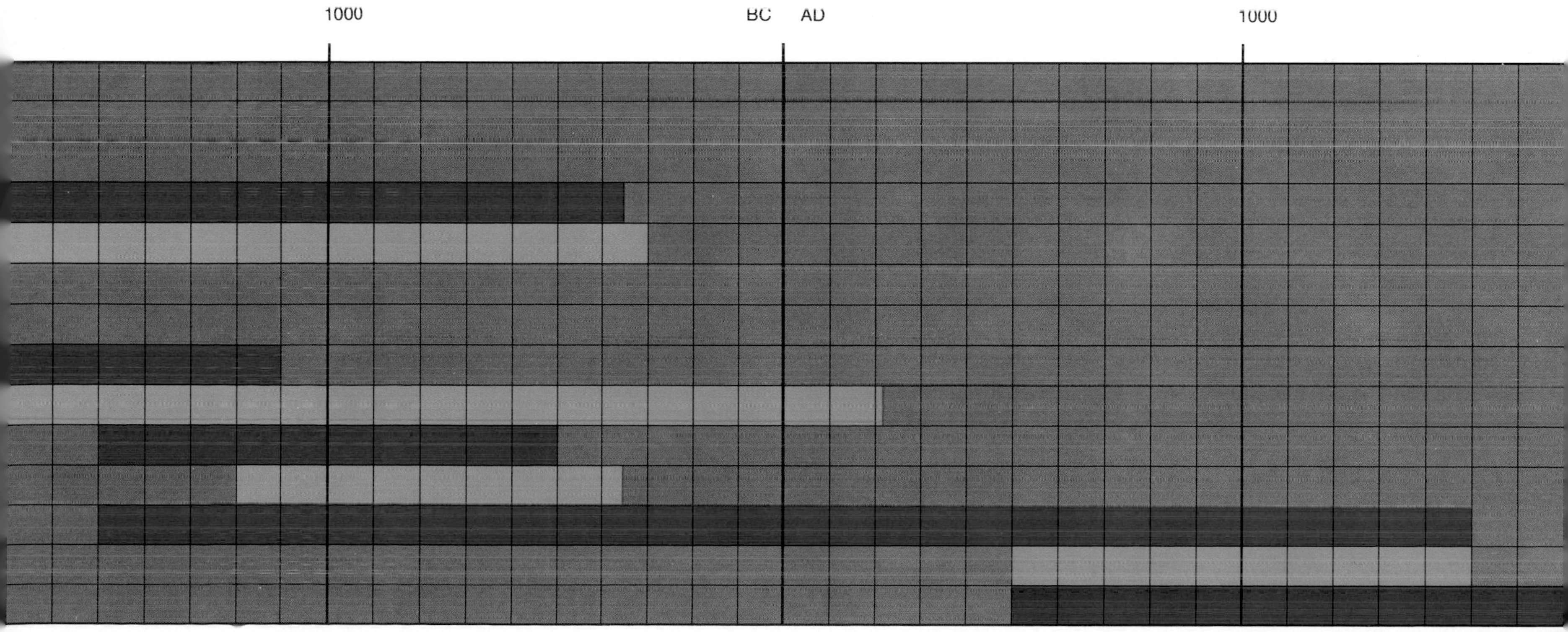

1000 BC AD 1000

Britain's Avebury Rings, a neolithic monument more than 4,000 years old, may resemble an early stage in the development of nearby Stonehenge. Circular earthworks a mile in circumference enclose a ring of sandstone blocks. The largest of its kind, Avebury may have been a center for religious activities.

Previous page: Danish priest-astronomer of the Bronze Age probably used this solar chariot in sun worshiping ceremonies. Both sides appear. Golden orb at far left is the sun at day, while the dark disk at right symbolizes the extinguished sun at night, drawn underground by the sacred horse for a new sunrise.

thing I know about from personal experience. After having lived most of my life in cities, I moved to an old farm near the Blue Ridge Mountains in 1974. Within a few years, I found that I had become much more aware of the motions of the sun and the moon than I ever had been before. This didn't happen because I set out to learn astronomy first hand, but occurred as a normal part of my new life. I would glance at the sun to see how much time there was to finish a job before dark, or notice where I could park the car so that it would be shaded on a hot afternoon.

Now I can point to the notch in the mountains where the sun sets at midwinter, where it will be at the equinoxes or at midsummer. I know without thinking what phase the moon is in at any given time. If a city boy can acquire this kind of appreciation of the sky, and by accident, what could hold back Neolithic people—immersed as they were in the heavenly spectacle.

It doesn't surprise me in the least that primitive people marked out the turning points of the sun and moon in the sky. It is, after all, only a short step from the kind of offhand observation I've described to a system of wooden posts marking out sight lines for the simpler observations. The more complex problems, such as eclipses, might require the full-time efforts of several generations of priest-astronomers, but this is still only the work of a few individuals.

The actual hauling, working, and placing of the stones, however, was a major construction project. For this reason we may suspect that the Stonehenge we see today had a more religious and memorial significance than astronomical. As a proportion of the resources of the society involved, it may well have surpassed our own Apollo project, which put a man on the moon in 1969.

Egypt and Babylon

The traditional histories of Western astronomy do not usually begin in Europe at all, nor on the rainy English plains, nor in the Big Horn Mountains, but in the Valley of the Nile and near the Tigris and Euphrates rivers in what is now Iraq and Syria. The great achievements of Egyptian civilization are well known to us—we've all seen pictures of the pyramids and temples that still stand along the river. We are somewhat less familiar with the civilizations of Mesopotamia, although many of the people who lived in that area in the last three millennia B.C. are mentioned in the Bible.

Among their many other achievements, the Babylonians of Mesopotamia developed the first systematic collection of astronomical measurements which survived long enough to form the basis for later work. We know that the builders of Stonehenge deserved to be called astronomers, but their work had little impact on modern thought. The roots of our astronomy really lie in the Middle East, with a different group of priest-astronomers. Indeed, the Bible suggests that the famous spire on the Plain of Shinar was the original observatory—known better to us as a landmark of linguistic confusion—the Tower of Babel.

The Egyptians built with stone, and their papyrus manuscripts were preserved by the warm, dry Egyptian air. Though Babylonians built with sun-dried brick, they baked their clay tablets in furnaces, a process ensuring great survivibility. In both cases, the archeologists had to dig for the astronomical documents, but all that enduring Egyptian stonework and sculpture caught the world's eye and imagination. Thus it comes as a surprise to most people that early Egyptian astronomy actually lagged far behind that of the Babylonians.

There is no general agreement among

scholars as to why things should have turned out this way, although it is possible to identify a number of the factors involved. For one thing, the Egyptians developed an extremely awkward and cumbersome number system. Whole numbers were written in a system resembling Roman numerals, while fractions, for some obscure reason, had to be written in a very strange form indeed. A fraction like 7/12 could not be written in the Egyptian system. Instead of this relatively simple notation, the number would have to be rendered as 1/2 + 1/12. Every fraction, in other words, had to be written as a sum of other fractions, each of which had a one in the numerator. If you think back to your grade school arithmetic, you will quickly realize how little progress you would have made in carrying out any complex calculations if fractions had to be done this way.

Their number system didn't keep the Egyptians from developing great practical skill in building and surveying, nor did it keep them from developing a calendar. They chose to make their year coincide with the motion of the sun—the choice that makes the most sense for an agricultural society. Their calendar was once described in a student's term paper as "twelve months of thirty days each followed by a five-day party." They missed the extra quarter day in the year, so their dates would slip as time went on. In the case of Egypt, however, the annual flooding of the Nile determined the planting time, so the slow sliding of the calendar probably had no more effect on them than the variable date of Easter has on us.

The Babylonians, on the other hand, were superb calculators. They almost had to be, because they chose the phases of the moon as the basic units of their calendar time. The time from one new moon to the next, the lunar month, is about 29.5 days. A moment with your calculator will convince you that dividing the length of the lunar month into the length of the year does not give a whole number. From the beginning, then, Babylonian astronomers had to deal with fractions, for the simple reason that they had chosen the wrong clock to measure out their year.

In fact, the lunar calendar that finally resulted from their deliberations was a pretty good one. It was based on the fact that there are 235 lunar months in 19 solar years. They developed a calendar system in which some years had 12 months, others 13—sort of a "leap month" system. It's clear that putting together a calendar like this required both a high level of mathematical skill and the ability to observe and record the heavens over long periods of time. It should come as no surprise, then, that people capable of constructing and maintaining a lunar calendar were also capable of developing a sophisticated astronomical system.

We are so used to associating astronomers with telescopes that it is important to note that the Babylonians had to do all of their observing with the naked eye. We do not know what sorts of instruments they used, but they were probably simple sighting devices. In essence, the instruments were long rods along which the astronomer sighted, the way you might sight along a rifle barrel. The direction of the rod could be recorded and the movement of an object traced through the sky by a series of measurements.

The Babylonians recorded the movements of objects in the sky—particularly the sun, the moon, and the planets. They became

Endlessly fascinated with astrology, medieval Europeans might have pored over these manuscript pages from a German almanac around 1450. In addition to astrological advice, such pages included tips on when to plant and harvest crops.

Solar charm and lunar calendar wrapped into one, this Peruvian gold disk is an artifact from the Huari-Tiahuanaco culture of about A.D. *1000. Leprous boils and discolorations on the face of the Aztec sun god Tonatiuh may symbolize sunspots, below. Turquoise mosaic masks were probably worn to ward off evil spirits.*

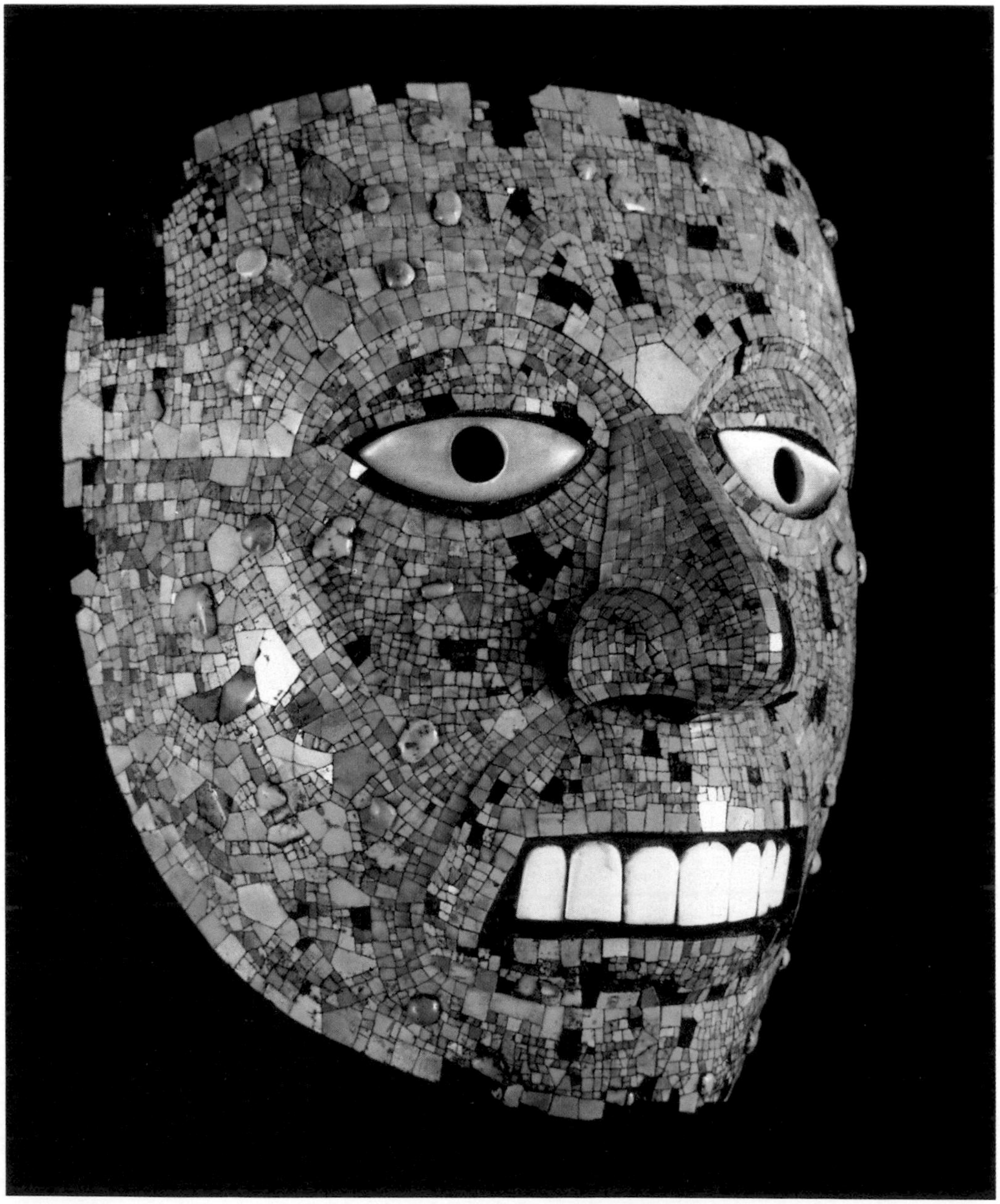

quite adept at describing these movements—so much so that they could predict the likelihood of eclipses of the sun and the moon. Unlike all the astronomers who followed them, including those of the present day, they did not seem to have had a mental picture of the solar system to go along with their mathematical calculations. It's almost as if they recorded the lights in the sky without worrying about what the lights were or why they moved the way they did. They were content to predict the movements they saw, without creating a mechanical model of the sky—an achievement that was left for the classical Greeks.

Mathematical techniques from Mesopotamia actually prefigured methods that are very familiar to modern scientists. The idea was that they would take the motion of an object in the sky and break it down into a sum of separate motions. For example, the motion of the sun could be represented by a daily motion across the sky superimposed on a yearly motion. For many centuries, Babylonian astronomers kept records; a continual process of refining went on so that eventually their predictions of sky events became quite accurate.

In a sense, the Mesopotamians were like today's weather forecasters who contribute to farmers' almanacs. In both instances, the accumulation of a large data base over a long time reveals cyclical patterns that suggest the course of future events.

A Word About Astrology

The Babylonians produced the first systematic written astronomical accounts. They also created astrology. Present-day scientists prefer to accept the former accomplishment and sweep the latter under the rug. But the Babylonian mind worked differently. Despite civilization (they all but invented it) and despite high technology (ditto) the Babylonians regarded the world with a good deal of what we would call superstition. It is still part of our cultural heritage, and hard to shake, but science and 40 centuries of experience have helped us to surmount some of our fears.

Mesopotamians needed to feel secure—as we do—and they came to believe that some of the threat could be removed from an uncertain world by the perusal of omens. In an attempt to catch a glimpse of the forces operating to create the future of each individual, they interpreted dreams, read the entrails of slaughtered animals, and watched the heavens. The belief that the process of keeping track of the skies would also help them with their earthly endeavors provided, no doubt, much of the motivating force behind the Mesopotamian's intense interest in astronomy.

One of the oldest texts we have from them states "If the sky is bright when the New Moon appears . . . the year will be good." Although this is clearly an astrological statement—telling us that the condition of the sky foretells the future—other old texts deal with very different omens. For example, in an omen series known as the Shumma Izbu, we find the following: "If a woman gives birth to an elephant, the land will be laid waste." (I expect that this prediction would prove true.) The point is that the Babylonians believed in all sorts of omens, and omens associated with the heavens were only one kind to which they subscribed.

The system of sky omens developed by the Babylonians has come to us essentially unchanged in modern astrology. (No one appears to believe in the other omens any more.) The idea is that the band of the zodiac is divided up into 12 familiar "signs." During the course of the year, the movement of the Earth around the sun makes the sun appear to be in each of these "houses" at various times. The signs corresponded with our familiar stellar constellations in A.D. 150 when Ptolemy froze astrology in his "tetrabiblos." Today, however, the constellations and the signs have diverged due to a cyclical displacement of the Earth in its rotation called precession. They will match up again in 24,000 years.

But returning to basics: when the sun is actually in a sign the light from the stars is masked by the sun's glare; but it is possible, by observing which constellations appear just after sunset and just before dawn, to deduce the sun's location in the zodiac. The sign in which the sun is located at the moment of your birth is called your "sun sign." It's what people usually mean when they talk about their "signs" and forms the basis for the kinds of astrological predictions you run across in newspapers.

A more complex bit of astrology consists of casting a natal horoscope. In medieval Europe, astrologers actually came into the home when a woman went into labor so that the horoscope could be cast at precisely the right moment. The visit was important as not only the sun, but the moon and planets are located in various celestial bailiwicks. Long lists of characteristics go with the appearance of each planet in each house, although these lists seem to vary from one astrologer to another. This may be what you get if you answer one of those ads for a personalized computer horoscope.

Attitudes vary. Some modern scientists regard the practice of astrology with a bemused tolerance, lumping it with the harmless superstitions associated with ladders and black cats. Others wax indignant over the fact that Americans spend more money each year on astrology than they do on serious astronomy.

For myself, I think there's nothing to worry about as long as I read about astrology in the section of the newspaper reserved for comic strips and other such entertainment. If astrology starts making its way into the news columns—as it does from time to time—that's a different matter.

Detail from the Bodley Codex, a pre-Columbian Mixtec manuscript, pictures what scholars believe is an astronomer sighting through crossed sticks. One thousand years ago Mayan priest-astronomers at sunset may have stood atop Chichén Itzá's Caracol, awaiting the rise of Venus.

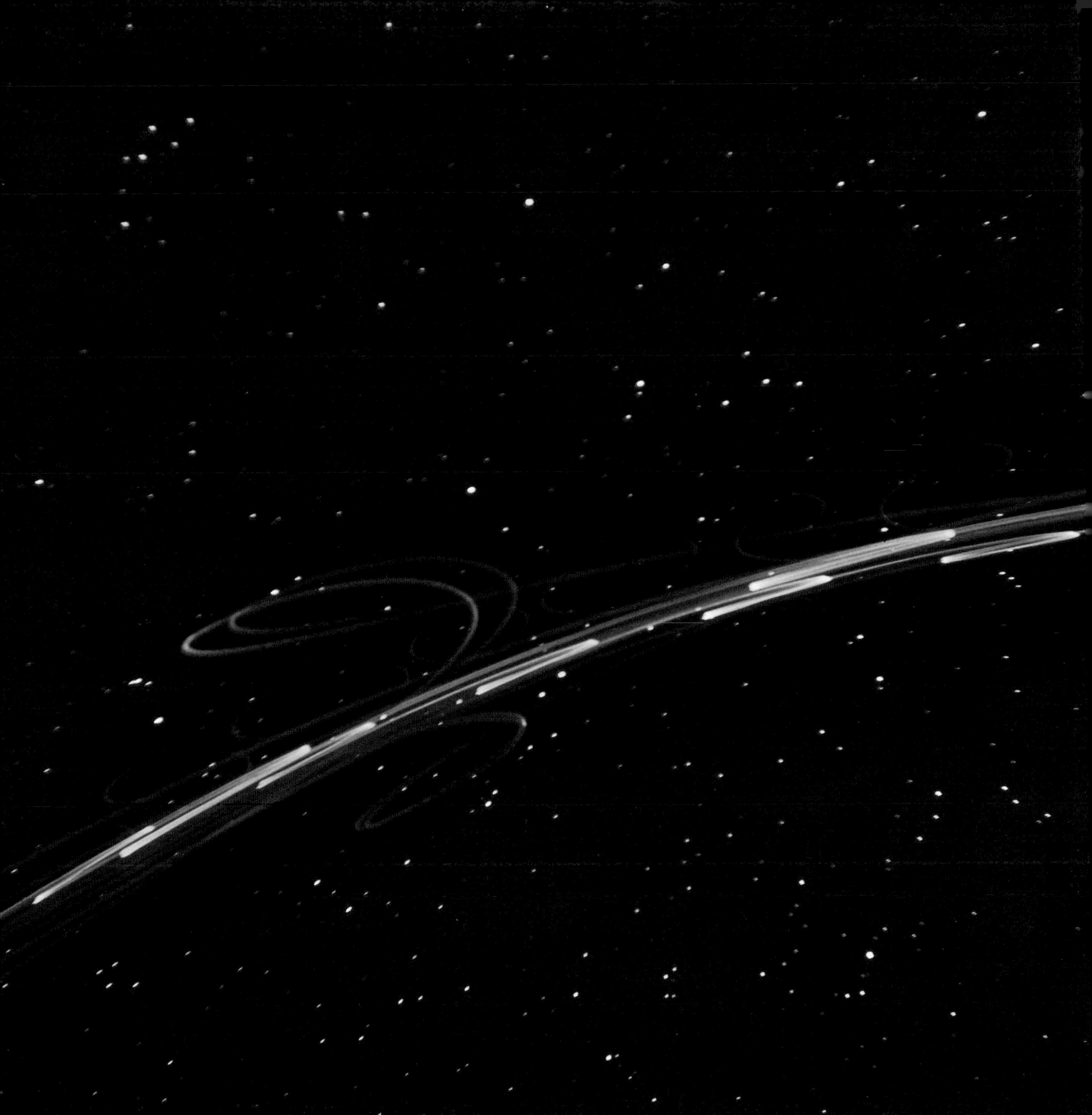

Saving Appearances

The first people to develop an astronomy in the modern sense—one that combined careful observation of the heavens with a theory about those observations—were the Greeks. Beginning in the period around 600 B.C., men in the Greek colonies of Ionia, along the coast of Asia Minor, began to think in ways that are easily recognized in the twentieth century. While the Egyptians and Babylonians were content to explain the universe in terms of the actions of the gods, the Greeks insisted on thinking in terms of natural processes. Instead of simply accepting the world as they found it, they searched for simple physical explanations for everything—at least in the early days.

The first of these new men we know about was Thales of Miletus. We know little about him aside from the fact that, in the marvelous language of historians, he "flourished" in 585 B.C. We know this date because he was supposed to have predicted an eclipse of the sun at that time. He formulated the doctrine that the primary matter of the universe was water; and it became air when rarefied, fire when incandescent, and earth when condensed. In this sense, by describing an underlying unity to the universe, Thales was the first true scientist.

The point of this picture of the universe isn't to show that it's correct—it's not. But here, for the first time, we see people looking at the world in a new way, no longer content simply to observe and express awe. They required rational explanations based on natural laws that can be discovered by the human mind.

Why the Greeks, relative newcomers to the family of civilized nations, should have been the ones to make this breakthrough is a subject of debate among social historians. But this Greek miracle really did occur, in addition to several other factors working to-

Planets occasionally appear to stop in their orbits, then reverse direction before continuing on—a phenomenon called retrograde motion by modern astronomers. It confused ancient scientists who believed that the earth stood still while the stars moved. Ancient philosopher and mathematician, Pythagoras appears in relief on the Chartres cathedral in France. He took delight in perfect circles and related musical scales to the planets.

Ptolemy's genius lay in his creation of a complex cosmological system accounting not only for the Greek idea of celestial perfection, but also for his rationalization of the retrograde motion of planets. Accepted by theologians and scholars alike, the Ptolemaic system became the bedrock of astronomical belief until shattered by the work of the Polish scholar Copernicus after 1543.

gether to advance Hellenic thought. For one thing, the colonies were part of a tight triangle including the older centers of Babylon and Egypt. Several important settlements developed upon islands that hugged the coast of Asia. Miletus itself was on the mainland. The Greeks were active traders and travelers, observing and gathering ideas as well as the goods of commerce. In contact with both of the older cultures, they realized that the accepted and established fact of one place was rejected in the other. It is easy to see how skepticism concerning religious claims might arise.

Secondly, these colonies were rough and ready places, with something of a frontier atmosphere. Everyone was expected to take part in the commercial life of his city. In other words, educated men could be expected to know something about engineering, and it is reasonable to expect that Thales of Miletus and his pupils would have spent some time around forges and blacksmith shops observing, for instance, how materials behave when they are heated and cooled. What would be more natural than for them to speculate about the formation of the earth in much the same terms as they thought about the formation of a plowshare in the forge?

Such a lifestyle was foreign to Egypt and Babylon, and to Athens of the Golden Age. Practical work was left to slaves—educated men would not sully their hands. Perhaps this is one reason, as we shall see shortly, why classical Greek astronomy failed to live up to its auspicious beginnings.

After the sixth century B.C., some of the vigorous spirit of intellectual adventure diminished. Astronomers concerned themselves with accurate measurements of the heavens so that the courses of all objects would be well known. They also thought about a coherent picture of a universe in which the motions of the objects agreed with the observations. In the language of Plato and his followers, the astronomer's task was "saving the appearances."

Unfortunately, the Greeks interpreted this mandate to include two major constraints. First, they insisted that the correct picture of the heavens must place the earth at the center. The evidence of the senses is quite clear. Our earth sits still and the stars and planets revolve around it. What could be more obvious?

The second constraint on Greek astronomical thought was purely philosophical. Since the heavens were associated with the gods, whatever happened there had to be a representation of perfection. It is obvious that the most perfect geometrical figure is the circle (or the sphere, if we're talking about three dimensions). It follows, therefore, that the demands of reason require that all motion in the heavens be circular. Besides, since motion in a circle is perfect, there is no need to worry about what keeps the stars moving in their tracks. Once perfection has been achieved, argued the Greek astronomer, it will continue forever.

Thus arose a split personality in science, a separation of astronomy from earthly studies. Possessing the power of religion and the scientific institution, the ancient view of the world persisted until the time of Galileo and Newton. The Greeks bequeathed to later scientists the first coherent, well-thought-out view of the universe, yet they put the study of astronomy on the wrong track until the coming of modern times.

When a Greek spoke of the task of astronomy as "saving the appearances," then, what he really meant was that astronomers were required to produce a picture of the universe showing the earth at the center and depicting circular motion in the heavens. And this picture was to represent exactly the motion of everything that could be observed.

Quite an assignment! One of the main problems was the apparent motion of the planets. On any night when they are visible, planets move across the sky like stars. But from one night to the next they change their positions among the stars. Sometimes they move ahead of the stars from one night to the next, then slow down, reverse direction and then continue on course. This effect is easy to understand in a system where the Earth and the planets orbit the sun—the motion is apparent not real, as with trains on parallel tracks appearing to go backward or forward as their relative speeds change. But the effect—assumed to be real and divinely ordained—was difficult for the Greeks to accommodate.

A number of other small effects added to the complexity of the task of anyone "saving the appearances." The direction of the Earth's axis of rotation does not stay fixed, but rotates around in a cone every 26,000 years. Right now, the axis points to Polaris, the "North Star," which explains why that star alone, in all the heavens, does not appear to move. But the alignment is not permanent. The North-Star role was assumed by Polaris only four to five hundred years ago. Such shifts, though never very much at any one time, are easily detected by naked-eye astronomy.

Given the severity of their self-imposed constraints, it was a major accomplishment that the Greeks were able to devise such a picture and to produce such a system.Their work stood as the bedrock of astronomy for more than fifteen centuries.

What the Greeks Really Knew

In grade school we all learned that before Columbus, everyone believed that the earth was flat. Unfortunately, this notion, like so many others, simply isn't true. The Greeks not only knew the earth to be round, but even estimated its radius!

As far as the shape of the earth is concerned, the second theorem stated in the *Almagest* of Claudius Ptolemy, written in the second century A.D., is: "That also the Earth, taken as a whole, is sensibly spherical." To prove this proposition, Ptolemy cites the following facts:

1. Stars do not rise and set at the same time everywhere.
2. An eclipse (an event taking place at a single specified time) is recorded as occurring at different hours of the day by different observers—later in Babylon than in Egypt, for example.
3. Some stars visible in the south are not visible in more northerly locations.
4. The apparent size of a ship sailing over the horizon does not dwindle away to nothing—the hull vanishes before the top of the mast.

After considering other possible shapes for the earth—a pyramid, a cube, a flat plane, and a cylinder—Ptolemy concluded

Ptolemy is directed in his use of a quadrant by one of the nine Greek muses, Urania, the patron of astronomy. By crowning Ptolemy, the illustrator of this sixteenth-century manuscript may have confused the astronomer with the long line of Egyptian kings bearing the name.

Angels escort the Prophet Muhammad during his assumption into heaven. He rides the winged mare Buraq. The Prophet passes through the celestial spheres—features of the skies as outlined by Ptolemy and others of the classical world. According to Islamic theologians, Gabriel appeared unto Muhammad, proclaiming him "messenger of God." Inhabitants of the celestial realms, angels are common to both Christian and Moslem traditions.

If the Lord God Almighty had consulted me before embarking upon the Creation, I would have recommended something simpler.

With these words Alfonso the Wise, thirteenth-century King of Castile, summarized the reaction of most people who have studied the Ptolemaic system. Indeed, the approach has spawned a mild epithet—*you're just adding epicycles*—among scientists. It is aimed at colleagues who produce enormously complicated theories to try to salvage their ideas.

The central problem faced by Ptolemy, of course, was to produce a model which reproduced the apparent motions of the stars, sun, and moon and yet which had the earth at the center and the planets moving in circular orbits. That he succeeded as well as he did is a tribute to his cleverness. Also, he passed on the supposed wisdom of his peers and predecessors.

First of all, Ptolemy had to find a way for a planet to move backward as compared to the motion of the fixed stars. He surmised that the planet must be attached to a small sphere (the epicycle) whose center was attached to the larger sphere (the deferrant). The epicycle turned uniformly, but at a different rate from the deferrant.

Unfortunately, the epicycle cannot explain why the planet appears to move at different speeds in different parts of its orbit. Nor can it explain why the retrograde motion of a given planet does not always appear to be exactly the same. In modern terms, we know that the latter variation occurs because the orbits of the planets are all tilted slightly with respect to the orbit of the earth. But Ptolemy did not know this. To account for the motion, he introduced two more complications. First, he put the center of the deferrant away from the center of the earth; thus the sphere would appear to be slightly off center as seen by terrestrial observers.

In addition, he had the center of the epicycle move around the deferrant at a rate that was uniform as seen by someone standing on the opposite side of the earth from the center of the deferrant. This point is known as the equant.

Still confused? Try a practical example: imagine a record turntable centered at the equant. The turntable causes a ball bearing to roll around a track in the shape of the deferrant. Then imagine watching the ball bearing from a stationary point halfway between the two centers. If—in addition to all this—you picture the planet as attached to a small sphere turning around the ball bearing, you have a good idea of the way the Ptolemaic system worked.

King Alfonso was wise indeed to react the way he did!

that only if the earth were a sphere could all of these facts be explained. This conclusion was known to the astronomers who preceded Ptolemy—his book is in part a summary of all knowledge available in his time. There are references to a round earth before Ptolemy, and with a few querulous monastic exceptions, they remain in the scientific literature right up to the time of Columbus.

Eratosthenes of Cyrene (276? B.C. to 194? B.C.) lived a full three centuries before Ptolemy. Not only did he know the earth to be round, but he even devised a clever way of measuring its radius. He knew that at the summer solstice, people in the town of Syene (modern Aswân) in southern Egypt saw the sun directly overhead at noon. In modern terminology, we would say that the town was located on the tropic of Cancer—the apparent limit of farthest northward advance of the sun.

Eratosthenes measured the length of a shadow cast by a pole of known length in Alexandria at noon on the solstice, thereby determining the angle of elevation of the sun at Alexandria. This measurement, coupled with the known distance from Alexandria to Aswân, allowed him to estimate the radius of the earth in terms of the distance between Alexandria and Syene.

Accounts differ as to how he knew the distance between the two towns. In some renditions he got the number from leaders of camel caravans. In others, he used the results of royal surveys. It turns out that the rulers of Alexandria employed a core of professional pacers—men whose job it was to walk from one place to another counting their steps. (Of all the jobs that have been eliminated by new technology, this is surely one of the most unusual.) Eratosthenes determined that the circumference of the earth was 250,000 "stadia."

A great deal of ink has been spilled over the question of the accuracy of his result, with the main problem being the definition of the unit of length called the stadium. At least three different stadia appear in the ancient literature—Pliny refers to one (about 517 feet); in addition, there are references to the Olympic stadium (about 607 feet); and the Royal Egyptian stadium (about 689 feet). If one assumes that Eratosthenes used the first of these values, he was within a percent of the modern result for the circumference—an incredible level of accuracy.

If one assumes that Eratosthenes used one of the others, the amount of his error was in the neighborhood of 20 percent. In either case, however, it's clear that this measurement demonstrates both a knowledge of the earth's shape and an ability to make quantitative use of that knowledge. It was, in fact, an important contribution to the new science of geometry, a word whose literal meaning is "to measure the earth."

No discussion of the Greek vision of our place in the universe would be complete without at least some mention of a courageous minority of astronomers who rejected the geocentric assumptions and argued that the sun, and not the earth, was the center of the universe. The best known of these was Aristarchus of Samos, who lived in the third century B.C. Unfortunately, the text of his writing about the solar system was lost long ago—perhaps when Christian mobs burnt the library of Alexandria, perhaps earlier.

We know of the theories of Aristarchus only because Archimedes commented on them in *The Sand-Reckoner*. Archimedes' words are: "Aristarchus brought out a book consisting of certain hypotheses . . . that the fixed stars and the sun remain unmoved, that the earth revolves about the sun in the circumference of a circle, the sun lying in the middle of the orbit, and that the sphere of the fixed stars . . . is so great that the circle in which he supposes the earth to revolve bears such a proportion to the distance of the fixed stars as the center of the sphere bears to its surface."

From this passage, we can conclude that Aristarchus not only realized that "saving the appearances" could occur without a stationary earth, but that the relative immobility of the stars is due to their great distance from us. Unlike the Greek knowledge of the shape of the earth, this idea did not survive and had to be rediscovered.

Claudius Ptolemy

The man who summarized four centuries of Greek astronomy and put together a model of the universe that was accepted for a mil-

Ottoman and other Islamic astronomers, like those shown in an observatory at Istanbul, helped to save ancient astronomy after the fall of Rome and the disintegration of the classical world. While originating little, the Arabs transmitted both instruments and data and translated Greek manuscripts, including Ptolemy's famed works. Such Arabic star names as Aldebaran, Betelgeuse, and Deneb have endured.

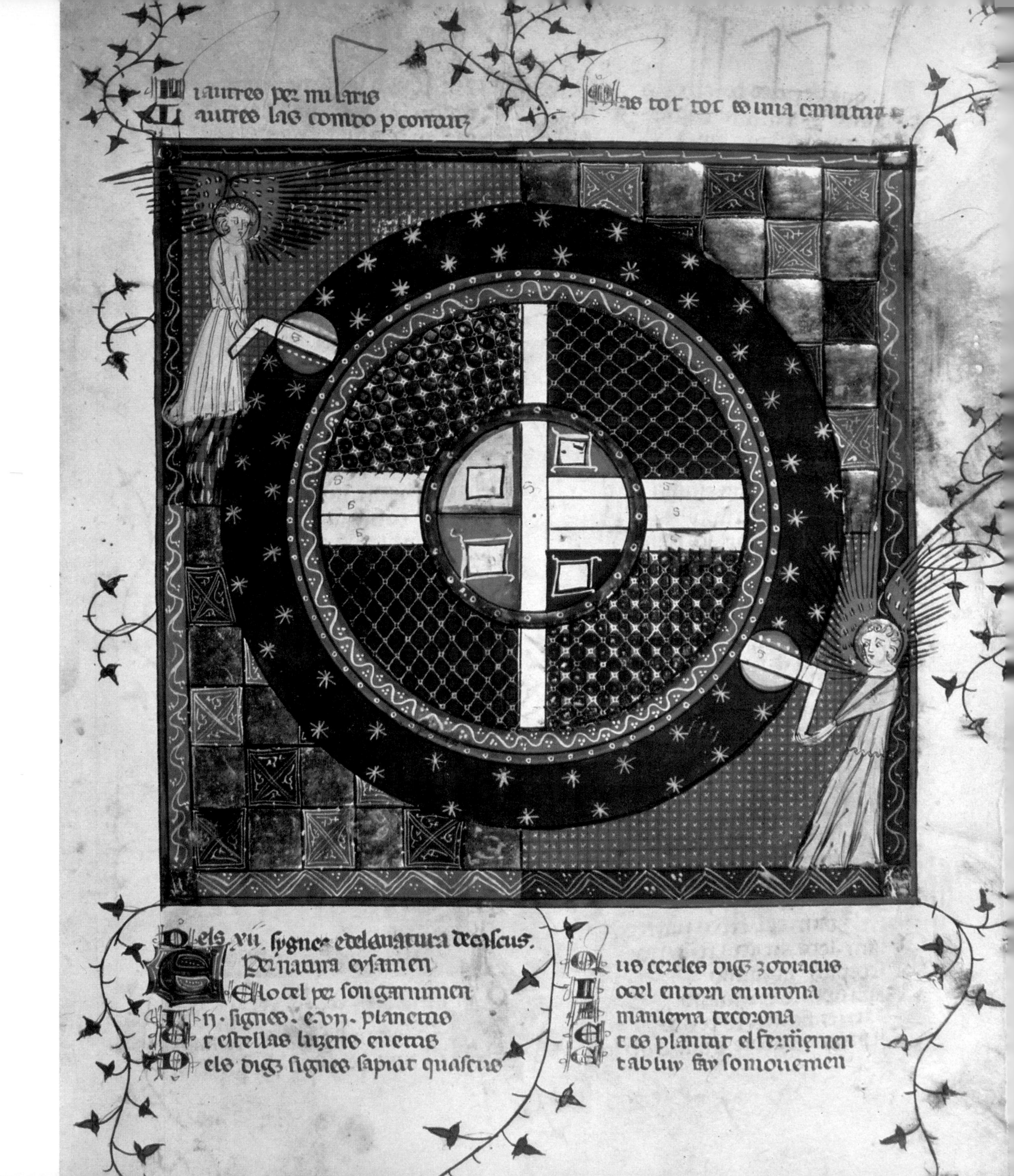

lennium and a half is almost unknown as a historical figure. We realize that he lived sometime during the second century A.D., and we know there is an Arab legend that he died at the age of 78, so his dates are sometimes given as A.D. 100–178, but this is largely guesswork. In fact, Ptolemy is such a shadowy figure in history that one of my colleagues has suggested (tongue-in-cheek, of course) that he wasn't a person at all, but a committee! He would fit today's description of a scientific popularizer. Though the Ptolemaic Dynasty did rule in Egypt during this period, and even included Cleopatra, Claudius Ptolemy was probably not related to the royal family. He certainly was not a Pharaóh, as some people believed in medieval times. We do know that one of the most important books in the history of science is ascribed to one Claudius Ptolemy. The original title was *The Mathematical Composition*, but Arab scientists called it "The Great Astronomer." The Arab article *Al* was added to the Greek *megiste* "great" to give the book the name by which it has been known for centuries—the *Almagest*.

In this book Ptolemy recorded his own observations along with those of previous Greek and Babylonian astronomers. Most important, he made a model of the universe that explained past observations, predicted future ones, and at the same time incorporated both of the Greek assumptions about the world. In his model, the earth sat immobile while the stars, planets, sun, and moon moved around it in a more or less circular motion. Hence the Ptolemaic system marked the completion of the task that Greek astronomy had set for itself. As far as we can tell, the system was accepted by Ptolemy's contemporaries and followers without much debate, and it quickly acquired the status of accepted wisdom.

There are a number of reasons for this attitude toward the Almagest. For one thing, it was the first successful system which incorporated both geocentrism and circular motion. Thus, Greek astronomers *wanted* to accept it. This situation bears a faint resemblance to modern attitudes toward the general theory of relativity. The theory is so beautiful, and so in tune with twentieth-century prejudices, that it was accepted enthusiastically long before a convincing body of experimental verification became available. Secondly, Ptolemy wrote at a time when Hellenistic science, as embodied in the great institutions of learning in Alexandria, was past its peak.

In the eyes of the very early Christian phi-

Opposite, angels crank a large celestial gear activating the planetary spheres. A fourteenth-century Provençal manuscript contains this delightful interpretation of the Ptolemaic system in which the heavens revolve around a central, and motionless, earth.

Ancient Astronomers

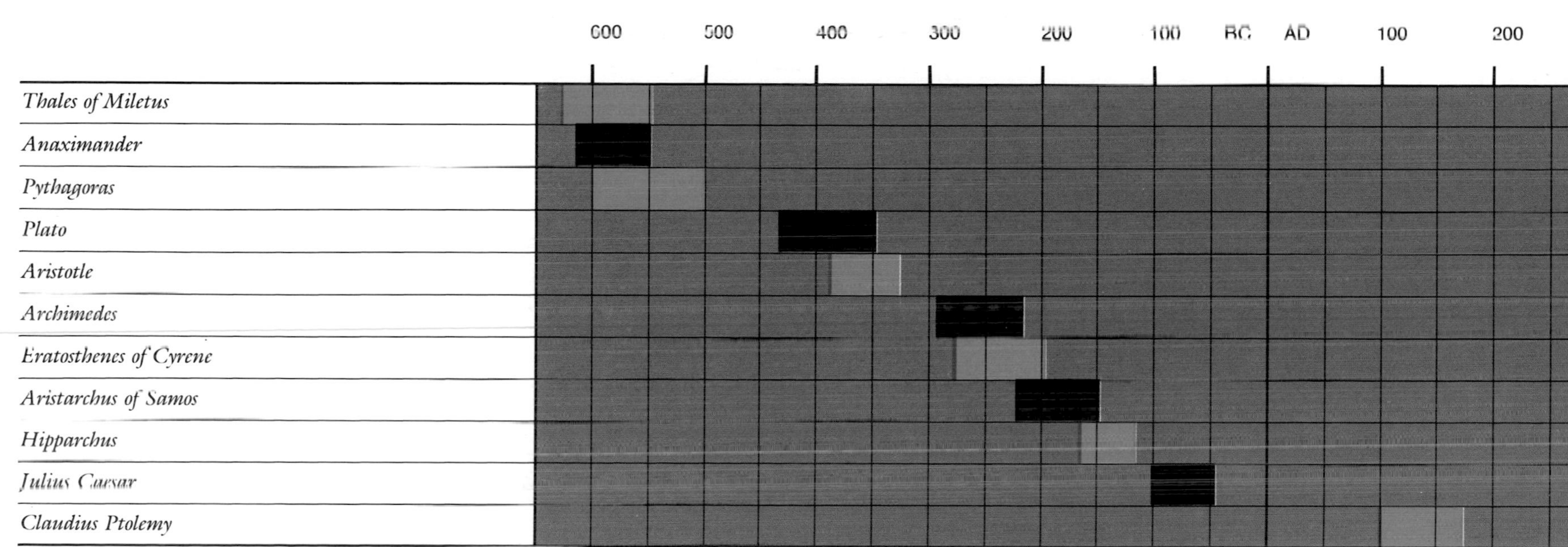

The astrolabe, among the oldest of scientific devices, measures the angular distance of stars above the horizon. Arabs and Persians of the ninth through eleventh centuries developed the astrolabe into an object of great beauty. Using an astrolabe, at right, a medieval monk observes the positions of stars, while an assistant records the readings.

losophers, Ptolemy's system represented pagan learning and therefore was to be excised as quickly as possible. This way of thinking culminated in the burning of the library of Alexandria, the great storehouse of Greek knowledge, in A.D. 391. By the time Ptolemy's work resurfaced among the Arabs, it had already acquired the status of being part of the wisdom of the ancients, and its high standing made the work very difficult to question. It's sometimes hard for us, accustomed as we are to the idea of progress, to imagine what it must have been like to live among the ruins of classical civilization. The remote Golden Age must have seemed like a period of almost superhuman achievements, and there would have been little inclination among Arab scholars to question a complex astronomical system which represented the summation of the best science that system had to offer.

Indeed, we owe our knowledge of the Ptolemaic system to the Arabs, who translated and preserved the work, when not available in the West. It returned to Europe via Moorish Spain, being translated from Arabic into Latin in 1175. For the next 400 years, until the time of Copernicus, the Ptolemaic system reigned supreme.

Was Ptolemy a Fraud?

In 1977 there was a minor storm in scholarly circles over the publication of a book titled *The Crime of Claudius Ptolemy* (Johns Hopkins University Press, 1977). Written by geophysicist Robert Newton, the book argued that many of the observations Ptolemy claimed to have made were fudged to fit his model and conform to his preconceived notions of how the heavens were constructed. The book closes with these words: "Thus Ptolemy is not the greatest astronomer of antiquity, but he is something still more unusual: He is the most successful fraud in the history of science."

While working at the Johns Hopkins Applied Physics Laboratory, Newton had spent many years studying the minute details of the rotation of the Earth. This rotation isn't as steady as you might think, and understanding its details is of obvious interest to anyone involved in navigation. Newton reasoned that ancient astronomical observations, even if imprecise by modern standards, would give him valuable data for his work. This led him to look closely at the observations reported in the Almagest. He quickly ran into problems: Ptolemy seems to have reported observations that were hours and even days from where they should have been. How could the greatest of ancient astronomers have been so wrong?

Perhaps the best way to understand Newton's solution to this problem is to look at a specific example. In the years A.D. 132, 139, and 140, Ptolemy reported several observations of the solstice and equinox. His figures seem to be quite different from those a scientist today would find by using modern techniques to extrapolate back nearly 2,000 years. Newton noted, however, that in 146 B.C. the astronomer Hipparchus (the greatest Greek astronomer before Ptolemy) had measured the equinoxes and used them to arrive at a value for the length of the year. Newton took this length and multiplied it by the number of years that elapsed between the measurements of Ptolemy and Hip-

Most ancient and very complex, the reconstructed Antikythera machine sits before Derek de Solla Price, the scholar who brought it to life. A geared computer of sky movements, its design originated nearly a century before Christ. Found in a shipwreck from Roman times, its gears had corroded and a calcareous nodule had formed around the device itself. X rays revealed shadows of gears, still properly meshed. Upon this evidence, ancient technology has gained greater respect among many researchers. The Antikythera machine may have been a forerunner of astrolabes.

Mathematician in a fourteenth-century manuscript records a sighting taken from his armillary sphere—a skeletal globe encompassing a model of the Earth. Classical Greeks used armillaries to plot equinoxes, and by the late 1500s Tycho Brahe had brought the device to perfection, just in time for telescopes. Suddenly such apparatus became obsolete. Opposite, Earth nestles within a magnificent armillary sphere of wood from medieval Italy. Six shells indicate the celestial spheres that hold the moon and five planets visible to the naked eye.

parchus. He found that the result was very close to that reported by Ptolemy. He concluded that Ptolemy had used this same technique to predict when the solstices and equinoxes ought to have occurred, then adjusted his data accordingly.

What can you say? Anyone who, like myself, has graded freshman lab reports can recognize in an instant what has probably happened here. An observer, knowing what the result was supposed to be, has produced the expected answer.

Does this make Ptolemy a fraud? In Newton's opinion, the answer to this question must be yes. In the opinion of other historians of science, including Owen Gingerich of the Harvard-Smithsonian Center for Astrophysics, the answer is not so clear. The difference in opinion depends on the standards one chooses to apply. By twentieth-century rules, there is no question—Ptolemy fudged his data. Had he worked among the ranks of today's scientists, he might be charged with intellectual dishonesty and drummed out of the corps.

But Ptolemy did not live in the twentieth century. He was, in fact, one of the first men to try to explain what was happening in the sky. In our time, we have learned that it is all too easy for an experimenter to convince himself that he is seeing the expected result, rather than the correct one. We have learned to treat an observation that is exactly as expected with as much skepticism as one which is off the mark. But how was Ptolemy to know this? Perhaps it is best, after all, to retain a measure of charity in judging his work, remembering his advances and keeping in mind that his observations may not have been up to the high standards we have come to expect.

In any case, Ptolemy's failure to correct the length of the year came back to haunt his followers. By the time medieval astronomers got around to checking his predictions, this initial error had compounded to such an extent that the Ptolemaic system was getting more and more out of synchronization with the heavens. By the year A.D. 1000, Islamic astronomers were incorporating a variable rate of rotation into the Ptolemaic system to make up for the errors (they called it "trepidation"). But by the sixteenth century, it was clear to astronomers that there was something wrong with the Ptolemaic system. By this time, however, the system had become so entrenched among scholars that it could justifiably be said to represent the dead hand of the past. How, indeed, might modern science emerge when so many learned men continued to serve the cause of ancient authority? Who would champion the future?

Copernicus and the Few

Nicolaus Copernicus was a Pole, a churchman, an intellectual recluse and a somewhat enigmatic figure. So much is unknown, yet it is very clear that he was able to spark the scientific revolution which has so powerfully influenced the past half millennium.

We know more of the lives of Galileo, Tycho, Kepler, and Newton—the four Old World savants who followed and built upon the work of Copernicus. They were all unusual individuals, so we can remark a bit on their personal traits, foibles, and fates. They were directly responsible for overturning key beliefs of medieval times. After a brief introduction to this select club, we will view the contributions of each member.

An Italian scholar and telescope maker, Galileo Galilei has probably attracted the most editorial comment. Admired by our age, he was a gadfly in his own. He finally pushed the Roman Church too far, ending his years in house arrest after recanting to the Inquisition his early claims about the motion of the Earth.

Tycho Brahe was the world's most famous observational astronomer with planetary orbits as his specialty. His personal life was bizarre: he lost the bridge of his nose in a sword fight; he gave up his native Denmark and grand observatory and went into self-imposed exile. He settled in Bohemia and hired an assistant before he died. This assistant, Johannes Kepler, had the good sense to "capture" his mentor's notes to keep them from probate and the heirs.

Kepler was a bit of a fanatic yet loyal to a fault and possessed of a deep belief—or obsession—in the idea that the universe represents a divine work of art. A professional astrologer, he added to his income by casting neatly drawn horoscopes. His scientific findings aided the Englishman Isaac Newton. Although Newton was, by all accounts,

a somewhat unpleasant person and a bit of a snob, he was nonetheless one of the greatest scientists who ever lived.

Copernicus: Chief Revolutionary

Guided by his uncle, a Roman Catholic bishop, Nicolaus was elected to a position as canon (business manager) at the Cathedral of Frauenburg in his native Poland. He traveled widely, studied in Italy, and was the very model of a professional scholar and churchman. From about 1512, Copernicus developed a scheme of a planetary system in which the planets moved and the sun stood still. He confided his manuscript to the printer only in 1540, at age 67. As the story goes, he received a copy of the book on the day he died, three years later.

To our eyes, his book titled *On the Revolutions of the Celestial Spheres* is a queer mix-

For the first time, planets circle the sun; from De Revolutionibus *(1543). Its author, Nicolaus Copernicus, appears opposite. Scholars of the skies, left to right: Tycho Brahe; Ptolemy; possibly St. Augustine; Copernicus; Galileo with pointer; and Andreas Cellarius. The last was author of* Harmonia Macrocosmica, *a scientific work of the 1800s and source for these idealized portraits. Urania, one of the nine Greek muses, also appears.*

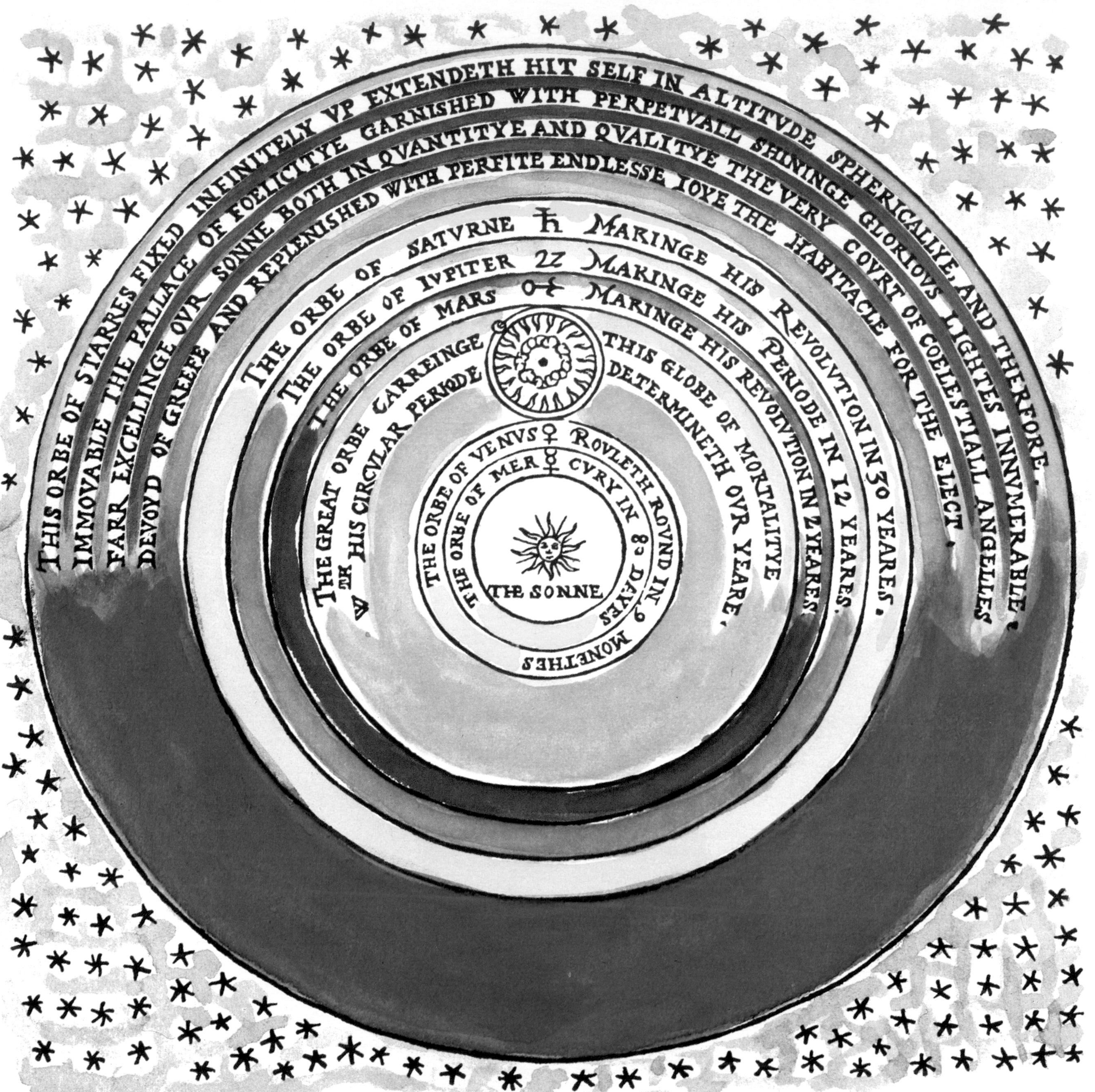
THIS ORBE OF STARRES FIXED INFINITELY VP EXTENDETH HIT SELF IN ALTITVDE SPHERICALLYE, AND THERFORE
IMMOVABLE THE PALLACE OF FOELICITYE GARNISHED WITH PERPETVALL SHININGE GLORIOVS LIGHTES INNVMERABLE.
FARR EXCELLINGE OVR SONNE BOTH IN QVANTITYE AND QVALITYE THE VERY COVRT OF COELESTIALL ANGELLES
DEVOYD OF GREEFE AND REPLENISHED WITH PERFITE ENDLESSE IOYE THE HABITACLE FOR THE ELECT.
THE ORBE OF SATVRNE ♄ MAKINGE HIS REVOLVTION IN 30 YEARES.
THE ORBE OF IVPITER ♃ MAKINGE HIS PERIODE IN 12 YEARES.
THE ORBE OF MARS ♂ MAKINGE HIS REVOLVTION IN 2 YEARES.
THE GREAT ORBE CARREINGE THIS GLOBE OF MORTALITYE WTH HIS CIRCVLAR PERIODE DETERMINETH OVR YEARE.
THE ORBE OF VENVS ♀ ROVLETH ROVND IN 9 MONETHES
THE ORBE OF MER ☿ CVRY IN 80 DAYES
THE SONNE

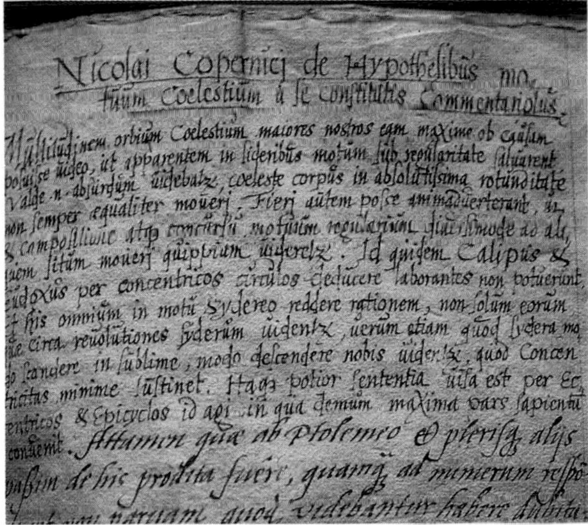

Nicolai Copernici de Hypothesibus motuum Coelestium a se constitutis Commentariolus

ture of revolutionary and traditional ideas. Of course we have the advantage of more than 440 years of familiarity with his breakthrough and its correction and amendment and diffusion by an army of others. But perhaps we are not aware of the magnitude of the Copernican Revolution, how momentous a change it really was.

Copernicus realized that the daily motion of the stars across the sky could be understood as an effect of the Earth's rotation, and that the complex motion of planets could be explained naturally as an effect of movement around the sun. His system also had the advantage that, unlike other ideas that had been introduced to modify Ptolemy, it did not require that the crystalline spheres ever pass through each other. The reader may recall that in the old view the sun, stars, and planets were embedded in their own clear and brittle sheets in concentric spheres around the earth. According to medieval tradition, God lived on the outside of this contrivance and turned the mechanism.

Now with Copernicus all that changed. The sun stood stationary and the planets circled in their orbits. It's important to realize that the Copernican system was not identical to the modern one. To account for the true planetary orbits Copernicus was forced to put his planets on epicycles (circles within circles). The epicycles moved on circles whose centers lay not in the sun, but at a point in space between the sun and the Earth. Nonetheless, even if it could not be immediately proved, his view had an immense allure for adventuresome minds. It was a lively proposition indeed: a seed with the future inside it.

Though the scheme was only marginally simpler than Ptolemy's, students of astronomy (at least from 1543 on) were aware that it was possible to question the wisdom of the ancients. Human reason had begun to free itself from the burden of the past. And for this reason alone we can begin to appreciate the vigor and appeal of the new idea in a Europe that had just participated in the Reformation, Martin Luther's break with the monolithic authoritarianism of Rome. These were heady days—at least for men of learning in northern Europe.

Another consequence of the Copernican system—one that is often overlooked—is that it greatly expanded mankind's concept of the universe. With a stationary earth, the sphere of the stars need lie only a little way beyond the orbit of Saturn, and the entire universe need only be as big as the solar system. If the Earth really were to move around the sun, however, the only way that the stars could appear to be stationary is for them to be exceedingly distant. In one fell swoop, Copernicus moved the Earth from the center and set it moving in a new heaven of wider horizons. Both he and Christopher Columbus lived and worked at the same time. Both revealed new worlds; with Copernicus beginning to chart a realm of whose ends we have yet to discover.

On the Revolutions of the Celestial Spheres spread quickly throughout Europe, encountering far less of the ecclesiastical opposition that was so familiar to Galileo. For one thing, Copernicus was well connected in the church establishment. For another, the unsigned preface of the book makes it clear that the reader can think of the Copernican

Early English version of the Copernican universe (1576), opposite, by Thomas Digges. Both he and Giordano Bruno suggested that stars fill the sky to infinity. Disclaimer to De Revolutionibus *left, says that the work is intended as a mental game, not a depiction of reality. It has been suggested that the addition was a ploy to keep the work off Rome's index of banned books. Some scholars believe that it was the work of Copernicus's proofreader, a Protestant named Osiander.*

Domes cover underground chambers on the Baltic isle of Hveen (now Ven), site of Europe's greatest observatory complex in the late 1500s. At this small annex, called Stjerneborg or "Star Castle," Tycho Brahe's assistants prepare instruments for the night's work. Before the era of the telescope, Tycho perfected positional astronomy—the recording of movements by stars, planets, and comets.

system as merely a mathematical exercise, and not a statement about the real world. This allowed plenty of room for maneuver between theologians, scholars, and others.

Tycho Brahe: One of a Kind

The Danish nobleman Tycho Brahe took Copernicus seriously, but he never had been conventional. In a sense, Tycho's unusual life had begun even before he was born.

Like Copernicus, Tycho had a powerful uncle who influenced him greatly. The Pole's uncle Luke was a Roman Catholic bishop while Tycho's uncle Jørgen served as a vice-admiral in the Danish Navy. He was childless, and had extracted a promise from Tycho's father that he would be given a boy to raise. Tycho's twin brother was chosen. This sibling died, however, and uncle Jørgen apparently felt cheated. He kidnaped Tycho and raised him. Evidently, in the Brahe family this wasn't considered particularly eccentric because, aside from a few threats from his brother, Jørgen managed to get away with his avuncular abduction.

Young Tycho was sent to university to prepare for a career in diplomacy. As might be expected in this family, Tycho had his own ideas. Profoundly impressed by a partial eclipse of the sun in 1560—not so much the eclipse itself as the fact that heavenly events could be predicted by mathematicians—he took up astronomy. The family objected and at one point sent a tutor with explicit instructions to see that their son stopped wasting his time with stars. To counter this maneuver, young Tycho hid his books and instruments under the blankets. Eventually, however, Tycho's family became reconciled to his headstrong behavior.

At the age of 20, Tycho fought a duel with a fellow student over the question of who was the better mathematician. In the course of the duel, a piece of his nose was cut off. He had a gold alloy replacement made and for the rest of his life he frequently rubbed the bridge of his nose with a special salve.

Tycho had a lifelong obsession with measuring the heavens accurately. He was one of the first persons to think seriously about the problem of observational accuracy. Observation in his time was really no more accurate than it had been during the time of Ptolemy. Tycho, born before the invention of the telescope, pushed the accuracy of naked-eye astronomy to its limits. He built huge instruments (some almost 40 feet across) to reduce the errors associated with the reading of scales. He considered the fact that his brass instruments would shrink and expand as the temperature changed and devised tables to correct his readings for this effect. He even built an underground observatory to cut down on vibrations due to the wind.

Tycho lived in a time when accuracy in astronomical observation began to assume the central role it does today. In part, such precision grew from the need to distinguish between the Copernican and Ptolemaic systems, and also because people of the mid-sixteenth century witnessed unusual events in the heavens. On November 11, 1572, a new star appeared in the constellation of Cassiopeia—a star so bright that during the next month it could be seen in daylight.

Tycho repaired to his beautifully crafted oak and brass instruments and took a series of readings. These established beyond a doubt that the object (now called Tycho's supernova) moved less than the most distant planet in the sky and was therefore beyond the sphere of the stars, in fact beyond all the crystal spheres. The heavens seemed to be crumbling, or at least not immutable, and by demonstrating this surprising fact the 25-year-old Dane established himself as Europe's premier astronomer.

Danish nobleman, Tycho Brahe ruled in splendor on an island full of marvelous instruments. His favorite for charting star positions was the astronomical sextant, right. He designed such equipment on a grand scale, and had the individual pieces built with great precision in his own workshop. Uraniborg appears on a recent postal stamp, as does Tycho's star, a supernova which flared in 1572.

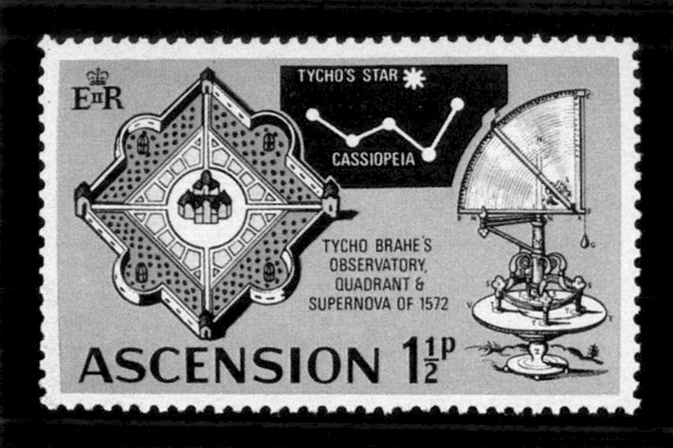

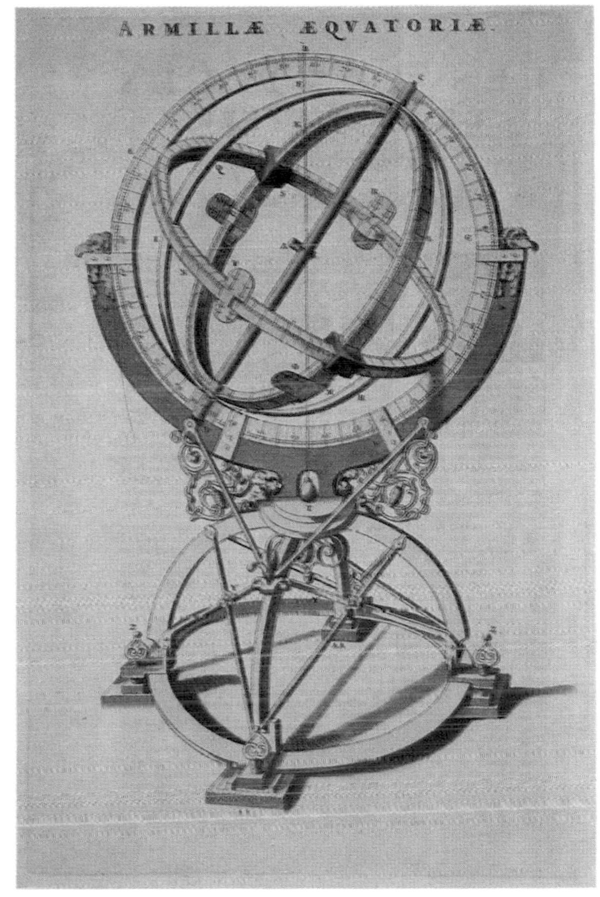

Tycho's large brass quadrant appears at Uraniborg. Behind it is a wall painting, or mural, which gave it the name of the great mural quadrant. In the picture Tycho appears before a cross-section of the castle, with an alchemical laboratory in the basement. The brass instrument itself was used to fix the altitude of stars above the horizon. The device above, an armillary sphere, may have been invented in ancient Greece.

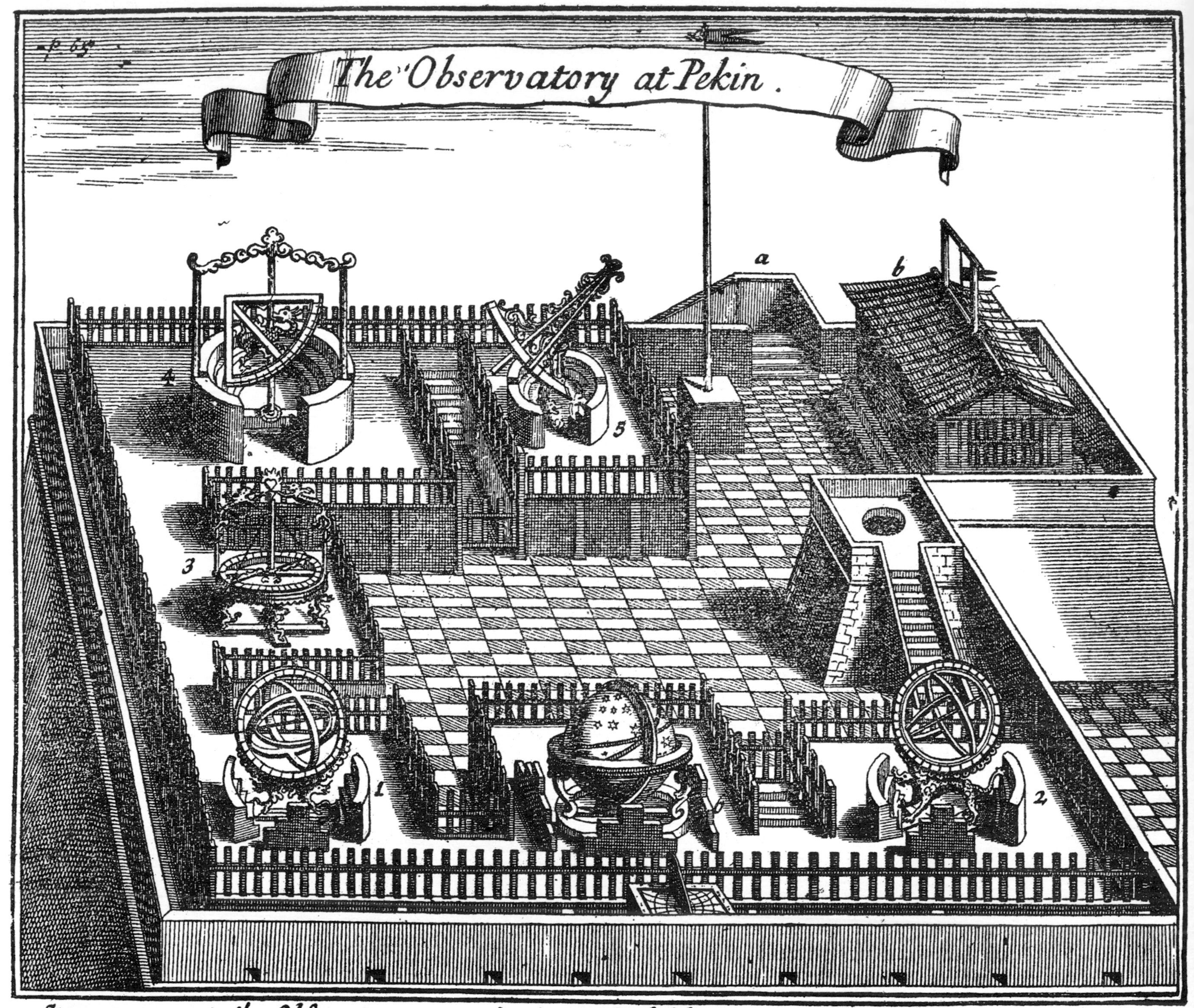

a. Steps going vp to the Observatory
b. A Retiring Room for those that make Observations

1: a Zodical Sphere
2 an Equinoctial Sphere

3 an Azimuthall Horizon
4 a Quadrant

5 A Sextant
6 a Cœlestiall Globe

China's own scientific firsts include the compass, as above. Important Western advances reached the Celestial Kingdom by a Jesuit astronomer, Ferdinand Verbiest (1623–1688). He added new instruments to the Imperial Observatory in Beijing's Forbidden City, including models perfected by Tycho Brahe in Denmark during the late 1500s.

So impressed was the King of Denmark that one of his subjects (and a nobleman to boot) had snatched such fame from the skies that he installed Tycho on an island in the Baltic and provided the money to construct the world's largest astronomical observatory. There Tycho built instruments and gathered a set of data unprecedented in both volume and accuracy. Unfortunately Tycho fell afoul of the succeeding monarch over a number of matters, including the question of whether or not he had the right to throw peasants into his private dungeon. The astronomer had a flair for the feudal life. Packing data, instruments, and his court jester, he left the island of Hveen, eventually alighting at the court of Emperor Rudolph II in Prague.

The events surrounding Tycho's death were as noteworthy as those surrounding his birth. At a banquet attended by much of Prague's high nobility, he partook copiously of the good Bohemian beer. Not wishing to appear impolite, or so the story goes, he refused to excuse himself during the evening, but kept on eating and drinking. Bladder stones may have been his undoing. In any event, he fell into a fever that night and died after 11 days.

Tycho's data tables fell into the hands of the impecunious Austrian mathematics instructor he had hired after his arrival in Prague—young Johannes Kepler.

Kepler's Laws

The Austrian was a mystic by nature, a man of his times. Yet confronted with the full details of the data collected over a lifetime by Tycho, he was compelled to ask certain fundamental questions, however unsettling the answers might prove. Instead of trying to force the data into epicycles and uniform circular motion, he finally went back to square one and considered which orbital shapes would best fit readings.

It may not seem like much, but remember that the persistent failure to discard ancient assumptions had held up progress in astronomy for many centuries.

The work wasn't easy. Sixteen chapters into his book, Kepler says: "If thou, dear reader, art bored with this wearisome method of calculation, take pity on me who had to go through at least seventy repetitions of it . . . " But he kept going.

Kepler established that planetary orbits are elliptical rather than perfectly circular. His results are stated in what are known as Kepler's first and second laws of planetary motion. The first law says that a planet's orbit assumes the shape of an ellipse, with the sun at one focus. The second law indicates that planets move faster when nearer the sun than when farther away. A pretty good way to visualize a planet in motion around the sun is to think of the old schoolchildren's game in which you take a long run at a post in the playground and then grab the post and swing around. As a planet passes near the sun it "swings around," speeding up as it does so.

Kepler published these two laws in 1609. A third and final law was published in 1619, relating the length of a planet's "year" to its distance from the sun. Thus it finally became possible to think about shedding the excess baggage of epicycles, deferants, and equants that had been imposed on nature by the demand that motion in the heavens be circular.

But there was still a distance to go. In the overall scheme, Copernicus had stated a logical deduction that others could examine and test. Tycho had amassed data of suitable quality. This allowed Kepler to hammer out a hypothesis, but others would come forth to forge powerful theories—science and scientists can aspire to no higher goal. In this an Italian had his contributions to make.

DE MAGNETE

In 1600, the English physician William Gilbert suggested that Earth is a gigantic magnet. Here he explains the attractive force of static electricity to Queen Elizabeth I, his most important patient. Gilbert gained the title of "the Queen's Electrician." Her interest in science helped to pave the way for the Enlightenment.

Galileo

Galileo Galilei is one of those men who is famous for the wrong reason. Because of his notorious trial by the Roman Inquisition he has, perhaps undeservedly, become enshrined as a "martyr of science." It is on this that his popular fame rests. The legend is that he stood alone as a champion of the heliocentric universe against the forces of dogmatism and authority. This is an unfortunate situation, because Galileo did many things during his life that were worthy of lasting fame. He was, for example, the founder of modern experimental physics. He also made the first break with naked-eye astronomy by starting a systematic study of the heavens with a telescope—an enterprise still going strong. He was largely responsible for bringing the ideas of Copernicus to the attention of the intellectual community in seventeenth century Europe. It was this activity, of course, that eventually caused him to run afoul of the Inquisition.

Born the son of a musician in Pisa, Galileo studied at the university in that city and soon entered on a career as a teacher of mathematics. According to the story his early interest in physics is associated with observations conducted at church. He noted that a chandelier required the same amount of time to complete a swing, no matter the distance of the swing. Later, Galileo applied this principle to develop a pendulum clock. His studies of physics and mathematics eventually helped him win a position in the court of the Medici in Florence.

While in Venice in 1609, Galileo learned of the recent invention of the telescope in Holland. He quickly devised a superior technique for making lenses and produced a telescope capable of magnifying an image 32 times. Although this is the sort of telescope you might buy for children today, at the time it was an immense step forward in observational power. For the first time it was possible to examine the heavens with more than the unaided power of the human eye. He opened a window on the cosmos and was not slow to exploit his advantage.

In the years that followed the building of his telescope, Galileo and others saw many new things. Mountains loomed on the

The Copernican Revolutionaries

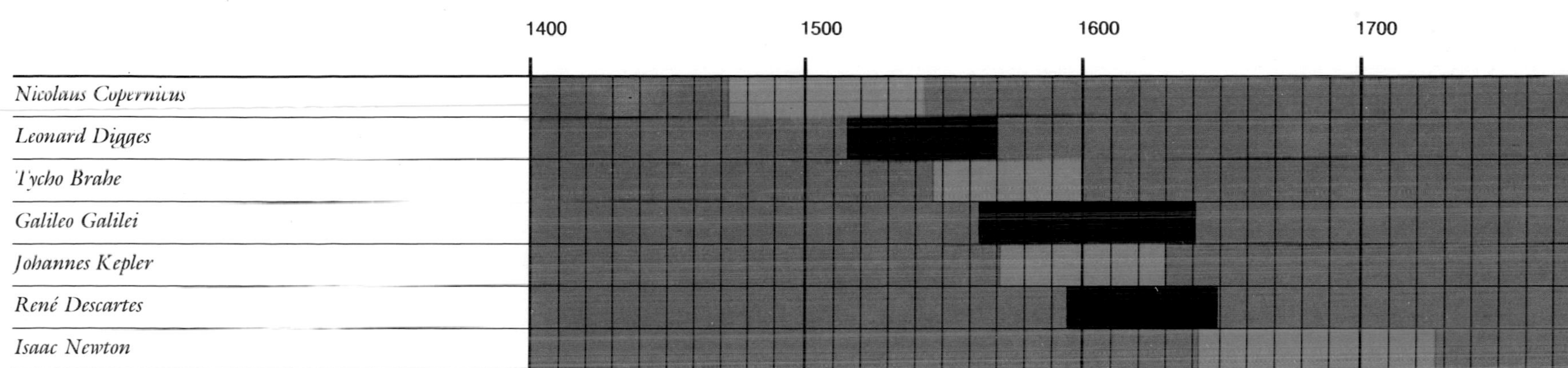

IOANNIS KEPPLERI,
Mathematici Cæsarei,
hanc Imaginem
ARGENTORATENSI BIBLIOTHECÆ
Consecr.
MATTHIAS BERNECCERVS.
Kal. Ianuar. Anno Chr.
M. DC. XXVII

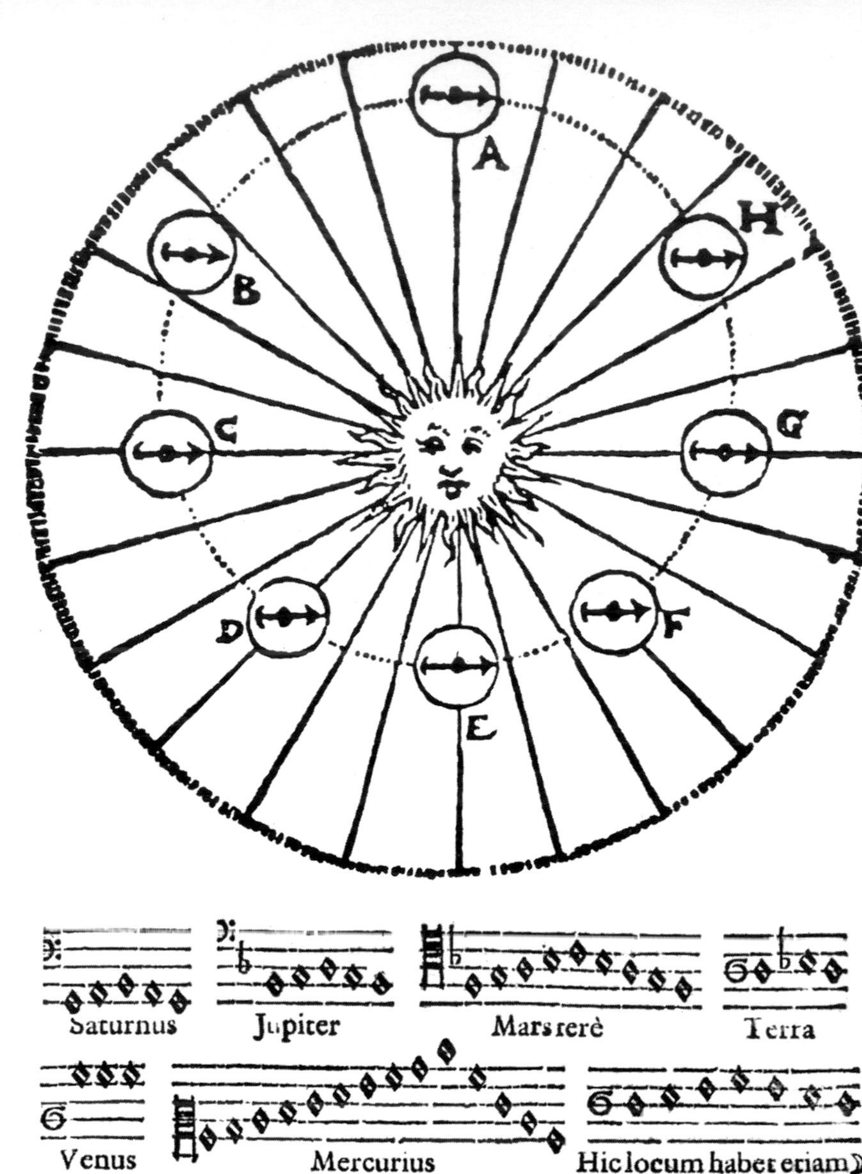
A
B
C
D
E
F
G
H
Saturnus
Jupiter
Mars ferè
Terra
Venus
Mercurius
Hic locum habet etiam ☽

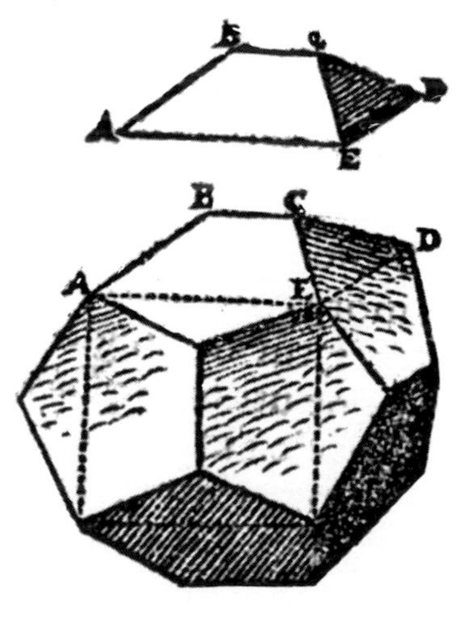
A
B
C
D

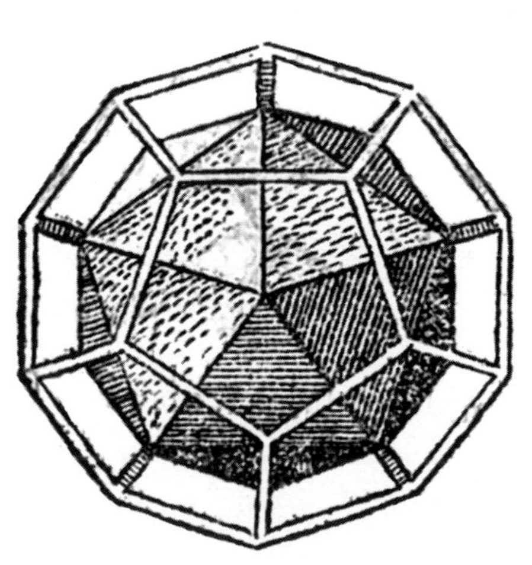

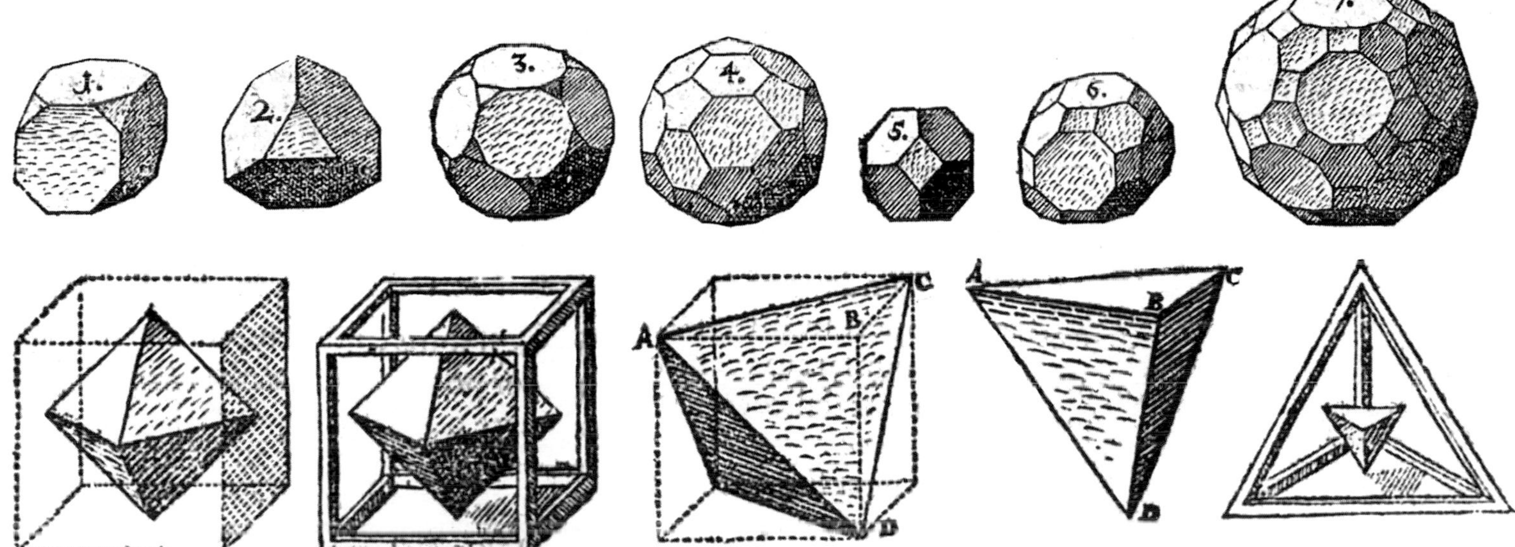

Beset by personal and family problems, Johannes Kepler perhaps found solace in the precision of geometry, endless calculations, and the "music of the spheres." In these he may be thought of as a latter-day disciple of the ancient Greek philosopher Pythagoras. One might imagine that the portrait, opposite, captures Kepler's nature better than the statue, left, reflecting romantic—even mystical—Bohemia of 1600. At this time, Kepler received his charge to analyze Tycho Brahe's data and fully describe the planetary orbits. Geometric shapes may have helped him to visualize various relationships of time and space, as did the musical notes, far left. They represent the changing speeds of the planets in orbit. The worlds were held in their orbits around the sun, Kepler believed, by a force resembling magnetism. This last tenet of his belief inspired both Pascal and Newton, with the latter going on to draft the laws of universal gravitation. As a force, gravity is still puzzling scientists who can find no waves, rays, or other signs of its transmission through space.

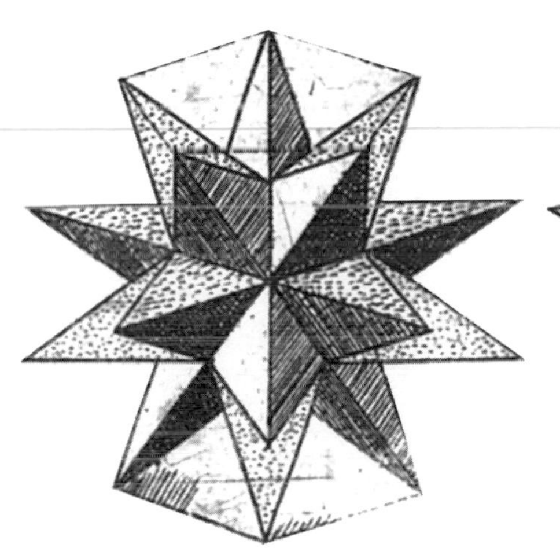

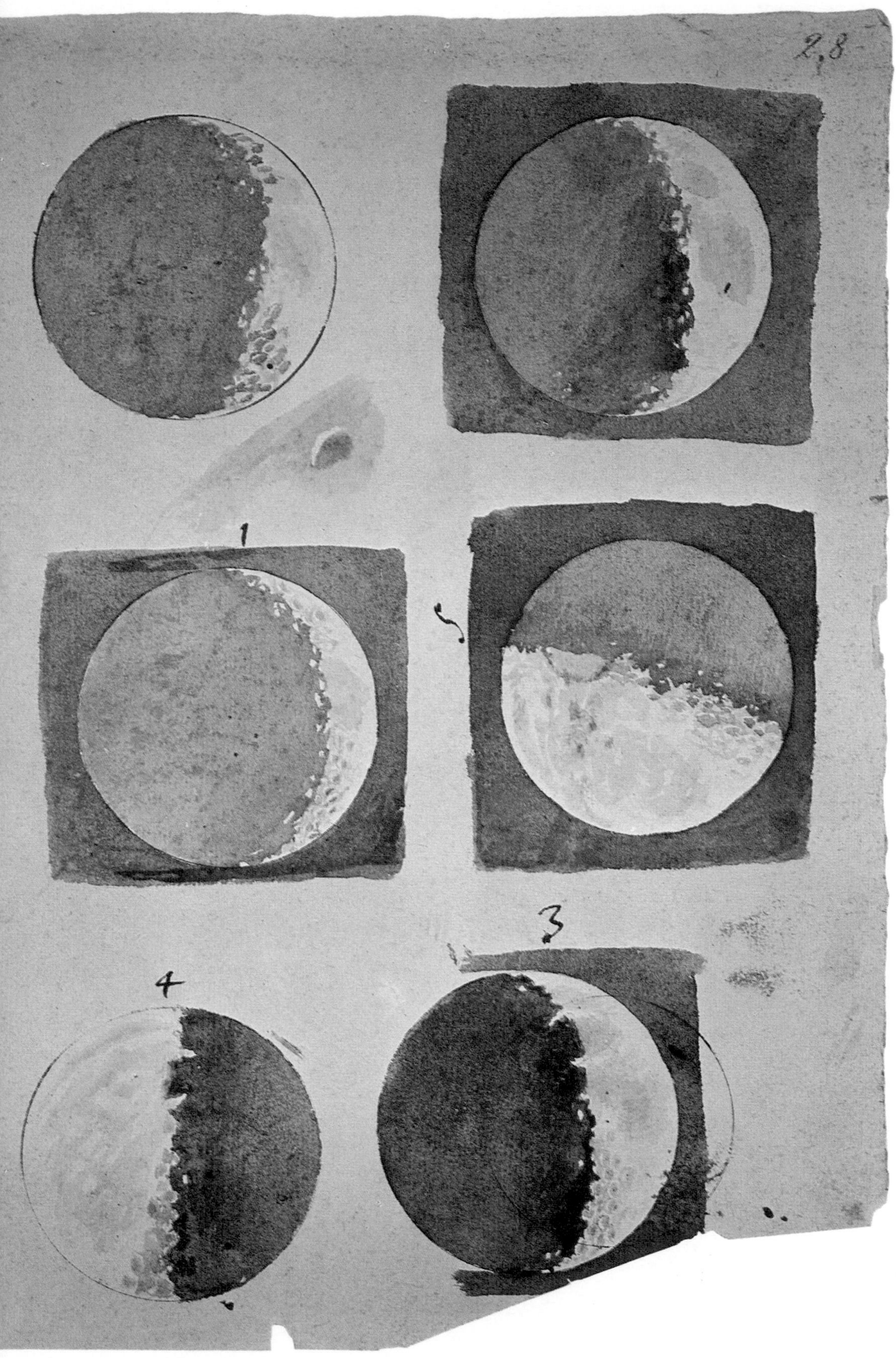

Galileo's precise artwork shows the moon as seen by the first telescopes used to study the skies. The Italian scientist ground his own lenses, and was able to see—and report—the presence of lunar craters, Jupiter's moons, and spots on the sun. We see a scene from the trial of Galileo, called before the Papal Inquisition, opposite. Here in 1633 he recants his earlier teachings and affirms his support for a geocentric universe, one in which the sun, stars, and planets revolve about a stationary earth.

moon where no mountains were supposed to be. The unblemished sun—at least as tradition dictated—clearly had spots on its face. Venus was seen to go through phases as does the moon. Galileo observed the four largest moons of Jupiter and caught a hint of Saturn's rings. As has happened ever since, whenever a new window on the sky is opened, the first glimpse shows an undreamed of richness and complexity.

Why were these discoveries so important in the Copernicus-Ptolemy debate? The first two—lunar mountains and sunspots—showed that the Greek ideal of heavenly perfection was incorrect. Also, the fact that Venus could be observed to pass through phases like the moon proved that at least one planet orbited the sun and not the Earth. Further, the existence of Jupiter's moons belied the assumption that everything orbited Earth. These four objects, at least, seemed perfectly content to circle Jupiter. These facts had enormous psychological impact in the seventeenth century.

Galileo announced the first of these findings in his book *The Starry Messenger* and called Jupiter's satellites the "Medicean Moons" to flatter his hoped-for patrons, the Medici family. The ploy worked, he received support from Florence, yet today we call these satellites the "Galilean Moons."

The maestro certainly had a way with words and, unlike Copernicus and Kepler, he wrote in the vernacular, Italian in this case, and in a manner that any literate person of his time could understand. Through

The Trial of Galileo

The publication of *The Starry Messenger* caused such a stir that complaints were made to the Church about the Copernican doctrines, which were thought to be heretical.

In 1616 the Qualifiers (theological experts) of the Holy Office considered the question and concluded that, while the idea of heliocentrism was indeed heretical, the idea of the motion of the earth was merely "erroneous." As a result of this decision, Cardinal Robert Bellarmine was instructed to summon Galileo and admonish him to give up his ideas. In the event he did not, the Cardinal was to command him to abstain from teaching, defending, or discussing the doctrine.

What happened (or failed to happen) at this meeting played a central role in Galileo's later trial and has been a source of conflict among historians ever since. The question is this: did the Cardinal simply warn Galileo about the new doctrine, or did he forbid him to discuss it further? If the former, then Galileo could have done as Copernicus had done before him—treat heliocentrism as a working hypothesis. If the latter, any further discussion of the subject would have put him—to use a modern analogue—in contempt of court. There are three documents that shed light on this question: first, the minutes of the College of Cardinals for March 3, 1616 state that Bellarmine "admonished him [Galileo] to abandon his opinion [about the Copernican system]." Second, Galileo obtained a letter from Bellarmine stating that "Galileo has not abjured . . . any opinion or doctrine held by him . . . ." Finally, a document was produced at the trial which was supposed to be a report of the meeting between the Cardinal and Galileo. It claimed that Galileo had, indeed, been prohibited from further publications on the Copernican system. Some historians suspect it was a forgery.

The best we can say, then, is that in 1616 something happened between Galileo and the Church concerning the Copernican system. He was an arrogant man, however, and it's clear from what followed that he didn't take the warning seriously. In 1632 he published a book titled *Dialogue on the Great World Systems*. The two systems are, of course, the Copernican and the Ptolemaic, and Galileo tried to demolish the latter. He used a literary device; a conversation between three people, where a character named Simplicio defends the traditional view. Using some good science, some bad science, and some ridicule, Galileo attacks arguments put forward by Simplicio (whose name translates as "fool"). He closes the book with the Pope's favorite arguments, spoken by Simplicio.

This was not welcomed in Rome. The Inquisition summoned Galileo in 1633. He produced Bellarmine's letter and the prosecution presented its document. The verdict probably reflected a plea bargain. Galileo was convicted of "suspicion of heresy," but purged himself by denying he had ever held the heliocentric view. He then spent his last few years under house arrest in his villa near Florence.

In recent times, the Church has reopened the question of Galileo's heresy. By all appearances, Galileo Galilei may well be on his way toward good standing at this time.

his writings the Copernican ideas spread throughout Europe, not just to the scholars but to anyone who was interested enough to read. His trial had little effect on the spread of these ideas—indeed, its only outcome was to guarantee that the center of astronomical studies would move across the Alps to the Protestant countries of Europe and eventually to England.

Newton and the Well-Ordered Universe

Isaac Newton was born the same year Galileo died—1642. This is a coincidence, of course, but it symbolizes the continuity of the development of scientific ideas about the universe during the seventeenth century.

Newton helped to introduce the scientific method into Western thought. He founded the modern science of physics and gave us a view of the universe that we still hold today. His most important contribution to astronomy was the law of universal gravitation. Deceptively simple, it states that there will be a force of attraction between any two objects in the universe, a force proportional to their masses and one which changes with the distance between them. The laws that Kepler deduced from Tycho's data can also be derived from Newton's work.

In later years, a legend grew about how he came to realize that one law could govern the entire universe. The part that sticks in the public fancy is the fall of that apple in the orchard.

To understand Newton's insight in the orchard, it is important to remember that up until his time the science of astronomy (which dealt with the heavens) and the science of mechanics (which dealt with the motions of things on earth) were totally separated. There seemed to be no connection at all between the stately turning of the planets and the fall of an apple. It was Newton's gift to humanity to realize that such

Spectral colors from Newton's prism fall on pages of his notes, to be seen at Trinity College, Cambridge. In his works, he also described an invention for which he is acclaimed, the reflecting telescope. Newton's likeness appears on a British pound note and a French stamp.

A mental experiment with the flight of cannonballs enabled Newton to analyze the orbital mechanics of planets, moons, and comets, tying the science of terrestrial mechanics to the science of astronomy. The diagram at right shows a cannon of the era, with an angular sighting device of a type developed by Galileo, whose experimental approach helped Newton make his theoretical breakthrough.

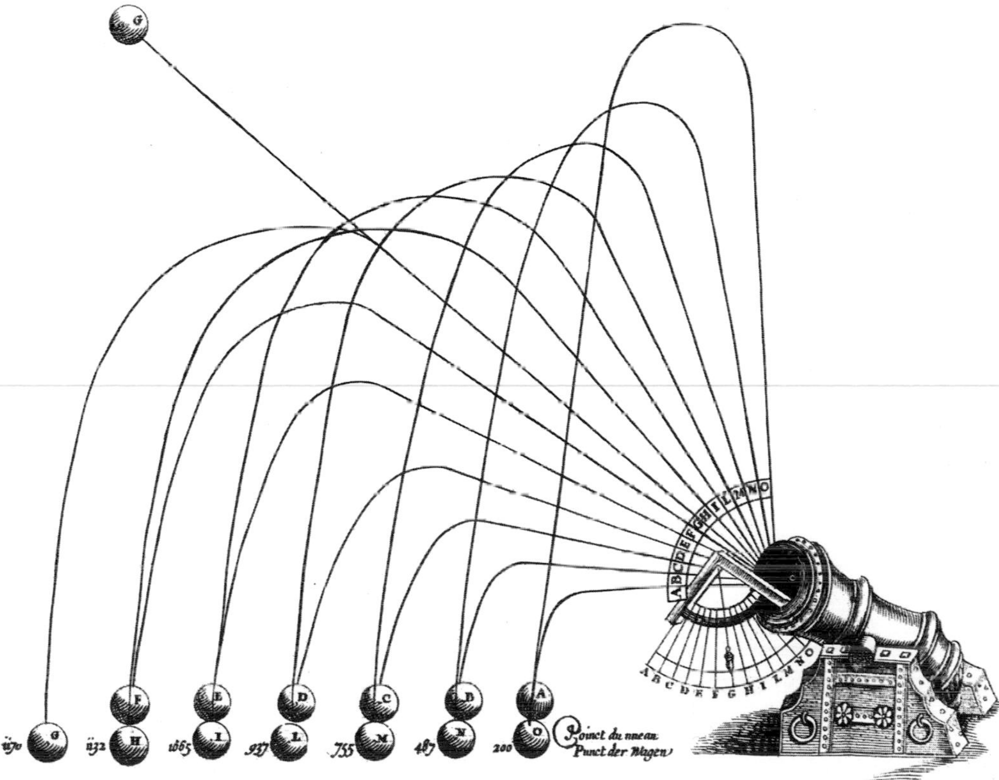

artificial distinctions do not really hold in nature—that the universe is a single seamless web, and the force that guides the moon also causes the apple to fall.

Earlier, Galileo had founded the modern science of mechanics. He understood how objects at the earth's surface fall under the influence of gravity, and how projectiles like cannonballs move through their trajectories. Newton built on this work to show the unity of what we call the gravitational force.

He tried to imagine what would happen if you put a cannon on a mountaintop and fired one projectile after another, increasing the charge of powder for each succeeding shot. Obviously, successive cannonballs would fall farther away from the mountaintop. Eventually, if there is just enough powder in the imaginary cannon, the cannonball would be moving so fast that it would be able to get all the way around the world. In this situation the downward pull of gravity would have been effectively overcome and the altitude of the cannonball would be the same after one orbit as it had been at the beginning, at least in Newton's brain. An interesting situation indeed.

One might fire the cannon, pull it aside, and wait for a little over an hour. At that time the cannonball would come whizzing by. Neglecting wind resistance, the rotational effect of the globe, and other influences the master gunner cannot afford to forget, our theoretical cannonball would be moving just as fast on its return as it had been moving when it left the cannon's mouth. In such an abstract situation the cannonball might just keep on going around the earth forever.

Newton realized that his hypothetical missile was behaving exactly like our moon or any other satellite. In his own words, "[I] compared the force requisite to keep the Moon in her Orb with the force of gravity at the surface of the Earth, and found them to answer pretty nearly." What Newton saw was that the moon and the Earth are continually falling toward each other, but that their orbital motion keeps them going around, just like the cannonball. With this realization, any nice distinction between earthly science and the study of the heavens (though an article of faith since it was first taught by the ancient Greeks) crumbled. There was only one force of gravity and it governed both the moon and the falling apple. And just as the Earth's gravitational attraction acting on the moon kept it in orbit, the sun's attraction acting on the planets kept them going. Using the methods of calculus, a mathematical method that he originated, Newton worked out the orbits of the planets and demonstrated that they matched Kepler's laws.

This picture of the bodies of our solar system in perpetual motion, and with continual influence upon each other, led naturally to the kind of clockwork universe we normally associate with the term "Newtonian." The same regime of nature, all-encompassing and inflexible, holds sway throughout the universe. Once the solar system was created, its future history was ordained, at least in the well-defined realm of Newton's celestial mechanics. Movement of heavenly bodies appeared as steady progression, even more regular than that of the gears of a clock of the era.

A debate ensued along these lines: G.W. Leibniz contending that God made the universe so that it worked properly all by itself; and Samuel Clarke saying that God made continual adjustments to the works. Either way, the Creator had more leisure than with Ptolemy's system, also geared, which ascribed to God (or appointed angels) the turning of cranks. Newton, we find, believed that God not only created the universe, and wound it up, but fine-tuned the mechanism as it operated.

How obvious that such a change of world view would have wide ramifications in philosophy and religion. Some people's eyes and minds—quite a few in England—were opened to the possibilities of scientific explanation of heavenly goings-on.

It is all but impossible to overemphasize the importance of this new movement, the Enlightenment, and of Newton's place as its prime mover. He culminated the work begun by Copernicus and his successors. Instead of a closed set of spheres revolving eternally around a motionless earth, the universe was revealed as a vast collection of suns, stretching away toward infinity. The slow majestic circling of the planets was revealed to be the consequence of the same law of nature that governs events on earth.

An important insight in itself, the Newtonian Synthesis leads to an even more powerful idea. Conceding that the laws of nature are the same for the sky as for the earth, it follows that we can investigate events anywhere else in the universe through work done here and now in our laboratories. If we assume that the laws of nature are unchanging, we can hold that what happened at any time in the past as well—right back to the creation of the universe itself—is accessible to our investigation.

We will see that the unraveling of the secret of the moment of creation is one of the prime goals of modern cosmology. It is comforting, in the face of such advances in scientific knowledge, to reflect on how it all started. An obscure Polish scholar, his energetic insights cherished and perfected by others, was able to set in motion a scientific revolution capped by (of all things) a view of all space and time based on an inspired interpretation of the fall of an apple in an English orchard.

Candlelight bathes the faces of English children of the mid-1700s, a time of wide popular interest in Newtonian physics and other aspects of natural philosophy. Called "Philosopher Lecturing on the Orrery," this painting by Joseph Wright of Derby (1734–1797) shows a clockwork model of the planets as they orbit the sun. The unseen candle represents our central star which shines with a pale yellow color.

Part 2

Exploding Horizons

Overleaf: Dwarfed by his 100-foot-high radio telescope, an astronomer pauses to read and reflect. The entire array of nearly 30 dishes in New Mexico tunes into galaxies millions of light-years away. Radio image, opposite, represents the nucleus of our galaxy as pictured in 1984 by National Radio Astronomy Observatory scientists van Gorkom, Schwarz, and Bregman.

In science as in other fields, certain headliners attract public attention. For instance, the planetary system adopted by most people was that proposed by Copernicus, described by Kepler, and explained by Newton. Yet the first real proof that the earth moved was set up by someone whom only astronomers remember. In 1675, observations made at the Royal Observatary in Paris by Olaus Rømer indicated that light had a finite velocity.

Building on Rømer's work, James Bradley discovered a slight displacement in the direction from which starlight arrived at the earth. He was able to show that this was a combination of the velocity of light and the velocity of Earth in its orbit around the sun. Bradley's proof of earthly motion had been totally unpredictable up to the time of his demonstration. Up until then, everybody pretty much accepted the Copernican-Newtonian scheme on faith.

Again and again in science, we see that the work of the pioneers—the finders—is brought to fulfillment by others, often of different temperament and talents. We are even tempted to repeat the old business cliché that there are three types of people behind every successful enterprise: these are the finders, the minders, and the grinders. Copernicus and Newton were certainly the finders; Rømer and Bradley minded the store. And in astronomy there are, quite literally, the grinders—optical technicians who produce lenses, prisms, and mirrors.

One might even consider the main astronomical work of the 1700s to be the improvement of observational techniques. New and sometimes better telescopes were constructed. As instruments and the field of optics improved, the chief aim of several astronomers was to survey the sky, to find what was there. If you don't know the inventory, you can't run the store.

One of the best instrument makers and users of them by the last part of the eighteenth century was William Herschel. Not only did he make the best telescopes, but he was most assiduous in their application. He was a combination grinder and finder, discovering a new planet, ultimately named Uranus, as well as so-called double stars, and cloudy spots we know as nebulae—all while making sky "sweeps."

No one really doubted that the sun and its entourage of planets were effectively isolated from the remote stars. But people wondered how extensive was our system of stars, the universe. In 1826, H.W.M. Olbers asked, "If the universe is filled with stars and extends to infinity, why is the sky dark at night?" His point was, given his conditions, no matter where one looked in an infinite sky, there would be stars. An infinite amount of stars would fill the sky like a bright sheet of light, filling all gaps. His question and the obvious darkness of the sky became known as Olbers' paradox. The obvious answer was that the universe had a finite extent. But how far away was the edge? And what was beyond?

As observing techniques improved, so did our inventory of celestial objects. One prominent class grew in size and diversity. It contained the clouds of hazy light we call nebulae—Latin for clouds. Again as telescopes improved, these nebulae came into sharper focus and astronomers began to classify them according to their appearance. Some were very hazy, others rather granular, still others had a spiral shape. Herschel himself had discerned a particular type he called "planetary." He knew they were not relatec to planets, but they looked like planets at first glance—they had round surfaces.

In order to learn the reality behind the images of stars and nebulae, progress was required on what seemed to be an entirely unrelated front, the work of the physics laboratory.

One of the things Newton—that paragon of a finder—accomplished in those halcyon days at Woolsthorpe was the observation that sunlight passed through a glass prism was arrayed into all the colors of the rainbow. Further, when this colored beam was passed through a second prism held in a complementary way, the colors were recombined to resemble sunlight. Newton noted the fact but did not pursue it.

The next advance in this direction came in 1802 when fellow Englishman William Hyde Wollaston repeated Newton's experiment. He used a narrow band of sunlight arranged to pass through the prism, crossing its long axis. He noticed that some colors were missing in very narrow regions of the rainbow that we call the spectrum. What caused the gaps? He had no answer, nor did Joseph von Fraunhofer who made a map of over 500 such spectral lines by 1815. The problem was solved in 1859 when Gustav Kirchoff and Robert Bunsen (who invented the burner) showed that the dark lines in sunlight corresponded exactly to the bright and narrow color lines emitted by chemical elements heated in a gas flame.

Laboratory work over the next many decades showed that spectral lines were related to changes in energy conditions inside atoms. The analysis of light by the spectroscope and the development of our ideas of atomic structure went hand in hand, and make a fascinating story in themselves.

By the first years of the twentieth century, astronomers using very clever statistical tools had found that the universe, as we recognized it, was indeed finite. We were sensibly near the center. Among the forms of star clusters found, there was a whole catalogue of a kind called globular from their obvious shape. A sky map of these spherical clusters showed them to be located in only one-half of the sky. They seemed to be centered on a region in the neighborhood of Scorpius and Sagittarius.

Harlow Shapley (an American we shall encounter again) reasoned that because of the laws stemming from Newton's understanding of gravitation, the center of the cloud of globular clusters was most likely the same as the center of our universe. He worked this out as about 50,000 light-years away. He concluded that we are nowhere near the center of the universe.

Now a controversy raged over the location of the spiral nebulae. Were they in our system of stars, or were they beyond the edge of our "universe?"

They were beyond our Milky Way. And those universal horizons have been expanding, explosively so, ever since. Where will it end? Will it end?

Even today we are not sure that these questions have answers! But—as revealed in the chapters that follow—the theoretical trailblazers, the minders of observatories, and the instrument makers still pool their talents to probe the unknown. K.L.F.

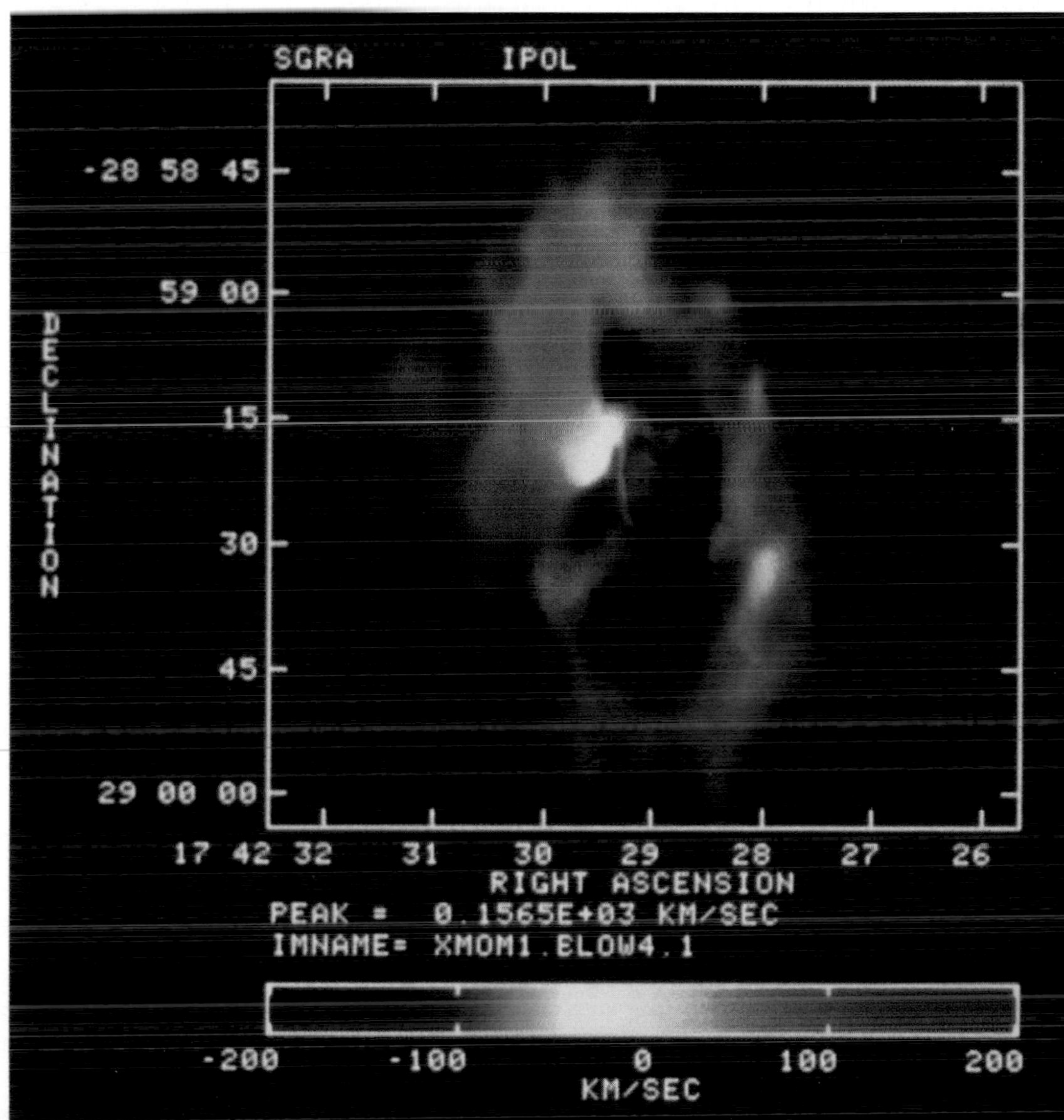

Our First Long Look

In the 200 years that followed Newton's discovery of the workings of the solar system, astronomers developed two improved tools. One of these was instrumental. Bigger and sometimes better telescopes allowed astronomers to collect more and more light from objects farther and farther away, thereby extending our ability to see at a distance—and to understand our surroundings better than naked-eye astronomers had ever dreamt possible.

The second improvement was theoretical and involved the increasing ability of scientists to use the calculus and Newton's laws to analyze (and therefore predict) the behavior of ever more complex systems. The delicate interplay of these two fields of science was like a waltz through history—first one partner leading, then the other, but with each dependent on the other to get from one place to the next. In similar fashion the development of our present knowledge of the solar system is a beautiful model of the interaction between theory and experiment, between science and technology—an interaction without which modern science could not exist.

We have already seen that even a primitive telescope of the type that Galileo first turned toward the heavens was capable of uncovering important new knowledge about the solar system. To go beyond Galileo, however, it was necessary to build better telescopes. This was a far from easy task.

Isaac Newton concluded that there was no future in the type of telescope used by Galileo. Called the refractor, it relies on a series of lenses to collect and focus the incoming light. But the design of lenses is fraught with problems, and almost a century passed before optical technicians could build a large telescope of this type.

Newton therefore decided to try to build a different type of telescope—one without

glass lenses. In Newton's device, light is focused by a curved mirror at the back of the instrument. Newton made the mirror on his telescope from polished metal. His first models were not much more powerful than Galileo's refractor, but by the latter part of the seventeenth century, William Herschel in England was building telescopes with mirrors measuring four feet across. With these sorts of instruments the exploration of the solar system went into high gear.

By mid-eighteenth century, the creation of mirrors from metal had been perfected. By the twentieth century, mirrors were ground from glass and then coated with reflective metal. Today, such highly efficient light-collectors are the workhorses of astronomy. The most famous (and most productive) of these giants is the 200-inch telescope located at the Hale Observatory on Mount Palomar near San Diego, California.

Completed in 1948, Hale's main mirror is 17 feet (or five meters) across and weighs more than 14 tons. Technicians ground and polished away more than five tons of glass to form the concave surface, which became

Observatory staff pose with the University of Pittsburgh's Thaw 30-inch refractor just before its completion in 1913. Stephen Thaw sits atop counterweights needed to keep the telescope in balance. European astronomer views the heavens with what appears to be a hybrid telescope, part reflector and part refractor, opposite, from about 1650.

reflective when coated with less than an ounce of aluminum. To construct the immense disk, molten Pyrex glass was poured into a form, then allowed to cool for an entire year to keep the glass from cracking.

The telescope itself is so big that the astronomer actually sits in a cage inside it when he is observing. On the other hand, it is so well-balanced that it can be moved by an electric motor no more powerful than the one that drives the food processor in your kitchen! Although there is now a larger optical telescope in operation in the Caucasus Mountains, technical troubles have limited the usefulness of the Soviet apparatus.

The new generation of telescopes concentrated in the southwestern United States uses computerized systems for light collection to compensate for what they lack in sheer size. Also, a national observatory at Kitt Peak, Arizona, holds one of the world's largest concentrations of astronomical instruments. And while the Hubble Space Telescope (a reflector) will operate outside the earth's atmosphere, big land-based mirror systems appear to have a bright future.

The Outer Planets

Steady improvement in telescope design has made it possible to expand our inventory of the solar system. William Herschel, born in Germany, was a musician-turned-astronomer who lived in England during the eighteenth century. He took to building his own

Above left, "Leviathan of Parsonstown," with a six-foot metal mirror, was the world's largest telescope when built by the third Earl of Rosse (William Parsons) in the early 1800s. John Herschel, son of William and known on his own as an early observer of the southern sky, became famous when a New York newspaper falsely reported that he had seen life on Mars. Above, one of the first photographs of a celestial object, this daguerreotype of the moon was taken in 1852 at the Harvard College Observatory.

reflecting telescopes because he couldn't afford to buy those made by craftsmen. Following his belief that studying the heavens was a way of seeing into the mind of God, Herschel set about his ambitious task of cataloguing everything in the sky.

On March 13, 1781, Herschel observed a fuzzy object, hitherto unknown. His telescope was good enough to allow him to see that this new object was not a mere point (as most stars appear), but something with an extended structure. Subsequent checking showed that the object moved against the background of the fixed stars, which meant that it was either a planet or a comet. Since there was a 2,000-year tradition limiting the planets to the six that are visible to the naked eye, European astronomers took a hard look before concluding that Herschel really had found another planet—one located too far from the sun to be seen by the naked eye. It was christened Uranus after a classical deity—the father of Saturn and grandfather of Jupiter—and became the first planet discovered in modern times.

Astronomers all over Europe worked to chart its orbit. It quickly became apparent that applying Newton's law of gravitation to the new planet did not give a correct description of its path in the sky. Working independently, an English and a French astronomer came to the same conclusion. In 1845, John Couch Adams and Urbain-Jean-Joseph Leverrier showed that this orbital discrepancy could be explained if there was yet another planet beyond Uranus. On September 23, 1846, astronomers in Berlin saw it, the planet we now call Neptune.

While the discovery of Uranus depended on the development of better telescopes, the discovery of Neptune depended on the ability of theoreticians to predict the orbit of the new planet. In fact, once they were told the general location, observers at Berlin took only a half hour of telescope time to pinpoint Neptune. The ninth planet, Pluto, was also found through computation and search.

About the same time that Herschel was expanding our perception of the solar system, another event took place that served to provide dramatic confirmation of the clockwork universe developed by Newton. In 1682, the British Astronomer Royal observed a large comet approach the sun and swing away. He was Edmond Halley, and from historical records he found that a bright comet with roughly the same orbit had appeared in 1531, 1607, and 1682. Using Newton's laws and the positions of the planets, Halley calculated the orbit of the comet and predicted that it would again be near the sun in 1758. Its appearance, on Christmas Day of that year, provided a major verification of the Newtonian universe. Halley's comet, as it was named, is due for a visit again in 1986. This time, it will be greeted by a small swarm of space probes.

You might think that today, with telescopes and satellites routinely probing the farthest reaches of the universe, there would be few surprises left in the relatively mundane study of our own neighborhood in space. This just isn't true. In 1978, scientists at the U.S. Naval Observatory in Flagstaff, Arizona, obtained high-grade photographs of Pluto showing that the planet has a moon. It was christened Charon, after the boatman charged with conducting souls of the dead to the underworld, Pluto's realm. This discovery allowed astronomers to estimate the mass of Pluto, a value insufficient to explain all of the vagaries of the orbits of Neptune and Uranus. Thus, there still may be pages to be written in the story of the solar system—the possible tenth planet.

The Stars

Beyond our own star system lie other stars, perhaps with their own planets. With our growing knowledge has come what might

Scientists of Many Spheres

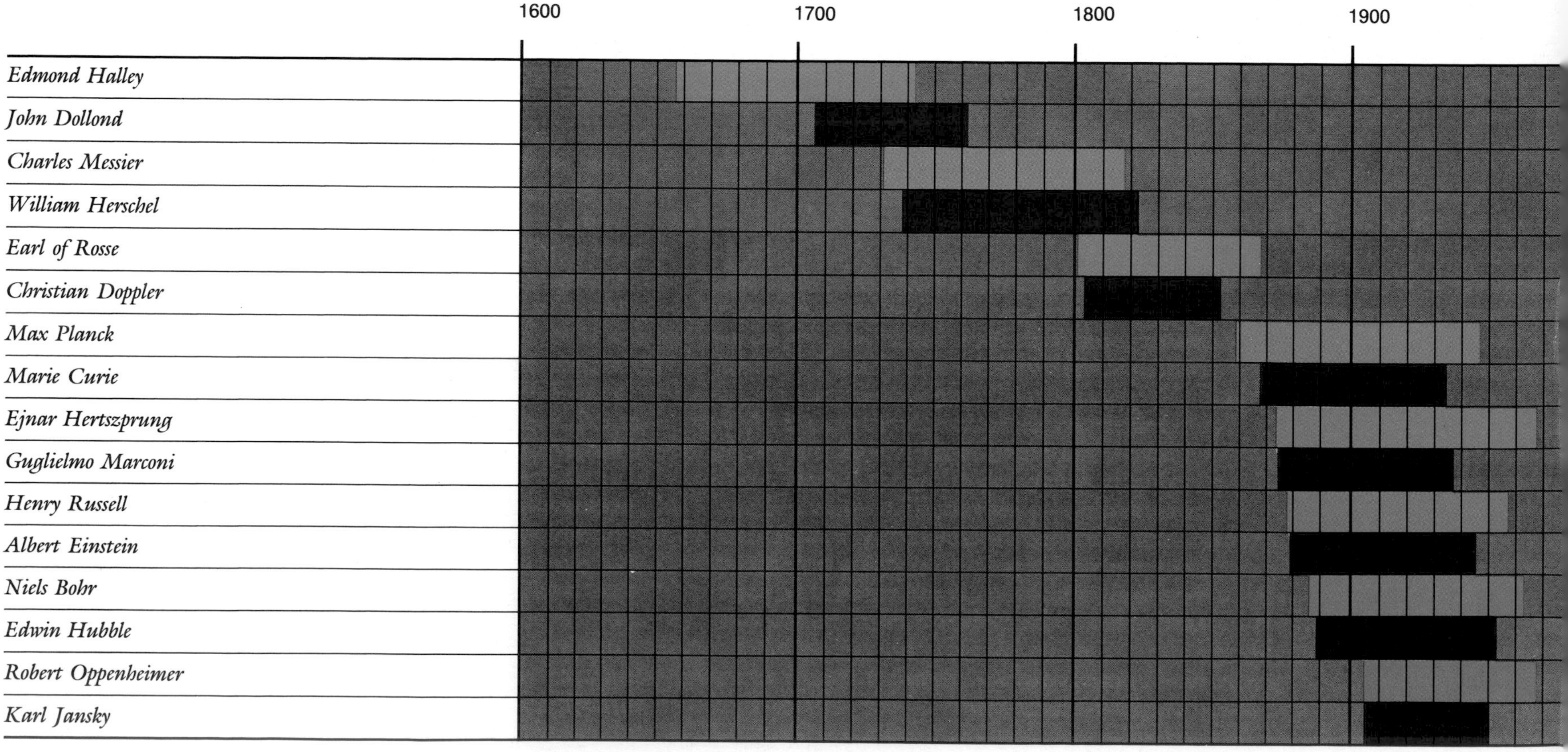

1600 1700 1800 1900

Edmond Halley
John Dollond
Charles Messier
William Herschel
Earl of Rosse
Christian Doppler
Max Planck
Marie Curie
Ejnar Hertszprung
Guglielmo Marconi
Henry Russell
Albert Einstein
Niels Bohr
Edwin Hubble
Robert Oppenheimer
Karl Jansky

be called the cosmological breakthrough. From a science concerned with determining *where* stars and planets are, the new discoveries changed the focus of astronomy to the question of *what* they are. The new science of astrophysics emerged as an exciting complement to astronomy. It seeks to reveal the nature of the stars through an understanding of the intimate and intricate relationship of matter and energy.

The basis for this new departure in our view of the heavens was a famous experiment by Isaac Newton in which he noted that a glass prism held up to a beam of sunlight broke the light into its constituent colors. In modern terminology, we say that Newton produced a "spectrum" of sunlight.

For a long time, this peculiar property of light remained nothing more than a nuisance in the making of lenses. Then in 1802 William Hyde Wollaston found stripes in the spectrum where colors were missing. By 1814 Joseph von Fraunhofer made the first map of these lines which have come to bear his name. Their origin remained a mystery until 1859 when Gustav Kirchoff, working with Robert Bunsen at Heidelberg, showed that the lines were caused by the presence of certain familiar chemical elements in the outer atmosphere of the sun. This connection between the light emitted by a distant star and the types of atoms in it became the central feature of the new astronomy. In fact, we can think of this discovery as the point at which the study of the sky began to shift from astronomy to astrophysics.

A useful way to understand the light-atom connection is to pause for a moment to contemplate the atom as most popularly portrayed. At the center is a small, massive, positively-charged structure known as the nucleus. Around this center the light negatively-charged electrons circle, much like planets circling a star. The analogy is more than figurative—the atom is knit into a unit by the electrical force in a way similar to that of gravity as it holds the solar system together.

Research has shown, however, that electrons can't be located just anywhere in an atom; only at certain well-specified distances from the nucleus. This is different from a planetary system in which, presumably, any planet could occupy a different orbit. There is no reason in principle, for example, why the Earth couldn't have been a little closer to the sun than it is. But with electrons, such variations aren't allowed.

Whenever we have a situation like this, in which something can have only a certain number of well-defined and prescribed values, we say that the system is "quantized." At the level of atoms and nuclei, nature appears to be completely quantized, and the branch of science that deals with such systems is called "quantum mechanics." Electrons must circle the nuclei in well-prescribed orbits; thus if they wish to move

Eight Canadian scientists and one central timekeeper, wait for signs of meteor activity in 1957. Each observer pushes a button as a shooting star appears in his sector. Large cameras at a nearby observatory open to photograph the fireball. "Pickering's Harem," below, were the women astronomy assistants who worked for Edward C. Pickering, famed director of the Harvard Observatory, in 1917. These pioneers in classifying star spectra included such illustrious astronomers as Henrietta Leavitt, sixth from left, who investigated Cepheid variables, and Annie Cannon, fifth from right, the founder of modern star classification.

Berlin's Treptow public telescope was built in 1896 and still receives 70,000 visitors a year. It originated in an era when the Industrial Revolution promised technology for all. At sixty feet, it remains the world's longest refractor tube.

from one orbit to another, they must make what is known as a "quantum leap," going from the initial to the final orbit without tarrying in between.

But such a leap changes the energy of the electron, just as rolling down a hill changes the energy of a ball. When a quantum leap occurs, excess energy can be radiated away from the atom as light. In an inverse process, light (of just the right energy) striking an atom can be absorbed, pushing the electron from a lower orbit to a higher one, in sort of a reverse quantum leap.

Since no two species of atoms have exactly the same orbits, the light emitted by one type of atom will differ slightly from the light of another. Thus we have something of an atomic fingerprint. If we measure the spectrum of light emitted by an atom in our laboratory, and then see that same spectrum repeated in the light from a distant star, we can be sure that the atom in the star is the same as the one in our laboratory. Similarly, in the laboratory we see that light which has passed through a group of atoms is absorbed at certain frequencies, and we then observe dark lines in the spectrum at the same frequencies in the spectrum of stars like the sun. We can be sure that we have identified at least one species of atom through which light from the sun's interior has passed on its way to our telescopes. For future reference, when we look at light being given off by an atom, we speak of an "emission spectrum;" but for dark bands, we talk of an "absorption spectrum."

This correspondence between atoms and the light they shed is actually part of our everyday experience, although we may not have thought about it this way. We know that a light bulb filled with neon will glow red, that sodium-vapor street lamps give off a yellow light, and mercury-vapor lamps are bluish-white. Each element has its own characteristic color. We have no trouble telling the difference between these types of light. Sodium lights are often used to mark freeway entrances and exits, and mercury is used widely for street lighting. The former casts a straw color and the latter creates a sickly green on some color film.

The discovery of the connection between atoms and light was tremendously important for astronomy, of course, but it would be a mistake to think that this was the only area where it was useful. It also played a role in chemistry. As early as 1868, bright lines were observed in the sun's spectrum—lines that had no counterpart in any known element on earth. It was concluded that there was a new chemical element present on the sun, an element that was given the name helium (from the Greek word for sun, *helios*).

There was, as far as anyone could tell, no helium on the earth. In 1895, however, helium was discovered in certain uranium-bearing minerals. Once again, it turned out that the earth was not so different from the rest of the universe, as some people had thought. Since that discovery at the end of the last century, helium has become a fixture in many laboratories. A quart of liquid helium costs $6.00—about the same as a cheap brand of Scotch whisky.

From these early days, the technique of identifying chemicals by the light they emit or absorb has penetrated into every corner of modern technology. Today spectroscopy finds extensive use in industrial quality control (to monitor the presence of impurities), in medicine (to identify substances taken from the body), and in many other areas where it is important to determine the chemical constituents of materials. It even figures in courtroom dramas, where substances identified by this sort of analysis are accepted as legal evidence.

The Power Source

Once it became obvious that the sun and the other stars are made of the same chemical elements as those we find on earth, another question arose. How could the stars shine so brightly for so long? We know that there are chemical reactions like burning that give off light and heat, but scientists quickly calculated that even if the sun were made of pure anthracite coal (the best fuel around), it could have shone for only 20,000 years before being reduced to cinder.

Throughout the last decades of the nineteenth century, scientists tried to determine the sun's fuel source. The answer came from a totally unexpected quarter—the study of radioactive materials. By the 1930s, a number of things had become clear: first,

The Lens

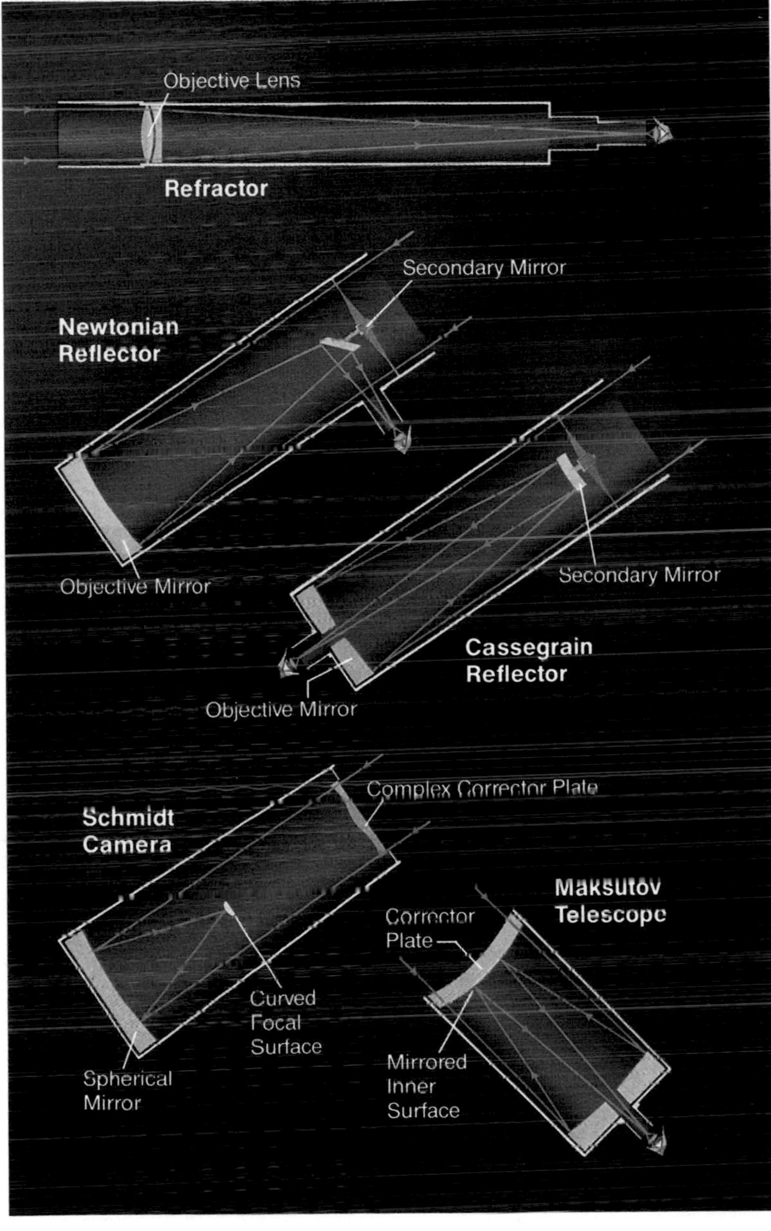

Telescopes collect and focus light with the help either of glass lenses or silvered mirrors. The former, called refractors, were first used for astronomical observation by Galileo. Reflectors, generally attributed to Isaac Newton, gather light in concave mirrors. Refractors employ various light paths to convey an image to the viewer's eye. The Schmidt camera and Maksutov telescope—often referred to as catadioptric—possess features of both types.

The same property of glass that produces spectra from a prism causes a major problem in lens design. When light enters the front surface of a lens it is bent in such a way that all of the beams converge on a point known as the focus. If, however, each different color is bent by a different amount by the glass, each color component of a beam of white light will be focused at a different spot. This means, for example, that it would be impossible to arrange things so that both red and blue are in focus at the same time. If the lens is used to project an image upon a screen, that image will be surrounded by a halo of varicolored light. Thus, an astronomer looking at a star sees a blurred image, an effect known as chromatic aberration. Early astronomers thought of it as an inevitable consequence of using a glass lens. This is one reason why Isaac Newton went to the trouble of inventing the reflecting telescope.

Chromatic aberration is not insoluble, however. As one of Newton's contemporaries pointed out, there is at least one lens—the one in the human eye—that manages to correct for the problem. In fact, by 1758 the English scientist John Dollond had designed telescopes with lenses made from a glass doublet, two pieces of shaped glass, one behind the other. Each lens element was ground from a different type of glass, and was so arranged that the aberration introduced by one lens is canceled by the aberration introduced by the other. Each lens, on its own, exhibits chromatic aberration, the two taken together do not. This is the secret of the achromatic lens of the type that you have in your camera. Yet even the best glass lenses are suitable for only relatively small devices.

Since the time of Dollond, the design of lenses has been brought to near perfection through the use of powerful computers. These electronic tools apply simple optical principles to design systems with many lenses. The zoom lens in a modern TV camera, for example, may contain more than 20 different lenses, together with electric motors to move them. For all of these complex systems the principle is the same. Multiple lens systems can often succeed where single uncorrected lenses are doomed to failure.

As telescopes have grown larger, therefore, the concave mirror has come into its own, since large glass lenses soon sag of their own weight. The largest lens used in a telescope was about three feet in diameter while the largest mirror measures nearly 20 feet across.

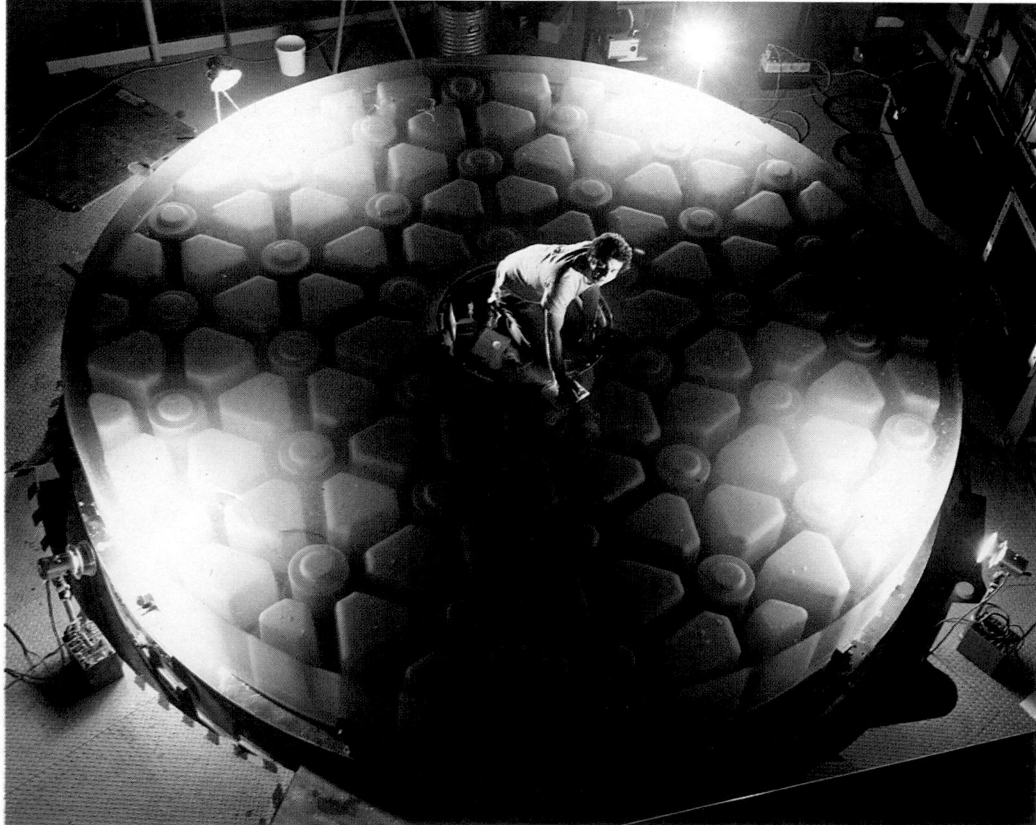

certain nuclear processes altered the weight of atoms; and second, the change could be related to energy by means of Einstein's famous formula, $E = mc^2$. Arthur (later, Sir Arthur) Eddington, working in England in the 1920s, had suggested that the conversion of mass to energy might be the process that provided the sun's energy. But no one knew enough about nuclear physics at that time to make Eddington's suggestion much more than an educated guess. Actually the sun shines through a fusion process in which lighter elements are transmuted into heavier ones with the liberation of energy.

Our detailed knowledge of the mechanisms that power the stars grew out of a small conference held in Washington, D.C., in April 1938. The purpose of the gathering was to bring together astrophysicists and nuclear physicists. The former knew about stellar structure and the latter understood something of the reactions that actually take place in stars. The interchange must have been extraordinarily effective because Hans Bethe of Cornell University worked out the earliest model of the process before dinner in the train diner on his way back home. The theory was so successful that Bethe was awarded a Nobel Prize for physics in 1967.

His idea of nuclear reactions in our sun (and most "stars" are either suns like our own or contain many stars) allowed scientists to begin to understand the very fires of creation. At the center of a star we find a nuclear furnace, a region of temperatures so high that small nuclei (including protons) collide with each other and stick together to form larger nuclei. The mass of the final large nucleus is smaller than the sum of the masses of the small nuclei that fuse during the process. The "extra" mass appears as energy in the center of the sun. In our sun, hydrogen is being "burned" to form helium with the solar body consuming its hydrogen at the rate of more than 10 billion pounds per second. Even at this rate, there is enough readily-available fuel around to keep our own star in its present state for at least another five billion years—half its predicted life span.

While the nuclear furnace is burning, the energy and hot gases streaming outward create a pressure which prevents the collapse of the star. Once the fuel is used up, however, the inexorable collapse begins again.

With the discovery of nuclear fusion, then, the old question of the sun's power source was resolved. But there is more to the development of fusion theory than this. We saw that the study of light from stars led us naturally to think about the atom—the smallest unit in which recognizable chemical elements come. Now we see that to discuss the ultimate source of the sunlight that feeds life on earth, we have to think about the reactions of protons with each other.

Once again we see that an intimate connection exists between the large-scale bodies studied by astronomers and the smallest building blocks of matter studied in the laboratory of the physicist. It is difficult to think of a better proof of the seamlessness of the laws of nature. After all, who would have thought that you could learn about the structure of a star light-years distant simply by studying atoms and protons on earth?

Although the controlled conversion of mass to energy through fusion is beyond our technical capabilities at the moment, another such process called fission is used to provide an appreciable fraction of the world's electrical power. Although this kind of energy generation appears prodigiously efficient compared to mundane processes like the burning of coal, fission is relatively wasteful as nuclear processes go.

The Birth of the Solar System

Once we have understood the basic workings of stars like the sun, we can begin to talk about how stars are created in the first place. For the sun, this question is inextricably bound up with the formation of the rest of the solar system, for the planets emerged during the same process that shaped the sun, our neighborhood star.

This simultaneous creation of the sun and the planets is an old idea, going back to the eighteenth century. It has not always been popular, however. I can remember being taught in grade school that the planets were formed when another star passed close to the sun and ripped huge pieces from the solar surface. These chunks then cooled to form the planets. This sort of close encounter would have been catastrophic in nature. It would also have been an extraordinarily rare event. Other problems with the catastrophic models (such as the inability to explain the enormous differences in chemical composition among the planets) have led the scientific community back to a set of ideas first worked out by the French mathematician Marquis Pierre-Simon de Laplace, in 1796—ideas which go under the general title of the "nebular hypothesis."

According to this body of theory, the solar system started out as a cloud of thin gaseous material, some of it ejected from dying stars, some left over between the primordial matter that collected between the Big Bang and the formation of our Milky Way Galaxy. Soon, the cloud started to contract under the action of the force of gravity. There are many ways such a collapse could be triggered. For example, there is some evidence that at about the time the solar system started to form, a nearby star exploded in a supernova. (Such events are not uncommon—they happen a few times a century in our Galaxy.) The shock wave from this explosion sweeping through the gas could compress some material. Regions where matter was more dense would then tend to attract more material to themselves, since they would exert a greater gravitational force than the less dense regions. Thus, a dense region will tend to become denser, exert a still greater gravitational force, attract more material, and so become denser still. Simple Newtonian gravity can explain how a dust cloud, in which irregularities of density occurred, could have developed into a system in which most of the mass is concentrated in a single compact object.

One aspect of this contraction process bears close consideration, however. It is the rate at which the contracting body spins. In general, the original cloud will have some slow rate of rotation. As the contraction begins, the rate of spin will increase for much the same reason that an ice skater will spin faster if he pulls his arms to his body. A problem arises from the fact that the original cloud was so much larger than the sun that the growing rate of spin would tear such a system apart long before it could reach its present state. This realization trig-

Opposite above, light collected by the main mirror of the Hale 200-inch telescope, the large bright disk below the tube, comes to its focus in the pedestal of the observing capsule in this drawing by Russell Porter. The honeycombed construction of the Hale's large Pyrex mirror lessens weight without reducing overall strength. Here the concave surface receives a polishing so it can be aluminized. Seated in the prime-focus capsule, an astronomer acting in total darkness guides the entire telescope to assure accurate photographic imaging, above.

gered the renewed interest in the catastrophic models during the middle part of this century. In the jargon of physics, the nascent sun needs to "shed its angular momentum"—to slow its spin down to the speed observed today—if we want the nebular hypothesis to work.

As it turns out, there is a mechanism that can accomplish this task. The original cloud, in addition to containing gas and dust, would have been permeated by the magnetic field that exists throughout the Galaxy. The contraction of the cloud served to concentrate this field. As the contraction proceeded, particles were blown out from the center and moved away from the new sun along these field lines, like beads sliding along a wire. This material, now moved to the outside of the solar system, acted as a brake on the spinning sun, just as a skater who extends his arms will spin more slowly. It was the realization that the cloud could shed angular momentum in this way that brought renewed attention to the nebular hypothesis.

Thus we arrive at the general outline of the formation of the solar system as taught today. The process started when the original cloud contracted as it began to heat up. The spinning of the cloud also tended to flatten the material into a disk. At this stage, the solar system possibly resembled Saturn and its rings, with the sun (only barely glowing) in the center. The contraction and the heating were more severe near the center than at the edge, of course, so the composition of the dust cloud surrounding the sun began to change. Throughout the system, materials containing iron and silicon formed into solid grains, but materials like methane and water could become solid only in the outer reaches where the temperature was below their freezing point. At some point the temperature at the center of the cloud became so high that the protons began to fuse into helium via the process we've just described. At this point, about five billion years ago, the nuclear furnace ignited and the sun began to shine.

While this was going on, solid grains out in the cloud were colliding and sticking together, forming solid objects measuring a few miles across. These bodies, planetesimals, in turn collided and began to assume globular shapes as gravity did its work. Such protoplanets traveled in their orbits, sweeping up other materials the way a car windshield accumulates bugs on a summer evening. Eventually the sun ignited, new forces came into play. Radiation may have blown some of the dust and vapor outward at the same time heavier materials rained toward the newborn star. Planets in the line of fire were pommeled and cratered by meteorites. The rain of rocks continued.

Though far less destructive, this process of growth by accretion still goes on today, and planets like the Earth are still being bombarded with materials from space. The next time you see a shooting star, you might reflect on the fact that you are seeing the tail end of the process which formed the Earth billions of years ago, and that the Earth is heavier by about one grain of sand for every shooting star that falls.

In a natural-color photograph, the shady collection of cool dust and gas called the Horsehead stands in silhouette against the Orion nebula's bevy of bright young stars. Below, computer-processed data reveals topographic relief of the Horsehead nebula in the manner of a geographic map of earth.

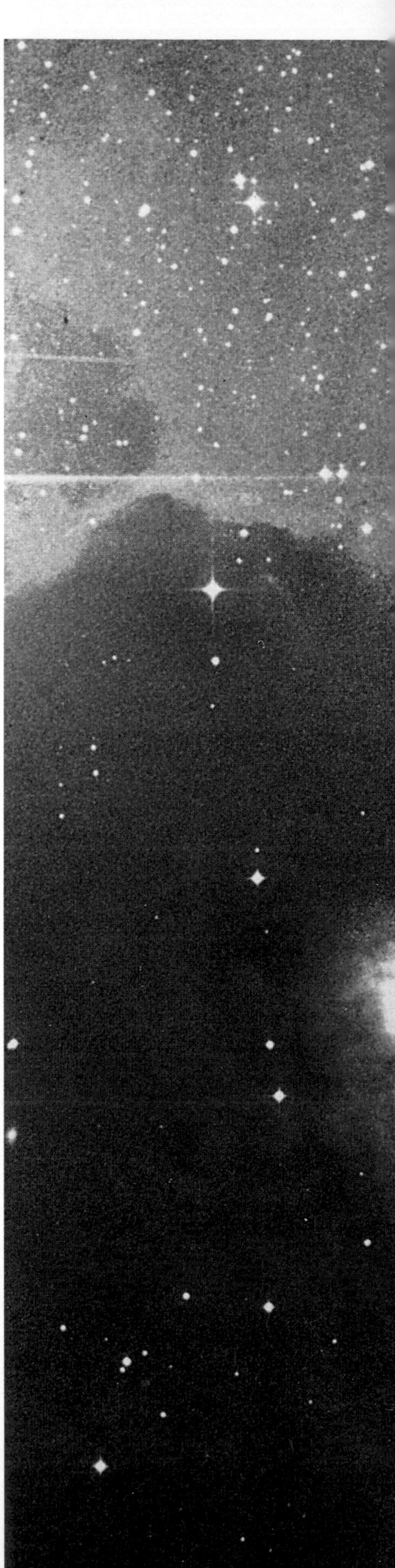

We Are Made of Star Stuff

One of the most vital realizations made by astronomers up to Newton's time was that stars are suns and suns are stars. A great realization in the era between Newton and Einstein was that some "stars" are galaxies, the separate units of hundreds of millions of stars that lie outside our own Milky Way Galaxy. A very important understanding of our contemporaries may be that some remarkable stellar objects—often active radio sources—may actually be galaxies in birth. However, if true or not, the primal importance of stars to astronomy and astrophysics is beyond question.

Stars are profound objects. But what indeed is their true nature? And how can it have any practical bearing on our daily existence? Answers to such questions have been found, but the finding was not easy.

Imagine for a moment that you had lived all your life in the Antarctic and had never seen a tree. Then imagine that you were put down in the middle of a forest and allowed one day to make all the observations and tests you wanted to make, with the understanding that at the end of the day you would have to come up with an explanation of your new environment. What could you do? How good would your conclusions be?

You could walk around the forest and note the fact that there were seedlings, saplings, mature trees, and dead trees on the ground. This would suggest that trees have a life cycle. You might observe the growth rings on exposed areas of fallen trees and come up with a theory about annual growth patterns and periods of dormancy. You could note that there were groups of trees that resembled one another—all the firs and pines and varied evergreen conifers, for example. You might even perform chemical analysis to assist in the process of deduction and classification. Or, if you were very lucky, you might see a rare event—a falling tree or a bud opening—that would confirm your theories about trees.

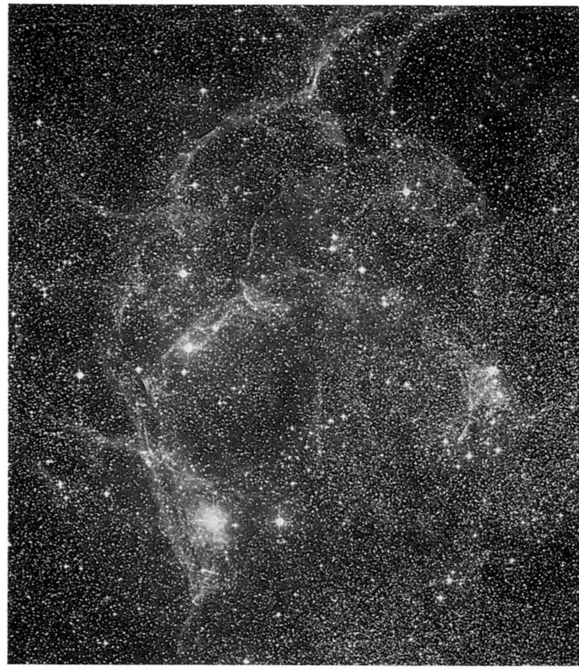

Dark mane of the Horsehead, opposite, consists of dust and gases—materials from which stars are born. Stars themselves gleam beyond this famous nebula of the Milky Way. Rich stores of minerals glow, right, in the Vela supernova remnant. When a star exploded here 10,000 years ago, its chemical contents began gradually to unfold into lacy filaments. These may find their way into galactic nurseries full of new suns.

The astronomer contemplating the heavens and our hypothetical natural historian are in much the same situation. The universe is billions of years old; we have been making careful observations of stars for only a few hundred of those years, too short a span to have seen a wide variety of changes. All of our information about the stars can be thought of as a snapshot of the universe taken at one particular moment. Through observing as much as we can of the stellar "forest" during our brief period of investigation, we have begun to reconstruct the entire majestic spectacle of the growth and evolution of the galaxies. The major difference between the astronomer and the forester is that the astronomer can never touch the stars. We have learned that stars, like trees, have life cycles—they are born, live out their allotted time, and die. We also

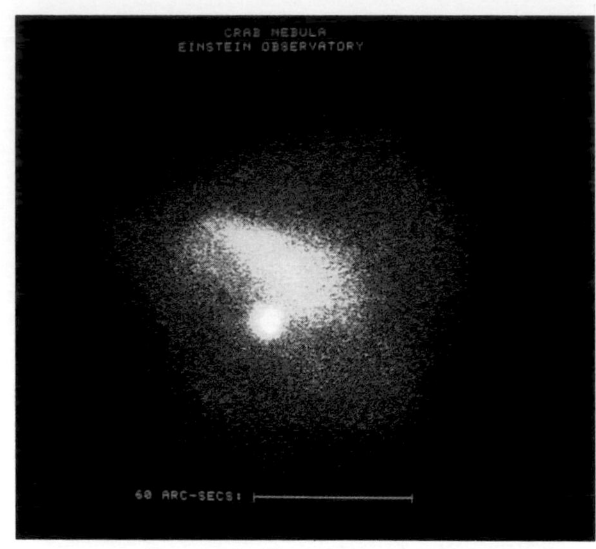

Vela supernova remnant creates its own bright image through emitted X rays, right. At its heart lies a pulsar, or blinking neutron star—the core of an exploded star. Most pulsars shine in wavelengths invisible to the human eye. Only Vela, and the Crab nebula at far right, pulse with light in the visual range.

know that almost every chemical element beyond helium and hydrogen was created in a large star somewhere.

The idea that stars are not eternal beacons in the sky came relatively late in astronomical history. Indeed, it is less than a century old. The reason isn't hard to understand. Most stars just don't change fast enough for humans to notice, much as our imaginary naturalist could not be expected to see a tree grow in the single day allowed him. But the idea that stars have fixed lifetimes is implicit in the fact that nuclear fusion is the energy source allowing them to shine. In a given star, there are only so many hydrogen atoms, and when they are all used up the fusion of hydrogen into helium will stop. It is as sure as the death of a campfire when there is no more wood to burn. The finite lifetime of a star, then, is less surprising than the fact that astronomers were able to discover it long before anyone had ever heard of nuclear fusion.

The technique they used was similar to the one we suggested for our imaginary naturalist. Just as he could deduce the life cycle of trees by cataloguing everything in the forest, so astronomers were able to deduce the life cycle of stars through cataloguing. Walk outside on a clear night and you will understand the enormity of this task.

You note that the stars differ in brightness—some flash like diamonds, others are milky. Look a little more closely; see that some are white, others bluish, and some have a reddish tinge. These characteristics—brightness and color—turn out to be the most important aspects of a star's appearance in classification schemes.

If you put a piece of metal into a fire, it will warm up and glow red. If the fire is hot enough, the metal will eventually turn orange, then white, and finally a bluish white. Gauging the state of a metal by its color in the forge is one of the most important skills that a blacksmith acquires in his training. For our purposes, however, this homey example illustrates the possibility of gauging an object's temperature by observing the color of the light it emits. What is true for a horseshoe is equally true for a star—blue stars are hotter than red ones.

The classification of stars by analysis of their emitted light is actually a bit more complicated than this. We have already seen that each atom emits and absorbs light of specific frequencies, depending on the state of the electrons. In very hot stars, collisions between atoms will have knocked most electrons away from their nuclei. Such stars reveal few absorption lines in their spectra, since there are few atomic electrons to absorb the light coming from the interior.

At the other end of the scale, cool stars may have such mild internal collisions that even molecules (atoms joined in chemical compounds) can survive—something impossible in their hotter cousins. Molecules produce characteristic absorption lines, ones different from those of atoms. Thus we have clues to the surface temperature of a star under observation. Astronomers classify stars into spectral classes—their names are set by historical precedent with little scientific significance.

The standard mnemonic to help students learn the spectral classes is Oh, Be A Fine Girl, Kiss Me. If the sexist aspects of this sentence bother you, substitute Guy for Girl—it still works. The stars are indifferent to change in fashion down here on earth.

Our sun, with a surface temperature around 6,000 Kelvin (10,340°F) and absorption lines of calcium prominent in its spectrum, is classed as a G star. As such, it is typical of the stars seen in the sky.

If we shift our attention from a star's

Harvesting supernova ashes—a source of minerals—unformed planets circle a nascent star, our sun before its nuclear fires burst forth.

Creation of our sun depended on the destruction of other suns. At least one star's violent death added chemical elements to the solar nebula, and supplied the energy that helped to trigger the condensation of interstellar dust into our own star system.

color to its brightness, we immediately run into a problem. A distant object, though bright, may appear faint while a dim object close up may appear bright. The brightness of stars as seen from the earth is generally rated in terms of a quantity called apparent magnitude, following a scheme introduced in the second century B.C. by Hipparchus. He rated the brightest star he could see as magnitude one, the faintest as magnitude six. Notice that the larger the magnitude, the fainter the star. Hipparchus worked with his unaided eye, of course, and since his time the scale has been changed somewhat. Several of the brightest stars needed to be reclassified, Sirius, for example, at a magnitude of minus 1.4. At the other end of the scale, large telescopes now routinely detect objects with magnitudes beyond 24.

Setting the scale for apparent magnitude does not, of course, solve the problem we posed earlier. Given that a particular star is first magnitude, for example, how do we know whether it's bright and far away or dim and close? To remove this ambiguity, we introduce the concept of absolute magnitude. This is defined as the magnitude a star would have if we observed it from a certain fixed distance. In practice, absolute magnitude is the apparent magnitude of a star as it would be viewed at 32.6 light-years, or ten parsecs away. A parsec is the astronomer's standard of angular measurement.

Here's an example of the way these things work. Sirius, the brightest star in the sky, has an apparent magnitude of minus 1.4. It is, however, only 8.8 light-years away. If it were viewed from our standard distance, it would appear to have a magnitude of 1.4. Thus Sirius has an apparent magnitude of minus 1.4 and an absolute magnitude of 1.4. It appears brighter because it is close to us. On the other hand, Polaris (the North Star), lies 680 light-years away. It has an apparent magnitude of 1.99 but an absolute magnitude of minus 3.7. It is really more luminous than Sirius, but appears dim because of the great distance that separates us.

It is clear that establishing the absolute magnitude of a star requires that we know its distance from us. With this information, a simple measurement of the light received in our telescopes tells us how much energy is actually being radiated from the star. For future reference, the total energy radiated by a star in one second is known as the star's *luminosity*. If we know the luminosity, then the amount of energy passing an observer 10 parsecs from the star (the quantity we have defined as absolute magnitude) is also easy to calculate.

Finding the distance to most stars is difficult. For stars within a few hundred light-years of the Earth, however, simple geometry suffices. First, the position of the star is measured on days six months apart. Thus the Earth has moved halfway around its orbit between observations. From the measured angles and the known distance between the Earth and the sun, we can cal-

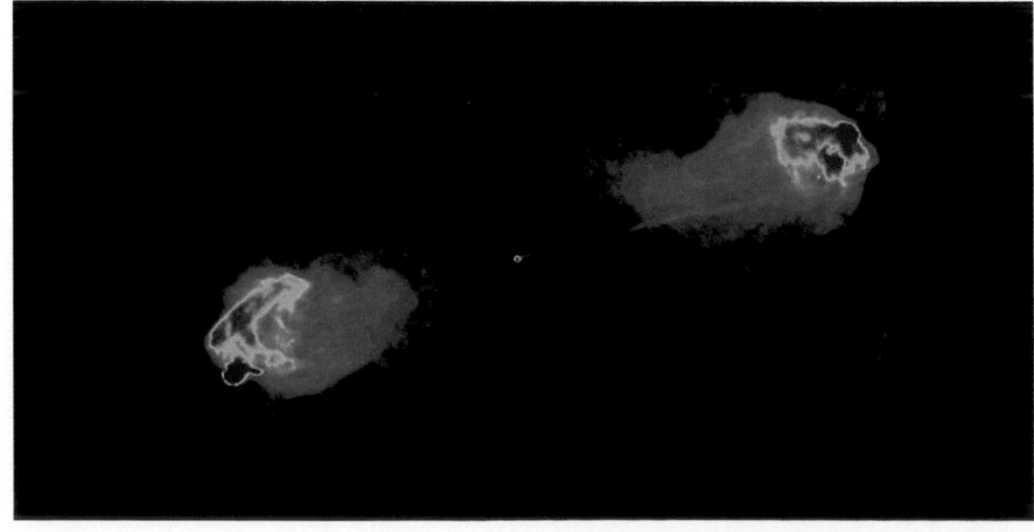

Huge lobes shoot out from the comparatively tiny active core of Cygnus A, one of the sky's most energetic sources of radio energy. Visible only to radio telescopes these "waterwings" outside the Milky Way may be regions of star formation. In the Orion nebula, at center, lies the Trapezium or star nursery. Opposite, Orion as seen by radio telescope and, bottom right, by an optical telescope.

A quick glance will convince you that heavy nuclei, so rare in stars, are common on the earth. In our bodies, for example, calcium appears in bones, carbon in our soft tissues, and iron in our blood. Even the water that makes up most of our body is 88 percent oxygen by weight. As we shall see during our discussion of the Big Bang, only hydrogen and helium could have been formed before the appearance of stars. This means that everything on earth other than hydrogen and the miniscule amounts of atmospheric helium was produced in one of those giant nuclear pressure cookers we call stars.

From the discussion of the death of stars, we know that the sun will eventually synthesize elements including carbon. The carbon made in the sun, however, will almost all remain locked up in the white dwarf the sun will become. Very little will be returned to the cosmos.

Large stars are different, they expel matter back into the interstellar medium from whence stars come. The fact that large stars burn out rather quickly, leads to a simple yet beautiful picture of how the atoms which form our bodies were made.

The first galaxy was a cloud of hydrogen and helium. Some of the stars that formed were very massive. In a short time (as these things go) they burned up their fuel, exploded, and injected a cloud containing heavy nuclei back into space. New stars drew dust and gases into themselves and thus the enrichment cycle continued until the interstellar dust approached its present composition.

A relative newcomer, our sun was born a mere 5 billion years ago and hence the dust from which it grew already contained many heavy nuclei from generations of supernovae. Thus calcium can be detected in the outer atmosphere of the sun. Thus the Earth, a child of the sun, contains calcium. So we, children of Earth, share the bounty with calcium in our bones.

You might ask whether there have been enough supernovae to manufacture all of the heavy elements. Supernovae are relatively rare events as seen from the earth—the last was the one which impressed Tycho Brahe in 1572. The galaxy is a pretty dusty place, however, and it's not at all certain that we'd be able to see every supernova that occurred. In fact, from watching other galaxies and from theoretical considerations, most astronomers now believe that supernovae occur every 50 to 100 years in the Milky Way, and that we're due for a visible one any day now.

If you require further convincing that supernovae manufactured the elements of the earth, I would point out that if the universe is 20 billion years old, and if the sun is 5 billion years old (while the lifetime of a heavy star is 20 million years), then enough time has elapsed between the Big Bang and the period before the sun's birth for a single atom to cycle through 750 large stars. Such material was incorporated into the dusty nebula from which our solar system took shape. Thus there was plenty of time for hydrogen to be transmuted into the more than 100 chemical elements we can detect.

So when humans finally leave the solar system, moving out into the Galaxy, in a sense we will just be going home again.

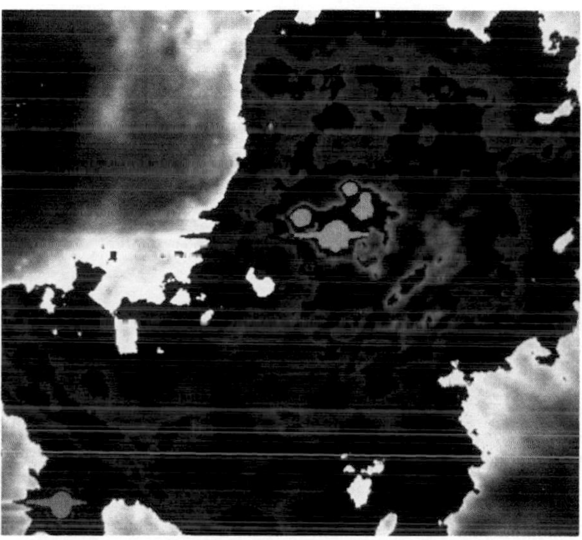

culate the distance to the star. For stars more than a few hundred light-years away, this simple technique is insufficient and more complex means were developed, with interesting results.

The Danish astronomer Ejnar Hertzsprung recognized differences between stars in 1905, cataloguing giants and dwarfs. In America, Henry Russell produced a remarkably interesting graph to compare star masses with spectral types. We now call it the Hertzsprung-Russell (or H-R) diagram and it shows the luminosity of a star plotted on one axis and its temperature on the other. In the H-R diagram, each star can be represented by a point. A surprising pattern emerged, one that set the stage for the modern interpretation of star life cycles.

On the H-R diagram, most star points cluster into a few well-defined areas. One band contains most of the observed stars, and is called the main sequence. For stars in the main sequence, we have a general rule that as the temperature increases the star radiates more energy (i.e. its luminosity increases). This seems reasonable. Two families of stars present us with important exceptions. There are red giants (very luminous, low temperatures) and white dwarfs (high temperatures, not much radiation). The sun is comfortably in the main sequence—quite an ordinary star.

If it all sounds pretty abstract, consider a simple analogy. Suppose you intend to organize a collection of motor vehicles. You might make a diagram in which each specimen is represented by its length and weight. Most of these would fall on the "main sequence"—the longer the vehicle, the greater the weight, from motorcycles up to semi-trucks. On the other hand, there could well be exceptions. A dune buggy, with a body of open tubing, would be large but light. A military tank, on the other hand, would be very heavy for its size. Nevertheless, this "H-R diagram" for vehicles establishes two things: first, there is a general rule relating the length and weight of most vehicles; and second, there are a few important classes of vehicles which are exceptions to the general rule.

The H-R diagram also provides us with a convenient way of thinking and talking about the life cycle of a star. The contraction of a dust cloud, as described in the last chapter, eventually produces a relatively cool, glowing mass of dust. As the cloud heats up and the nuclear fusion reaction is ignited, the temperature increases, and the new star joins the main sequence.

Once afire, the star settles down to burn its initial endowment of hydrogen fuel. How long the star remains in the main sequence depends on how much material it contains. The relationship is not straightforward, however. The gravitational attraction in a very massive star raises the temperature of the nuclear furnace to a very high level, and the star burns its fuel with profligate splendor. While a playboy can go through a

Thick dust clouds reflect light and break it into colorful displays within the nearby Rho Ophiuchi nebula. Only one star's light is strong enough to assert its own true color, Sigma Scorpii at bottom. This sky locality, filled with dark and heavy particles, provides both fuel and substance for new stars.

fortune in a few years, a less wealthy but more sober individual can remain in the black for a lifetime. Similarly, a massive star will burn up its hydrogen in 20 or 30 million years, while the sun nurses its smaller fuel supply for 10 billion. But whether for 20 million or 10 billion years, both stars will sit on the main-sequence line in the H-R diagram, with the massive star located somewhere in the upper left-hand corner. The interesting question is what happens when the fuel runs out. We have only begun to find adequate answers.

Stardeath

We recall that every star is the product of a constant struggle. Gravity tends to pull the star in upon itself while radiation and hot gases exert a powerful force for limitless expansion. From the moment two particles come together to form a concentration of mass in a dust cloud, the star fights a losing battle against gravity. No matter how big the star and how fierce its internal fires, gravity always wins in the end.

Take our own sun as an example. For five billion years or so, energy created by the fusion process has kept the sun in dynamic equilibrium. Heat output has probably risen by 25 percent while the core may have contracted slightly. At the same time outer solar layers have expanded. These gradual trends will continue for another five billion years while the sun consumes hydrogen in its core. A day will come when the core of the sun consists primarily of helium, the ash of the nuclear burning. The fusion fire in the center of our sun will die, though reactions will continue in a shell around the core while the hydrogen fuel holds out.

No longer able to counteract the pull of gravity, the core starts to collapse, heating up as it does. The heat from the core raises the temperature of the hydrogen-burning layer and the outer part of the star begins to expand. The sun becomes a red giant star with a large, cool envelope and a slowly contracting core. Eventually, the solar atmosphere will balloon, perhaps reaching well into the region of the planets. The sun will move off the main sequence into the upper right-hand corner of the H-R diagram.

The collapsing core grows hot enough for the fusion of helium into carbon. Nuclear fires re-ignite. Energy pours out of the core and the inevitable end is staved off. During this penultimate phase the giant star contains two separate and concentric fusion furnaces. At the center, helium nuclei are combining in groups of three to form carbon nuclei. In the outer layer, hydrogen atoms continue to fuse into helium. Note that the stellar furnace is the ultimate in efficient recycling design; the ashes of one reaction (helium) become the fuel for the next. This general pattern is characteristic of the final stages of all stars.

Eventually, of course, the helium in the core is used up, and the central fusion furnace is clogged with the carbon "ash." For

Key to understanding the stellar makeup of our own Galaxy, the Hertzsprung-Russell diagram arranges stars by size, luminosity, and primary color of their light—spectral class. For purposes of standardization, the value for the sun in the luminosity scale at left is one.

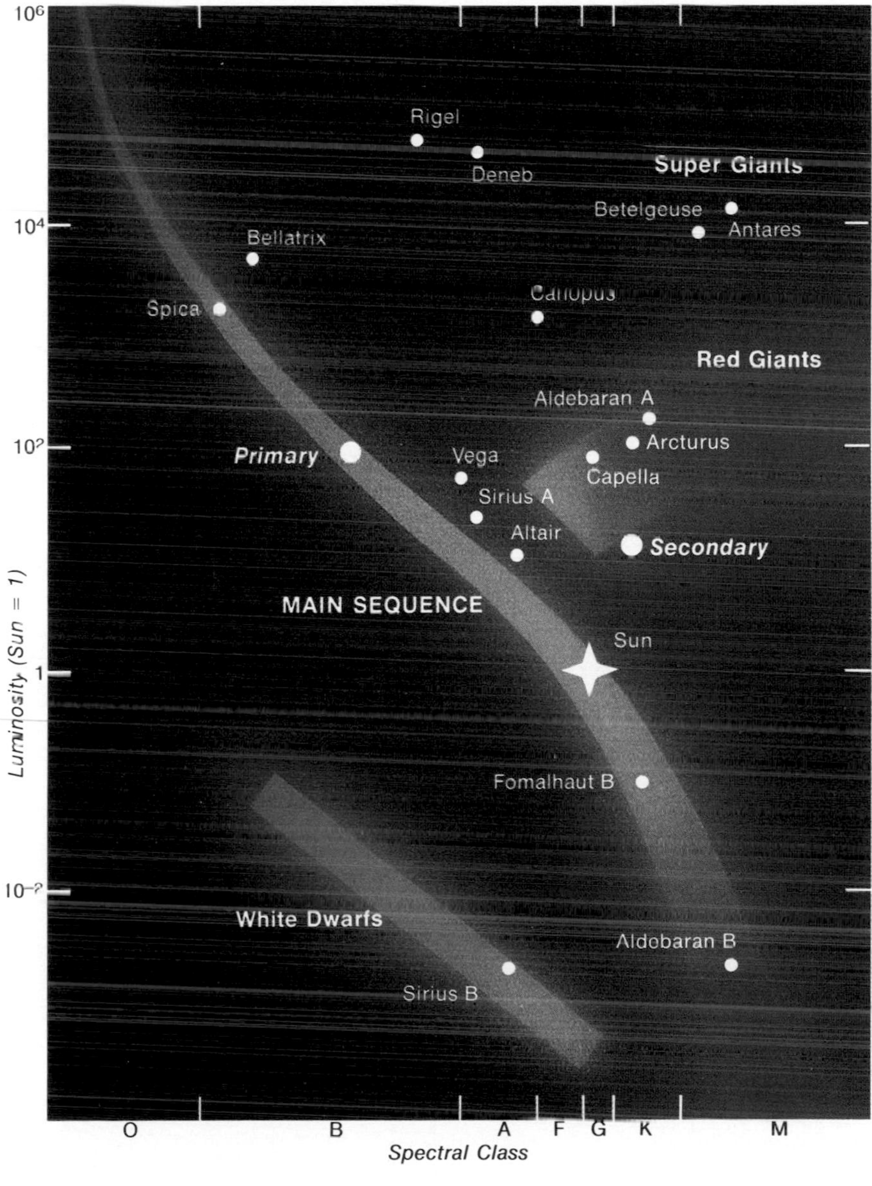

stars the size of the sun, there is not enough mass to crush the carbon core any further. The electrons associated with (but not attached to) the individual nuclei are packed densely in the core—now about the size of the Earth. We know that electrons can't be squeezed together; think of each electron as requiring a certain amount of elbow room. In this unstable situation the outer layer of the star may billow out, forming a globular cloud called a planetary nebula.

A star full of closely packed carbon nuclei and free electrons remains at the site of the old sun. It weighs about as much as the sun, though its size is that of the Earth. If anybody remains to observe, it will be classed as a white dwarf. Further contraction is unlikely. The fires are gone. The star slowly cools down to its end product—a black dwarf. Think of it as a galactic cinder. If you are of a romantic frame of mind, you can think of the dwarf as a giant diamond in the sky, though it's just as correct to call it a lump of coal.

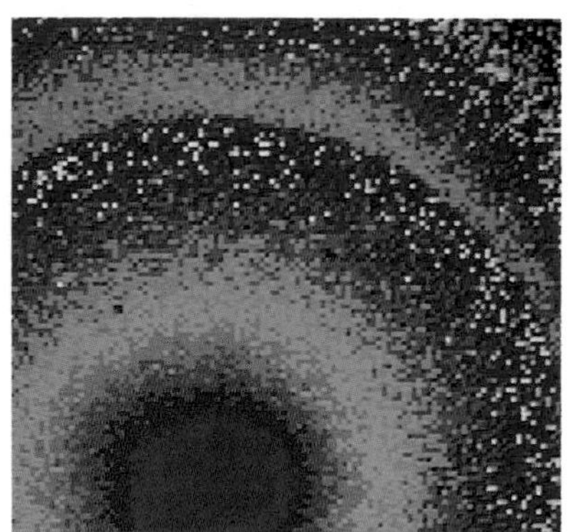

International Ultraviolet Explorer originated this UV image of Sirius, the brightest star in our sky. Knowledge gained from the study of stars and the nuclear reactions in their cores helps scientists unravel secrets of the atom, symbolized by an artistic conception of the heart of an atom of uranium, at right.

In 1930, astronomer Subrahmanyan Chandrasekhar from India proved that the force exerted by the electrons in a white dwarf can balance gravity provided that it is no more than 1.4 times as massive as the sun. This figure is one of the contributions to science that brought him a Nobel Prize for physics in 1983. In practice, the existence of the Chandrasekhar limit means that stars up to four times the mass of the sun will have a chance to end up as white dwarfs providing that they are able to shed enough mass to bring them below the limit.

A much more interesting path is followed by stars much more massive than the sun. As we have seen, large stars stay on the main sequence for relatively short periods—20 million years if the mass is 15 times that of the sun, for example. During their sojourn on the main sequence, these heavy stars burn hydrogen, but because their interior temperatures are so high the star quickly goes through its allotment. Then, much as we described above, the core collapses until helium burning starts. Some hydrogen fusion continues around the original core. The star becomes a red giant, converting its helium core to carbon and oxygen. The difference between a large star and the sun becomes apparent when the helium at the core is used up. Because of the large mass involved, the gravitational contraction following that event is strong enough to raise the core temperature to the point where carbon will undergo fusion. Once again, the ashes of one fire become, at higher temperatures, the fuel for another.

While the core burns carbon, creating "ash" in the form of nuclei of different elements, helium fusion continues in a concentric shell, with hydrogen afire in a shell closer to the surface. Eventually, the central parts of the star begin to resemble an onion, with different reactions in successive layers. Each re-ignition represents another attempt by the star to stave off the effect of the ever

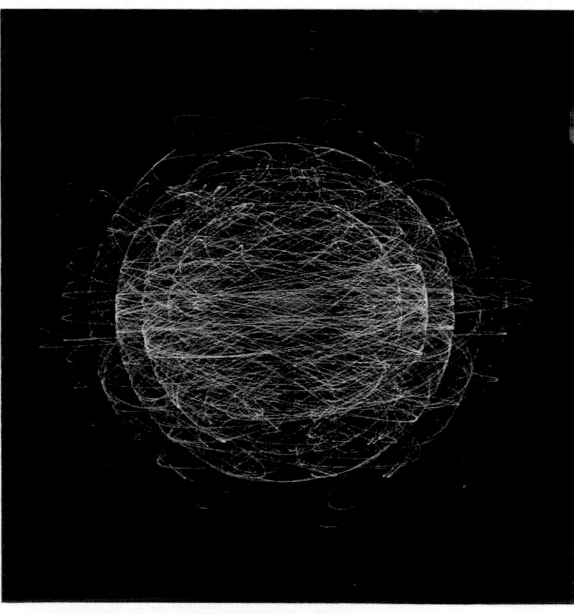

stronger gravitational forces pulling its mass inward. Finally, silicon at the core becomes transmuted into iron.

As the concentric burning continues, more and more iron accumulates in the core. Iron is the ultimate nuclear ash. It cannot be "burned" in the sense we have used the term. In each previous ignition, the star has found a way of producing energy from nuclear combinations. With iron, however, this is no longer possible. Iron is the most efficiently bound of all the nuclei, requiring extra energy to break it down or to fuse it.

Theorists have several scenarios of just such disastrous transitions. One suggests that when the iron core builds to 1.4 solar masses, the outward push of the electrons can no longer counteract gravity and the core collapses. The outer regions of the onion-like star suddenly find (so to speak) the rug pulled out from under them, and they fall in, heating up rapidly. All kinds of nuclear reactions are ignited as these layers heat up, and the atom-building process is augmented by the flood of neutrons and protons streaming out from the disrupted core. Larger and larger nuclei emerge as fragments stick together. All of the known elements are fabricated during this disastrous death throe of the giant star, a process that may well last for only a few minutes. Then the energy of the fall and of the nuclear reactions combine for the most titanic explosion known in our Galaxy. The star is literally torn apart and blown into space during its brief existence as a supernova.

Meanwhile, a number of different fates could await the original core, depending on the mass of material involved. Gravitational attraction in the core may be strong enough to force electrons to combine with protons, converting the core material into a collection of neutrons. Like electrons, neutrons need elbow room, and if the mass of the core is not too large the forces they exert will stabilize the star when its diameter reaches 20 miles or so. The result is known as a neutron star, a remarkably massive body, though not as solid for its size as one other thing in the universe—the nucleus of an atom.

If the original star core was rotating at the time of collapse—even very slowly—then its speed of rotation would increase. It happens for much the same reason that an ice skater spins faster by pulling the arms close to the body. A rotating neutron star will emit radiation mainly from its north and south magnetic poles. If, as is the case with Earth, the axis of rotation does not pass through the magnetic poles, the radiation will sweep through the sky like a beam from an airfield beacon or a lighthouse. A detector on Earth will catch a regular pulsating radio signal, a fact that explains the use of the word "pulsar." Of the more than 300 known, only two of these bodies have been found to show pulses of light. Some pulsars emit X rays.

The first evidence for pulsars was discovered in 1967, when a radio signal that recurred every 1.337 seconds was picked up by two English astronomers. The folklore in astronomy says that the discoverers, Anthony Hewish and Jocelyn Bell Burnell, first referred to the signal as the LGM for "Little Green Men" because of its similarity to what you might expect an interstellar message to look like.

There was great excitement in 1968 when a pulsar was discovered in the center of the Crab nebula—for it is the expanding shell of a supernova—the original explosion seen from earth in 1054. The existence of the pulsar in the Crab showed that ideas about the evolution and death of large stars at

In 1912, a year after her second Nobel Prize, Marie Curie works in her Paris laboratory. Investigation of radioactive elements led to the modern science of atomic and particle physics. Applied to astronomy, knowledge of nuclear reactions spawned an important new science, astrophysics.

least predicted the right end state.

Other supernovae may not end up this way, however. If the collapsing core is massive enough, the neutrons will not be able to overcome gravity and the collapse will continue to a black hole—the ultimate triumph of gravity over matter. The mass of the core is packed into so small a volume that nothing—not even light—can escape the gravitational pull at its surface. In a very real sense, when matter enters a black hole it has isolated itself from the rest of the universe. Henceforth it can be detected only by the gravitational force it exerts on other things. As Winston Churchill once said of Russia, it is a mystery wrapped in an enigma.

In its death throes a star resembling our own sun has puffed out a perfect sphere of dust and gases—materials which might one day be incorporated into a world like our Earth.

Research Frontiers

The main outlines of the stellar life cycle and the creation of the elements are pretty well established, but a lot of details are still being worked out. For example, we know that stars with a mass of less than four times that of the sun can end up as white dwarfs, while if they have more than 10 solar masses, they will become supernovae. What about stars between these two limits? What about those supermassive stars of 60 solar masses or more? Is there a single number like the Chandrasekhar limit that predicts the difference between evolutionary paths, or is the situation more complicated?

On the observational side, the black hole is expected to be created as the end product of the life cycle of very massive stars, but finding a black hole isn't easy. By definition, you can't "see" a black hole, and its presence can be detected only through its gravitational interactions. There are a few good candidates in the sky—objects which might be black holes—but everyone would rest easier if the evidence were better.

Finally, there is still a very active program in the area of nuclear astrophysics, the branch of science devoted to the study of the creation of the elements. Not all heavy elements are created in that last moment of the supernova process. Some (up to iron) can be created in a more leisurely manner in the outer regions of red giant stars, and others (rare elements like beryllium and boron) by the collisions of nuclei with other particles in the interstellar medium. In addition, light elements like helium (and a small amount of lithium) were probably made in the Big Bang. Sorting out the details of all these processes and determining where and when each of the chemical elements emerged still occupies researchers. This is one area where the laboratory can play a crucial role; many nuclear processes that go on in stars can be duplicated on earth. In 1983, William Fowler of the California Institute of Technology won the Nobel Prize in physics for his work in this area.

Affirming his link to the stars, American astronomer James Lick (1798–1876) had himself buried within the concrete foundation of the famous telescope bearing his name.

Galaxies and the Edge of the Universe

The development of the telescope allowed astronomers to peer deep into the heavens for the first time. With the newly expanded horizons came new questions and new challenges. William Herschel, whom we have already encountered as the discoverer of the planet Uranus, undertook an ambitious project with his new instruments. He proposed doing a complete survey of the sky, charting the positions of the stars. In this way, he hoped to learn what was in the mind of God when he created the universe.

But the universe does not yield its ultimate secrets so easily. Herschel discovered something fundamental but not revolutionary, and it can be verified by a casual inspection of the sky on a warm summer evening. Look in one direction—toward the band of light we call the Milky Way—stars are close, crowded. In other directions, you see that stars appear farther apart.

The obvious explanation for this state of affairs is simple. The sun and the planets are members of a huge collection of stars arranged in the general shape of a disk. This arrangement would explain Herschel's observations in a neat and natural way.

Someone located deep inside of the disk would have two very different lines of sight. Looking up or down, he would see few stars between himself and the void. Looking either inward or outward (in the plane of the disk) he would see a large number. Many of these stars are so far away that they do not appear as individuals but their collective

As if caught in spun sugar, colorful stars reveal the composition of their galaxy, NGC 2997. Old ones lie in the nucleus and provide yellowish light. Younger bluish stars populate the spiral arms while the pink and youngest suns most often gleam at the outer fringes—born here from dark, cool nebulosities. Charles Messier, his personal emblem above, created the first catalogue of celestial objects. His M prefixes many galaxy numbers, as does NGC, referring to another classification system.

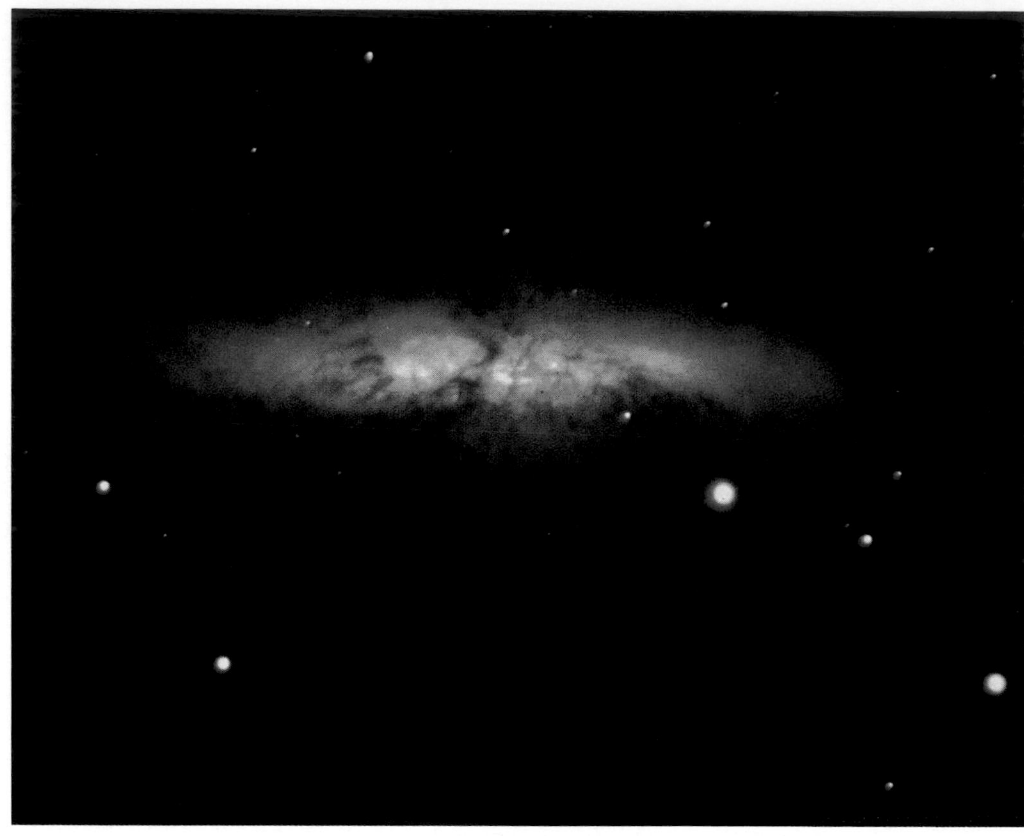

Ages ago a galaxy erupted, its violent burst of energy creating a multitude of hot new stars. Known as M 82, it appears in normal colors above, while a computer-enhanced image, opposite, accentuates huge filaments of gas and dust at the galaxy's center. Strong radio signals emanate from the heart of M 87, right. They may escape from the source of a mysterious explosion.

light forms a haze. Such a collection of stars is called a galaxy. The Milky Way is simply the galaxy which we most easily see and to which we belong.

So, the obvious question presented itself. Is the Milky Way Galaxy, with its 200 billion stars, the entire universe or—as Immanuel Kant guessed—do others exist as well? Certainly there are objects in the sky that look as if they might be large collections of stars. Some of these are visible to the naked eye as small, smeared-out patches of light. Arab astronomers recorded the presence of these objects. Through Herschel's telescopes some of these so-called nebulae were seen to contain individual stars immersed in dust clouds.

In the 1800s, Lord Rosse noted the spiral structure of some hazy nebulae. The question of the identity of these objects was intimately related to the question of their distance from us. Two possibilities present themselves. First, the nebulae are other galaxies that seem small because of their great distance from the Milky Way. Or, second, they are clouds of interstellar dust lit up by the stars within them. They shine for the same reason that low clouds glow with city lights. Through one of those fixed ideas that now and then perturb the history of science, there was a general feeling (one that lasted well into this century) that whatever explanation was proposed to explain the nebulae had to explain them all.

It does not seem to have occurred to anyone that both of the possibilities cited above might be true—that some nebulae were galaxies, while others were dust clouds within the Milky Way. So everybody was wrong—something not all that rare in science.

It is clear that the question of the nature of the nebulae leads to the same question we faced in classifying the stars in the last chapter—how can we find the distance to a given star or collection of stars? How do we know whether what we're seeing is bright and distant or dim and close? Again we face the problem of establishing a distance scale for the heavens.

In some ways, the problem isn't so different from those encountered in measuring distances on earth. You might use a micrometer to measure the thickness of a wire, a hand ruler to measure the dimensions of this book, a carpenter's rule to measure a table, a tape measure to find the length of a house, a car odometer to measure the distance to the next town, and so on. You wouldn't insist on using the same instrument to measure each distance. It would be silly to measure the distance to the next

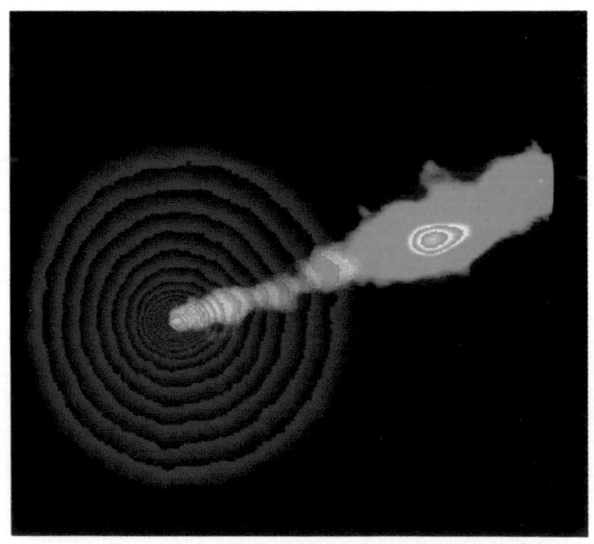

town with a ruler, for example. Besides, you know that the various instruments will all give you equivalent answers for any particular measurement. If you were of a suspicious mind and wanted to check your array of rulers, you might find some object of intermediate size and measure it twice, using a different instrument each time. You might, for example, measure a chair with both the hand rule and the carpenter's rule, or the porch with the carpenter's rule and the tape measure.

Like people in their everyday pursuits, the astronomer also uses many rulers, and also checks one against the other to help assure continuing accuracy. For nearby objects—the solar system and neighboring stars—we can use a method called parallax. A simple analogy makes this technique understandable. If you were driving by a field with a large tree in it, you could find the distance from the tree to the road by measuring the angle of the line of sight to the tree at two different places. One way of doing this would be to notice when the tree appeared to line up with specific peaks on a distant mountain range. With a knowledge of the car's velocity, the elapsed time between sightings, and the angles, some simple geometry will give us the distance to the tree.

If the two lines of sight originate from telescopes on different sides of the Earth, you can get sufficient precision with this technique to measure the distance to objects in the solar system. If the two lines of sight originate from points on opposite sides of the Earth's orbit (a situation you could create by waiting six months between measurements), then you can gain sufficient precision to measure distances of about 150 light-years. While this is a large distance, it is only a fraction of the size of our own Milky Way Galaxy.

To measure even larger distances through such descriptive geometry, we observe clusters of stars which move in relation to our solar system. And while this technique allows us to measure distances of a few hundred light-years, we are still within our own Galaxy.

With moving clusters, we have come as far as we can using simple geometry to determine distances. From here on out we will

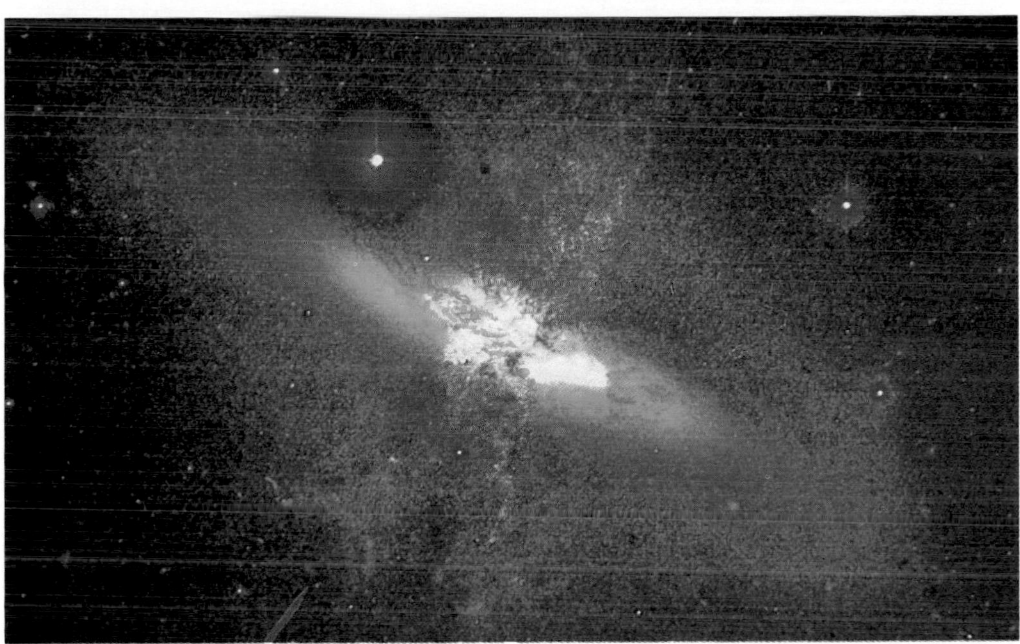

The Astronomical Distance Scale

The following five rulers can be used to establish the distance to objects out to the limits of the detectable universe:

Stellar parallax: triangulation of nearby stars, using the Earth's orbit as the base; good to 150 light-years.

Stellar motion: using the apparent motion of the stars as a base, good to about a few hundred light-years.

Cepheid variable method: good to about 13 million light-years, far enough to figure the distance to several nearby galaxies.

Relative luminosity: when galaxies are too distant for us to distinguish individual Cepheid variables, we need to find some other characteristic of the galaxy to relate to its true luminosity. We might, for example, note that the brightest stars in galaxies of a certain type seem to have the same luminosity. We calibrate this new ruler by establishing the desired relationship for those galaxies within which we can see the Cepheids, and then assume the same relationship holds for galaxies where we can't. With this technique we can reach out to distances of about 80 million light-years. At this point our telescopes can no longer distinguish individual stars in galaxies. With the Hubble Space Telescope we should be able to resolve things 10 times better than before.

Red shift: for the farthest of the galaxies which we can measure by means of our fourth ruler. The red shift is correlated to the distance. The greater the red shift, the farther away the object. We use the "red shift ruler" to the farthest limits of observability. Here visible objects, mostly quasars, exhibit extreme red shifts.

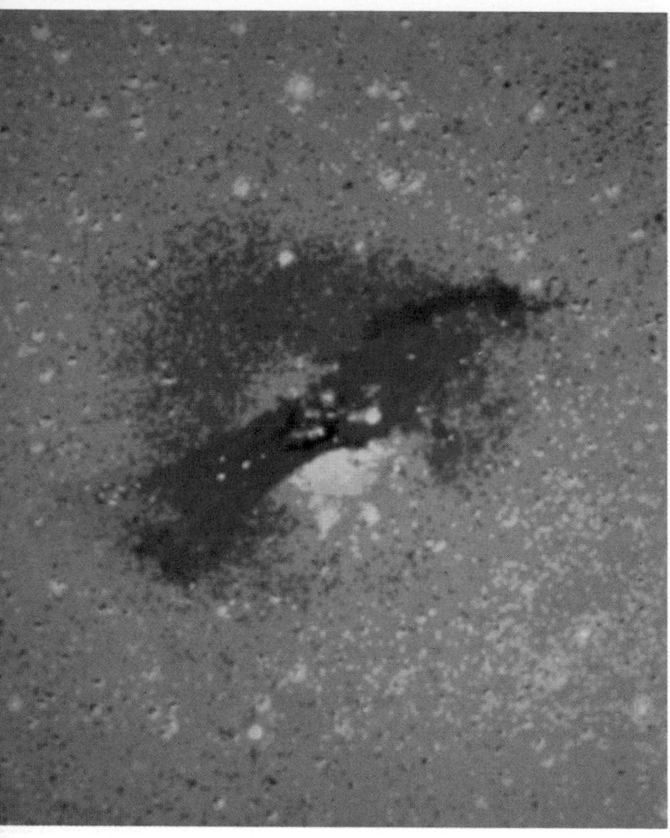

Centaurus A, above left, and right in color-enhanced photography, was described in 1830 by John Herschel as "cut asunder . . . by a broad obscure band." Unusual for an elliptical galaxy, the dust lane, gas, and abundance of young stars seems more typical of a spiral galaxy.

have to use totally different logic. We will need some other way to estimate the true luminosity of a distant object, and then compare that true luminosity with the actual amount of light received at the earth. From the comparison, we will be able to deduce the distance to the object, just as you would be able to tell how far away a 100-watt bulb was by seeing how bright it appeared to be.

The first scientists to use this new measuring scheme depended on a discovery made by Henrietta Leavitt at the Harvard Observatory in 1912. She noticed that certain stars (called Cepheid variables) exhibit a regular behavior—they grow dimmer and brighter with a periodicity ranging from a few days to a month or more. Leavitt was able to show that this period was proportional to the luminosity of the star. Generally, the longer the period, the brighter the star. Thus, if we can find a star of this type and watch it for a while, we can deduce the amount of light it is emitting by measuring the time it takes the star to brighten and grow dim. By comparing this number with the amount of light actually received at earth, we can work out the distance to the star. This scale allows us to calculate distances out as far as we can distinguish Cepheid variable stars in our telescopes. This is a great advantage as it allows us to reach out across tens of millions of light-years, though the scale becomes harder to establish at extreme distances.

Edwin Hubble and the Expanding Universe

Once the Cepheid variable distance scale was established, the stage was set for the resolution of the old question of whether there are other "island universes" as they were called by Frederick Wilhelm von Humboldt. Edwin Hubble, a former lawyer and soldier with a fresh Ph.D. under his arm, arrived in 1919 at Mount Wilson Observatory near Los Angeles. He was ready to undertake a study of the question. Like Newton, he was a cold, overbearing person. He was also a Rhodes Scholar and his Oxford accent grated on the ears of his colleagues, especially those who knew he had been born in Missouri. Nevertheless, like Newton, he opened up a new vista of the universe.

Concentrating the new 100-inch reflecting telescope on the nearest spiral nebula—the Andromeda galaxy—Hubble took a series of photographs that clearly showed the existence of no fewer than 40 distinguishable Cepheid variable stars. From the periods of these stars and the light received, Hubble was able to show that the Andromeda nebula was too far away to be part of the Milky Way. Hubble placed a provisional value of almost a million light-years on the distance between the two galaxies. Today we know that the figure is about two million light-years, 20 times greater than the diameter of the Milky Way itself. The publication of this result in 1923 ended the island universe controversy once and for all. The Milky Way was only one of many galaxies in the wide universe. We still do not know for certain, however, if what Copernicus called the "universe," the solar system itself, is unique within our Galaxy.

Another astronomer, Vesto Slipher of the Lowell Observatory of Flagstaff, Arizona, discovered another feature of the light from distant galaxies that provided the key to our modern view of the universe. Light emitted by atoms in distant galaxies didn't appear to be exactly at the frequency one might expect from looking at the same atom in the laboratory, but had shifted toward the red end of the spectrum. Hubble correctly interpreted the shift as an indication that the galaxies emitting the light are receding from Earth. The key to making this logical step is the phenomenon known as the Doppler effect.

Proposed by the astronomer Christian Doppler in Vienna in 1842, the effect is easy to understand. Suppose you have some system emitting waves. Crests of each wave will move out from the source in concentric circles. Observers anywhere will see the same number of these crests pass by them each second, and will therefore agree on the frequency of the emitted waves.

If the source is moving however, the situation can be different. Each emitted-wave crest moves out in a circle, of course, but that circle is centered on the spot where the source is located at the moment of emission. This means that the circles will tend to be off-center because of the motion of the source. An observer standing in front of the source will see the crests bunched up and will conclude that the frequency of the moving source is higher than that of the stationary one. Someone standing behind the source, however, will see the wave crests spread out and will conclude that the frequency is lower.

If the wave emitted by the source happens to be light, then the forward observer will see the light shifted toward the blue, while the observer in back will see the source shifted toward the red. If the wave happens to be sound, then the forward observer will hear a high pitch, the rear observer a lower one. You have probably witnessed the Doppler effect yourself. When a passing train blows its whistle, the pitch drops abruptly as the train goes by. This change in pitch is simply the Doppler effect associated with the transition from a source moving toward you to a source moving away from you.

In one of the most colorful and musical physics experiments ever performed, Doppler's conjecture was verified three years after it was proposed. With a style seldom if ever equaled, Christoph Buys Ballot of the Netherlands assembled a group of musicians with perfect pitch next to a railroad track, and then had a group of trumpeters pulled by. Though the trumpeters hit sweet notes, the Doppler effect soured the music. A microphone and tape recorder undoubtedly does the job more efficiently now, but how dull they seem!

Once Hubble had noted the relationship between the red shift and the motion of the galaxies, he noticed that the more distant galaxies exhibited exaggerated red shifts. He was forced to conclude that the universe itself was expanding. A useful analogy involves a loaf of raisin bread rising in an oven. As the dough expands, the raisins will move farther apart.

Hypothetically speaking, of course, an observer standing on one raisin will see all of his neighbors receding from him. If the loaf were as large as the universe and expanding at the same rate, beams of light shined from distant raisins would exhibit the red shift of the Doppler effect.

Furthermore, the observer on our raisin will notice that one raisin twice as far away as another will be receding twice as fast.

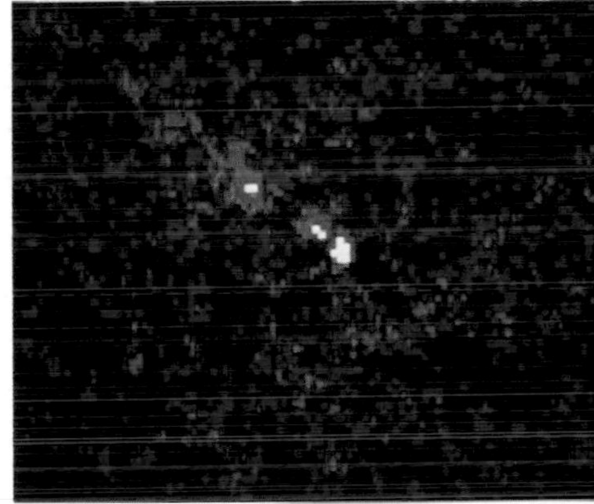

X-ray image of Centaurus A reveals a strange jet invisible to light-gathering telescopes. Spiralling, highly-charged particles emitting synchrotron radiation may cause the jet's strong X radiation.

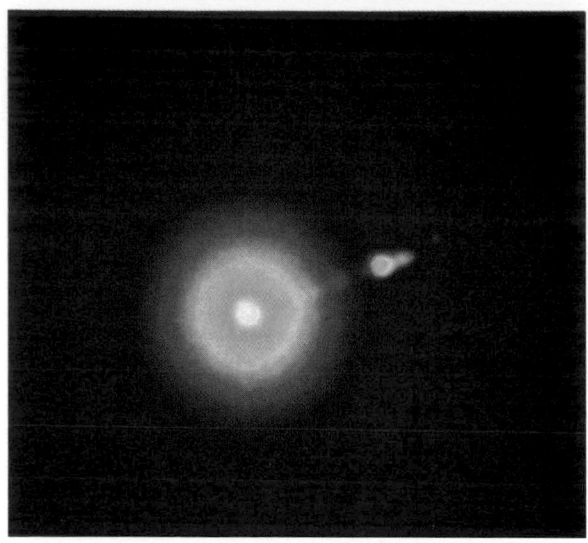

Active elliptical galaxy M 87 lies at the hub of the Virgo cluster, nearest neighbor to our Milky Way's Local Group of galaxies. From its mass of 30 million suns a knotty jet of synchrotron radiation shoots out a distance of 5,000 light-years. The galaxy and its jet appear in four computer-enhanced variations, each selected to reveal different aspects of this unusual body.

The simple reason: twice as much dough intervenes between him and the second neighbor as between him and the first. The farther the raisin, the greater the red shift. This, of course, is exactly what we see when we look at distant galaxies—the farther away, the more the wavelength of their light is shifted, and the more the color of that light changes.

However, I should qualify our discussion with one important point. It appears to us that the Earth is the center of Hubble's universal expansion. Everything is moving away from us, a fact that seems to imply a special place for the Earth in the grand scheme of things. It isn't necessarily so. Let us return to the raisin.

An observer on any raisin in the system will think that he is stationary and unmoving. Looking outward, he will see all the other raisins moving away from him, and the farther away a raisin, the faster it appears to be moving. Thus, he will conclude that he is at the unmoving center of the universal expansion. But an observer on *any* raisin will come to the same conclusion. The end result, then, is that we are indeed at the center of expansion, but so is everyone else. In the great universal raisin bread there is no privileged center.

It is important to realize that once we have understood the connection between how fast something is moving and how far away it is, we have a powerful tool for establishing a distance scale. In our bread analogy, the speed of recession of a given raisin depended on the amount of dough between us and it. In the same way, once we know the red shift (and hence the velocity) of a distant object, we know roughly how much space and time separates us from other parts of the universe. We are still refining the distance scale with its implications for the age and evolution of the universe.

Once the idea of the expanding universe is established, another fundamental insight follows immediately. If we could imagine the expanding universe as a movie and we were to run the film backwards, we would see a situation in which the universe got smaller and smaller as we moved backward in time. It's not hard to see that if you pushed this idea to its limit, you'd wind up with a picture of the entire universe packed into a single, infinitely dense point. This point is called a singularity.

If we begin with this singularity and run the film forward again, we'd see the universe begin in a single expansive event and eventually evolve into its present state, with galaxies flying apart from each other. This scenario—called by scientists the Big Bang—is the basis for today's most advanced cosmological thinking.

We will describe the Big Bang in detail elsewhere. But before leaving the subject temporarily, a few points are well worth mentioning. First, it is tempting to think of the initial event in terms of an explosion, with the galaxies spinning off like pieces of

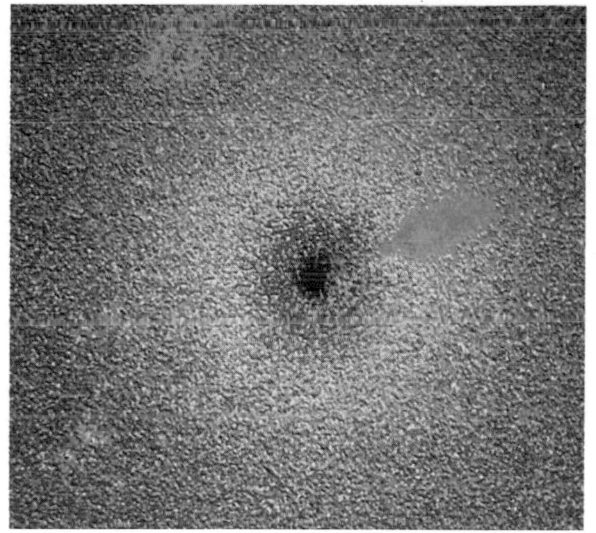

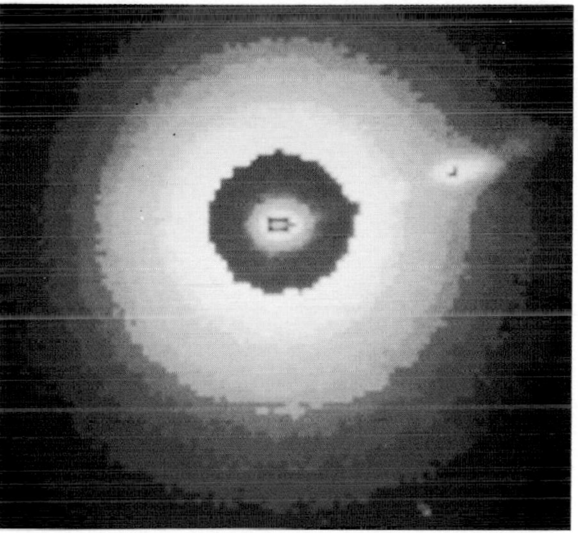

M 87 may contain a supermassive black hole, some astronomers contend. Attracted by the pull of gravity, ten thousand globular clusters swarm around this remarkable object, creating a halo effect.

debris or the starbursts thrown off from big fireworks rockets. This isn't the way scientists see things—the event is not an expansion *in* space, but an expansion *of* space itself. The rising bread dough provides us with a much better analogy than does a starshell or artillery burst.

Secondly, the term "Big Bang" is used to refer both to the initial event and to the entire event-plus-expansion-and-evolution picture. This leads to some confusion; we shall see that it is possible to have a Big Bang (in the latter sense) without any Bang (in the sense of an explosion). Finally, in our discussion we have talked loosely of galaxies as receding from each other. As we shall learn elsewhere, galaxies tend to be grouped together in clusters. And, in point of fact, the clusters rather than just the individual galaxies are receding from each other. Now, having brushed-up on our basics, let us return to the celestial realm we know best.

The Milky Way—Our Home Base

We are used to thinking of the Milky Way as a typical spiral galaxy, made up of billions of stars. It is certainly true that if someone looked at the Milky Way from outside, using the type of telescopes we have on earth, he would see stars in the familiar spiral pattern. Our own sun is located about two-thirds of the way out along one of the arms.

The prevalent spiral structure we see in galaxies isn't hard to understand. In the case of the formation of the solar system from a gas cloud, for example, the theory showed that as the cloud contracted it would almost certainly rotate. The same is true of the cloud from which the galaxy formed, a fact which guarantees that every spiral galaxy will rotate slowly about an axis through the center of its disk. The sun, for example, completes a grand circuit around the Milky Way about every 250 million years. You can see something very much like it in a full cup of hot coffee. Just stir up the coffee first and then pour in the cream to see the white spirals form. The vortex in the coffee persists for only a few turns, while in our Galaxy (and others) the basic structure persists much longer, and there are other differences limiting the use of the analogy.

The structure of our Galaxy is a disk, a spiral that is not perfectly regular. We also find a general thickening at the center of our Milky Way. It is called the nucleus. In addition, rounded masses of stars called globular clusters, naturally enough, appear throughout the region of the Galaxy, but are not confined to the galactic plane. By studying these clusters, and noting that they appear to be concentrated in the direction of the galactic center, the American astronomer Harlow Shapley first showed that the sun was not at the center of the Galaxy.

Near the main part of the Milky Way are two small collections of stars known as the Magellanic Clouds. They are actually small galaxies associated with the Milky Way and connected to it by a bridge of hydrogen gas.

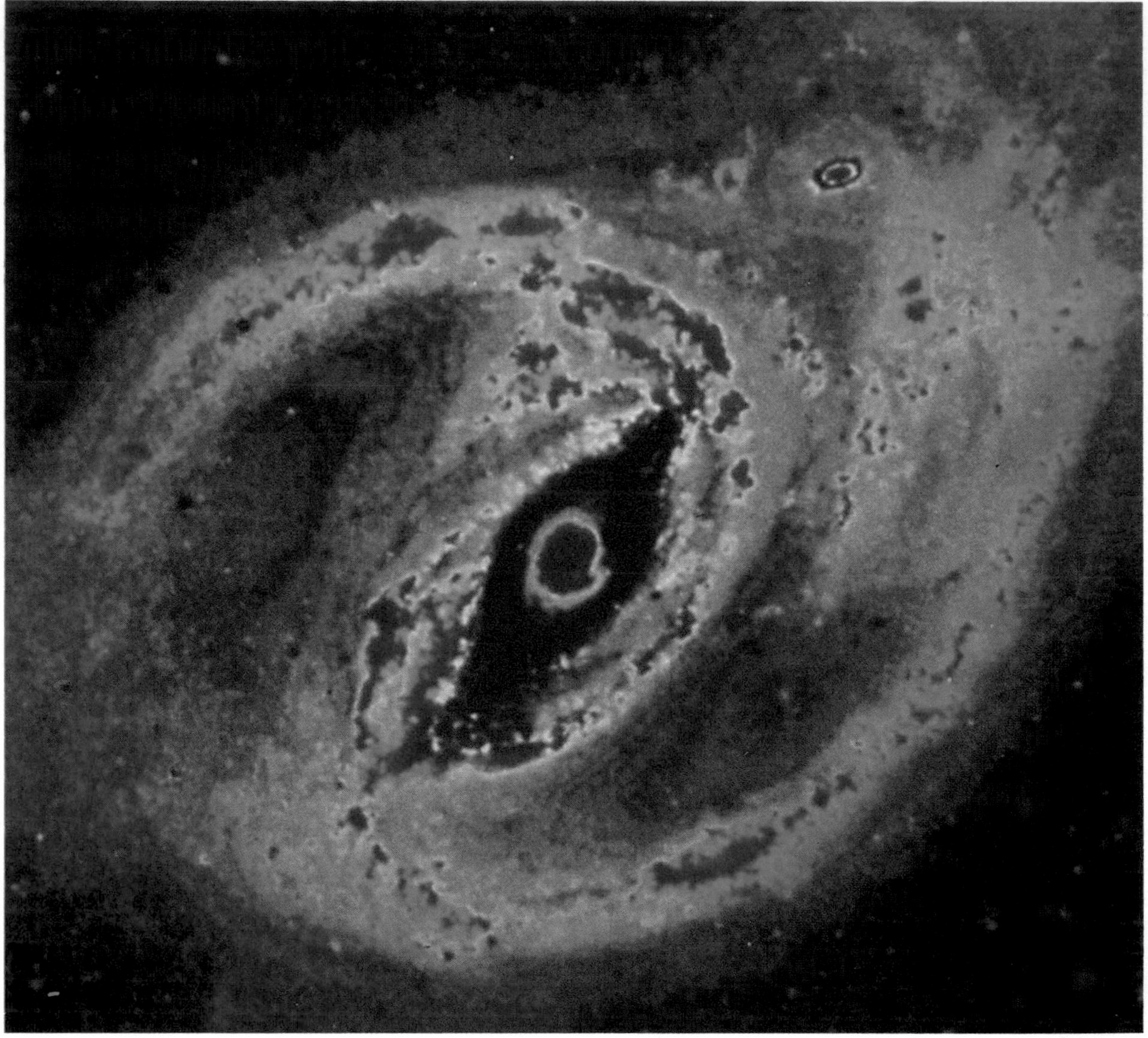

Double feature, NGC 1097 consists of two galaxies, one large barred spiral, and a small, hostage elliptical which appears in the upper right-hand corner.

In fact, a good many other galaxies have such satellites and some are apparently drawn inside. Others are characterized by jets or features created by material leaving the galaxies.

Because our eyes and our telescopes are sensitive to visible light, we have a tendency to stop the catalogue of the Milky Way at this point, for we have described all of the luminous matter. It would be a serious mistake. We already know of gas, dust, and the remains of exploded stars. This medium scatters the light so we have a visual clue to its existence. Note that this cast of distant stars, often reddish, is not caused by the Doppler effect—it's not a red shift.

In fact, light itself may lead us astray, when we seek the overall structure of the universe. Many scientists suspect that all of the matter of the galaxy—stars, nebulae, dust, clusters, gas, and other chemical substances—amounts to only a few percent of the total mass present. As we will see, knowledge of both visible and invisible components of space is necessary to determine the ultimate destiny of what we know of as space and time.

A study of galactic rotation suggests a wider dispersion of matter than meets the eye. For instance, if most of the mass were concentrated in the center (as you might expect from looking at the distribution of stars), then as we reached the outer parts we would see the rotation start to slow down.

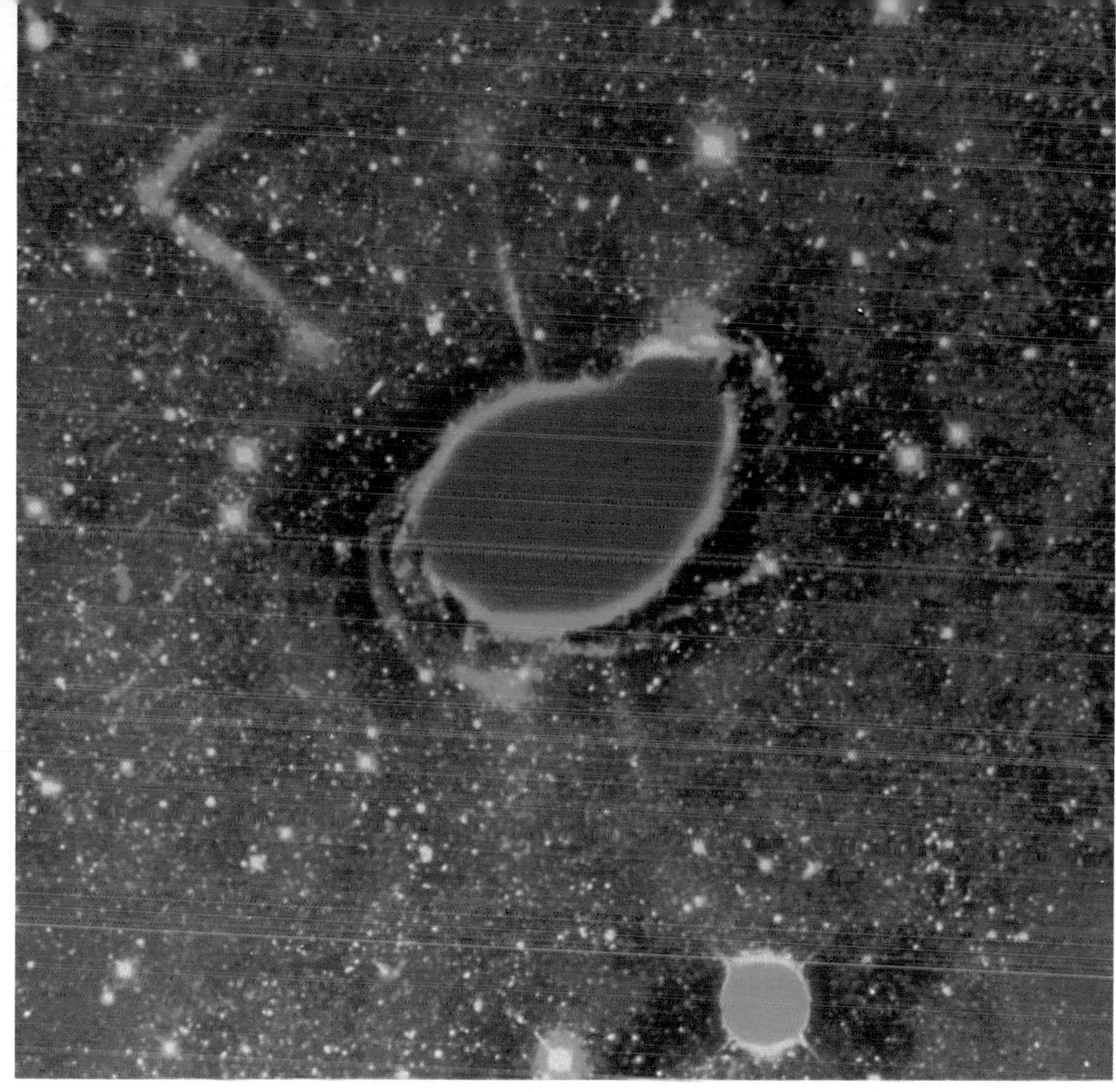

Radio close-up of the nucleus of NGC 1097 reveals mysterious jets emanating from the polar regions.

The effect is clearly visible in our solar system, where the outer planets move much more slowly than the inner ones. However, we do not detect this expected slowing down in galaxies, even at distances from the galactic centers that mark our limits of observation. We might assume that unseen matter exists here.

According to models current in 1985, dark matter forms coronas (haloes) around galaxies, thus increasing the galactic masses many times over. The composition of the dark matter is unknown—scientists have conjured up the specters of black dwarfs, black holes, Jupiter-sized objects, and any number of strange new (and as yet undetected) particles. We say with certainty, however, that enough dark matter is present to produce the kind of galactic rotation we observe. A good many scientists would not be too surprised if it were to account for more than 95 percent of the mass of the Galaxy.

For the moment the mystery lives. We simply do not know what exists either at the hub of our Galaxy or on its fringes.

It is an old and respected rule of thumb in astronomy that the study of nearby bodies can lead to an understanding of those far away. Let us apply this rule to our own galactic center and the globular clusters, both composed of stars with very few heavy elements in them. Thus, we suspect, these stars are probably old, having formed from an interstellar medium poor in mineral content. Those in the spiral arms of the disk, on the other hand, resemble the sun in their richer chemical composition, and hence appear relatively young.

Very unusual things are going on in the center of our Galaxy that we cannot see with optical telescopes. There is simply too much material in the way. Quite recently, radio telescopes and various sensor satellites have allowed us glimpses into that central bulge. We receive images of expanding shells of gas, almost as if the debris of past explosions is hurtling outward. As we approach the center, stars become densely packed. Several million stars may shine in the central 100 light-years of the Milky Way, for example. This means that, on the average, the distance between stars will be a fraction of a light-year (as compared with average separations of many light-years for stars near the sun). At the very center lies one of the most mysterious objects in the sky. Packed into a volume smaller than the solar system is something with a mass 50 *million* times that of the sun. This object can be detected by its radio and infrared emissions, yet we can only guess as to its nature. It may be a large black hole in the center of the Galaxy. If so, then such entities may be found at other galaxian centers, and the space telescope may reveal more of their anatomy and function.

Galaxies

Hubble quickly realized that not all galaxies are identical. Spiral forms abound, while only 20 percent are elliptical. The latter are large collections of stars with little obvious internal structuring arranged in a generally elliptical pattern. While most galaxies have their little quirks, some are outlandish. Professor Halton Arp of the California Institute of Technology had catalogued nearly 7,000 by 1985, and several appear in this chapter. Perhaps it is a good thing that astronomical realization comes to mankind only a little at a time.

In Hubble's wake, we discover that galaxies seem to be grouped into clusters, rather than spread uniformly through space. The Milky Way and the Andromeda galaxy are the largest members of what is called the

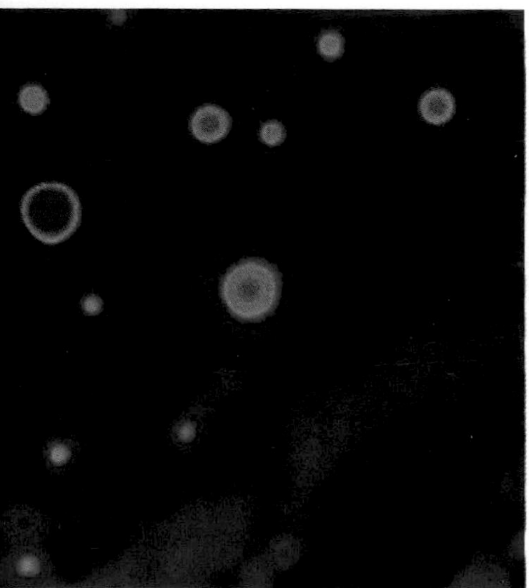

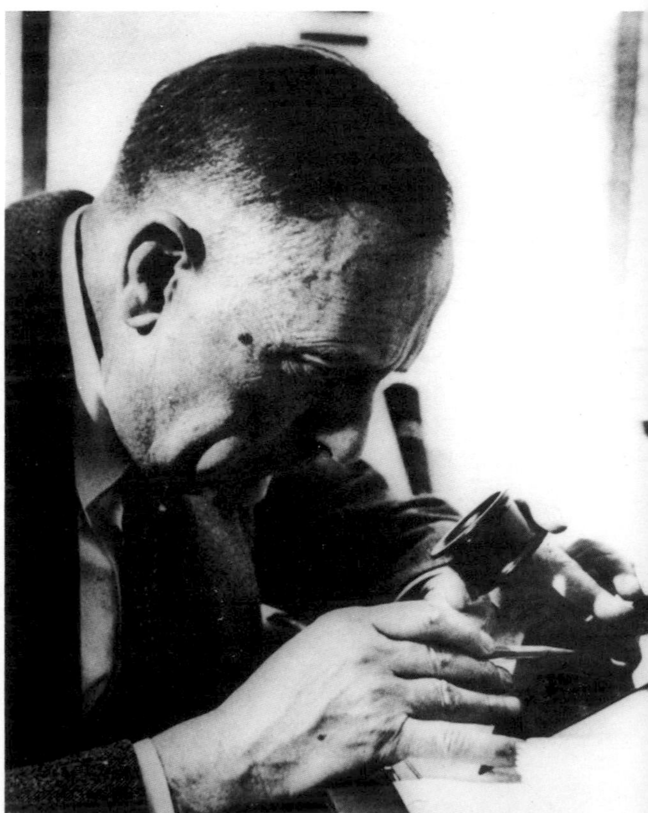

Stars rich in cosmic rays and complex magnetic fields shine in Andromeda, above, reaching us through the radio "window." For our own Milky Way, Henrietta Leavitt, shown at right in the Harvard College Observatory, charted the period-luminosity relation of Cepheid variable stars. Her work enabled other scientists to calculate distances to these stars. Edwin Hubble, far right, extended the Cepheid yardstick to Andromeda and other galaxies as he furthered his theory of an expanding universe.

Local Group, a smallish fleet of 20 or more lesser galaxies held in by the gravitational attraction of the two giants. We are unsure of the exact number of neighbor galaxies because dust in the Milky Way might keep us from seeing some of the fainter ones.

Some other clusters contain thousands of individual galaxies. Astronomers are currently addressing the question of whether clusters of galaxies themselves form larger groupings called superclusters. Delineation of such a large-scale arrangement has become very important in modern astronomy, and we will examine it in considerable detail in a later chapter.

All of the galaxies in Hubble's original classification scheme (and the additions and elaborations since his time) are relatively quiet places. The stately process of star formation, element creation, and star death goes on in each of them, and the fact that they radiate energy can be explained simply. The stars are hot. In the jargon of physics, we say that the galaxies emit a thermal spectrum. Philip Morrison of MIT calls this sort of galaxy "hearthlike." These are places where planets like Earth could circle stars like the sun.

Active Galaxies

If we confined our attention to the universe as it appears in ordinary visible light, we would conclude that most of it is hearthlike. The advent of radio astronomy, however, has shown that there are things in the sky that most emphatically do not deserve this description. Certain galaxies appear quite unexceptional when viewed in visible light, but broadcast prodigious amounts of energy in radio-wave frequencies. It is common for such galaxies to emit 100,000 times more energy than the entire Milky Way! Objects that show this sort of unusual behavior are called active galaxies, an appropriate name if ever there was one. Only in very recent years have radio astronomers been able to gain the kinds of detailed images of radio sources shown throughout this chapter and elsewhere in the book.

In addition to being very bright, the radiation emitted from active galaxies is not of the type associated with hot objects. In the

Edwin Hubble ended the island-universe controversy in 1923 by discovering that the Andromeda nebula, below, is in fact a galaxy in its own right, far too distant to be a part of the Milky Way. Scientists superimposed UV, red, and blue wavelength photographs to create this close up of Andromeda.

active galaxy, of course, is that in the latter there is no attempt to control the emission for purposes of communication.

Some active galaxies are compact, with the emissions sometimes coming from regions no more than a few light-months across. Other sources are extended—a typical situation might involve two huge jets emitted back-to-back from a galactic nucleus, with the intense radio emissions coming from the jets. Whether the active galaxy is compact or extended, it often involves energy sources that measure only a few light-years across. How so much energy can be generated in so small a volume is a major question in astronomy.

Finally, there are a few types of rare active galaxies that may figure prominently in future theories of galactic evolution, so we mention them here for completeness. Seyfert galaxies, named after the American astronomer Carl Seyfert, are small spiral galaxies with very bright nuclei, violent gas motions, and (usually) a source of radio emission. Another group of strange objects in the sky are called BL Lacertae objects. They have no visible structure and their brightness can vary by a factor of 20. (The last part of the name comes from the constellation Lacertus where the first such object was seen.) And then there are quasars!

Digital electronic detectors, charge-coupled devices or CCDs, significantly enhance the detail of this bright elliptical galaxy, NGC 4472. It lies 50 million light-years away in the Virgo cluster.

jargon, it is non-thermal. Somewhere in the nucleus a cataclysmic event occurs, sending material streaming into the intergalactic medium. This material carries tangled strands of the galactic magnetic field with it. Electrons in the emitted material turn in tight orbits around these magnetic fields, so the particles follow a corkscrew path through space. As they move along, they radiate energy that our radio telescopes detect.

This connection between moving electrons and radio emissions shouldn't be surprising. After all in an ordinary transmitting tower, electrical current (moving electrons) is manipulated to produce the waves that you pick up in your radio receiver. The difference between a broadcast antenna and an

Quasars: The Beginning or the End?

During the late fifties, when radio astronomy was in its springtime, the locations of many radio sources in the sky were catalogued. It got to be something of a cottage industry for optical astronomers to try to find and photograph objects at the locations of the radio emission. When these identifications were made, many of the objects appeared as stars—merely simple points of light—so the name *quasi-stellar radio sources* emerged, only to be shortened to quasar. We should also note that although the first quasars discovered were radio sources, most are not. The modern definition of a quasar refers to any very luminous starlike object with a large red shift.

For a time they presented a unique puzzle to astronomers: the spectral lines from these objects simply didn't seem to match any atoms known on earth. In 1963, the Dutch astronomer Maarten Schmidt, working at the California Institute of Technology, finally solved the problem. The light from the quasars had been shifted so far to the red that the spectrum had become unrecognizable. It was as if someone had superimposed a map of New York City in the spot where we would normally expect to find Los Angeles. There's nothing particularly mysterious about the New York map, but until you had figured out the shift, you'd certainly have trouble navigating. In just the same way, spectral lines that astronomers expected to see in the visible region had been pushed down into the infrared band in the quasar data, and the visible region was taken up by lines normally appearing in the ultra violet range.

Schmidt's discovery was initially greeted with a sigh of relief, soon to be followed by puzzled expressions. If the red shifts were really as large as he claimed (and there was really no way out of that conclusion), and if we believe that large red shifts correspond to large distances, then some quasars are among the most distant objects in the universe. The one that Schmidt was working on, for example, turned out to be moving away from us at about 16 percent of the speed of light, or 30,000 miles per second. Early estimates put the quasar at three billion light-years away. The light we receive left its source three billion years ago and has been traveling toward us ever since. In the meantime, the quasar itself may have vanished altogether or have changed into something else.

If the quasar were really that far away, it would have to put out enormous energy to be visible from earth. Today we know that quasar radiation outputs of 100 to 10,000 times greater than that of the Milky Way are common. With active galaxies, we really don't have a very good idea of the processes that generate this energy.

If three billion light-years seemed like an unheard of distance in 1963, it quickly paled in the light of subsequent discoveries. The "world champion" quasar discovered to date, which goes by the mundane name of OQ 172, recedes from us at 91 percent of the speed of light, or 169,500 miles a sec-

Stephan's Quintet, a grouping of five intertwined galaxies, was discovered by French astronomer M.E. Stephan in 1871. Four of the galaxies exhibit similar red shifts indicating their proximity to each other. The fifth, a dwarf, seems to reside inside the large galaxy in the lower left-hand corner. This tiny body puzzles astronomers since its red shift is significantly smaller than the others. Thus it seems closer to Earth.

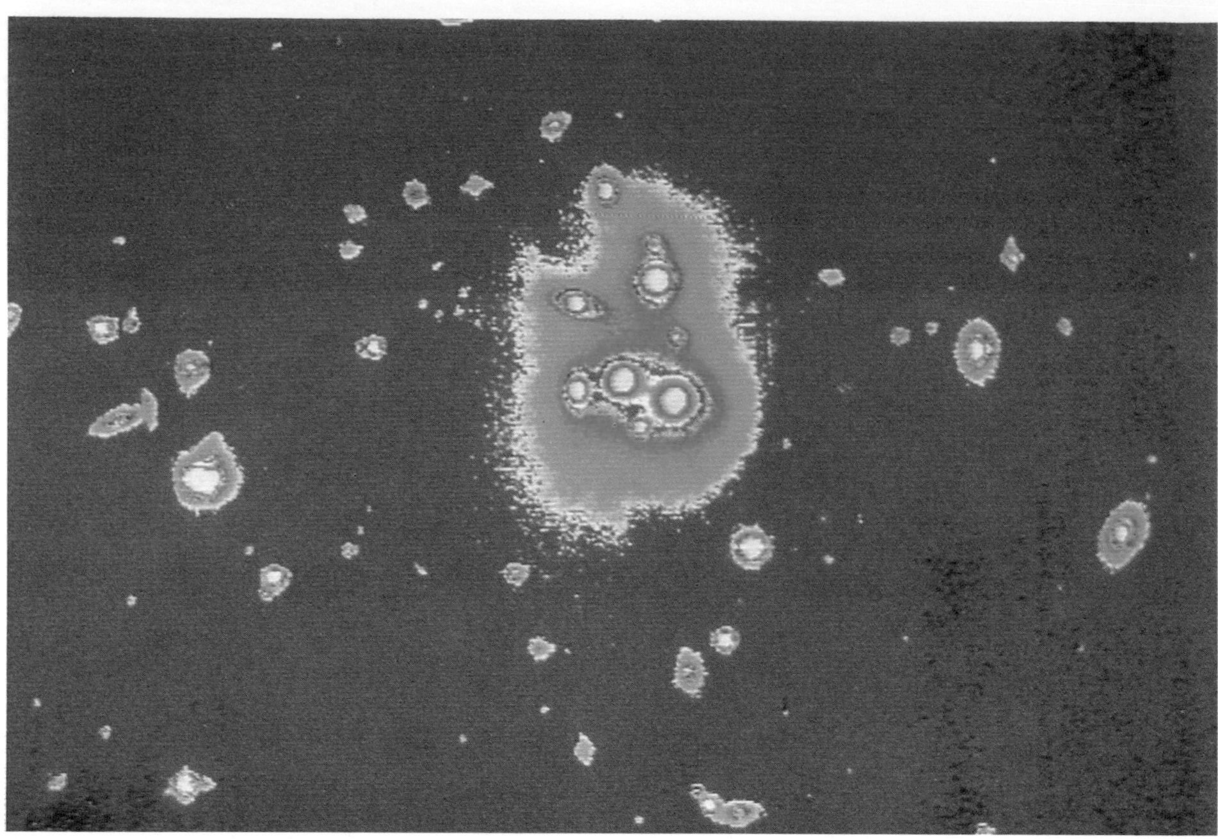

Light that we see today first shined a billion years ago from the distant cluster called V Zwicky 311, at right. Known as a multiple nucleus giant, the central galaxy dominates other, smaller galaxies.

ond. Its red shift indicates a distance of 15 billion light-years, according to estimates from the early eighties. When we detect something this far away, we would do well to keep two things in mind. First, we may be seeing the very edge of the universe—something so far away that light from it has been traveling toward us almost since the beginning of time. Second, we are looking backward in time, detecting the state of OQ 172 *as it was near the very beginning of creation*. With the quasars, then, we seem to have reached the edge of observability.

Since looking outward in space is equivalent to peering backward in time, the conjecture is that quasars are nothing more than galaxies in birth. If by some magic you could see OQ 172 as it is today, it's possible that a galaxy much like the Milky Way would appear. Similarly, astronomers in OQ 172 looking at us might be seeing a quasar—the most distant thing in their sky.

As best we can tell, galaxies go through a series of evolutionary stages as they mature. A popular evolutionary chain for a galaxy would have it start as a quasar, then move quickly through BL Lacertae, Seyfert, and active galaxy stages, and finally wind up as a normal galaxy like our own. This is a very appealing idea. For one thing, it explains why so many quasars are so far away. They may represent an earlier stage of evolution, one close to the Big Bang. Then we would be observing things the way they were billions of years ago. The scarcity of nearby quasars could suggest, for instance, that the universe is no longer in the quasar producing stage. How comforting to think that all of the strange and violent things we see in the universe may be like dinosaur skeletons—fossils of an earlier and harsher time.

Frontiers of Knowledge

An obvious and important question is where does (or did) all the energy come from to power quasars and active galaxies. More to the point, how can the source of so much energy be so small? Many scientists find it absolutely incredible that an active galaxy should emit many thousands of times the energy generated by the Milky Way. Some of these exotic energy sources are only

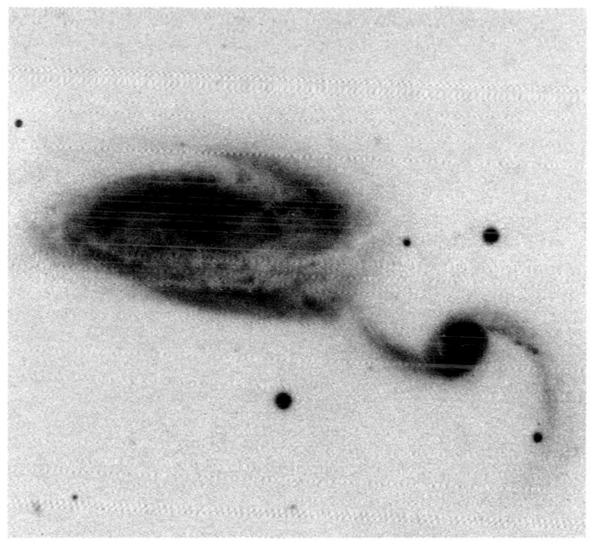
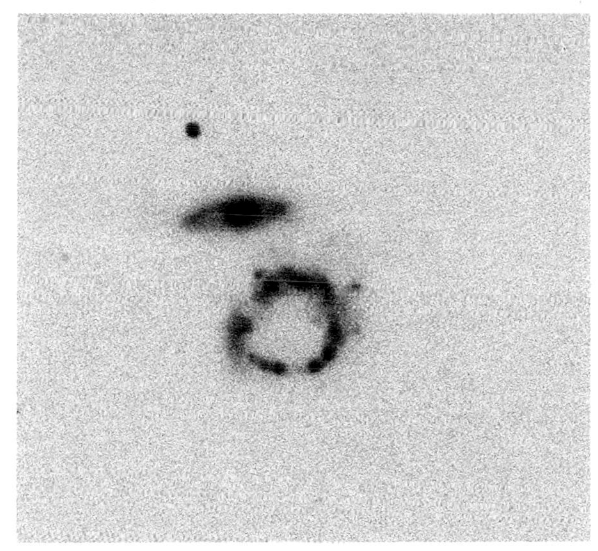
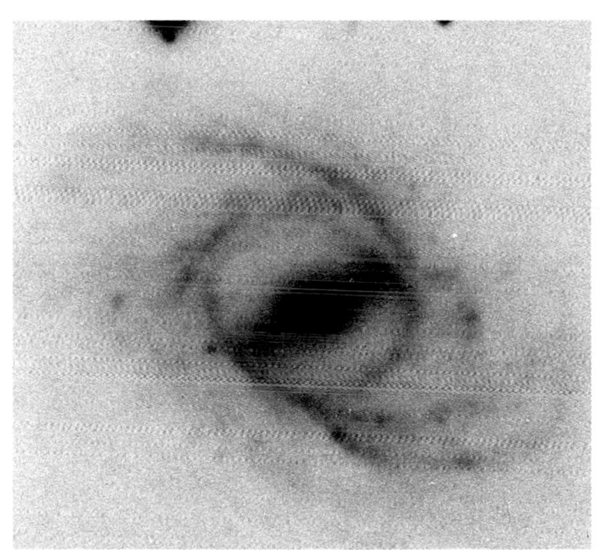
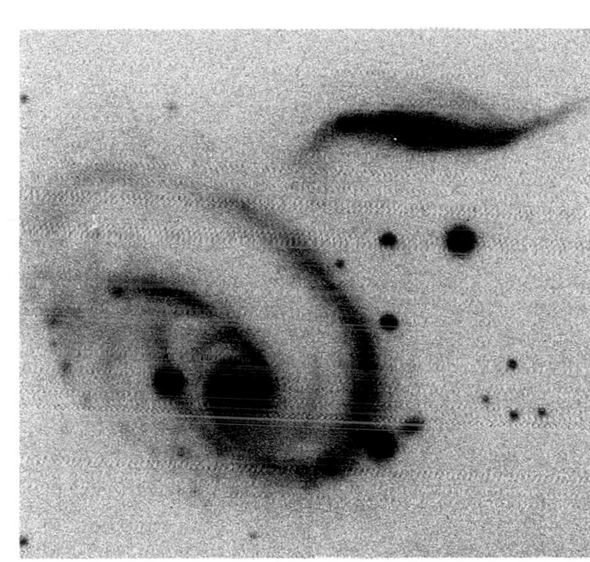

Rogue's gallery of perturbed and deformed galaxies originated with Halton Arp's Atlas of Peculiar Galaxies. *Though too faint to be analyzed and interpreted in detail, these images are nonetheless valuable in astronomers' search for clues about galactic formation.*

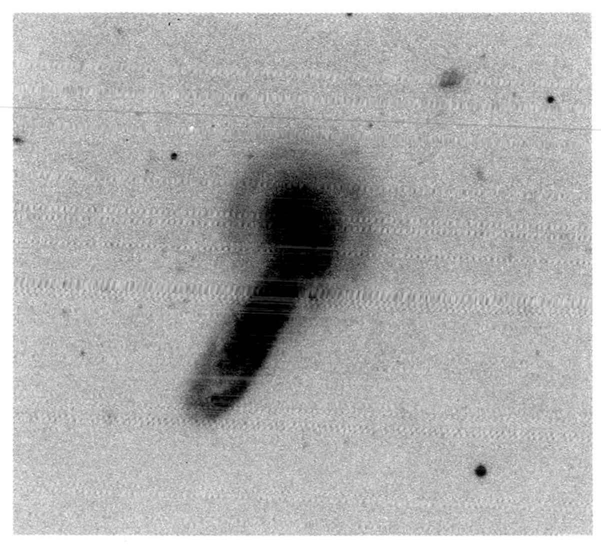
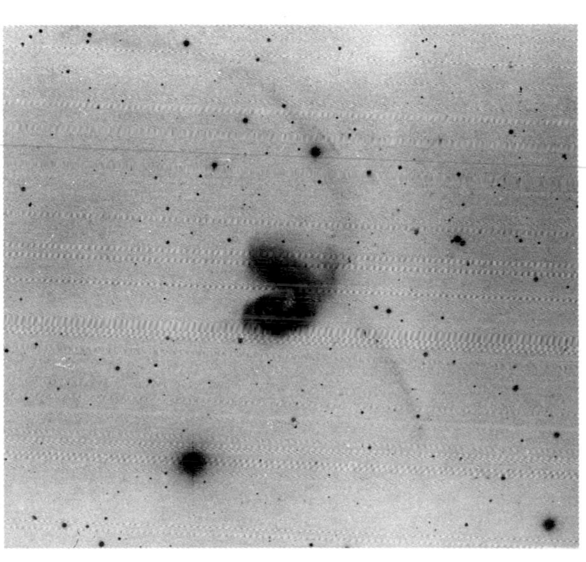

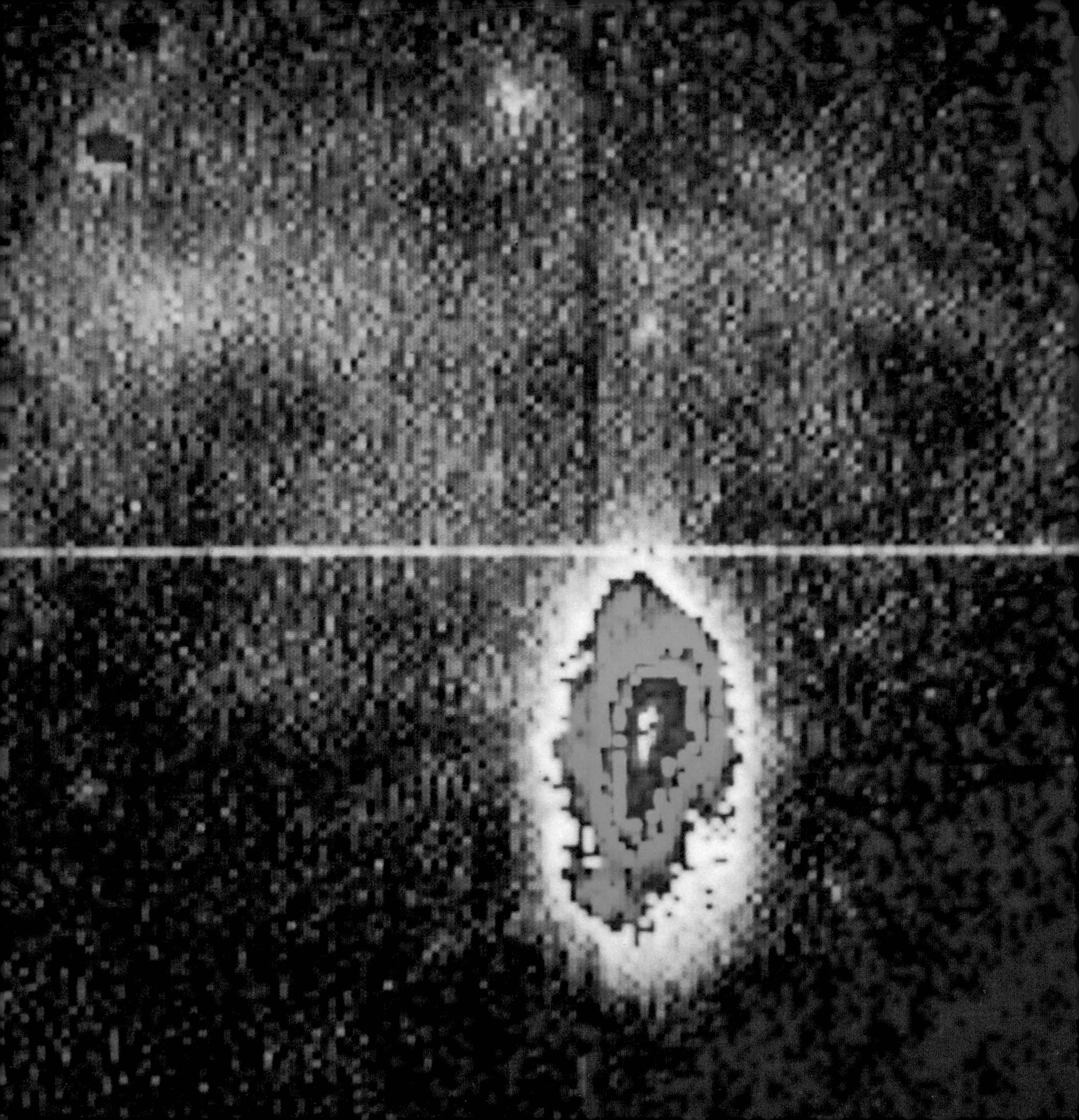

a few light-months (or light-years) across! Our Galaxy spans 100,000 light-years. There seems to be evidence that quasars, as well, emit most of their energy from small regions. What process could possibly produce all that radiation?

Most conjectures seem to center around the idea that massive black holes lie at the center of active galaxies and quasars. In one sense, this is an appealing thought, since the idea of galactic evolution would surely be strengthened by having black holes at the centers of both quasars and active galaxies. Moreover, as we have seen, a popular theory puts a massive black hole at the center of the Milky Way. Such consistency is certainly suggestive, but it has to be taken with a grain of salt. In the words of an astronomer whose judgment I have learned to trust, "Since no one has found a black hole, you can assume any properties for it you want." By the same token, you can solve any problem if you pick the properties of the black hole correctly.

Computer image of a quasi-stellar object or quasar, left. Scientists believe that such brilliant outbursts in the center of distant galaxies originated as many as 15 billion years ago. Thus we are seeing their "fossil light" in our telescopes. Such time-tripping reveals evidence of the origin of the universe. Tremendous red shifts indicate a recessional velocity of 90 percent the speed of light. Right, balls of stars from Thomas Wright's New Theory of the Universe *of 1750, may not be an accurate model of star or galactic formation. Yet this image is curiously suggestive of recent computer simulations of large-scale fluctuations of matter and energy in the universe.*

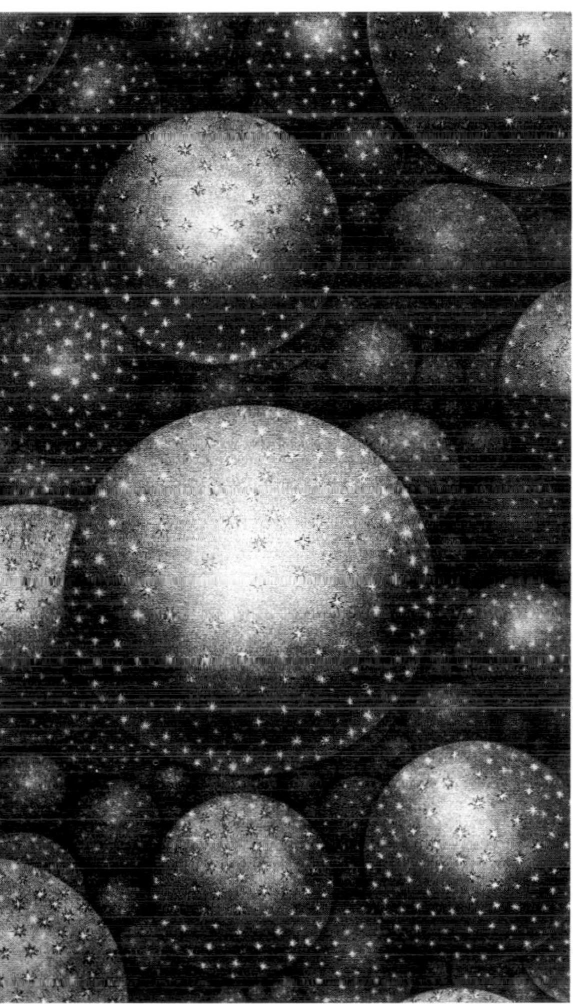

The second research frontier has to do with the limited distance range we find for quasars. All of the quasars in the sky seem to be associated with times between three and fifteen billion years ago. Are there fainter quasars, or is there an end to them? This is an observational (as opposed to theoretical) question. The best thinking now says that we have seen all the quasars there are. But will this be borne out by the next generation of astronomical instruments?

Another question concerns the exact value to be assigned to the Hubble age for the universe. At present, the uncertainty comes down to the question of whether the universe is 10 or 20 billion years old.

You will undoubtedly encounter headlines about this controversy, an important one for scientists. But it is more in the nature of a re-adjustment than a breakthrough. For example, should the age of the universe turn out to be 10 instead of 20 billion years, the distances to (and ages of) the distant quasars would simply be scaled down accordingly. On the one hand, this may look like a huge change. On the other, I regard it as a great tribute to the human intellect that we are arguing over a factor of only two in the age of the universe.

Windows in the Sky

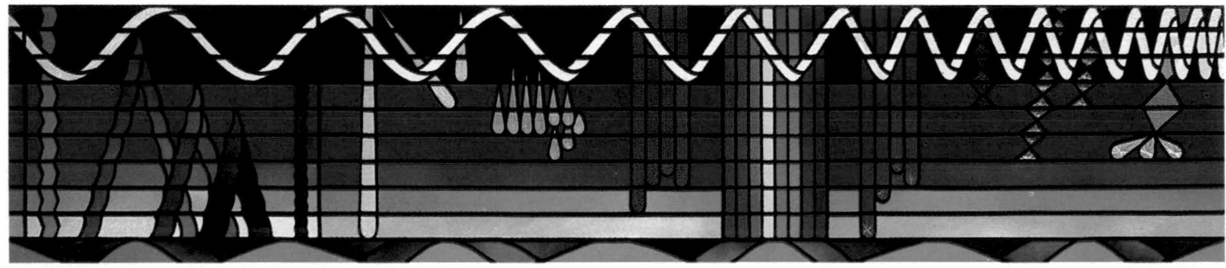

All in one: the sky's entire electromagnetic spectrum appears in stained glass at the Smithsonian. Our optical "window" shines to the right of center as a rainbow band. To its right, shorter wavelengths include the ultraviolet and X-ray ranges, and cosmic rays. To its left we see the infrared range, aurora and meteor "whistlers," and long radio waves.

Hold out your hand to a fire. You feel the warmth. Furthermore, you will still feel warmth when the fire has died down and the coals no longer glow. Your hand is detecting unseen infrared radiation from those coals.

If you overdo it your first day in the spring sun (as, alas, I did the day before writing this), you will discover that there is more to sunlight than one can see. Your skin will "detect" the invisible ultraviolet radiation streaming down, and then register it as a sunburn.

These homey examples make two points: first, there is more to the world than meets the eye; and, second, that even so crude an instrument as the human skin can detect the presence of some invisible radiation. In this chapter we will explore the world of unseen energy and discuss its importance to astronomical observation.

A glance at the spectrum shows that visible energy is only a small sliver out of the whole array of electromagnetic wavelengths. From the radio waves that wake you up in the morning to the microwaves that cook your food to the X rays that show your broken bones, they all have the same basic structure of oscillating electrical and magnetic fields. They differ only in wavelength. This is probably one of the least appreciated (and most beautiful) facts in science.

Our historical interest in optical astronomy, then, is not solely due to the fact that our eyes are sensitive only to visible light. The atmosphere effectively blocks almost all other forms of radiation, so even if we knew the radiation was there, we couldn't use it. In effect, our atmosphere possesses a window that lets in visible light. Only radiation that comes through such windows is of any use to the earthbound astronomer.

Electromagnetic Waves

To understand the nature of the invisible part of the electromagnetic spectrum, we need to think a bit about the nature of that visible radiation we call light. It falls into a general class of phenomena that physicists call waves. As such, light is related to such diverse things as the surf coming into a beach, the sounds you hear, and earthquakes—the waves propagated in solid material and through destructive ocean waves called tsunamis. Since most of us can visualize waves on water quite easily, we can introduce their properties by thinking in terms of what you might see on a quiet day at the surface of a lake.

We have several numbers with which to characterize the wave. One is the distance between crests, the wavelength. This number can range from thousands of feet in the open ocean to fractions of an inch for wind-driven ripples. The number of wavecrests that pass a given point in a single unit of time is called the frequency of the wave. At a beach, you might see a wave coming in

Great-great grandparents of today's space probes, these instruments from Smithsonian collections produced data for the Institution's pioneering astrophysical research around the turn of the century and later. They measured solar radiation that could reach Earth through the sky's visible or infrared "windows." Front, a pyrheliometer for measuring the components of sunlight. Left to right: mirror for observing sunspots; silver-disk pyrheliometer; light-sensitive cell; and a pyrheliometer designed for balloon work. The slender Crooke's radiometer is the familiar solar paddle wheel. Revolving sector radiometer measured the luminosity of the sun. Bolometer component held water to cool a device for measuring radiant heat.

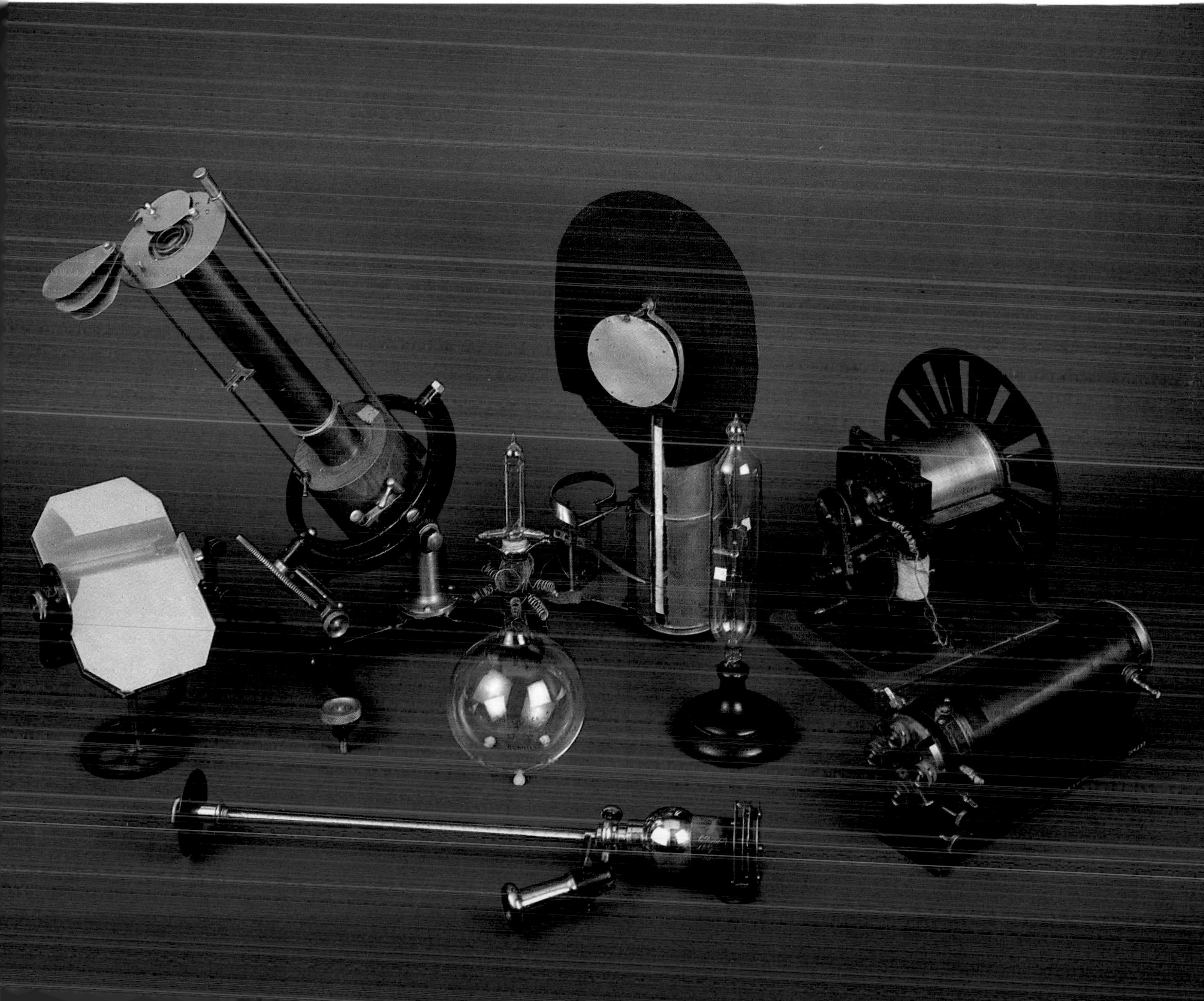

every 10 seconds. The frequency of such waves would be six cycles per minute or 0.1 cycles per second. Finally, the speed with which the crests of the waves move through the water is known as the wave velocity. The height of the wave is called the displacement or amplitude.

The wave has a special relationship with its medium. A wave on water may travel toward the shore, but the individual bits of water do not. If you watch a piece of floating debris for a while, you will realize that as a wave crest moves past a point, the debris does not follow it. This important observation shows that the debris is somehow connected to the surrounding water and its motion displays for us the actual motion of the water. Waves travel shoreward but the water moves up and down. The two movements are not the same. In fact, this simple example shows us that while the wave is a motion *on* the water, it is not a motion *of* the water. The wave is a traveler, the water a medium of transfer.

Seen in red light through the telescope, galaxy Abel 2199 appears as a fuzzy spot with few discernible features. Combining information from different sources opens a "window" into this unusual island universe. Now Abel 2199 is shown as a galactic cannibal—its large nucleus absorbing smaller star clusters.

This is true of waves in any medium. When your hear sound, you are actually hearing a wave that moves through the air. As with the water, however, individual air molecules do not move from the source to your ear, but vibrate back and forth in the same place—again, a motion *in* the air, but not a movement *of* the air.

From these examples, it becomes clear that the important characteristics of a wave are in some sense independent of the medium on which the wave moves. You could even imagine a "pure" wave, one which involved a motion with no medium at all. Physicists think of light in this way. To them, a light wave is a periodic up-and-down motion of an electric field accompanied by an oscillating magnetic field. This wave travels through space in much the same way that surf travels through water.

Unlike water, light waves always travel at the same speed in a vacuum, regardless of their wavelength or displacement. This speed, usually denoted by the letter c, is about 186,000 miles (or 300,000 kilometers) per second. The fact that every wave travels at the same velocity means that if we know the wavelength, we can work out the frequency (or vice versa). For example, if a wave crest travels at ten feet per second and two crests go by in a second, it's easy to see that the wavelength must be five feet. We can always do this sort of calculation with light; thus we can completely specify the wave by giving either the wavelength or the frequency—we don't need both.

When light enters our eye, its associated electric fields move electrons in the atoms of the retina. The resulting processes are complex, but the net effect is that we perceive the phenomenon we know as color. Which color we perceive depends on the wavelength of the light. If the wavelength registers 7,800 angstroms, we see red. If it's 3,800 angstroms, we see violet. This unit

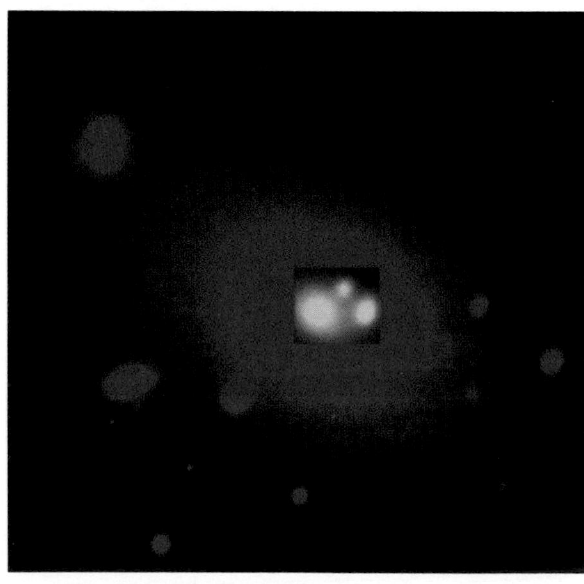

for measuring wavelengths, the angstrom, is about as long as the diameter of a hydrogen atom—the diameter of a human hair is 500,000 angstroms. The two wavelengths mentioned above mark the limits of visibility for the human eye. How bright the light appears to us depends on the displacement of the wave—the higher the displacement, the brighter the light.

It may help to picture these wavelengths by noting that if we stacked 7,800 hydrogen atoms end to end, they would stretch about as far as the distance between crests in red light. Similarly, 3,800 such atoms in a row would span a wavelength of violet. Wavelengths between these two are seen as intermediate colors in the spectrum—blue light would correspond to about 4,700 atoms, yellow to 5,800. All of these waves travel at the same speed in a vacuum.

The understanding that light is a mixture of electric and magnetic fields—the electromagnetic wave as we say—was reached in the latter part of the nineteenth century. As soon as this realization came, however, it presented problems. Why is the range of wavelengths so restricted? After all, we know that water waves come in all sizes. Why isn't light the same? If electromagnetic waves were indeed confined to the wavelength associated with visible light, it would be very restrictive; it would be like looking at oceans, ponds, rivers, and puddles and seeing midsize waves between five and six feet only—nothing longer, nothing shorter. This would be an amazing state of affairs, to say the least.

The German physicist Heinrich Hertz was the first to see the way out of this dilemma. The problem, he said, was not that electromagnetic waves longer and shorter than light didn't exist, but that we simply hadn't detected their presence. His discovery of radio-frequency—or Hertzian—waves was quickly followed by their use in radio by Guglielmo Marconi from 1896. Radio waves have the same structure as light—that is, they are oscillations of electric and magnetic fields in space—but they have wavelengths from hundreds of feet to miles in length. They bear the same kind of relation to light as a tidal wave on water does to the ripples on a pleasant lake: radio is just a stretched-out version of light.

Once scientists understood that certain electromagnetic waves were invisible to the eye, it was but a short step to the realization that electromagnetic waves could have any wavelength whatsoever, and the variety of electromagnetic radiation was no less rich than the variety of waves on water. The resulting collection of waves has come to be known as the electromagnetic spectrum.

The Radio Window and Beyond

There are two very important "windows" in the atmosphere that allow visible light and radio waves to reach the earth's surface from space. With the exception of a few very narrow windows for the infrared, everything else is absorbed high above the ground. The physical process of atmospheric absorption is different for each type of radiation. Oxygen and nitrogen atoms stop gamma and X rays while the ozone layer intercepts ultraviolet rays, and the lower-lying molecules of carbon dioxide and water drink up the infrared. Whatever the reason, however, the effect is the same. Only a few windows in the atmosphere allow information from the heavens to reach the ground. Radiation outside these windows is simply dissipated in collisions high above our heads.

Opening of the second window, radio astronomy, is generally reckoned to have occurred in 1931, during a period when electrical engineer Karl Jansky of Bell Labo-

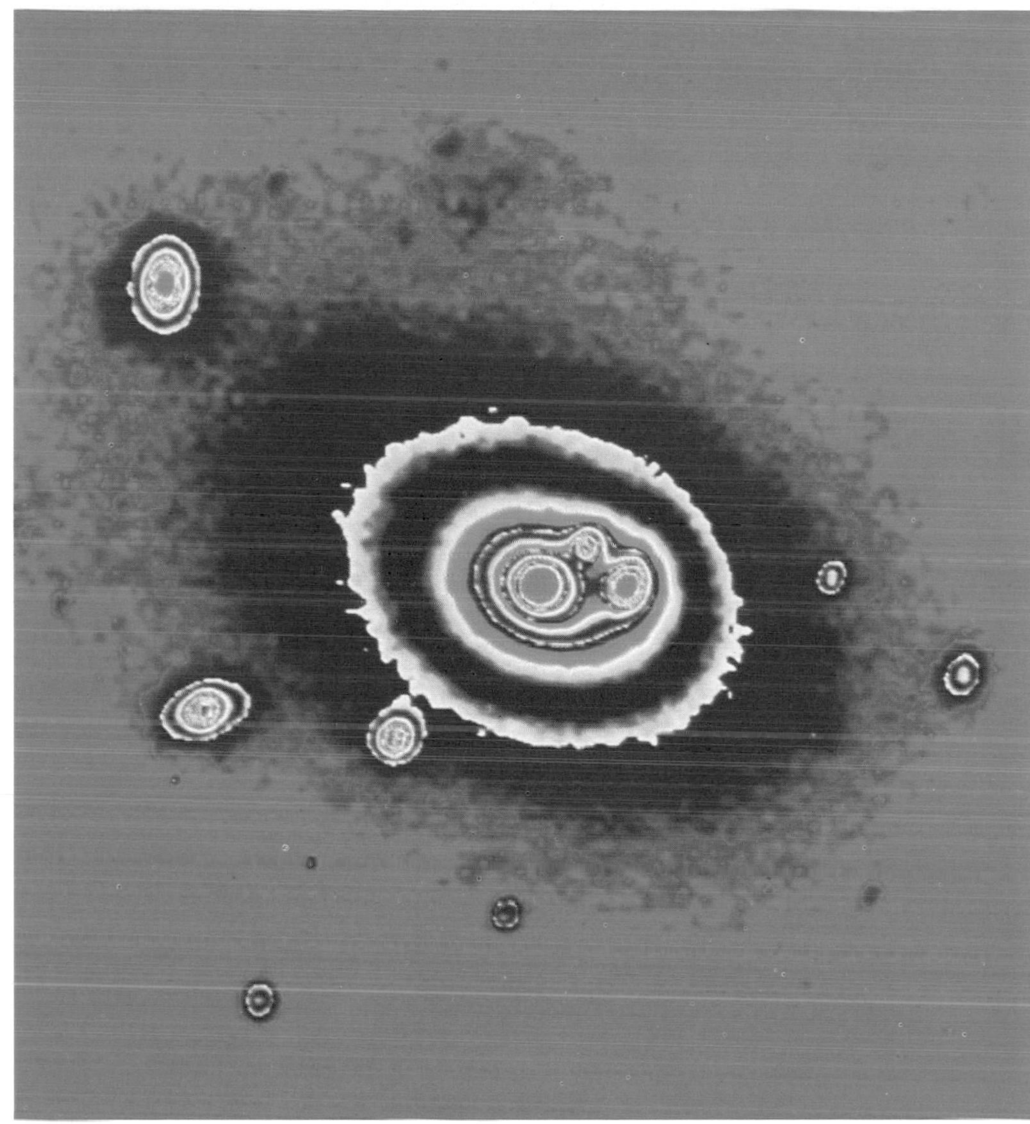

Through a computer-enhanced image, Abel 2199 seems to be sliced open, uncovering details normally hidden. For this intimate view, different levels of brightness have been artificially colored. Two smaller galaxies orbit near the central mass and gradually lose their stars. At greater distances, other galaxies move toward their eventual destruction.

Magnificent artwork, above, and photography, opposite, show just how much (and how little) can be portrayed through the visual window. Stars and nebulas on photographs were plotted by artists and technicians at Sweden's Lund University and then rendered into a consistent panorama—something nearly impossible by photographic methods alone. Only the closest star fields can be clearly seen, as they curtain off areas closer to the nucleus.

ratories was working on intercontinental telephone lines. He wanted to understand the causes of static in transmissions. He noticed a sporadic hissing noise in his earphones—one that simply refused to be explained. Eventually, Jansky realized that the hiss occurred every 23 hours and 56 minutes—a unit of time astronomers call the sidereal day. This is how long it takes for a given star to come back to the same point in the sky each day. Jansky concluded that something like a star was emitting radio waves, and his receivers were picking up these signals as static.

Jansky's work was followed by that of Grote Reber, a radio engineer in Wheaton, Illinois, who constructed a crude radio receiver in his backyard and produced the first radio maps of the sky. The biggest boost for the fledgling science of radio astronomy, however, was the tremendous development of radio and radar technology during World War II. The tools that had been developed to detect enemy aircraft were quickly redesigned to look at the sky. By 1957, Sir Bernard Lovell had constructed the first large radio telescope at Jodrell Bank, near Manchester, England, and the exploration of the sky through the second window had begun in earnest.

A radio telescope using a dish reflector is actually identical to the ordinary optical reflector, except that it concentrates radio waves instead of light. The waves coming from space are reflected by a parabolic dish to a receiver at the focus. In this case, the amount of energy carried by the radio wave under study is read out on an electronic recorder. You have undoubtedly seen these sorts of dish receivers, for they are used to receive all sorts of radio transmissions, including those from TV satellites.

Since the radio telescope (like its optical counterpart) needs to point at its target, the dish is mounted so that it can be aimed. In practice, this sets a limit on the size of a single dish. The large steerable telescopes operating today all have reflectors about 300 feet across—any larger and the dish would sag of its own weight. With the loss of its parabolic surface, the telescope dish loses its focusing power.

This is a very important limitation on radio astronomy because the larger the dish the more clearly the source can be seen. The unit that astronomers usually use to discuss the resolving power of a telescope is called the arc second. It corresponds to one thirty-six hundredth of a degree of arc in the sky. A good optical telescope with a one arc second resolution can distinguish the opposite edges of a dime a mile away, or distinguish between two objects located a mile and a half apart on the surface of the moon. The

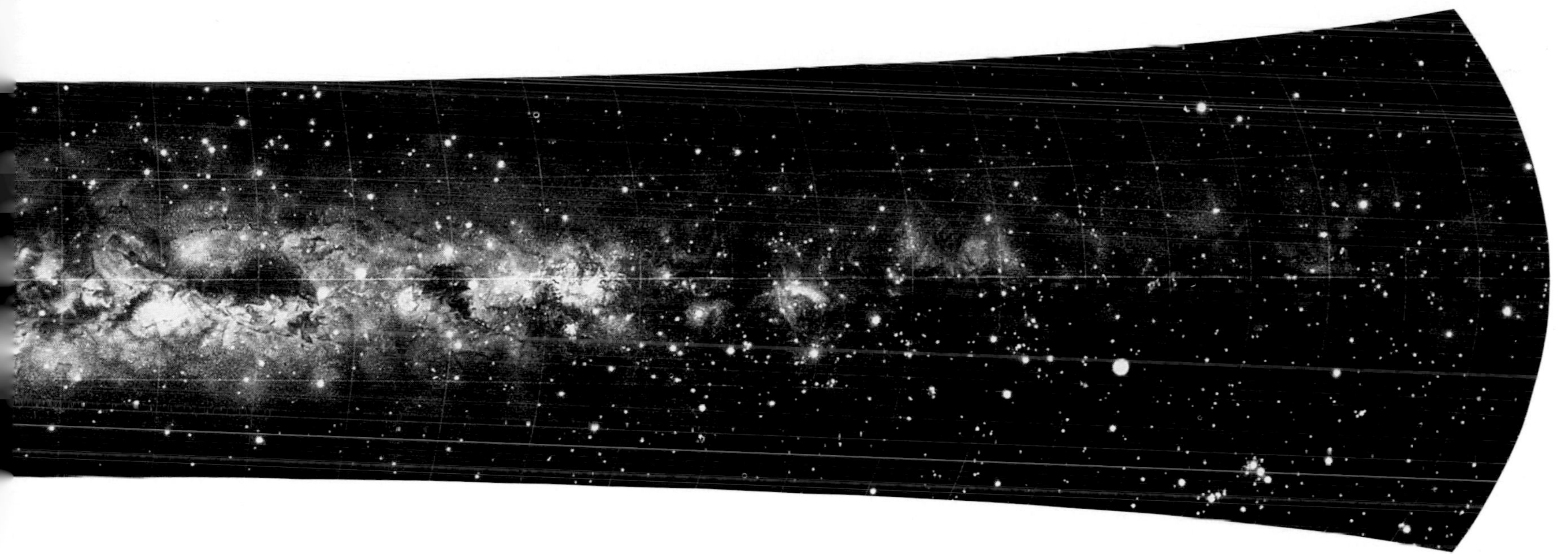

resolving power of a telescope depends on its size (the bigger the better), but it also depends on the wavelength of the part of the electromagnetic spectrum received. The longer the wave, the bigger the telescope needed by the astronomer. Since radio waves are so much longer than light waves, radio telescopes would have to be correspondingly bigger to achieve the same resolution. For example, if we wanted to build a single dish to match the resolution of the Palomar instrument, we would require a dish almost 400 miles across.

We have already begun to circumvent the size and resolution limits on radio telescopes. The National Astronomy and Ionosphere Center (operated by Cornell University) built the world's largest radio dish at Arecibo, Puerto Rico. It was laid out in a valley and does not move. It relies on the movement of the earth to bring different regions of the sky into its sight. What it lacks in mobility it makes up for in sheer size—the dish is 1,000 feet across.

The second (and more common) way to get around the size limits on radio telescopes is to use two or more telescopes and some fancy electronics to obtain a radio picture. The idea is that the crests of a radio wave will arrive at the two telescopes at slightly different times since, in general, the wave will be approaching the earth at an angle. As the observation continues, the rotation of the Earth changes the relative positions of the telescopes with respect to the beam. By timing the arrival of crests at the two telescopes, an extremely detailed radio "photograph" of the object emitting the waves can be obtained. The technique is known as radio interferometry. While the origin of the name is a bit obscure, it is well to realize that the process was perfected as a method to track rockets in flight.

The VLA (Very Large Array) located near Socorro, New Mexico, is an example of an installation built to utilize interferometric techniques. Completed in 1980, it consists of nearly 30 telescopes that can be moved

Below, edge of the famed Sombrero galaxy stands out in sharp relief—at the expense of the nucleus, however. Light has fogged the photographic plate and thus obscured the core, which appears unnaturally swollen. Light photos taken at different exposures can each reveal different aspects of a sky subject. The CCD, an electronic "film," gathers light quicker and provides a more detailed glimpse through the visual window.

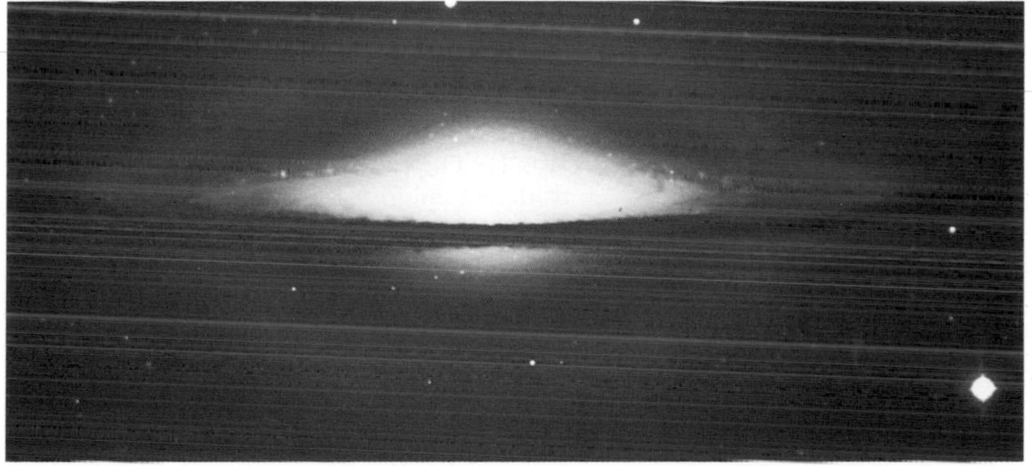

Below and opposite, images through gamma-ray and X-ray windows uncover regions of intense magnetic flux within our Milky Way, as seen looking toward the center from Earth. We lie two-thirds of the way out from the galactic center. On Earth, gamma rays and X rays have been produced in the detonations of nuclear and fusion devices.

over a Y-shaped track on the desert floor. Airline pilots flying over the VLA have dubbed it the mushroom patch. In effect, this technique of interferometry turns something like the VLA into a single radio dish several miles across; the individual telescopes sample the incoming wavefront and the computer reconstructs the wave from the data. Resolutions of a few arc seconds—close to those of the 200-inch telescope at Palomar—can be achieved by the VLA.

More recently, astronomers have started using radio interferometry to link telescopes separated by thousands of miles. Known as VLBI (Very Long Baseline Interferometry), this scheme takes the output from several telescopes in different locations and analyzes the data in the way we've just outlined. For example, one telescope might be in California, the other in Massachusetts, or Holland. The readings first are synchronized with extremely accurate atomic clocks, then recorded on magnetic tapes, and finally mailed to a central computer where the photograph is put together. Resolutions of 0.01 arc second have been obtained by this technique, a resolution better than that achieved by the Palomar telescope. In effect, VLBI can be used to produce a "dish" several thousand miles across. What brute-force construction cannot give us, brainpower can!

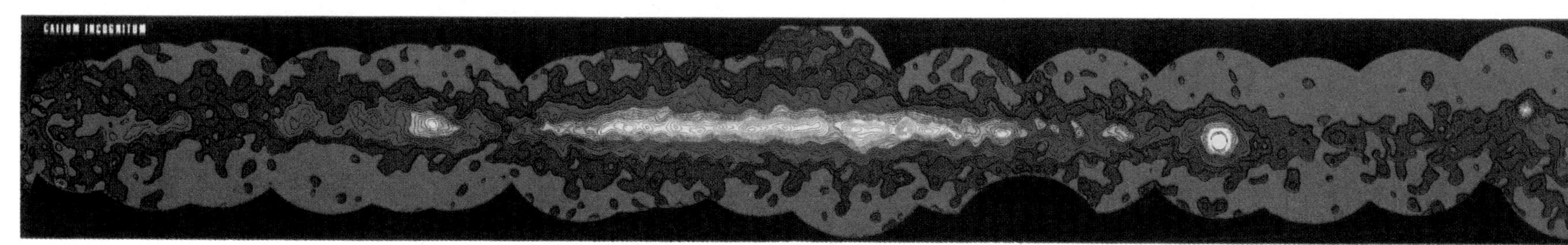

We already know that the sky seen through the radio window is much different from the sky seen through the optical. The brightest objects in the visible sky—the sun and nearby stars—shine feebly at radio wavelengths. Instead, we see radio sources like the center of our own Galaxy, quasars, pulsars, and active galaxies. While the optical window shows us a quiet, ordered, hearthlike universe, the radio reflects a world of cataclysmic violence.

There is one important source of radio emission that isn't nearly as dramatic as the ones we've discussed so far, but which plays an important role in many questions of fundamental interest. A good deal of the matter in the Galaxy consists of clouds of hydrogen atoms. Dark for the most part, they do not have enough energy to produce much visible light. They do emit energy in radio frequencies and thus reveal their whereabouts and extent.

By mapping radio emissions, the existence of unseen matter in galaxies has been established. Waves emitted by hydrogen have allowed astronomers to chart the spiral arms of our own Galaxy. They cannot be seen optically because of intervening dust but hydrogen radiation cuts right through.

All this happens in a very interesting way. A hydrogen atom is simply an electron circling in orbit around a proton. In addition to this orbital motion, both the electron and proton spin around their own axes. The atom can have electron and proton spinning together or in opposite directions.

These alternate states represent slightly different levels of energy, with the opposing directions of spin indicating a lower level. If the atom should gain sufficient energy through a collision or other event, it will spontaneously drop to the lower energy state, reversing the spin and emitting electromagnetic radiation. The radiation emitted by this particular transition has a wavelength of 21 centimeters (about eight inches). Since hydrogen is found everywhere, radiation at its wavelength is very common from all parts of the universe.

If we want to look at the universe through windows other than the radio or optical, we need to avoid atmospheric absorption. The only way to do this is to move our telescopes into space. Above the atmosphere, we can see the entire electromagnetic spectrum without distortion. The past 25 years have been a golden age for astronomy. This period of unprecedented discovery is due to the fact that now we can see the universe through all the windows in the sky. Many images of the same object, each revealing a single aspect or two superbly, can be combined in the scientist's (or the reader's) mind to create a powerful picture of reality. In other words, evidence from many sources can converge.

In this pursuit we have become used to the idea of putting large payloads into orbit. To us, the phrases "in space" and "in orbit" are almost synonymous. Yet a moment's reflection will convince you that one does not have to go into orbit to be above the atmosphere. Balloons were the first space vehicles and are still very cost effective. They stay up for hours at a time. If you're willing to collect data during brief periods aloft, a cheap and primitive rocket can hoist a payload into "space" for several minutes at a time. With captured V-2 rockets at first, groups of scientists began peeking at the sky in the late forties. Their rocket vehicles were much like dolphins leaping out of the water. A camera took a glimpse or two, then the rocket plunged back into our planet's ocean of air.

X-Ray Astronomy

Even peeks through the X-ray window showed exciting results. Early on we discovered that the sun was a modest source of X rays, a fact which caused little surprise. The first X-ray source in deep space was found more or less by accident in 1962. During its flight above the atmosphere of only five minutes, an X-ray scanner designed to view the moon had to track across some open sky to find its target. In doing so, it recorded the presence of an X ray background and one strong X-ray source in the constellation Scorpius—a source now called Sco X-1 (the name arises because it is the first X-ray source that we discovered in the constellation).

The first long-term X-ray observatory was placed into orbit from a launch site in Kenya on December 12, 1970—an anniversary of that country's Independence Day. The project name was Uhuru, "Freedom" in Swahili, to honor that event. The satellite performed our first rough survey of the X-ray sky, turning up more than anyone had dreamed. The Einstein Observatory, a satellite equipped to do much more sensitive and detailed studies of X-ray sources, followed in 1978. The orbiting observatory accumulated data which it broadcast to earth to be stored on tape. It collected so much information during three years that as of 1985 many miles of tape still remained for astronomers to analyze.

The X-ray sky proved to be unexpectedly bright—in fact, 10 percent of the radiation output of the Milky Way is thought to occur in this region of the spectrum. X-ray stars may blink, or pulse, giving rise to their name of pulsar. In a binary star system, the pulsar might hide behind its partner some of the time, introducing a series of eclipses on top of the normal pulsing—a rather common occurrence.

Matter falling into a black hole may generate X rays. We suspect that black holes consume matter a little at a time, and circular traffic jams may occur as stars wait their turn to be swallowed. Such disks contain material that spins very fast. During acceleration, this matter radiates at ever higher frequencies—to X rays and beyond.

One source, Cygnus X-1, shows a flickering in X-ray wavelengths that many astronomers associate with double-star systems

Sky spies returned valuable astronomical data in the form of an X-ray map of our galactic neighborhood from 1969 through 1979. The same sensors, designed to pick up nuclear detonations, documented natural radiation near the center of our Galaxy. Nuclear and thermonuclear reactions seem to characterize regions of black-hole and neutron-star activity in the heavens. Some X-ray sources, called bursters, emit radiation only during infrequent but intense outbreaks.

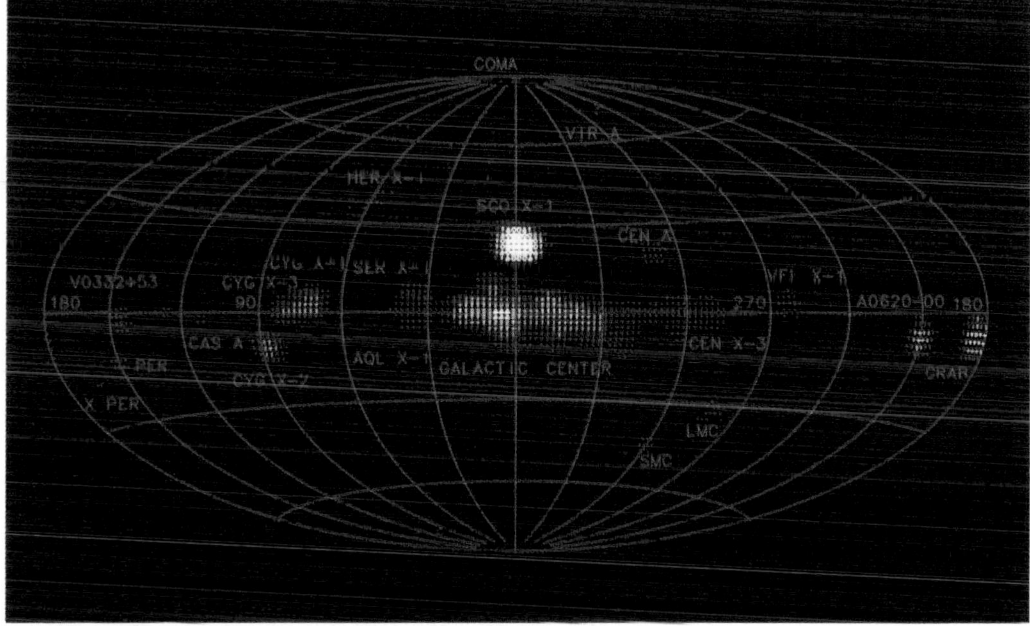

"Mushroom patch," as nicknamed by airline pilots flying over New Mexico, contains nearly 30 radio telescopes. They can line up in several patterns by moving along connecting rails. Called the VLA for Very Large Array, the dishes function as a single gigantic radio-telescope. For a close-up, see pages 58 and 59.

organized around black holes instead of neutron stars. The companion star may feed mass into the black hole. If so, the flickering could reflect irregularities in the transport of matter into the maw. If this explanation holds up, X-ray astronomy may have begun to uncover the first hard evidence for black holes. Their confirmed discovery would clear a lot of air. Heretofore, the existence of black holes has been based on circumstantial evidence, conjecture, and perhaps even some wishful thinking.

Whatever the source of their energy, active galaxies are powerful X-ray sources. Their brightness in the X-ray part of the spectrum seems to increase as we move from Seyfert galaxies to nearby quasars to more distant quasars. We have a ready explanation for this effect if a black hole lies at the center of each galaxy, as suggested by proponents of one current scheme of galactic evolution. In young galaxies (which we see as distant quasars) much luminous mass is available to fall into the central black hole. This supply dwindles as the galaxy evolves and matures. By the time it becomes a staid old spiral like the Milky Way it is a shadow of its former self. Facing an empty table, the X-ray source at the center dims as it starves.

Finally, the X-ray sky contains one true mystery that no one can explain. There are about 30 sources which appear to emit sporadic bursts of X rays. The source will brighten, sometimes by as much as a hundredfold, in about a second and then die out, often within 10 seconds. These "bursters" are every bit as mysterious as black holes. Some scientists associate this phenomenon with thermonuclear explosions on densely packed neutron stars. It has also been suggested that some neutron stars draw gas from a much larger but lighter satellite star and feed their X-ray bursts by transforming the stellar matter into energy.

Ultraviolet

We were reminded that as objects heat up their color changes from red to white to blue. If they are heated beyond this point, they begin to emit the bulk of their radiation as ultraviolet waves—in the ultraviolet, as we say. Therefore, we expect the ultraviolet sky to be bright where there are very hot objects. Paradoxically, we also expect it to be bright where there are very cool objects. In interstellar space, stable atoms such as those of oxygen, nitrogen, and silicon, and some very common molecules—hydrogen, for example—can emit radiation in the ultraviolet range.

Because of similar techniques for handling ultraviolet radiation and ordinary visible light, we find a long history of exploration in this field. Astronauts on the Apollo 16 mission, for example, carried an ultraviolet telescope to the moon. The two most recent ultraviolet satellites, Copernicus (launched in 1972, operated until 1981) and the International Ultraviolet Explorer, a joint European and American project launched in 1978, have given us a pretty good picture of the UV sky.

UV surveys have made interesting but not spectacular discoveries. It appears that many of the interstellar hydrogen clouds are made of molecular (as opposed to atomic) hydrogen. Also, the gas between the clouds has a higher temperature than anyone had suspected, upwards of a million degrees. Furthermore, some objects in the sky have very different signatures through the X-ray and UV windows, a fact we can't account for.

Infrared Astronomy

The infrared spectrum, located between visible light and microwaves, presents its own problems to the astronomer. Unlike X rays, infrared radiation from space can penetrate deep into the atmosphere since the carbon dioxide and water molecules that absorb it lie close to the earth. Telescopes located on mountaintops can catch some of these fleeting beams before they are completely absorbed. At Mauna Kea on the island of Hawaii, for example, telescopes are located nearly 14,000 feet above sea level, well above most of the water vapor and obscuring molecules in the air. Such observations can also be made at more modest elevations below 10,000 feet, as in the dry southwestern United States.

The infrared spectrum is particularly important because it is the one way we have of detecting the presence of cold, non-luminous matter in the sky. However cold, even a few degrees above absolute zero, everything radiates energy by virtue of its temperature. Thus, the infrared sky should show us where the relatively quiet, cold matter in the

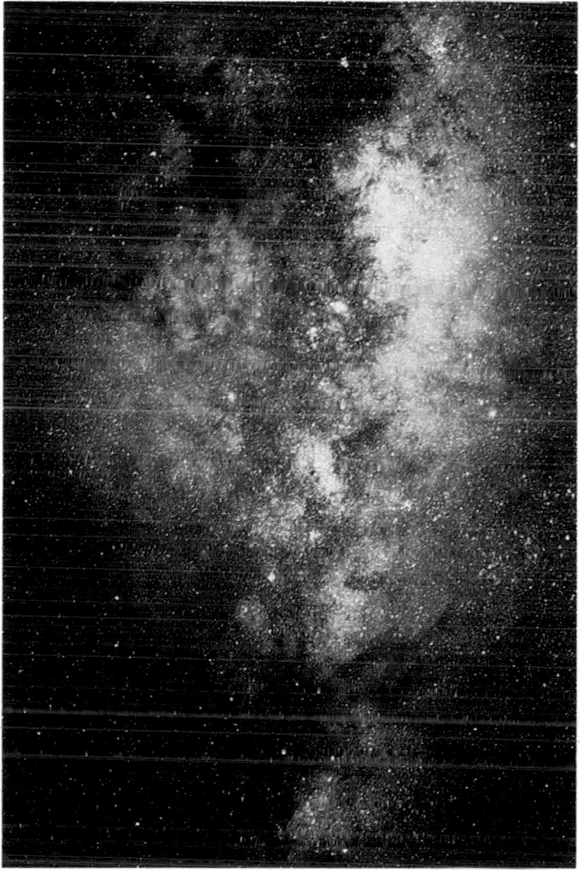

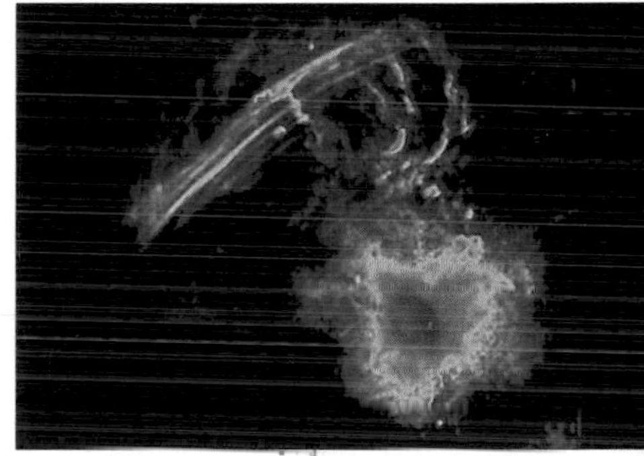

Radio signals, originating in a celestial object under observation, can cut through the normal light blockage. This is represented at left by a conventional photograph of the central region of our Milky Way. Strange magnetic arcs, as seen through the radio "window," above, appear related to the active core of our Galaxy. This enigmatic structure is thought to possess a black hole—often pictured as a vortex into which radiation and material are attracted, thus disappearing (or at least being sealed off) from what we think of as the universe.

universe lies. Since stars and planets emerge from dust clouds, we would expect the infrared sky to be particularly bright where star formation occurs.

In January 1983, the first major survey of the infrared sky began with the launching of IRAS (InfraRed Astronomy Satellite). The satellite itself was a small telescope encased in a large vacuum bottle of liquid helium. The function of the helium was to bring the telescope's temperature down to four degrees above absolute zero. Supercooling is necessary when dealing with the infrared because anything, including the telescope itself, gives off infrared radiation if it is warm enough. To keep the telescope's own radiation from blotting out faint sources in the sky, cooling must be maintained; hence the helium, which remains liquid below 452°F.

The sky was almost overwhelming in infrared, creating more new questions than it answered. Discovered early on was a ring of dust and rubble around the star Vega. The birth of planets? In any case, the resolution of IRAS was too poor to allow it to see individual planets. (But now we have hints that stars don't sit alone in space.) Also, a number of dust clouds were seen glowing with radiation from stars in birth—stars too young to be visible in the optical range of the electromagnetic spectrum.

At the other end of the stellar evolution cycle, the IRAS sensors detected clouds of cold matter, apparently from the surface of red giant stars—those approaching final collapse. IRAS also found streaks of dusty matter (rather like cirrus clouds) pervading the Milky Way.

Finally, surveys of galaxies reveal enormous differences in the rate of star formation. The Milky Way, for example, emits half of its radiation in the infrared spectrum, indicating many regions of star formation. Andromeda, on the other hand, emits only three percent of its radiation in this range, suggesting a rather meager number of new stars. Why should there be such differences in otherwise similar galaxies?

As with the X-ray satellites, data from IRAS will continue to be analyzed for years. The satellite itself ran out of helium at the end of November 1983, and thus data transmission ceased. It was an immensely successful venture. As one writer put it, IRAS was "good to the last drop."

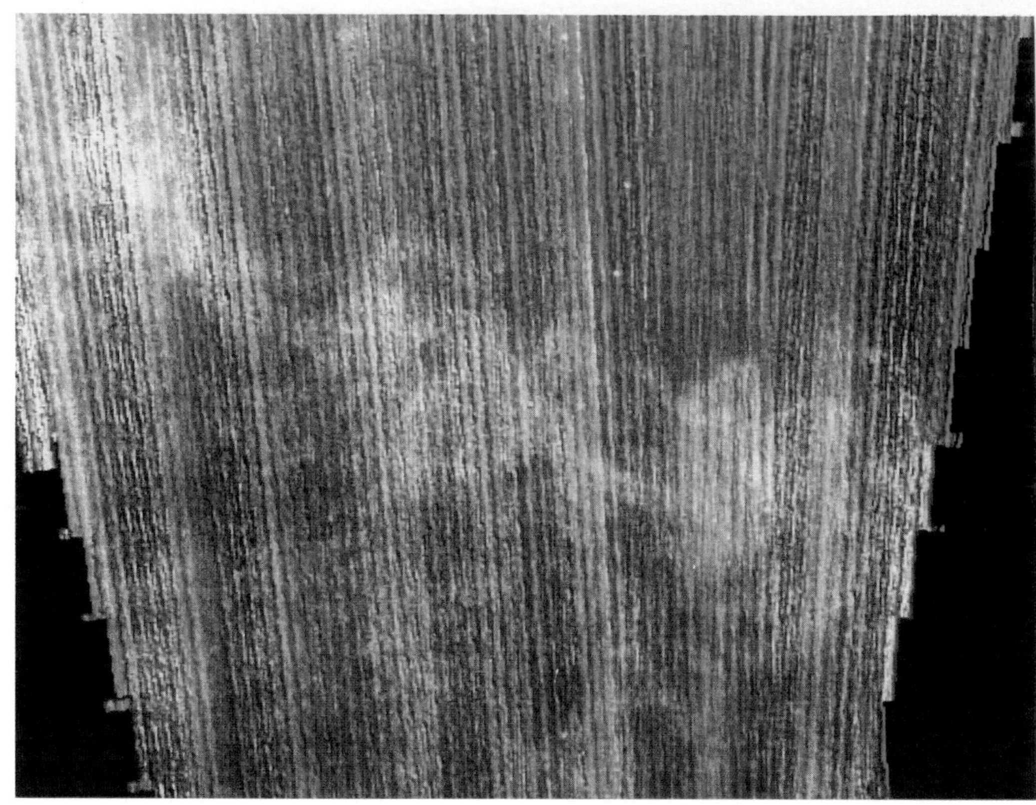

Derived from the Infrared Astronomical Satellite (IRAS), images resembling cirrus clouds appear in our Galaxy. The vertical strips represent scanning tracks of the electronic sensor. Similar stripes register on the surface of Capella, at right, a star imaged by the International Ultraviolet Explorer (IUE). Satellite imagery gives clues to its atomic components, which include silicon, carbon, and helium.

Other Visitors

By far the bulk of the data collected by astronomers concerns itself with the various forms of electromagnetic radiation that can be detected on the earth and its environs. There are, however, other ways of learning about what's out there. All sorts of visitors from other parts of the universe fall on the earth, such as meteorites (from our own solar system) and cosmic rays (some of which come from other galaxies). We can attempt to detect all sorts of unusual particles like neutrinos, gamma rays, and magnetic monopoles. Each of these has its tale to tell about its point of origin, and each, in a sense, is another window in the sky. Throughout this book astronomical objects are shown in several views—each taken through a different window. Thus the reader may gain several different slants as to the object's composition, energy production and flow, and influence on nearby space. We can all possess new eyes when we peer through our new windows on the universe.

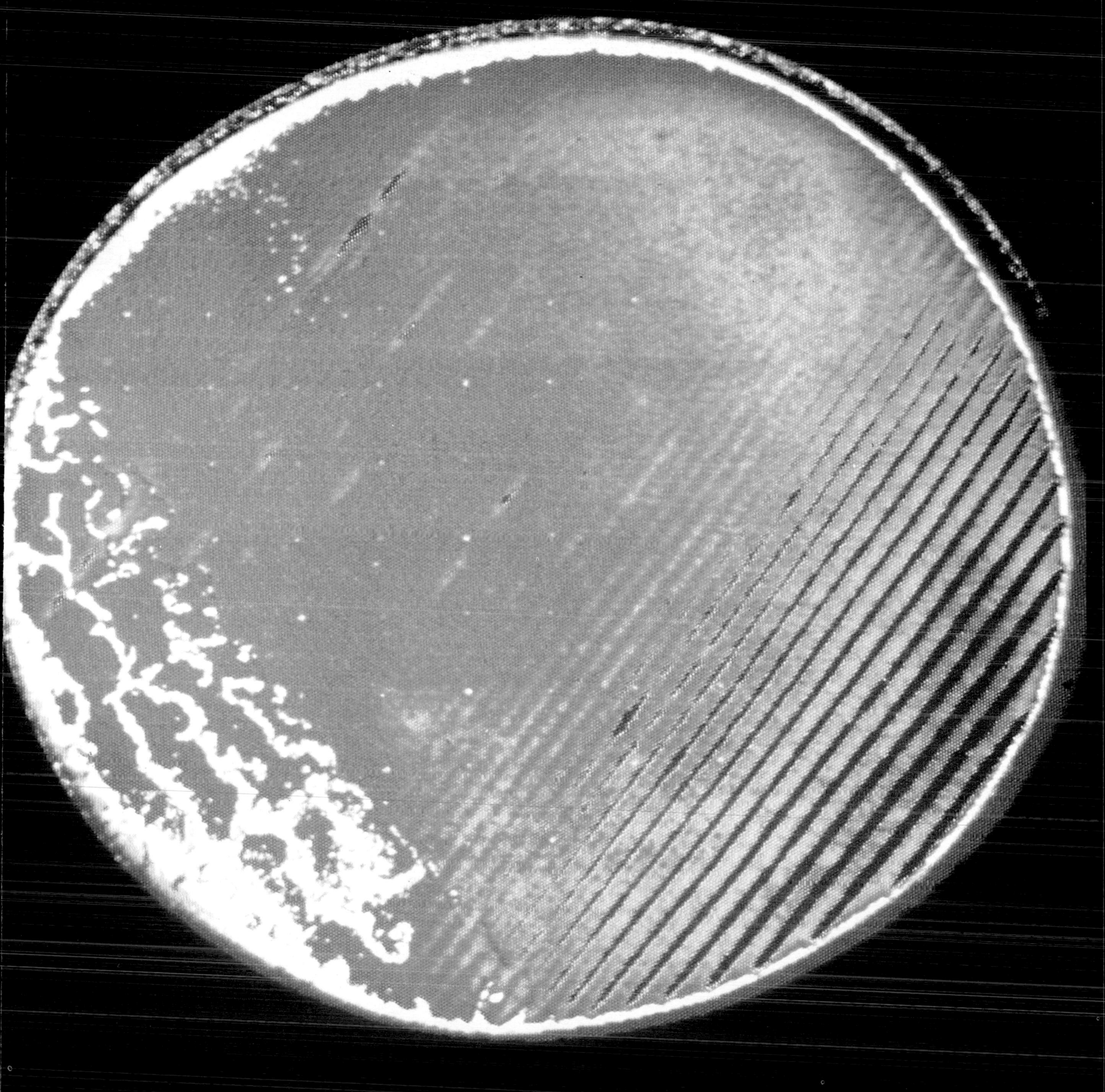

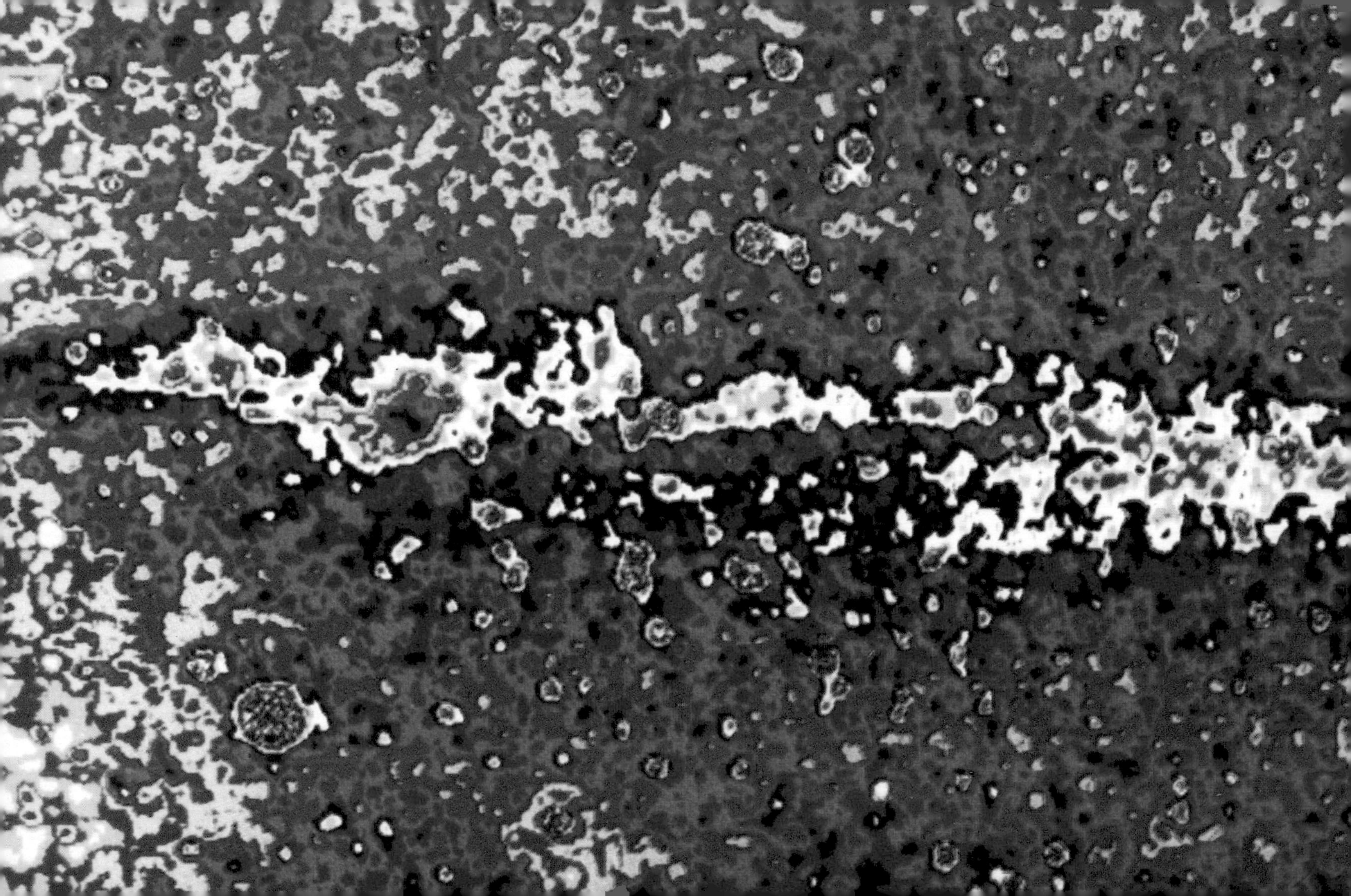

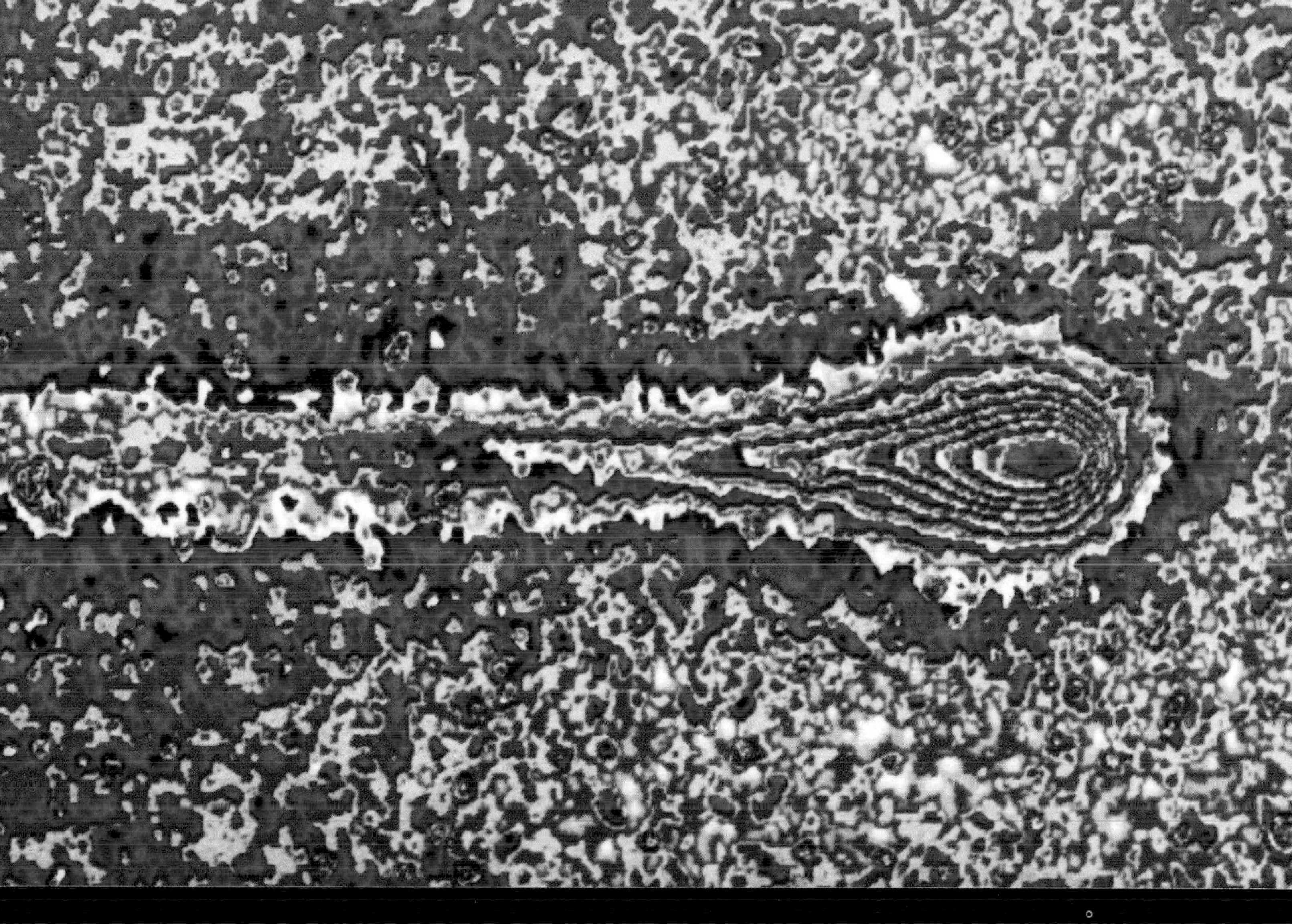

Part 3

The Solar System

Overleaf: Shimmering as if robed in antique Italian silk, a comet named Kohoutek traverses a computer-processed sky. The electronic transformation reveals details of the comet's head, swaddled in ice particles that catch sunlight. A comet, opposite, appears as the Star of Bethlehem in Giotto di Bondone's "Adoration of the Magi" of 1304. In fact, the fresco may reflect a spectacular return of Halley's comet visible in the Italian sky during 1301. For the 1985–86 appearance, scientists of the European Space Agency have launched a probe called Giotto in honor of the artist. Its rendezvous with Halley's comet is slated for March 13, 1986.

When Newton was barely in his twenties, London was ravaged by fire and plague. His mother insisted he return to the safety of the family place in Woolsthorpe. For a couple of years he enjoyed tranquillity and a time to think and to watch apples fall to the ground. Newton made most of his famous scientific discoveries in this period. He knew of Galileo's work and of the kinematic description of planetary motion deduced by Kepler, using the plan of Copernicus.

Drawing from Galileo, Newton drafted his famous three laws of motion: a force causes a change in the state of motion of an object; that this force is proportional to the product of the mass of the object and the change (acceleration) so produced; and that for every action, there is an equal and opposite reaction. (One must have three laws or fame will be elusive.) Following on Kepler's three laws, Newton deduced his law of universal gravitation.

Putting all this together, Newton determined the equations of motion of one heavenly body about another. We know this today as a differential equation requiring calculus for its solution. (Newton devised calculus to solve the problem.) As a result, he found that Kepler's laws expressed only a partial solution to what we call the problem of the attraction of two bodies. The orbit of one body about the other may be any cross-section of a cone: these include circles; ellipses; parabolas; and hyperbolas. He also explained how we might produce satellites, 300 years before our technology caught up.

It is understandable how Newton could declare that if he had seen further than others, it was because he stood "upon the shoulders of Giants." Soon other people began to share Newton's vision. Within a short time, humanity was shown as not occupying the hub of creation. We had finally discovered our actual place in a universe of undreamed of immensity.

Thus it took humanity nearly all of its existence—up to the time of Newton—to discover that there was such a thing as a solar system; and that Earth was a part of it, not vice versa. It remained for others, using the improved telescopes pioneered by Galileo and Newton, to begin to determine the nature of the planetary orbs themselves. Yet only in our day of space probes and satellites, have human eyes been privileged to see the sun and planets as we do here.

Just as important, science and scientists have begun to look beyond the cataloguing of planetary features and types. In one chapter, the author and two distinguished colleagues discuss the possibilities of finding intelligent beings among the stars. We also learn just how special our home planet is, and of conditions in the solar system which make life possible.

Since biblical times, people have been admonished to be humble in those endeavors which have to do with the heavens. Yet we now possess telescopes that soon may probe the edges of the universe. We hold secrets of the nuclear power of the sun; and with them we may blow ourselves to kingdom-come.

Thus, our understanding of the planets and the processes by which they came into existence also has application to the creation (and possibly even to the habitation) of other realms of the sky and to the ultimate fate of the human race. In the next five chapters of *Space, Time, Infinity*, readers will have the opportunity to appreciate both the fact and the implication of our planetary system. With knowledge to build upon, we may prepare ourselves to understand astronomical and cosmological discoveries in the future. We have finally gained a broad outline of the forces and processes which operate in the solar system, but mysteries remain. K.L.F.

Planetary Science

If you were to approach our solar system from deep space, the first thing to catch your eye would be the sun, swimming in lonely majesty while its internal fusion furnace pours energy into the void. As you moved closer, you would notice a few of the sun's companions—giants much like the sun in composition but shining only by reflected light. Closer yet, you'd discover other bodies circling close in to the star—small, rocky worlds totally unlike their great neighbors. As you reached the edge of the solar system, you would be able to see finer details—moons circling most of the planets, and rings around the large outer members of the system. Bits of debris—asteroids (small chunks of solid material in orbit around the sun) and comets would come into view. Finally, you might notice some special things about the third planet: an atmosphere; water on its surface; and, most amazing of all, life. We and the other living creatures have found a home in the void of space. If only for such a reason, this welcoming star system of ours—a complex collection of materials—deserves our special attention.

The Sun

The sun, our sun, is a star. It supplies virtually all the energy that maintains the planets. Giant magnetic storms rage on its surface. We see these as sunspots, small, apparently dark blemishes. They aren't really

Editor's Note: *Important! Never attempt to look at the sun directly, as naked-eye viewing may cause permanent eye damage. Indeed, instant and permanent blindness can result from viewing the sun through any lens system, including that of a camera.*

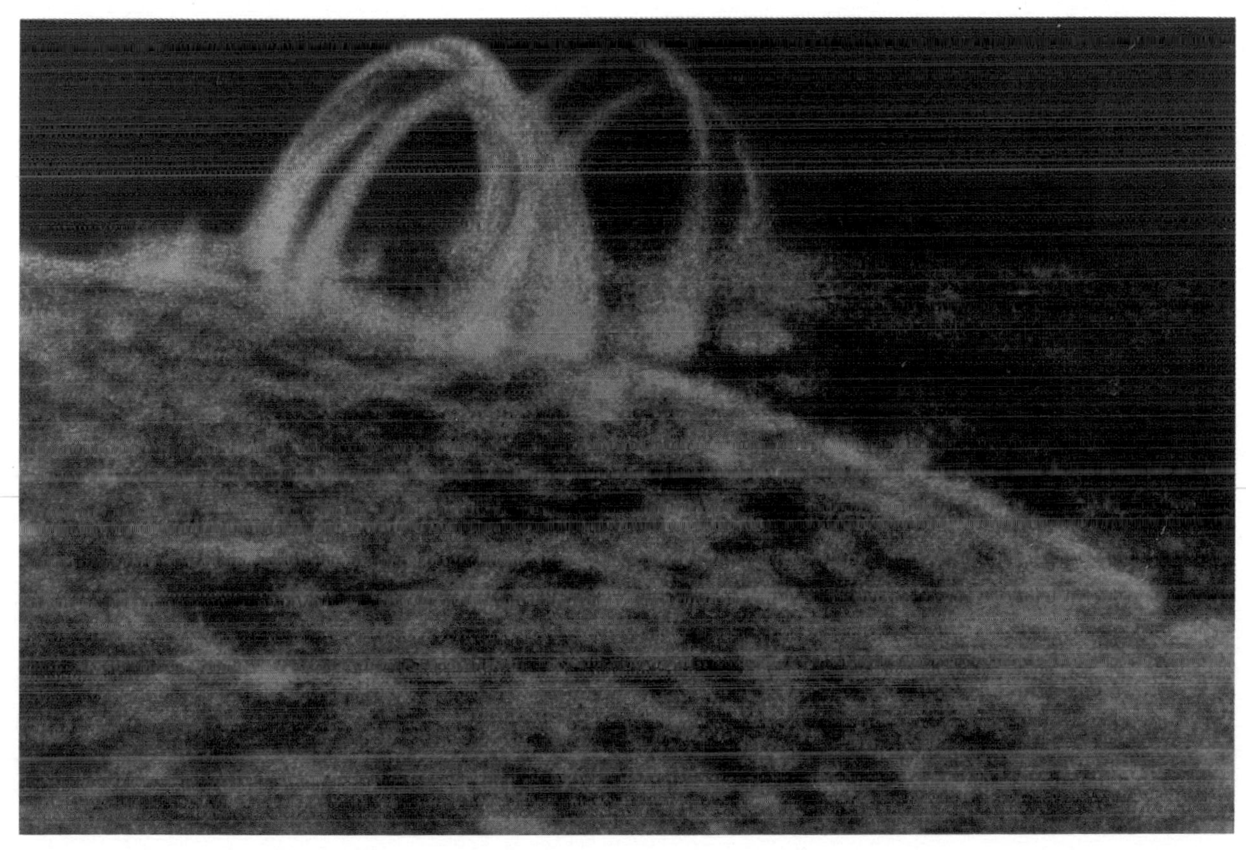

The battered rock-and-ice face of Callisto, far left, one of Jupiter's "Galilean" moons, bears eloquent witness to innumerable collisions with debris left over from the formation of the solar system. Left, the Earth could pass easily through this nearly 50,000-mile-high arch of hot gas looping along the lines of intense magnetic fields on the sun.

Artist Don Davis has pictured the sun as it might appear from the nine planets. Left to right: airless, scorched, cratered, Mercury circles the sun in only 88 days. Venus's dense carbon-dioxide atmosphere and clouds of sulfuric acid trap heat, raising the surface temperature to about 800°F. Earth nurtures the system's only life. The bleak, frozen surface of Mars lies beneath a rarified atmosphere of carbon dioxide. Great clouds of methane and ammonia crystals boil up in Jupiter's hydrogen-helium atmosphere. Saturn's rings cast a thin shadow over billowing cloud tops. Also gas giants, Uranus and Neptune receive little heat from the sun. From lonely Pluto and its moon, Charon, the sun appears scarcely brighter than other stars.

dark, of course, only cooler and thus less incandescent than the surrounding gases. These are a visible sign of the other important influence the sun has on the planetary system. The sun ejects a part of itself to form what is called the solar wind, a medium through which the planets move.

The outer regions of the sun are composed of plasma. Physicists define it as material in which some or all of the electrons are stripped from each atom, leaving matter in a state that has no overall electrical charge, but in which negative charges (the electrons) and positive charges (the stripped atoms) are free to move independently of each other. In such a system, magnetic fields tend to become "frozen in" to the plasma. The actual physical process is a bit complicated, but you can picture it by thinking about what happens at the edge of a pond when the water freezes. Long stalks of swamp grass are locked into the ice. If the ice moves (e.g., if a piece breaks off and is pushed away), the grass moves with it. If, on the other hand, you pull on the grass, the ice will cling and come along. If the grass in this analogy were replaced by the magnetic field lines, and the ice by the plasma, you would have a good picture of the way things happen at the surface of the sun. When the magnetic field twists into loops, fiery arches of hot plasma are dragged along with it, producing solar prominences, some of the solar system's most spectacular displays.

The sun's plasma doesn't end at its surface, however. A steady stream of particles flows from the solar surface, pulling the magnetic field with it, and forms that complex structure we call the solar wind. Instruments aboard the Soviet Luna 3 vehicle made the first direct measurements of the solar wind in 1959. Results from the U.S. Mariner 2 flight in 1962 indicated that the solar wind is a flow of particles (mainly protons and electrons) that stream outward from the sun into the solar system. The solar wind blows at several hundred miles per second by the time it reaches Earth's orbit. It isn't very dense, with only about 10 of its particles in a thimbleful of space. Yet the solar wind is felt as far out as our space probes have traveled.

It is tempting to think of the solar wind

Bombarded for billions of years by meteoroids and other space debris and exposed to intense solar radiation, Mercury's airless, pockmarked surface has probably known no tectonic activity since early in the planet's history.

as a series of particles ejected by the sun. It is more exact, however, to think of the entire solar wind as being a part of the outermost layer of the sun, the part we call the corona. This wispy, bubble-like structure has no sharp edge and expands as it moves away from the sun. Thus the solar wind is part of the continuously expanding corona where our planet's magnetic field warps and shapes the flow of particles that come close. Thus the old view of things, in which the sun sat at the center and the planets circled it in discrete and independent orbits, should be modified. In a very real sense, Earth and the other planets are all inside the sun, or at least inside the outer bit of the solar corona. Our system is not just a set of discrete and independent planets, but a curiously tangled system of solid matter held within a tenuous web of particles and magnetic fields.

There are many consequences of this point of view. For one, the magnetic field of a planet like the Earth does not simply die off as it moves into space. Eventually it merges with the solar magnetic field and the solar wind in a region known as the magnetopause. The magnetic field of the Earth, in fact, bunches up slightly in the direction of the sun, and then casts a long shadow "downwind." Furthermore, since the sun itself rotates, the movement of the outward-streaming solar wind resembles that of water coming from a lawn sprinkler. Each drop of water (and each particle in the solar wind) moves outward in a straight line, but the

stream appears curved because each particle is slightly offset from its neighbors due to the rotation of the source.

Finally, as if to prove that even a well-studied body like the sun has something new to teach us, X-ray studies in the early seventies have shown pretty conclusively that the particles of the solar wind do not originate over the entire surface of the sun. Instead, they come from certain well-defined regions that are less dense and cooler than their neighbors. Known as "coronal holes," these are where the solar magnetic field leaves the sun and swirls into space like some sort of impossible cowlick. Plasma particles stream from these holes and come together into the general solar wind that en-

Visionaries and experimenters of many nations contributed to the realization of space exploration. American physicist Robert H. Goddard, above, invented the liquid propellant rocket and proposed as early as 1919 that such vehicles be used to probe space. Parts of his first successful rocket, launched in 1926, were incorporated into a later rocket, right, now on exhibit at the National Air and Space Museum. German scientists and engineers who had developed the first large rocket missiles during World War II were used by both the United States and the Soviet Union in their rocket and spaceflight programs. These programs came together briefly in 1975 with the launch of a Soviet Soyuz spacecraft, far right, to rendezvous in orbit with a U.S. Apollo spacecraft.

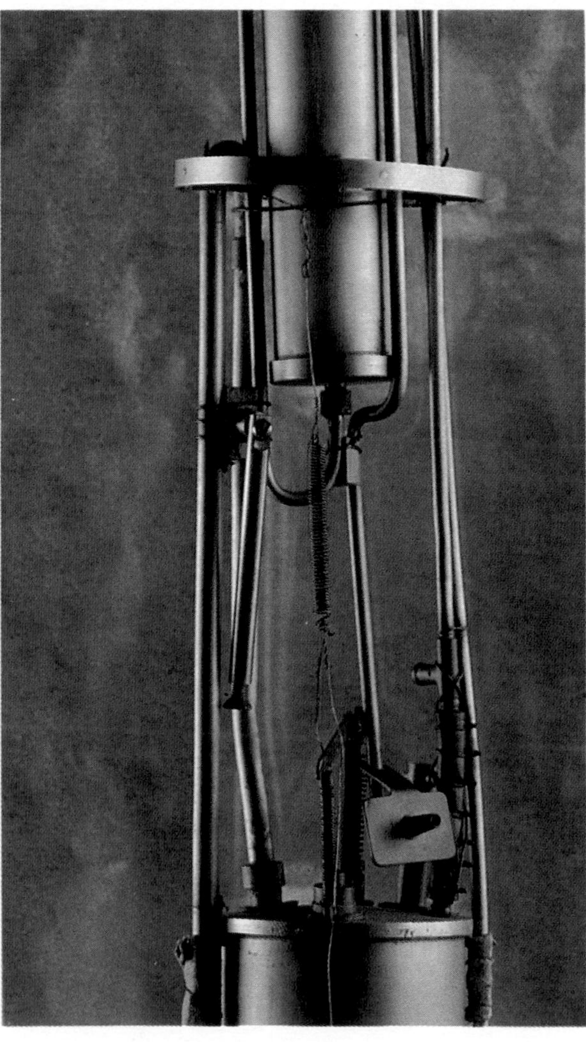

velops the planets and their satellites. Expanding spherically, coronal material even fills space beyond the planets.

The Moon and the Inner Planets

We note that the planets can be divided quite easily into two categories—the inner planets, which are small and rocky, and the gas giants that circle through the outer reaches of the solar system. Within each class, the planets bear a striking resemblance to each other, but the two classes themselves are very different. The inner planets—Mercury, Venus, Earth, and Mars—are sometimes called the terrestrial planets. As we shall see, the Earth's moon can also be included in this category (although, strictly speaking, it is not a planet in its own right). Earth is sufficiently different, and of sufficiently high interest to those of us who inhabit it, that we shall devote a chapter to understanding its astronomical aspects.

The terrestrial bodies, forming as they did near the newborn sun, eventually incorporated grains containing atoms such as silicon and iron—atoms that are relatively rare in the universe as a whole. These are the only materials that would have existed in solid form so near to the sun, and hence it is from these atoms that the terrestrial planets are built. Under the influence of gravity, these solid grains came together to form rocks a few miles across. Called planetesimals, these rocks become the raw material for larger bodies—perhaps the size of the moon—called protoplanets. How this aggregation from grain to planetesimal to protoplanet to planet took place is a subject of intense research in astronomy today. The Department of Mineral Sciences at the Smithsonian's National Museum of Natural History conducts significant work in the field.

I think it is fair to say that no one has yet produced a theory that explains all of the details of planet formation in a completely satisfactory way. Nevertheless, even in our present state of knowledge, we can discern the main stages in the evolution of each of these bodies.

According to theory, each planet was relatively cool as it started to accumulate loose material from space. As each body grew, its gravitational attraction was enhanced. This, in turn, allowed each growing body to capture more and more of the large pieces of space debris, including planetesimals. Repeated impacts helped to heat the protoplanets. At the same time, radioactive elements began to decay, providing another source of heat for the young worlds. The way in which each planet handled all this energy during the early stages of development determined, to a large extent, the future course of its history.

You know that on cold nights animals huddle together to keep warm. One way of thinking about why such an arrangement works is to consider what physicists call the surface-to-volume ratio. It works for planetesimals as well as for cows.

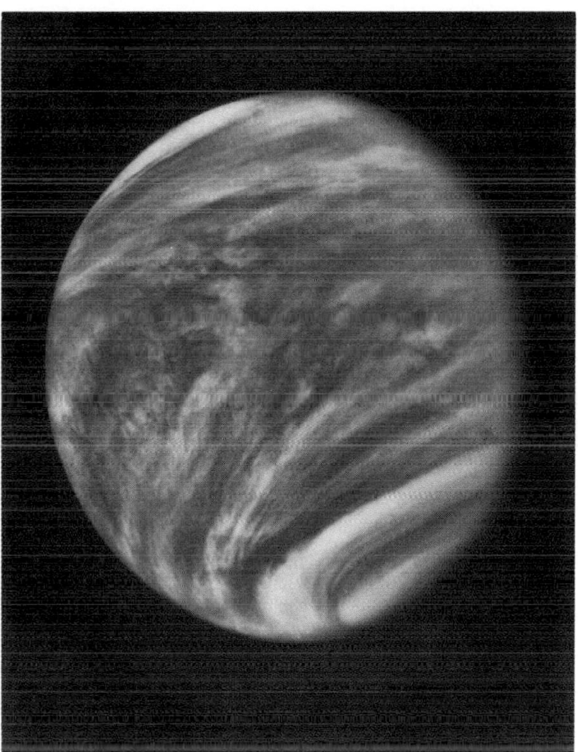

Perennially shrouded in dense cloud, Venus presented a mystery to earthbound observers until the sixties, when the first of a series of unmanned U.S. and Soviet spacecraft visited the planet. Since then, such probes have measured its atmospheric temperature and pressure, made radar maps of its topography, and even photographed its hellish surface. Left, the U.S. spacecraft Mariner 10 obtained this view of Venus on February 6, 1974, during a flyby that brought the spacecraft to within 3,600 miles of the planet. Above, Soviet artist Andrei Sokolov has depicted Venera 9 as it might have appeared after its soft landing on Venus in 1975. The reversed curvature of the horizon is caused by the refraction of light in Venus's dense atmosphere.

Unlike cloud-shrouded Venus, Mars and Mercury can be mapped by cameras using visible light. Above, the U.S. unmanned Viking spacecraft sent back images used to make up this striking mosaic of the surface of Mars and also the dawn view of the planet, opposite, with the great rift canyon, Marineris Vallis, at center. Below, Mariner 10 provided the images for this geologic map of Mercury's Shakespeare Quadrant.

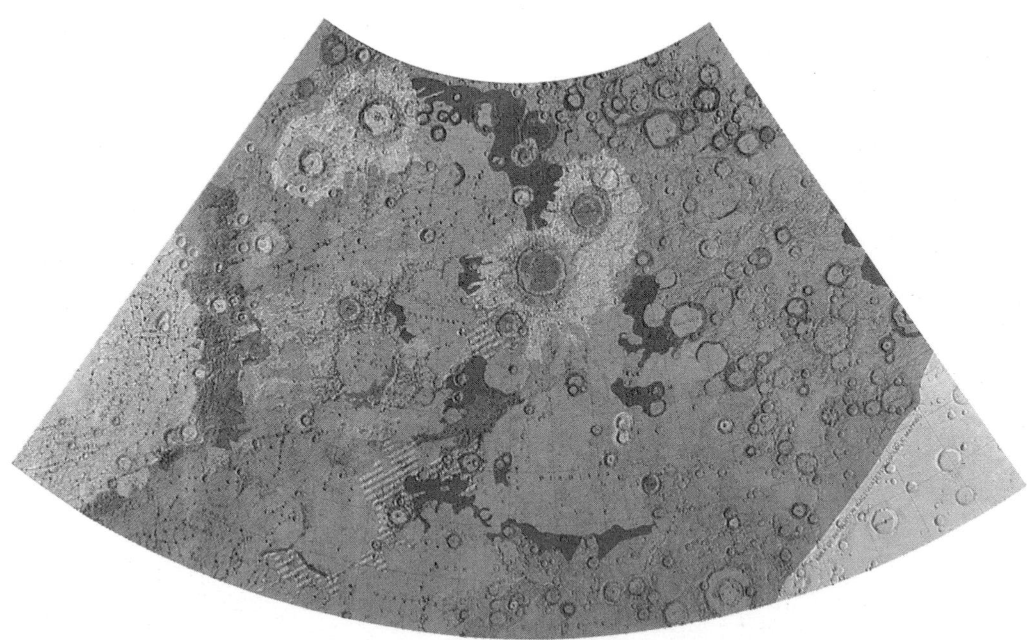

A single animal, for instance, radiates heat from every square inch of its body surface. This energy, of course, must be generated by the animal's metabolism. If animals group together, however, heat is lost to the environment only from the top and the outer perimeter. As physicists say, the animals have lowered their heat loss by lowering the surface-to-volume ratio.

The chunks of material in a new planet are like the animals in the huddle. They have a source of heat, and they have a surface through which that heat can be dissipated. What actually happens depends both on the intensity of the heat source and the surface-to-volume ratio of the body. If the surface is large enough in comparison to the volume to get rid of the heat being added, the planet will cool. If the surface isn't large enough to do the job, the planet will heat up. It's as simple as that.

As relatively small worlds, the moon and Mercury have a high surface-to-volume ratio. This means that when the planetesimals started falling and the interior began heating up with radioactive decay, these bodies didn't melt completely. The moon became plastic to a depth of only 100 miles. (Seismic instruments left behind on the lunar surface by Apollo astronauts have taught us a good deal about the interior of the moon.) We can conjecture that much the same thing happened to Mercury, although we have no direct data. Thus we can sketch that planet's early days only on the basis of what we know about the moon. The outer crusts of both probably melted about 200 million years after they formed, but remained plastic for only a short time.

Since the moon and Mercury are not very massive, whatever atmosphere they might have had in the beginning quickly wandered off into space. With almost no atmosphere, they had no weather to erode the evidence of impact. Craters have remained on their surfaces for the last four billion years, bearing mute testimony to the processes that worked to form our solar system soon after its birth. According to the standard model, the heaviest period of meteor bombardment occurred close to the time when the sun's nuclear fires began. With the emergence of light, anything not incorporated into solid bodies was blown away from the center. From this era, frozen gases and other icy leftovers of the solar nebula may have migrated outward to establish the Oort cloud, the distant realm from whence comets come. Light materials including ammonia and water vapor did not solidify, did not become part of the terrestrial planets, and were ultimately blown out of the inner solar system. These facts help to explain why Mercury, Venus, Earth, and Mars are so different from the gas giants.

The terrestrial bodies gained heat from impact and from their radioactivity. For Earth, Venus, and Mars, however, the surface-to-volume ratio was different than for the moon and Mercury. For example, the Earth has about 18 times the volume of Mercury but only about seven times as much surface area. Consequently, Earth was unable to get rid of its heat by radiation so the entire planet melted. Heavier ingredients such as iron sank toward the center, while the lighter silicate minerals floated toward the surface. As geologists say, Earth experienced *differentiation* about 100 million years after its birth. It did so because its surface area was too small to allow all of the heat being generated to be lost into space. Venus and Mars, we believe, went through the same process at about the same time.

The outer crusts of Earth, Venus, and Mars resolidified quickly and, in the process, gases were freed from the interior, primarily from volcanoes driven by the trapped

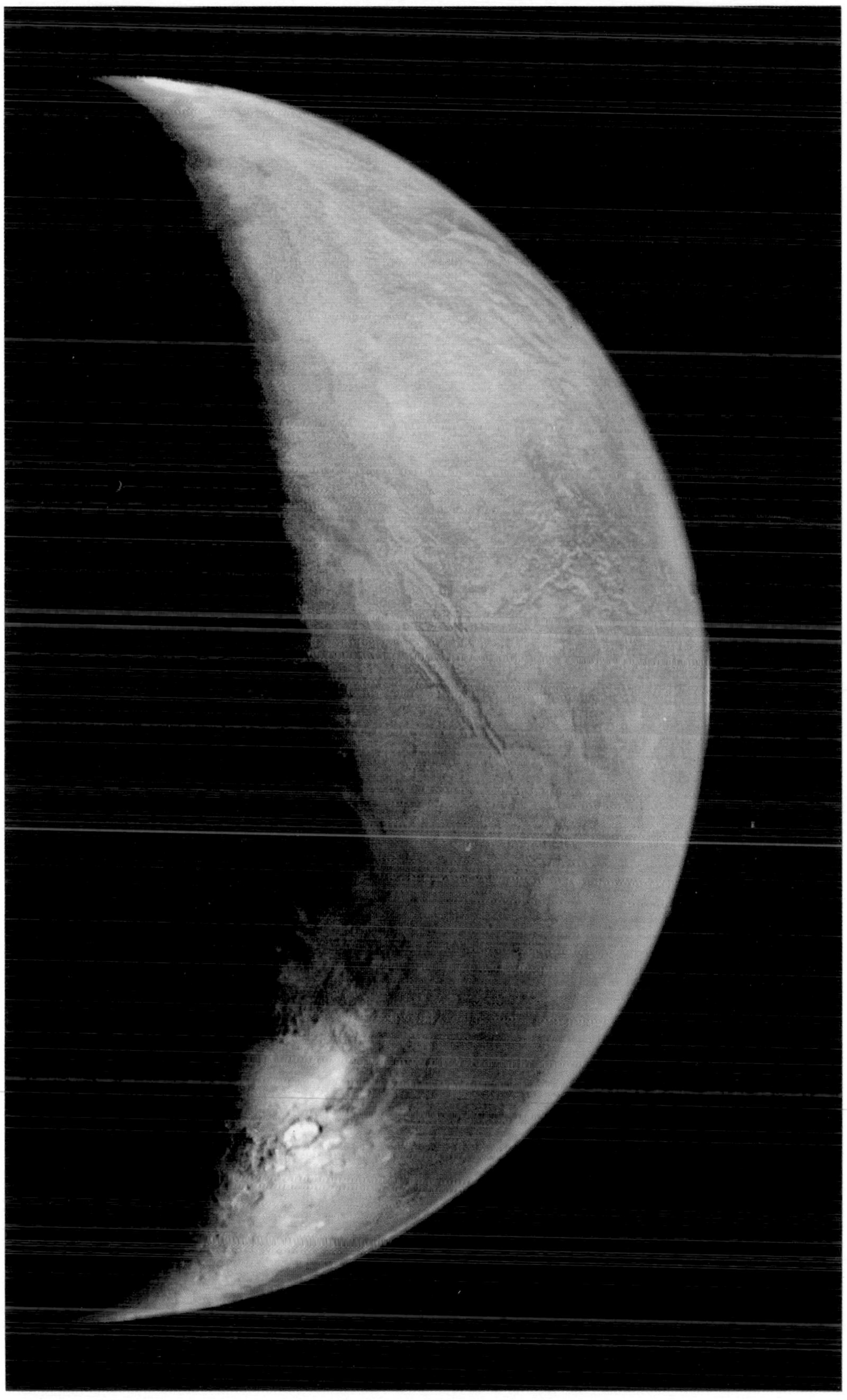

Below, a remarkable cut-away view of the interior of Mars, including a section of the volcano Olympus Mons, shows the relative sizes of the planetary crust, mantle, and metallic core. As with the other terrestrial planets, this body melted early in its history. Gravity acted upon the plastic materials, drawing metals and heavier minerals toward the center. Kurt Wenner, the artist, has retired and now occupies himself with drawing astronomical scenes on sidewalks in Rome. Opposite, Martian landscape reveals dry channels suggestive of liquid erosion.

heat. These gases formed a new atmosphere for each planet, and their masses were high enough to keep the new gases from escaping into space. In the case of the Earth, this primitive atmosphere included ammonia, carbon dioxide, water, methane, carbon monoxide, and nitrogen. Details of chemical composition, however, are less important than the fact that the planetary atmospheres remained once they had formed.

Such stable atmospheres meant that each planet would experience its own kind of climate and weather patterns. Over long periods of time, craters that marked the larger terrestrial planets were worn away. On the Earth, for example, no traces whatever remain of the bombardment that accompanied the formation of the planet. Those larger craters we have discovered date from later impacts. Only the airless worlds still carry their earliest scars.

All of the terrestrial worlds except the Earth formed a single continuous outer crust during the cooling period. On the moon and Mercury, this crust was occasionally broken by the impact of large objects, creating basins. Later, lava filled them. The ***maria*** (Latin for "seas") on the moon—the dark blotches visible from the Earth—developed in this way, as did the Caloris Basin on Mercury. At the same time, the internal heat occasionally caused volcanic eruptions and produced mountains. For the moon, this process ceased three billion years ago. Today a slow rain of meteorites causes almost the only erosion.

Once solid crusts had formed on the terrestrial planets, only a limited amount of evolution was likely. Volcanoes could form, regions could be thrust upward, and faults could appear as their crusts cracked. In fact, we see all of these features on the terrestrial planets. With the exception of the Earth, the crusts of the inner planets are resistant to general and fundamental change. The reason: heat added to or generated within these worlds can leak through their monolithic crusts and escape into space. Though only slightly larger than Venus, Earth has a significantly different surface-to-volume ratio. Consequently, the Earth's surface continually churns (somewhat like the surface of boiling water, though in slow motion) as it dumps heat from its interior. Thus arise the complicated motions we call plate tectonics. For present purposes, it is important to realize that because of its size and position in the solar system, Earth is the only terrestrial planet which still displays geological activity on a global scale.

Earth's Neighbors

Venus and Mars have long interested and even thrilled astronomers and the general public. In 1877 the Italian scientist Giovanni Schiaparelli looked at Mars through a telescope and reported a number of long, straight ***canali*** on the surface. In Italian, the word means channels. The English mistranslation, "canals," implied an intelligent life form as well. There is a lesson to be learned here.

The idea of Mars as the home of a dying civilization was taken up by the American astronomer Percival Lowell. He wrote a number of popular books championing the idea, and argued that the system of land use on Mars pointed to the existence of an efficient government. His theme was echoed in

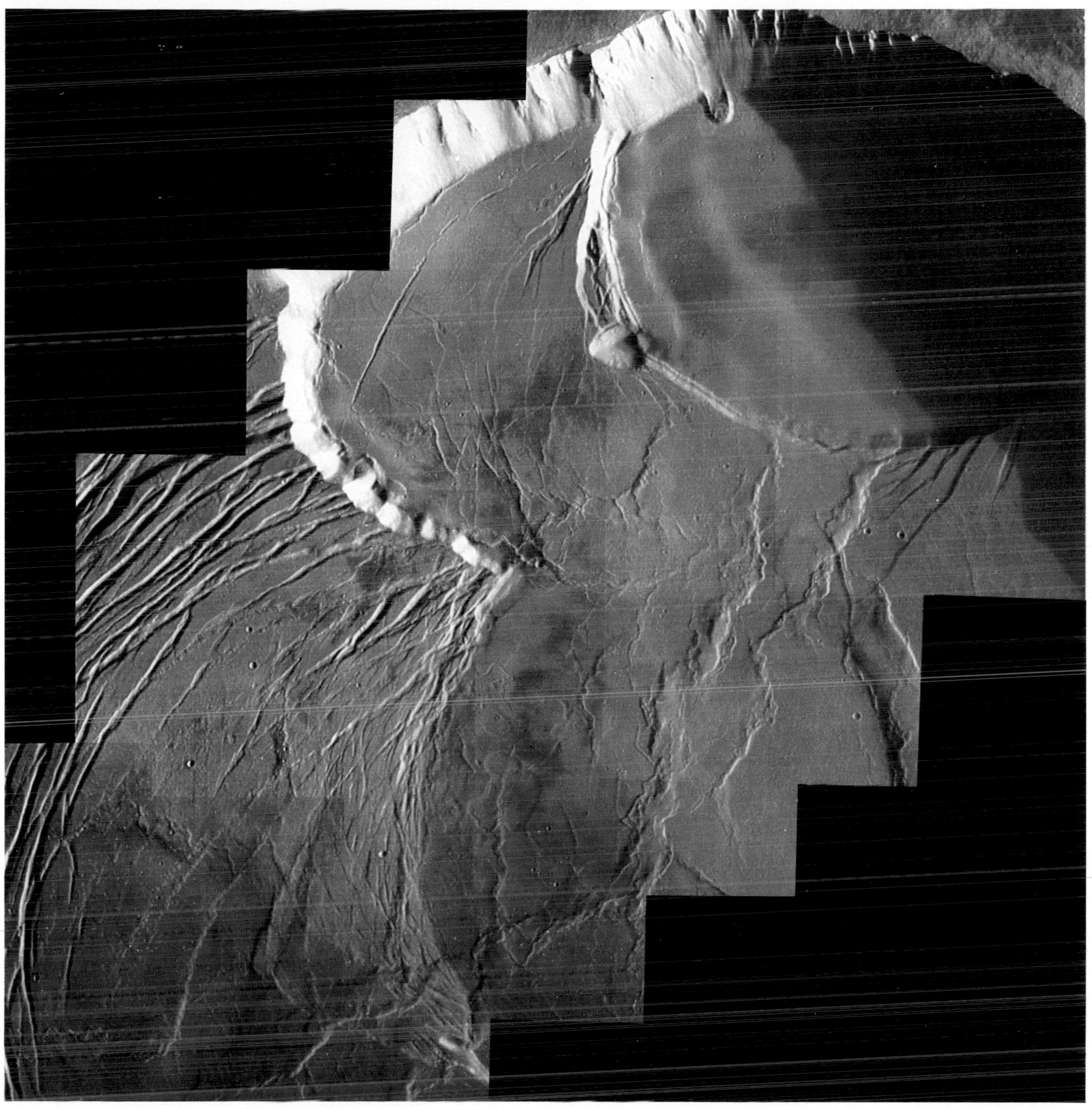

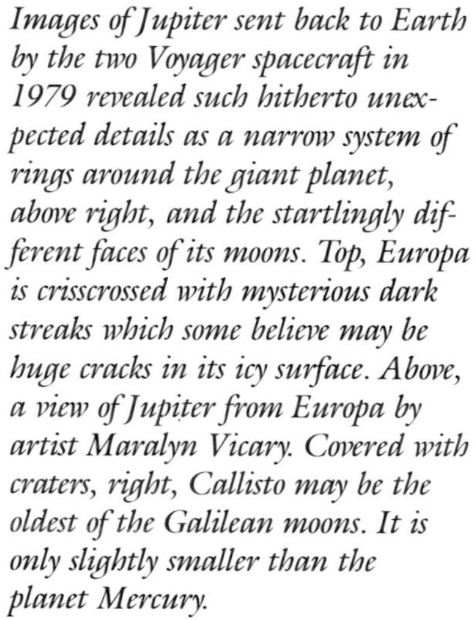

Images of Jupiter sent back to Earth by the two Voyager spacecraft in 1979 revealed such hitherto unexpected details as a narrow system of rings around the giant planet, above right, and the startlingly different faces of its moons. Top, Europa is crisscrossed with mysterious dark streaks which some believe may be huge cracks in its icy surface. Above, a view of Jupiter from Europa by artist Maralyn Vicary. Covered with craters, right, Callisto may be the oldest of the Galilean moons. It is only slightly smaller than the planet Mercury.

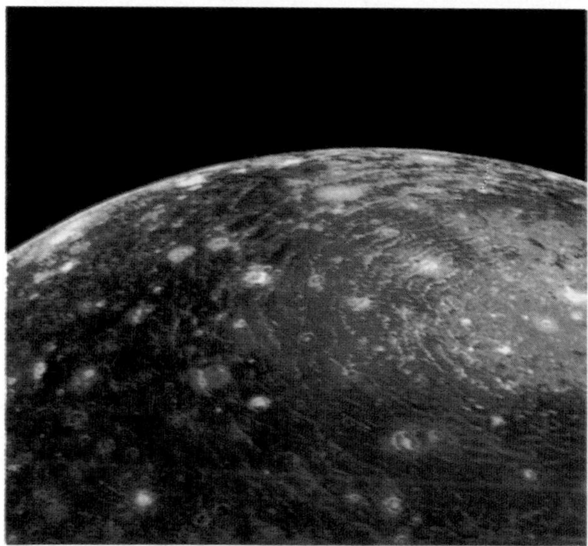

countless science-fiction novels, well into the 1950s. It took a while for everyone to realize that the argument about the Martian canals was a tempest in a teapot—there are no canals at all.

The Mariner mapping satellite, and the landing of the first Viking spacecraft on Mars in 1976, settled the issue. Viking sent back pictures of a lifeless, desert world of red sand and rock—nothing like Lowell's imaginings. Atmospheric pressure is very low—about equal to that found 30 miles above the surface of the earth, with the atmosphere itself almost all carbon dioxide. There is water on Mars; it can be found locked up in ice under the surface, or up in the clouds, and to some extent in the polar ice caps. These caps also contain dry ice (frozen carbon dioxide) and their melting and freezing leads to seasonal alterations in the area covered by polar ice. There are even channels on Mars, a fact which causes some astronomers to argue that once water must have flowed on the Martian surface. While this may be true, it is clear none flows today, and the chance of any sort of life—much less intelligent civilization—existing on the surface is small.

Venus has always been an enigma. Its surface is eternally hidden by clouds, and most science-fiction writers imagined it to be something like the Florida Everglades, only more so. The "swamps of Venus" joined the "canals of Mars" in popular imagination.

Two important space programs have helped to give us a more realistic picture of the planet most like the Earth in size. One involved the Pioneer Venus orbiter circling Venus and making radar maps of the surface. The clouds of Venus are transparent to radar, making it possible for these missions to give us detailed topographical maps.

Soviet investigations of Venus have been significant. Six probes from the U.S.S.R.'s Venera program soft-landed between 1970 and 1978, the last two sending back photographs of the surface itself. Venera 13 and 14 landed in 1982, Venera 13 enduring for 127 minutes. On other terrestrial planets, this would be no record at all. Why then is survivability so limited on our neighbor Venus?

The probes showed us many things: clouds composed mostly of sulfuric acid droplets, with the cloud layer extending to within 30 miles of the surface; and a clear region beneath the cover. We have also clocked winds—nothing short of ferocious—high above the surface and normally moving at several hundred miles an hour. In this respect, the Venusian atmosphere differs from our own, where the winds move at roughly the same speed as the Earth's surface. Atmospheric pressure at Venusian ground level is almost 100 times that of sea level on Earth, with a temperature of 800°F. No wonder the Soviet probes were unable to operate for more than two hours and seven minutes. Obviously Venus is an even more unlikely abode for life than Mars.

The Giants

If the inner planets exhibit such great variety based on small differences in their surface-to-volume ratios, the great outer planets, by contrast, display a certain measure of homogeneity. In fact, their satellites (moons and rings) are often studied with more avid attention than these immense planets them-

Above, Pele, one of Io's giant volcanoes, spews a 200-mile-high plume of sulfur dioxide over a wide area of the Jovian moon during the 1979 flyby of Voyager 1. Io's intense volcanic activity may be generated by tidal forces within the moon caused by Jupiter's powerful gravitational field. A technician at Pasadena's Jet Propulsion Laboratory, a major center for planetary studies, projects a computer created image of the surface of Io on a large screen.

On November 16, 1980, four days after it had flashed by Saturn, Voyager 1 looked back to the ringed planet to give observers on Earth the first view ever seen of Saturn from beyond its orbit, right. Since they were recognized as rings by Dutch astronomer Christiaan Huygens in 1659, Saturn's rings have been the first wonders of the solar system. However, not until the Voyager flybys of 1980 were the rings' astonishing complexity revealed. Shown here are parts of the B and C main rings, each made up of many ringlets, themselves composed of countless icy particles orbiting the planet.

selves. Because Jupiter is the largest of the outer giants—Jupiter, Saturn, Uranus, and Neptune—they are sometimes called the Jovian planets.

The formation of Jupiter and Saturn, according to some theorists, followed a different course than the one described earlier for the inner planets. In this process we saw grains grow into planetesimals which joined to form protoplanets and so on. In theory at least, the Jovian planets grew from the condensation of large gas clouds and in a manner similar to the formation of the sun. The chemical composition of the Jovian planets (almost exactly the same as the sun) provides evidence for this scenario. Direct gravitational collapse of gas clouds, requiring only a few months, might have done the entire job for Jupiter and the rest. Earth was framed across 100 million years.

Images from our probes reveal huge worlds with atmospheres so turbulent that storms can last for hundreds of years. One such perpetual hurricane, Jupiter's Great Red Spot, is big enough to swallow Earth, Mars, and Venus. Our knowledge of what

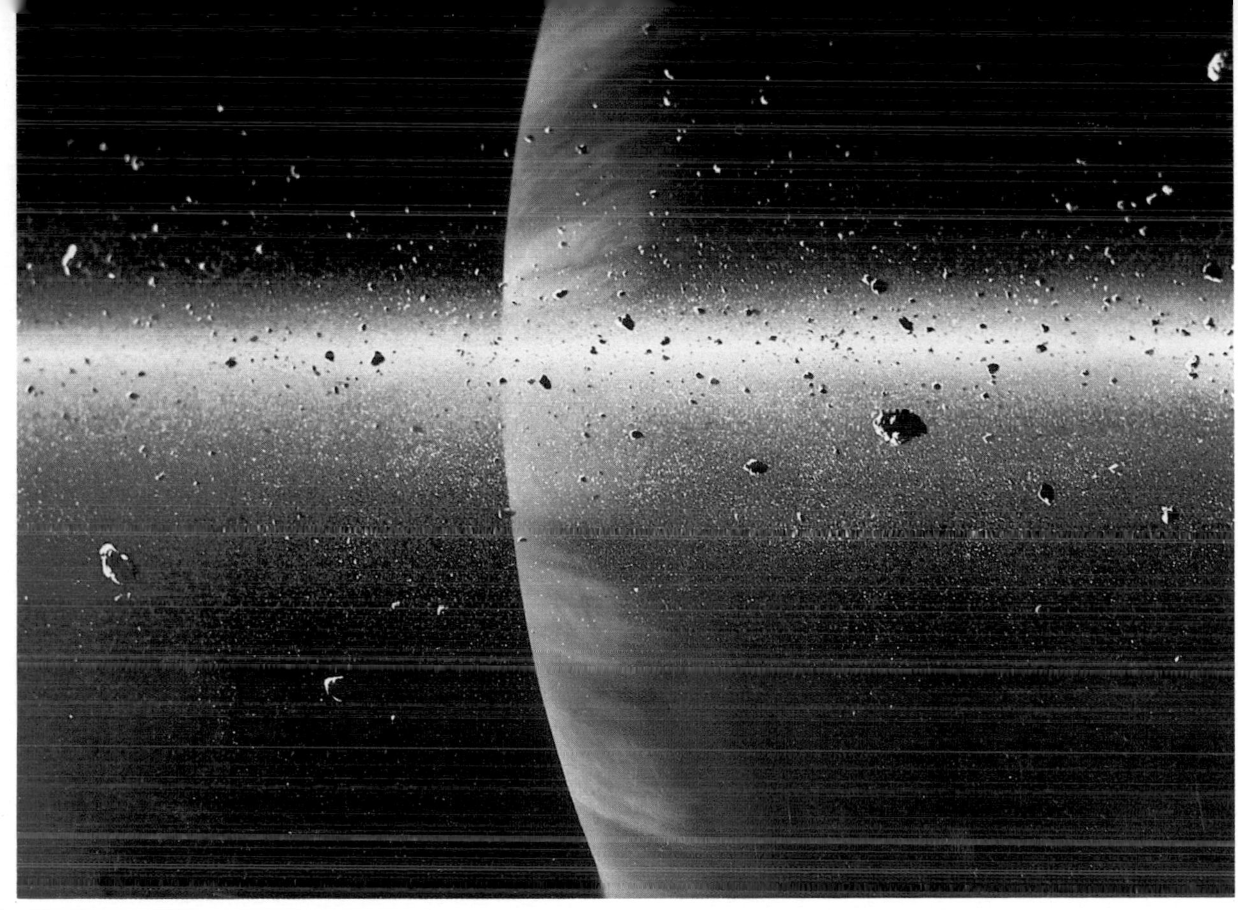

The particles seen in this artist's view of Saturn's rings are believed to be composed of ice containing small amounts of dust or elements such as iron and sulfur which give them distinctive colors. Their intricate promenade around the planet is choreographed by complex interactions among the gravitational fields of the large and small moons, many smaller bodies, and, of course, Saturn itself. These forces shuffle the particles into distinct bands where the chunks dance up and down, forward and back, in and out in response to the myriad gravitational tugs.

lies below the top of the Jovian atmospheres is less complete than for the terrestrial planets. The Galileo probe, scheduled for interception with Jupiter in late 1988, will probably be the first to penetrate that mysterious veil of swirling cloud.

Everything about the Jovian planets is great—except their density. They are often called the gas giants, though liquid and solid material may lie deep within. You could pack 1,300 Earths into Jupiter's volume and have room to spare. Its mass exceeds that of all of the other planets combined. In fact, from a strictly Newtonian point of view, it would be quite reasonable to think of the solar system as being made up of the sun and Jupiter, with a few bits of debris scattered around in other orbits.

The outer atmosphere of Jupiter presents us with a series of brightly colored stripes. These are the result of circulation in the atmosphere. Warm gases rise to the top, then cool, and finally sink. Very probably, if Jupiter didn't rotate, the top of the atmosphere would resemble the turbulence of boiling water. With its rapid turning, however, such zones would be spun out into bands around the entire planet, as we see. If it seems strange to you, remember that the gas at Jupiter's equator is moving along at speeds of nearly 30,000 miles per *hour*! Jupiter is thus the fastest-rotating planet in the solar system. The Jovian day is nearly 10 hours long.

The most arresting feature of the Jovian atmosphere is surely the Great Red Spot. Seen by the Englishman Robert Hooke in 1664, this is just what its name suggests—a large red spot that rotates with the planet. For a long time its nature was a mystery—I remember one science-fiction story portraying the Red Spot as a large island city floating in the Jovian sky. We now know, however, that it is a high-pressure region roughly 10,000 miles wide and 25,000 long. And because its appearance has not changed much since Hooke's observation, we are certain this weather cell has been churning along for three centuries; and for all we know, it has been going on for thousands of years and may very well continue for a long time into the future.

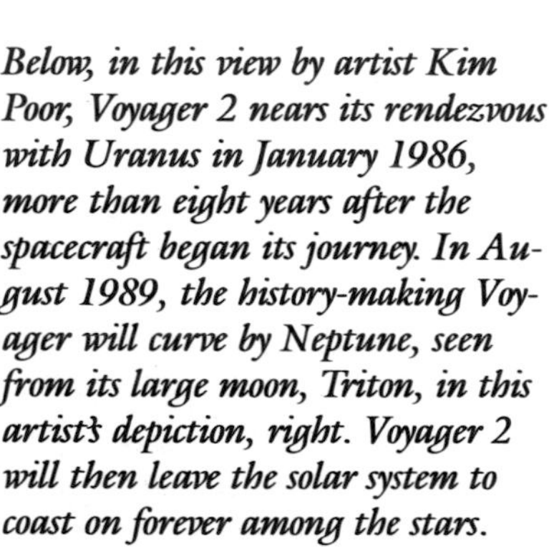

Below, in this view by artist Kim Poor, Voyager 2 nears its rendezvous with Uranus in January 1986, more than eight years after the spacecraft began its journey. In August 1989, the history-making Voyager will curve by Neptune, seen from its large moon, Triton, in this artist's depiction, right. Voyager 2 will then leave the solar system to coast on forever among the stars.

We know that, like all of the Jovian planets, Jupiter has a very low density. Beyond this certainty, we must rely on theoretical conjecture to tell us what we would find if we could penetrate the clouds. The upper atmosphere, however, contains a large percentage of hydrogen and a lesser amount of helium. The ratio, about 3:1 by measurement of mass, is roughly the same as the sun's.

From spectrographic studies, we know that the clouds we see are frozen crystals of ammonia, and that a number of other compounds (water and methane, to name a few) exist in the atmosphere. If we were to drop into the atmosphere, we'd notice a gradual rise in the temperature and the pressure as we move down through layers of ammonia crystals, water ice, liquid hydrogen, and (perhaps) gases. There really isn't a sharp boundary between "atmosphere" and "ground" on Jupiter—in fact, the descent we are describing would probably be more like sinking into a banana split than encountering a planet like the Earth. The atmosphere, about 700 miles thick, is subject to great pressure in its lower reaches and prob-

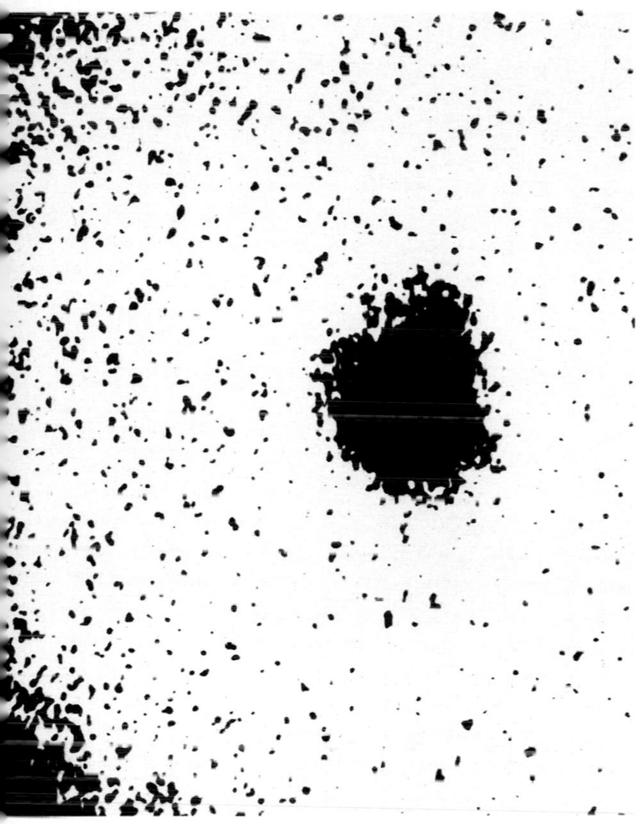

ably graduates into liquid hydrogen. About 30,000 miles from the center of the planet, the pressures are probably high enough to force the hydrogen into a very exotic form—metallic hydrogen. Some theorists claim there might be a small solid core at the center of the planet as well.

The appearance of Saturn, with alternating turbulent bands visible in the upper atmosphere, is similar to that of Jupiter. The composition of the atmosphere is also similar, though lower temperatures seem to have caused some atmospheric ammonia to freeze and migrate toward the interior. Voyager I even discovered a small version of Jupiter's Red Spot. Saturn's interior is probably similar to that of Jupiter, with liquid and metallic hydrogen surrounding a possible rocky core.

Details of Uranus and Neptune are to be revealed as probes reach their vicinity after 1985. Uranus, discovered in 1781, is too cold for ammonia to appear in its atmosphere, but both methane and hydrogen have been detected. The composition of the atmosphere gives it a pale greenish cast when viewed through a telescope. All in all, it should resemble its gas-giant neighbors. Uranus is unusual, however, in that it spins on its side, unlike other planets. The "day" on Uranus, then, would be much like the "day" at our polar regions. On one end of Uranus, the sun would set only every 42 years, while on the other end it would rise according to the same period.

Neptune, discovered in 1846, is similar to Uranus. It appears pale green, with indications that its cloud patterns may change every year or so. There is little profit in speculating further, especially since space probes will eventually reveal more than we could ever guess.

Pluto, usually considered the outermost planet, was discovered in 1930. Rather small and rocky, it is something of an anomaly in the outer solar system. Astronomers have even suggested that Pluto isn't a proper planet at all, but a lost moon of Neptune or perhaps a comet that has assumed a planetary path. Unlike those of the other outer planets, its orbit is highly elliptical. Curiously, in the late 1970s Pluto passed inside

Small and dark, Pluto was discovered in 1930 by American observer Clyde Tombaugh and named by 11-year-old English schoolgirl Venetia Burney, opposite. In 1978, using an electronic imaging technique, James W. Christy of the U.S. Naval Observatory discovered a moon in close orbit around Pluto. Named Charon, the moon appears in the historic image, above left, as a small blob at the top of the large blob which is Pluto. Above, in this painting by James Hervat, a remote sun shines feebly on Charon and the surface of Pluto.

Above, the sun sets on Mars—and on the Viking 1 lander, part of which can be seen in the right foreground. After a gentle landing in the Chryse plain of Mars, Viking 1 sent its first message back to Earth on July 20, 1976. For more than six years it faithfully transmitted images of the terrain around it, as well as meteorological reports and other data, until after a last transmission on November 13, 1982, it fell silent. Surely, in the not-too-distant future, a spacesuited figure will stride across the red desert of Chryse to the squat spacecraft and stand for a moment in admiration of this robot pioneer.

the orbit of Neptune and until the end of the century Neptune will, in fact, be the planet most distant from the sun.

Moons and Rings

The gas giants share one trait—they all seem to have a lot of debris floating around them. We know that all of them have moons, and at least three (and perhaps all four) have rings. These moons and rings make the gas giants the most spectacular objects in the solar system. In fact, we have already seen that the discovery of the moons of Jupiter was one of Galileo's first great findings with his telescope. He saw four moons—bodies we now call the Galilean satellites. Subsequent investigations with telescopes and space probes have uncovered another dozen, bringing the total to 16. At some point, however, moon-counting among the gas giants becomes more a matter of semantics and less a concern of meaningful astronomy. Whether a particular object is a large piece of debris or a small moon is hardly an intellectually exciting question.

The Galilean satellites are all large compared with our own, although Earth's moon is by far the largest satellite of the terrestrial planets. Like ours, each of these moons carries with it the story of its formation and evolution. Io, for instance, has a thin atmosphere of sodium and sulfur atoms spewed out by its active volcanoes. These eject about 1,000 billion tons of material a year. The volcanoes seem to be fed by sulfur compounds from within Io, heated and melted by tidal forces strong enough to create displacement of solid rock.

Europa's outer coating consists largely of water ice crisscrossed by large cracks. Neither Europa nor Io show craters so, like Earth, both may be geologically active. Astronomers believe that Europa retained a molten surface until long after the fall of meteorites ended, and that the cracks we see now are similar to those that occur in pack ice around Earth's polar regions. We note, as did the makers of the motion picture "2010," that these satellites seem more mysterious—and thus more interesting—than the great planet Jupiter itself.

Ganymede, the largest moon in the solar

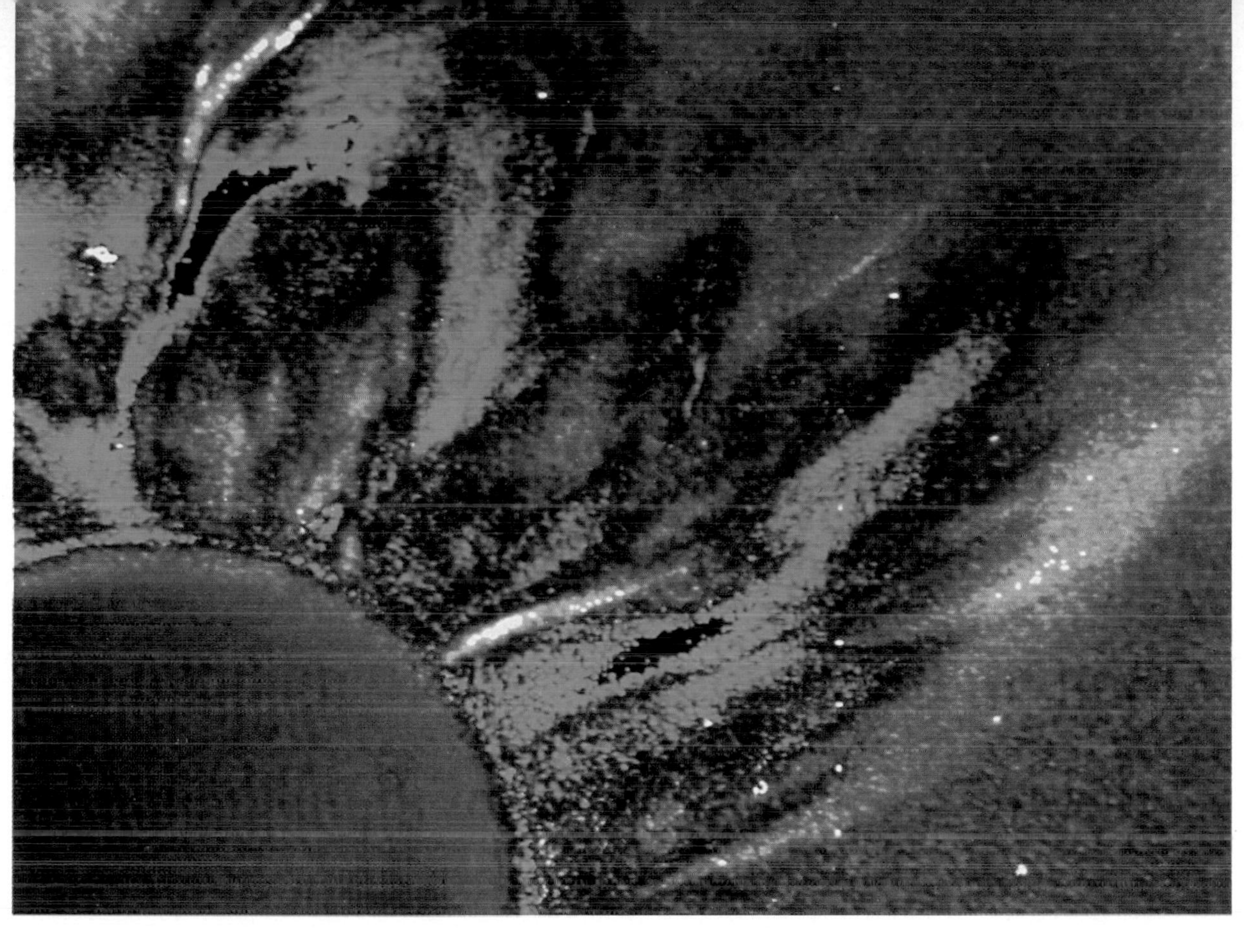

Left, the outer atmosphere, or corona, of the sun glows vividly in this "coronagraph" taken by the Solar Maximum Mission satellite on May 6, 1980. Normally visible only during an eclipse, the corona can be seen here enhanced in artificial color because a disk (lower left corner of the coronagraph) in the camera system blocks out the bright sun, allowing the much dimmer corona to appear. Many astronomers believe that the solar wind, the blast of charged particles that sweeps out through the solar system from the sun, is the outermost extension of the corona. If so, it may be said that we on Earth live not only because of the sun, but within it.

system, bears scars of meteoroid impact from the days of the sun's awakening. Also apparent are regions of grooved and cracked surface in the fashion of Europa. Like Europa, Ganymede may hold ice. The grooves we see could be fracture patterns. In a sense, great Ganymede appears to be a transition moon—midway between the inner moons, and dominated by the tidal pull of Jupiter, and the outer satellites. This picture is consistent with the fact that Callisto, the farthest of the Galilean moons, has a cratered surface closely resembling Earth's moon and the planet Mercury.

The Voyager mission made a surprising discovery about Jupiter itself. The planet has a series of small, thin rings around it. Very narrow and made of dark material, this feature is invisible to all but nearby observers. The discovery is not so important for what it tells us about Jupiter, but because it shows that the rings of Saturn, as spectacular as they are, are not unique in our system. Perhaps the greatest wonder of the varied worlds of our solar system—large and small—is that our study and knowledge of them has suddenly come of age. A few decades ago, some astronomy books were filled with speculation. The only truly accurate facts were the names of the planets and the information derived from Newtonian physics and the fuzzy images from our telescopes. Now we spin theories to help explain such details as Saturn's braided outer rings.

Our wonder about the planets will not cease. The next salvo of probes will carry charged-coupled devices (CCD), improved sensing elements which will enhance our vision. But their images will only add detail. We already possess the broad outline. And one day, though perhaps not in this century, men and women from Earth will set foot upon the red sands of Mars.

Sternbach

Debris

Fact catches up with science fiction. Richard Sternbach's painting at left portrays a proposed cometary rendezvous. The real thing comes to life in late 1985 and early 1986 as space probes close in on Halley's comet during its swing past the sun. Comet at right fatally grazed the sun in 1979, vaporizing instantly.

Between and beyond the planets, a large number of objects move in orbital paths. Those we call comets and meteors provide spectacular celestial displays. Asteroids, when we reach and analyze some, will probably enable us to solve the riddle of the formation of the solar system.

Comets loom large in mythology, usually as messengers of disaster. Throughout most of history, their visitations have appeared to be random events and no one really understood what comets were. Then, in 1705, the English astronomer Edmond Halley published a book called *A Synopsis of the Astronomy of Comets*. He noted that the orbits of comets sighted in 1531, 1607, and 1682 were so similar that the comet involved was probably the same one.

He used Newton's laws to calculate the orbit of this regular visitor and predicted that it would be sighted again in 1758. The reappearance of the comet within months of Halley's prediction was the first great triumph of the application of the law of universal gravitation to bodies in the solar system, and the comet was named after him. Since Halley's time many other observations of the comet have been found in the historical records, perhaps as far back as 240 B.C. It appeared just before the Norman Conquest of England and was last seen in 1910, when some people believed the world would end as we passed through the comet's tail.

The last visitation of the 20th century (late 1985 and early 1986), marks the comet's third return since Halley published his identification in 1705. In its approach to the sun, Halley's comet passes close to Earth on November 27, 1985, and even closer on April 11, 1986, when it swings out on its trip to the far planets and beyond.

Halley's comet, and the many other periodic comets that we know about, have elongated orbits that take them far from the sun

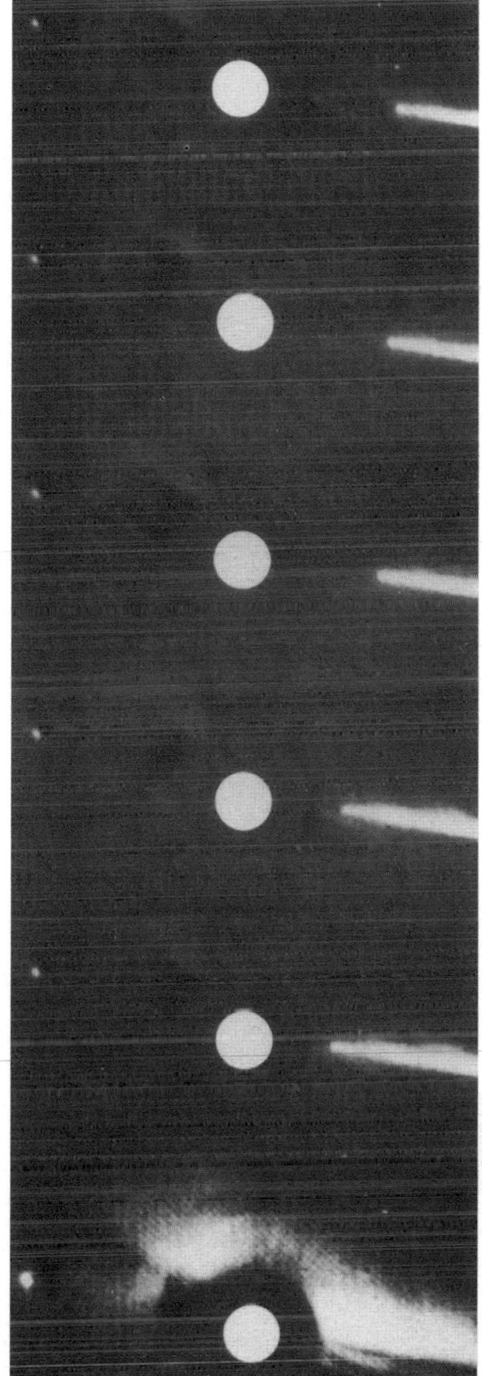

Fred Whipple, who proposed that comets are dirty snowballs, discusses details of comet anatomy with astronomer Brian Marsden, a colleague at the Harvard-Smithsonian Center for Astrophysics in Cambridge, Massachusetts.

before gravity slows them down. Then they curve back and fall faster and faster toward the center of our planetary system. Increased temperature and the solar wind begin to boil off material and the comet sprouts a tail, or, actually two tails: one of gas; the other of dust. The dust streams away from the path of the comet in a curving track as it encounters the solar wind. The gas blows out straight. The nucleus of a large comet is probably no more than six miles across, but the tail can stretch for millions of miles. From analyses of the material in the tails, scientists believe that comets are actually some sort of "dirty snowballs."

From Kepler's laws we know that any object in an elliptical orbit will move quickly when near the sun and slowly when far away. Given the elongated nature of cometary orbits, this means that they will spend the greatest part of their lives in the farther reaches of their orbits. The average comet has a period of about ten million years and makes its turn some 50,000 times farther from the sun than the orbit of the Earth. (Halley's comet is an exceptional object, since it has a short period.) This means that most comets will spend most of their time making a leisurely turn well outside the solar system proper. In effect, the comets form a cloud out there, and only occasionally come plunging in toward the Earth. This far-off region is known as the Oort cloud, after the Dutch astronomer Jan Oort, who first proposed its existence in 1950.

Like comets, asteroids are nonplanetary bodies in orbit around the sun. Unlike comets, however, they are solid objects and do not make spectacular displays in the sky. Most asteroids circle the sun in a tight set of orbits called the asteroid belt, located between the orbits of Mars and Jupiter. Some of these oddly shaped stones are little more than gravel in space, but the largest is 620 miles across. The best guess is that the outer asteroids are a group of leftover planetesimals, those primordial orbiting bodies that clumped together and were amalgamated into the planets. The asteroid belt itself probably represents a planet that never made the final step in the amalgamation process.

Occasionally, asteroids come near each

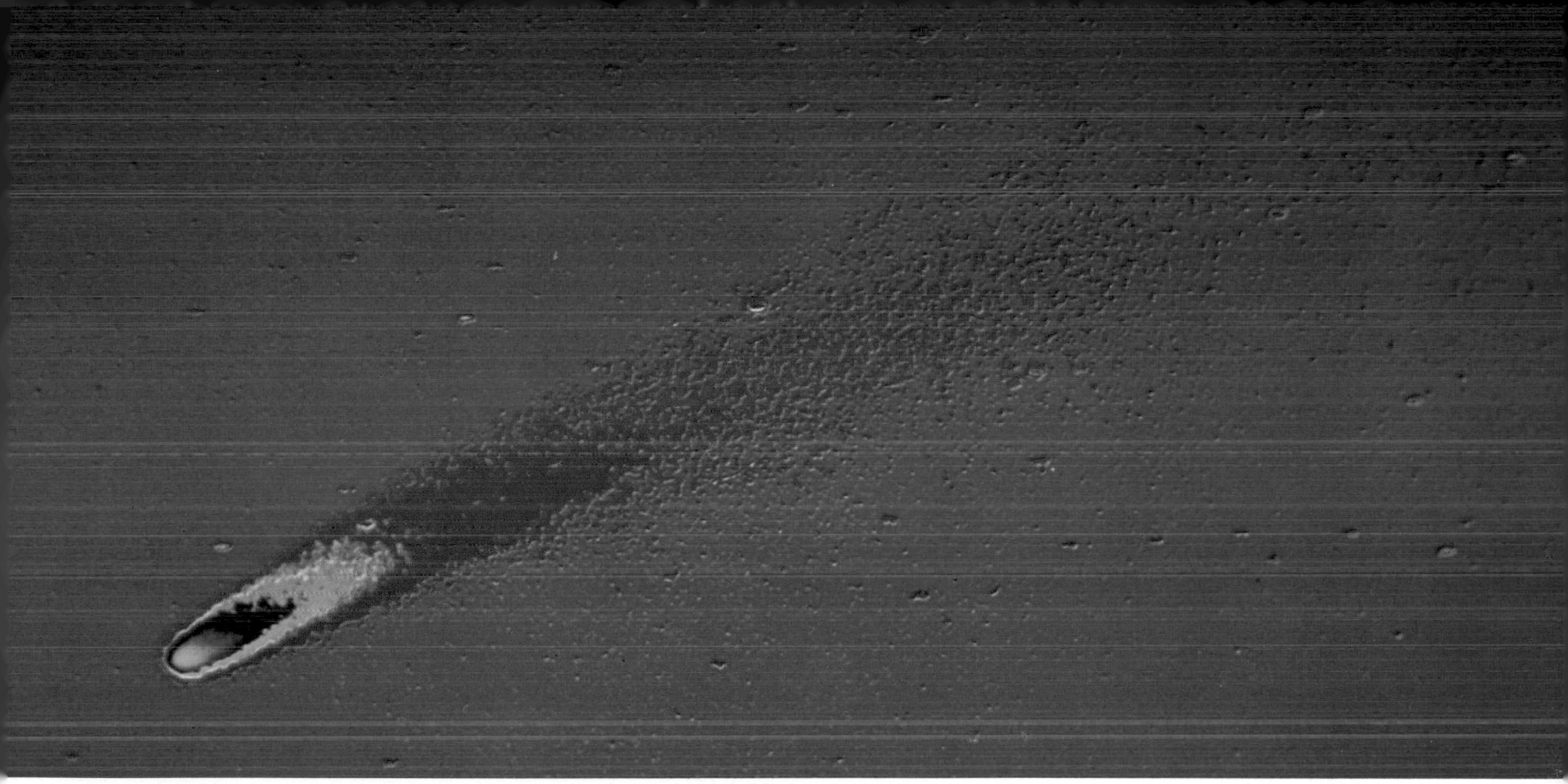

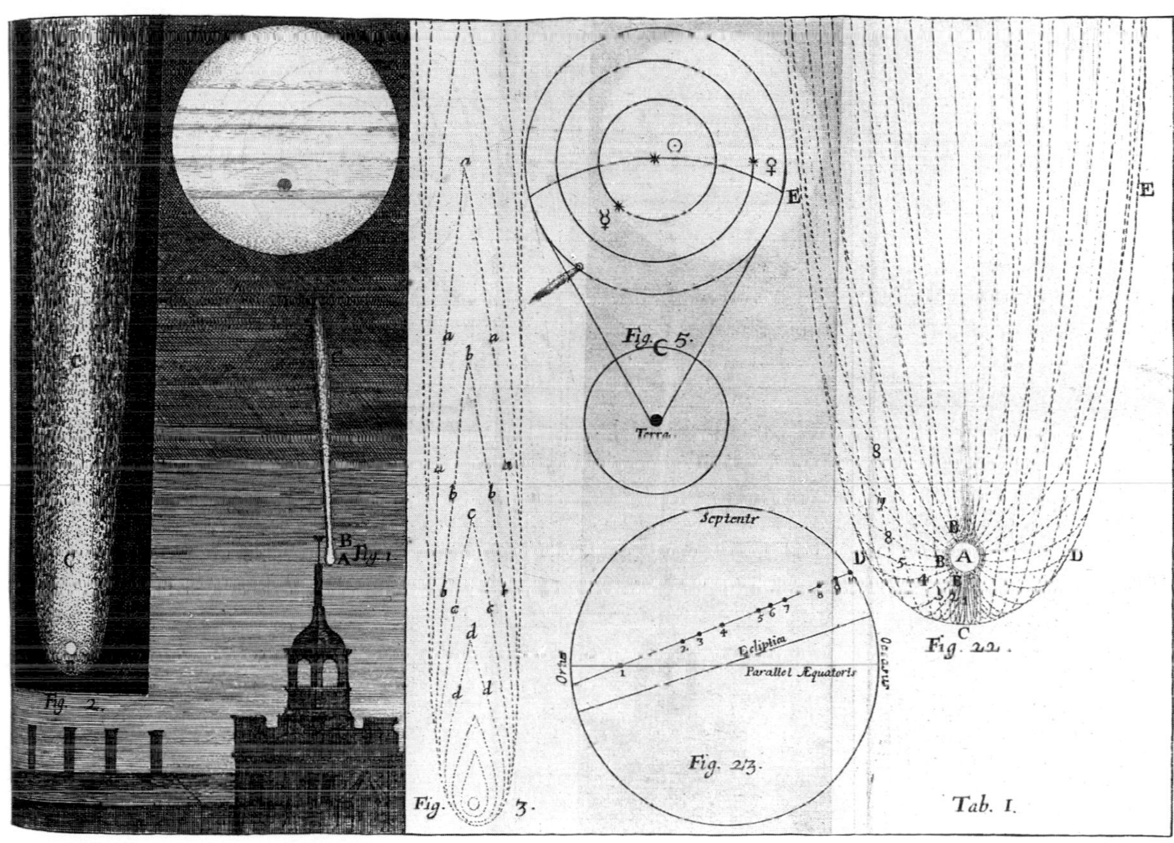

Above, Comet Bennett—namesake of the discoverer, a South African amateur astronomer—swept across the sky in 1970, appearing as bright as Polaris. Drawings of cometary heads and tails appeared in a book of lectures given by Robert Hooke, circa 1679.

other—either colliding or simply exerting a feeble gravitational attraction on each other. When this happens, the asteroids may enter new orbits that take them out of the belt. Some such bodies, known as Apollo asteroids, actually come inside the orbit of the Earth. There may be hundreds of Apollos measuring a mile or more across and, of course, many more smaller ones. It has also been suggested that some of these may be comets that have lost their tails and have gone into orbit in the inner solar system.

The existence of large asteroids whose orbits cross the path of the Earth is important for two reasons. First, these bodies occasionally collide with the Earth, either burning up in the atmosphere or (more rarely)

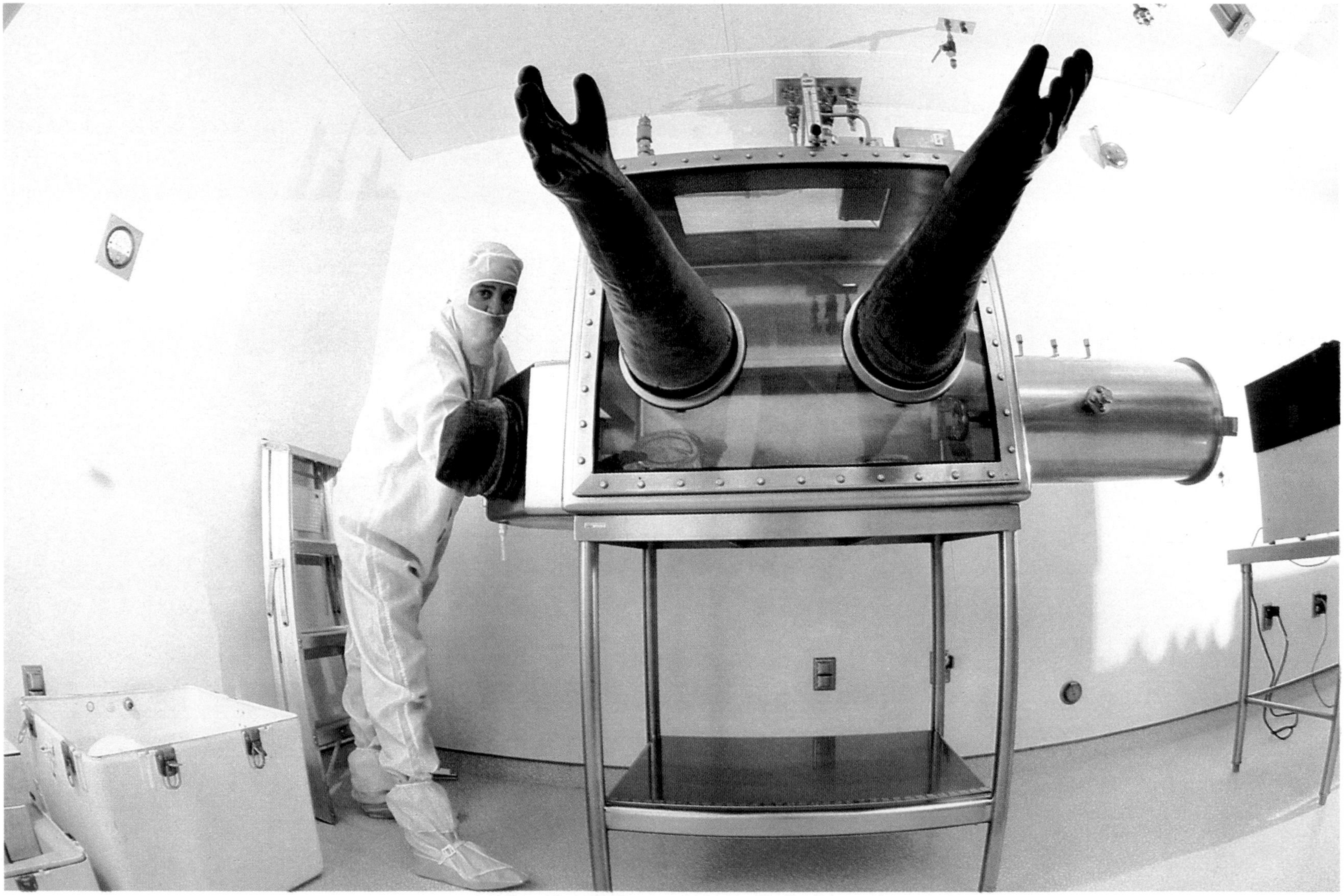

coming down to the ground if they are large enough. As we shall see, these intruders from space carry important clues to the history of the solar system.

Apollo asteroids are also important because they represent an important resource base that the human race, just entering its spacefaring period, can use. If meteorites are any indication, some of these asteroids are metallic, others stony. It's not too far-fetched to suppose that during the next century intrepid prospectors will start to look at this debris from the early solar system not as a scientific treasure, but as an economic resource. And a truly staggering resource at that, one that provides the primary motive for humans to venture beyond the orbit of our moon. At prices current in the early 1980s, the value of the gold in a single asteroid six miles on a side could be more than $500 *trillion*—enough to settle the national debt, pay for the space program, and abolish income taxes in the bargain!

Meteors and Meteorites

If you stand outside on a clear night for any time at all, the chances are good that you will see a "shooting star" streak across the sky. What you are seeing—a meteor—is usually something the size of a grain of sand that falls from space into the earth's atmosphere. Some larger specimens survive the fiery trip through the atmosphere, in which case the meteor is called a meteorite.

The study of meteorites is important for several reasons. First, they are the remnants of the materials from which the planets were built and, second, they have spent four billion years in space. In the words of Roy S. Clarke, Jr., curator at the Smithsonian's Department of Mineral Sciences, "They're the cheapest space probes we have."

The more I learn about meteorites, the more I understand the reasons for treating these rare falls from the heavens with a great deal of respect. Imagine first of all that you are standing outside of a magnificent new building. You notice that the building is several stories tall, that there are switches that turn on lights and taps that give you running water, but you can't go into the building to figure out how everything works. Suppose, however, that someone allowed

Flying 13 miles high, a U-2 meteorological aircraft scooped up samples identified as comet dust, opposite. Pressure pops rubber gloves inside out at the Johnson Space Center. The sterile chamber is of a type used to examine cosmic dust and moon rocks. Below, a snarl of orbits of short-period comets circle the sun. The highly elliptical path of Halley's comet appears in light blue at the upper left. A small, curved arrow represents Earth's orbit, the large one, Jupiter's. Linear arrow points to the vernal equinox, an astronomical reference point.

you to rummage through the scrap heap left behind by the construction crew. You might find some bricks, and scraps of steel beams, and lumber that would tell you what kept the building from falling down. If you were lucky, you might even find a few bits of wire and pipe that would allow you to guess how the electrical and plumbing systems worked. Having knowledge of the building's raw materials would actually tell you a great deal about how the structure worked.

The study of meteorites gives us a chance to look at the unprocessed building materials from which planets are made. For instance, in 1969, many fragments of one meteorite fell near the town of Pueblito de Allende in northern Mexico. Careful chemical analysis of some of the grains of material in the meteorite revealed greater amounts of a particular isotope of magnesium than is usually found. Isotopes are rare variants of the usual chemical elements, either slightly heavier or lighter than the standard. In this case the isotope, called aluminum-26, was present in excess of only half a percent over the expected amount.

Now this may not seem earth-shattering, but it can be of considerable value in explaining the origins of our solar system. We know that exploding stars called supernovae occur with some regularity in our Galaxy. What would happen if one went off near a gas cloud? For one thing, a shock wave would propagate through the cloud, an event that could easily trigger the collapse of the cloud into a protostar. At the same time, elements created inside the dying star would be blown into the cloud, there to mingle with the material from which the new system would form. Some of the hard stuff in the form of grains would contain radioactive isotopes of aluminum created in the last stages of the supernova. These grains would have been incorporated into planetesimals as they formed.

In most cases, of course, these planetesimals would be lost as they were compacted into the planets. The isotope of aluminum would decay into magnesium, but the excess magnesium would be swamped by the large amounts of normal stuff already in the system. In one case, however, we know this didn't happen. A particular rock (perhaps the size of a small car) carried its alien grains into orbit and escaped the planet-making process. For four and a half billion years it quietly circled the sun, its original complement of radioactive aluminum decaying into magnesium. In 1969 it entered the earth's atmosphere, broke up, and became what we call the Allende fall. This space rock had served us well, for we can still read parts of the record of how our solar system received its elements, the source of minerals.

Meteorites have other stories to tell. Some of them were taken into protoplanets, partially melted, and then blasted loose by meteroid impact. When they eventually fall to earth and are collected we can read their history through analysis of their chemical and physical features. Researchers at the Smithsonian Museum of Natural History help to classify some of the meteorites found in Antarctic ice. One of these was once on the surface of the moon, another probably from Mars. In each case, a major impact seems to have knocked them loose, to wander the void until they fell to earth.

In talking with Roy Clarke about meteorites, my thoughts turned to the question of how a man charged with collecting these rare objects goes about his job. "In the United States," he explained, "the meteorite belongs to the landowner. If it falls on government property, the Smithsonian claims them. In other cases, we can usually come to some sort of agreement. But our main job is to obtain as many as we can for study."

Later on, some of Roy's colleagues told me just how much this last sentence meant. Confronted with a couple of prospectors who threatened violence to anyone who tried to remove a meteorite they had found on government land, Roy enlisted the aid of a squad of U.S. Marines with a helicopter to whisk an important find out of its mountain fastness in the Mojave Desert.

What advice does he have for anyone who happens to see a meteorite fall? "Most meteorites are from common classes, but every now and then there's one that is absolutely unique," he said. "If they are kept as mementos, they are lost to science." So if you should be fortunate enough to come across one of these visitors from the sky, be sure it reaches the proper hands.

Teaching old photos new tricks, Tucson astronomer Steven Jastrow programmed his computer to process glass photographic plates taken of Halley's comet during its last flyby in 1910. By imposing colors and manipulating contrast, he revealed the comet's head in a new light. French postcard of 1910 proclaims the "End of the World" in reference to rumors of poisonous gases in the tail of Halley's comet.

Earth as a Planet

Editor's Note: *In the English language all planets except our own are named for classical deities. As for Earth, some prefer the name Gaia, the primordial Greek goddess of life in earth, of earth, and upon Earth. She is also the root of our prefix* ge, *as in geology, geography, and geometry.*

Africa appears to emerge from the clouds. This remarkable image of Earth as a planet originated with the European Space Agency's orbiting weather watcher, Meteosat. Jean de France, the Duc de Berry (1340–1416) commissioned a version of Eden as Earth, far right. Even after we have seen from space all the deserts of our planet, the ancient notion of Earth as a garden still applies.

Earth isn't the largest planet in the solar system. The honor goes to Jupiter. Earth isn't the most impressive, either—Saturn holds that distinction. Earth alone possesses one characteristic that makes it very special among the planets of the solar system and, for all we know, among all the planets in the Galaxy. Our planet is small and undistinguished, yet only here, as far as we know, has life unfolded.

As we have seen, one unique feature of the Earth is a function of its size. When the infall of meteorites and the decay of radioactive nuclei began to heat the planet soon after it was formed, the surface-to-volume ratio of the new world was too small to allow the heat to escape into space. The entire globe melted (or at least became plastic) and the heavier elements sank toward the center under the influence of gravity. This resulted in a variable geological structure, one in which the chemical composition of rocks changes as we go deeper and deeper. The outermost skin, or crust, is composed of rocks like granite and basalt—rocks made largely of rather lightweight atoms including silicon and oxygen. Though only 20 to 30 miles thick, this layer presents a formidable barrier. No human agency has ever penetrated below the crust of the earth, and all of our knowledge of it, and what may lie even deeper, has come to us through indirect measurements.

Below the crust is a layer of solid rock nearly 2,000 miles thick. This mantle contains heavier rock, composed largely of iron and magnesium. Beneath the mantle lies the core, more than 4,000 miles in diameter. This globular body consists of iron, molten in the outer portion but solid at the center.

This highly differentiated structure is a direct result of the melting of the entire planet just after its formation. The consequences of this early heating have affected our planet throughout its life. Because Earth is larger than the other terrestrial planets, it was unable to form a stable, solid crust. The heat generated by radioactive decay in the interior, perhaps augmented by heat left over from the great meltdown, continues to flow out of the surface. It churns the crust and leads to the phenomenon we call plate tectonics—the spreading of the ocean floor and the slow movement of the continents across the surface of the globe.

A useful way to visualize the modern view of the dynamic earth is to think of a few isolated films of oil on the surface of a pan of boiling water. The movement of the water caused by the heating element of your stove will make the oil films change position. Occasionally, two slicks will come together and coalesce, while at other times a large film will be broken up by the rolling water. Be-

Turning globe reveals the area of Africa's Great Rift Valley, a major geological fault which cradles the Red Sea, Africa's great lakes, and the Jordan River valley. Above the blocky Arabian Peninsula, the Persian Gulf represents a flooded fracture from India's collision with the Asian landmass. Opposite: Soviet Soyuz and American Apollo space capsules link-up in July 1975. They orbit above the Caspian Sea at the productive Volga Delta near Astrakhan. Soviet artist Andrei Sokolov produced this realistic depiction.

cause heated water rising from the bottom of the pan cools, then sinks, the oil films will be in continuous motion.

This motion of the water, which physicists call convection, also operates in the mantle of the earth. The motion of the rock is much slower than the motion of water in a pan, of course, but scientists believe that the same type of motion takes place in both the mantle and the water. The crust, like the oil film, floats on top of the churning mantle and moves in response to it. The major difference between the oil films in our analogy and the crust of the earth is that the crust completely covers the mantle. Thus, while the drops of oil on water can float around without touching each other, the crust of the earth must always cover the entire surface. How, then, can it respond to convection in the mantle?

In areas where heated material is rising in the mantle, the crust is split apart. The newly separated pieces are drawn apart as the crust floats along with the motion of the mantle. The gap created in this way is filled by warm material welling up from the lower regions of the crust and the upper mantle. Thus, in regions where warm material is rising, we expect to see the continuous creation of new crust.

Obviously, if new material is added to the crust at some points, some of the old must be removed. When two separate pieces of the crust collide, one can be forced beneath the other in a process known as subduction. Earth's internal heat may melt the covered rocks which could return as new crust at some future time.

If this picture of the Earth is accurate, then it ought to be possible to locate the places on the surface where new crust is being created and where old crust is being destroyed. When we find these places we discover that the surface is split up into six or more major plates, and several minor ones. Each moves with respect to the others in response to the churning of the mantle. Much of this action occurs under the oceans, where water hides the changing geological surface. For instance, the North American plate—on which the United States rests—is augmented and moved westward by the upwelling of magma along a mountain chain in the center of the Atlantic Ocean. At the moment, the North American plate is not being subducted (forced beneath an adjoining plate) but is sliding sideways along the Pacific plate at the Pacific coast of the United States. Subduction is occurring along the western edge of South America, and the Andes mountains are a visible sign of the geological forces at work here.

It is important to realize that the shorelines of the continents do not precisely coincide with the boundaries of the plates. The North American plate includes the floor of the western Atlantic Ocean and most of North America. The western boundary of the plate is indicated by, among other things, the famous San Andreas fault.

The boundaries between plates are the real dividing lines on the Earth's surface and not, as one might expect, the shorelines of the continents. In fact, you can think of the continents as light debris that has floated to the surface and is being carried along by the motion of the plates.

This model for the planet's surface and moveable underpinnings goes under the name of plate tectonics. An older term—continental drift—was used to refer to the idea that the continents moved, a feature which we now see as implicit in the tectonic picture. Thus, plate tectonics not only deals with the concept of continental drift, but with the entire surface as well.

We know that from the beginning Earth's geology has been active. Continents atop the lithospheric plates have coalesced and then separated, mountain chains have been uplifted and then worn down by the action of water and wind. Evolving species of both plants and animals have been challenged to adapt to new environments.

The Atmosphere

The motion of the tectonic plates may have been going on in its present form since the surface of the Earth solidified. Forces deep within the planet drive the plates—forces unaffected by changes at the surface. Two other important systems, however, have undergone radical changes during this same period. These are the atmosphere and the hydrosphere. The first is our evolving gaseous envelope, the second our total water-supply system including oceans, ice, surface water, and vapor providing clouds and precipitation. Both systems interact with each other and have gone through important and irreversible changes since the formation of the planet.

Earth's early atmosphere may have contained large percentages of helium and hydrogen, as do the Jovian planets even today. These chemical elements may have been torn away as the nascent sun finally ignited and sent forth an intense solar wind. For all practical purposes, however, we can regard the world as born with neither an atmosphere nor a hydrosphere.

Since the moment our star first began to shine, the atmosphere has continued to evolve. As the planet's crust cooled and solidified, volcanoes and meteor impacts aided in the release of gases from the interior. Hot water vapor condensed as soon as the earth's temperature fell below 212°F (100°C). Thus began the cycle of evaporation, rainfall, and runoff that dominates our weather. Condensation filled the earliest ocean basins.

As far as I am concerned, the most amazing fact about the formation of the hydrosphere is that virtually all of the world's water was produced in the early days. The molecules of water washing up on your favorite beach today are the same molecules that formed the Earth's first oceans over four billion years ago!

In addition to water vapor, the early volcanoes put a large amount of carbon dioxide

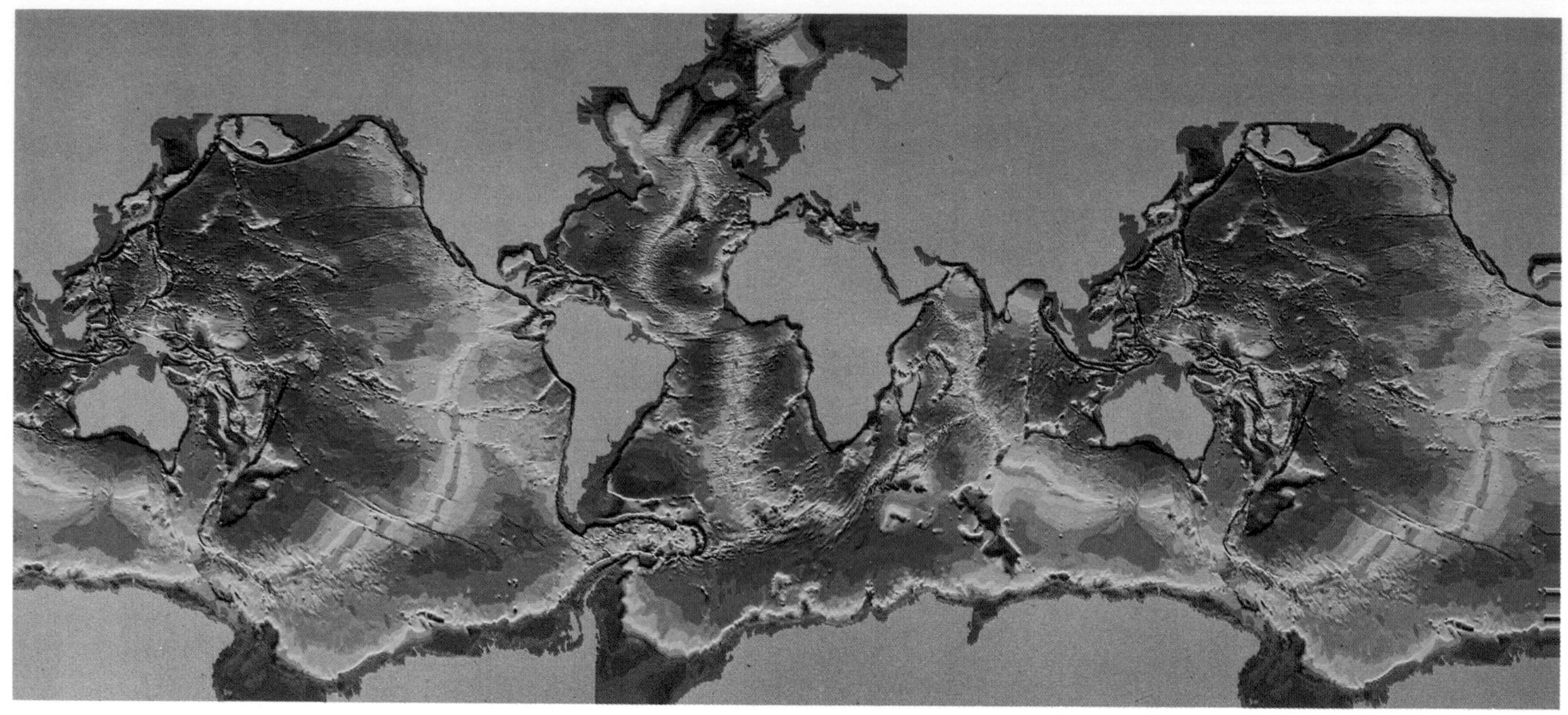

With oceans emptied, continents obscured, a new seafloor map reveals a region of ceaseless geological activity. Continents actually float on great moveable plates. Satellite data made this detailed view possible.

into the atmosphere. We believe that a sizeable fraction of this was quickly converted, via simple chemical reactions, to methane and ammonia. The earliest permanent atmosphere, then, was very different from that of today. The primary components of our atmosphere are nitrogen (80 percent) and oxygen (20 percent), with only small amounts of carbon dioxide and water vapor and no methane or ammonia to speak of. What caused this change? The appearance of living organisms contributed greatly to the transformation.

Up to this point we have discussed the evolution of the solar system in purely physical terms. Inert chemical interactions coupled with the force of gravity account for a great deal in the most primitive environments. With Earth's atmosphere, however, we encounter an active system that requires a far more involved interpretation. The equation must include something new—the effects of life within the planetary environment. Nowhere else in the solar system—or in the universe, as far as we know—does such a condition apply.

Paleontologists and others speculate at length about the process by which life appeared, but for the moment it is sufficient to realize that when the Earth was about a billion years old the new ingredient was present. We postulate at that time the existence of primitive single-celled systems which we would one day grace with the title "living." Although we are not sure how they came to be, we know of their spread because of fossils in the Australian rocks.

For billions of years, these cells and their descendants, the primitive blue-green algae, floated in the world's oceans. They took in carbon dioxide and put out oxygen as a waste product. About two and a half billion years ago, this particular pollutant had reached such a high level that a massive turnover occurred in the atmosphere. The oxygen produced by the plants reacted chemically with the methane and ammonia in the atmosphere. This process resulted in an atmosphere made up almost completely of nitrogen (derived from the ammonia) with a small mixture of oxygen. The increase in the oxygen content to its present 20 percent may have taken place about 600 million years ago.

Though rather slow, this turnover in the atmosphere had some revolutionary conse-

quences. Some of the oxygen in the air, for instance, formed an ozone layer high in the atmosphere and blocked off ultraviolet radiation from the sun. Many established organisms perished, yet this basic alteration allowed life to emerge from the sea onto the land. More important, a drop in the carbon dioxide levels allowed some of the heat normally trapped by the earth's atmospheric blanket to escape, and cool the earth's surface by about 20°F.

This drop in temperature influenced life on our planet in important ways, especially since—as we believe—the sun has gradually become brighter since its birth. Its luminosity has probably increased by up to 20 percent during the past 4.5 billion years. Had the adjustment not occurred, all life might well have ended as the oceans evaporated. On the other hand, the world might have frozen over had the cooling been a little more severe.

The narrow margin of survival between fire and ice has been emphasized by a series of calculations carried out by Michael Hart in 1978. These figures trace the history of our planet from its initial condition of no atmosphere, through the volcanic stages and the great turnover, to the present. His computer output revealed an astonishing fact. There is a very narrow band around the sun in which a planet can avoid the twin catastrophes of freezing and overheating. Hart called this band the "continuously habitable zone" and Earth alone occupies this crucial space. Thus the location of our planet helps to explain why only Earth can sustain living creatures on its surface. By changing his computer program slightly, Hart could also examine the behavior of planets of hypothetical solar systems as they circle various types of stars.

Had Earth ranged just one percent farther away from the sun, Hart showed, its surface would have been frozen solid for the past two billion years. Similarly, had Earth orbited five percent closer to the sun, the oceans would have boiled. Our planet would resemble Venus. Then he found that had the radius of the Earth been 10 percent larger, so much carbon dioxide would have been emitted during the volcanic period that the atmosphere would have formed a blanket around the earth, trapping heat and raising the surface temperature above the boiling point of water. If the Earth's radius had been less than 94 percent of its actual value, the gravitational attraction would have been too small for the planet to develop an ozone layer. According to the model, life never would have emerged from the sea.

When he turned his computer to the question of the effect of our star—the sun—on the continuously habitable zone, Hart found an even more surprising fact. Had the sun's mass been less than 83 percent of what it is, the zone would have vanished completely! In other words, planets circling stars slightly smaller than the sun will either freeze or boil—there is no middle ground. And while stars larger than the sun support larger habitable zones, they also burn their fuel faster and thus possess lifetimes shorter than the immense spans apparently needed for the evolution of life. Thus, the dynamics of planetary atmospheres are such that stars of only one type—stars like the sun—can have planets in which life based on the element carbon can develop and survive over billions of years. Such stars belong to a type designated by the capital letter G.

On the Kola Peninsula, above the Arctic Circle in the Soviet Union, technicians drill the world's deepest hole, bringing up rock cores from depths of more than seven miles. The 27-story derrick building houses pipes used to extend a turbo-drill into the borehole. Firsthand evidence is gained of subterranean temperature, pressure, and materials. A hole three times as deep might barely puncture Earth's "skin" or rocky crust.

Day meets night as Earth rotates. The dividing line, corresponding to sunrise here, is called the terminator. Light from American cities sparkles as a pale halo of the aurora borealis pulses across mid-Canada, sweeps east of Greenland and west toward Alaska. Our Earth rotates from west to east at 1,000 miles an hour—somewhat less than the speed of the Concorde at full altitude. The planet revolves around the sun at more than 1,000 miles a minute.

Hart's calculations explain why Earth is so different from the other planets in the solar system. While all of our neighbors circle a G-type star, Earth is the only one of just the right size and just the right distance from that star to meet all the requirements for the survival of life on its surface. Our home planet is a very remarkable place indeed!

The Evolution of Life

Few questions are more fundamental than that of how life came to exist here. How was it possible for a collection of rocks and volcanic gases to give rise to something as complex as the human brain? Only within the last 30 years have we been able to fit together a few pieces of this puzzle. Many gaps in our knowledge remain. Nevertheless, the general outline of the history of life on our planet is finally unfolding.

The chemical basis for all life on the earth is the interaction between carbon atoms. The electrons in each atom are arranged so that there are four in the outer orbit. When two carbon atoms approach each other, they begin to share a pair of outer electrons—one from each atom. This sharing creates a bond that holds the atoms together. The remaining electrons belonging to the atoms in the chain can be shared with other atoms like hydrogen. Carbon chains form the basis for all living matter on earth, from the simplest amino acid to incredibly complex molecules like DNA.

The simplest carbon chains—the ones that form the basic building blocks for more complex organic molecules that make up proteins—are called amino acids. All told, there are more than 100 amino acids to be found in living systems on earth, though just over 20 are required for adequate human nutrition.

One might ask, then, whether it is possible to assemble some of these chemical building blocks of life from ingredients of the primitive atmosphere. This question was answered in 1953 by Harold Urey and Stanley Miller at the University of Chicago. They took a flask containing likely materials and ran some electric sparks through it. This, they argued, would simulate the lightning in the Earth's early atmosphere. After a few days, the fluid they collected began to turn a dark brown, and analysis revealed the presence of amino acids.

Since that time, amino acids have been produced using ultraviolet radiation instead of an electrical discharge. Different chemical mixtures for simulating the early atmosphere have also been tried. In fact, during the last 30 years chemists working on the origins of life have been able to produce quite complex carbon chains using improved versions of the Urey-Miller experiment. Cyril Ponnamperuma at the University of Maryland has been able to derive the complex building blocks of DNA in this way.

If we take the rate of amino acid production from these experiments and extrapolate to the early Earth, we find that the building blocks of life would be created in the atmosphere at the rate of about a ton per second. At this rate, the amino acids raining down on the ocean would have produced a one percent solution in roughly 200,000 years—a mere blink of an eye on the geological time scale. Scientists refer to this mixture of organic matter and water in the early ocean as the "primordial soup."

It seems, then, easy to account for the accumulation of the basic building blocks of life very early in the history of the earth. Nature seems bent on producing such simple molecules. Indeed, amino acids are routinely found in meteorites. The problem comes in the next step—the joining together of these building blocks into what we call life, a system capable of its own development and reproduction.

In the early part of this century, people used to talk about finding the "missing link" in evolution, by which they meant the link between man and ape. Now that the evolutionary tree of *Homo sapiens* has been worked out in some detail, however, I think it would be much more appropriate to apply the term "missing link" to the gap between amino acids and the first living cell. How did that cell emerge? What physical processes shaped its creation? How did the laws of chemistry and physics join to produce a biological organism?

These questions touch on the very heart of the problem of life itself. And over the past few decades, scientists have come to understand some of life's basic requirements. A cell needs three different chemical constituents: proteins, to carry out the biochemical functions; nucleic acids (RNA and DNA) to pass on genetic information to the next generation; and lipids (fats) to form a membrane to protect the interior of the cell from its environment. The problem of how the simple molecules one might expect to find in the primordial soup could organize themselves into a functioning cell is the central question faced today by researchers who probe the origins of life.

There are some fascinating experiments that seem to indicate that this transformation may not be as difficult to accomplish as you might think. At the University of California at Davis, for example, David Deamer has found that lipids can be assembled from simple precursor molecules in the primordial soup. Furthermore, if he alternately dries the molecules and washes them with a solution containing DNA—a situation you might expect to find in early tidal pools—the membranes tend to wrap themselves around the DNA, forming what Deamer calls "protocells." Other scientists have investigated the way in which primitive chemicals interact when they are spread onto the surface of certain clays and then subjected to alternate heating and wetting. It turns out that quite complex molecules can be built up in this way in a matter of weeks—molecules that might then be incorporated into cells. It seems that the searchers for the first cell are in the position of someone trying to assemble a watch—they have the parts and are beginning to understand how they fit together into a complex system. At the moment, however, no one has managed to assemble life in the laboratory.

In any case, once the first cell came into existence in a tidal pool somewhere along the ocean border, we can guess what followed. The original cell would have taken chemicals from the pool to produce new cells like itself. Some of these cells would eventually have been washed out into the ocean, where they would have found a perfect environment for reproduction—plenty of building materials in the broth and no predators. It would not have taken long (geologically speaking) for the descendants of that first cell to fill the oceans. And, of course, the processes by which such cells occur may be unexceptional. There may well have been more than one tidal pool where the cells developed, and thus more than one center of origin and dispersal. Given the rate at which knowledge is accumulating about the missing link in the evolutionary chain, it is not too optimistic to think that we will know about the origin of that first cell within this generation.

The Future of the Earth

Having traced the evolution of our planet from its beginnings to the present, it is only natural to ask what the future may hold. Oddly enough, once again we seem to have reached a point in evolutionary history when the activities of living things may put the planet in danger. Two and a half billion years ago blue-green algae were abundant and through their photosynthetic activity large amounts of oxygen were introduced into the primitive atmosphere.

Today, human beings are the most dangerous creatures of all. The greatest hazards fall into two categories; the first is a reality

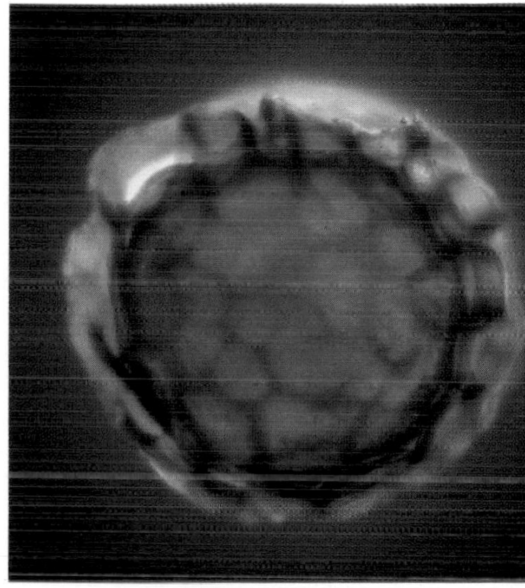

Like a tiny world, though hollow, the opalized spore of a plant symbolizes the many contributions of living things to the Earth. These include the formation of limestone from ancient corals and shellfish to the development of the atmosphere through the metabolic processes of plants.

Vincent van Gogh created his enthralling "The Starry Night" in 1889 near the end of his tormented life. Here he visualizes the heavens as a source of pent-up energy and perhaps tries to bring them into an aesthetic atonement with himself and his idyllic surroundings near Arles in southern France.

and the second a possibility. They are, respectively, the environmental effects that follow the overuse of resources, and the threat of nuclear war. Either of these hazards could make the earth a much less hospitable place for life, and might create environmental changes as great as those that occurred during several geological periods in which mass extinctions occurred.

To take one example of the danger, consider the widespread burning of fossil fuels like gasoline and coal. One outcome of this activity is an increase in the amount of carbon dioxide in the atmosphere—an increase that has been well documented over the past few decades. Some doomsday scenarios, such as those predicting the melting of the polar ice caps and the conversion of the Earth into a planet like Venus, are undoubtedly overblown. It is true nevertheless that most meteorological models predict an increase in the average temperature of the earth of several degrees by the end of the next century. Such a change is comparatively large, probably similar in magnitude to the drop in temperature accompanying the last great Ice Age. So it is logical to believe that human activity has the potential for causing drastic alterations in the Earth's climate.

Many scholars concern themselves with short-term solutions to these problems, and such work is extremely important. It is clear, however, that there is a basic conflict between an expanding technological civilization and the terrestrial environment. A small group of visionary scholars, led by physicist Gerard O'Neill of Princeton, have decided to look at this problem in a larger context, with some surprising results.

Back in 1969, O'Neill taught an introductory course in physics at Princeton. He took as his theme the question,"Is the surface of a planet really the right place for an expanding civilization?" Given the environmental problems that have plagued us in recent times, it's hardly surprising that the class answered this question in the negative. These young people suggested that industrial activities ought to be carried out in space, and that the surface of the Earth should be spared the ravages of further exploitation.

This statement seems less strange today than it did in 1969. We have, after all, seen numerous launches of the space shuttle, so the idea of large-scale movements of people and equipment no longer seems impossible. And, since the design of a permanent space station is now under serious study by NASA, the concept of permanent habitations in space no longer seems to belong to the realm of science fiction.

Both the nearby asteroids and the surface of the moon present opportunities for the acquisition of minerals. In addition, there is abundant free energy in space as sunlight, without clouds or nighttime darkness to lower the efficiency of the collection system. Space might, indeed, provide a useful environment for some of our industrial activities, especially as extraterrestrial mineral deposits come to light.

The presence of industry in space, of course, requires a place for permanent human dwellings. This is where the idea of the space colony comes into the picture. O'Neill and his co-workers have put together a design for a structure in space that would provide a pleasant home for a colony of 10,000 people.

The design calls for the construction of a doughnut-shaped ring about a mile across, with the habitable area being the "dough" in the doughnut. The ring would rotate once a minute, and this rotation would simulate gravity for the inhabitants. There would be plenty of room in such a structure for plants to recycle the oxygen in the air, and there are already technologies available for recycling such a colony's water.

In O'Neill's design, the material for the colony would be lifted from the surface of the moon by solar-powered devices known as mass drivers. Thus, the colony would be a true child of space—built with extraterrestrial materials and existing without dependence on Earth. Eventually, the colonies could produce generations of inhabitants who had never set foot on a planet.

And who knows—someday people may decide, or be forced, to install a propulsion device on a large colony. Once our descendants possess power enough for interstellar flight, the human race may finally set sail for the stars. Indeed, the human race might eventually provide the only space creatures to be found in our Galaxy.

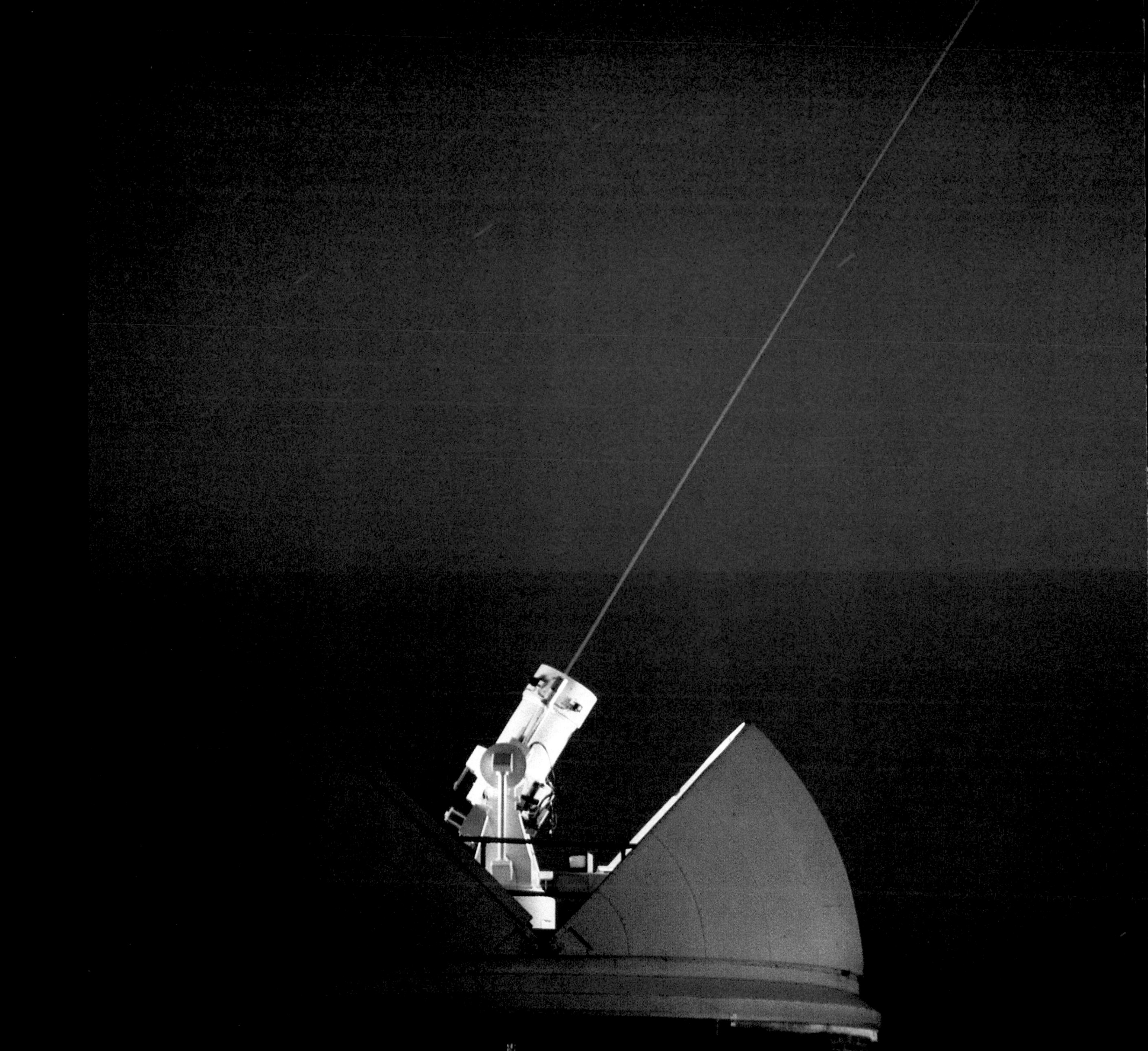

Open Questions

Though locked onto an orbiting satellite, a laser gun in the English countryside is no Star-Wars weapon. It and more powerful lasers make very accurate surveys—revealing the distance to the moon to within an inch, for instance. Such data help scientists map gravitational fields of the Earth-moon system. Above, our planet rises on the lunar horizon.

At first it may seem strange that after so much study there are still gaps in our understanding of the solar system. We expect, of course, that space exploration will bring with it an awareness of phenomena that will take some time to sort out—the braided rings of Saturn are a good example of this kind of thing. But in dealing with these newly discovered phenomena, we have the feeling that they are in a way peripheral to our basic understanding of the way things work. They are, to use a phrase common among engineers, the "bells and whistles" of the solar system. It is surely possible to understand the basic workings of the system even if we can't untangle an occasional complex phenomenon.

Other questions, such as those concerning the origin of the first cell, are more fundamental. Often, though, these problems have been studied for only a short time and scientists seem to be making progress.

Scientific passion, however, is thoroughly and generously invested in a third class of questions. These represent profound problems, ones we feel we ought to understand and that have been studied since the nineteenth century or earlier. Answers still seem to elude us.

Here we examine three of the great unsolved problems, and try to determine where we stand on each. First, where did the moon come from? Second, what exactly are the fusion reactions that drive the sun? Then, third, why does life on earth suffer episodic massive extinctions? A fourth concern is so basic and so elusive that we spend an entire chapter on it, asking, "Are we alone in the universe?"

The Origin of the Moon

Until the advent of modern astronomy, little thought was given to the question of the origin of the moon. Like the other heavenly bodies it was simply there. Once astrophysicists started talking about creative processes, however, interest in our satellite increased and was fed by the lunar landings.

Theories concerning the origin of the moon fall into three general classes. In fission theories, the moon is torn from the body of the Earth. In capture theories, the moon originates elsewhere and is drawn into its present orbit by the gravitational attraction of the planet. In simultaneous creation theories, the moon and Earth form near each other in space. In this latter case, the two bodies probably grew up together by attracting and sharing the same local materials within the large nebula that gave rise to the other protoplanets and the sun itself.

Each body of theory explains some of the features of the Earth-moon system, but each has drawbacks. In the capture theories, for instance, the low density of the moon can be understood because the moon formed in a different part of the solar system. On the other hand, calculations indicate that the capture of one large body by another is an extremely unlikely event.

In the mid-eighties, a variation on the capture theories gained some popularity among scientists. Called the Big Splash, it held that the moon formed after a large sphere hit the young planet and tumbled back into orbit. The impact itself broke material loose from the Earth, presumably some of it molten or hot. The alien object then attracted the loose material to itself and emerged in much its present size through the fusion of local and foreign substances. Following closely upon this theory's reemergence in 1984 (it had been around for a long time, something of a Cinderella) some criticisms arose. Calculations suggest that such a celestial sideswipe could not loosen enough material and thrust it into orbit to make the moon by this process.

Nearly close enough to touch, our newborn moon may have almost grazed the mountaintops some billions of years ago, above. Thus, according to some theorists, our moon could have stirred gargantuan tides to batter the land. As evidence of such an encounter, scientists reveal that the moon moves away from Earth at more than an inch a year. Vigorous tides of long ago may have helped to stir the chemical cauldron from whence life emerged upon our planet. Today's tides help maintain Earth's life.

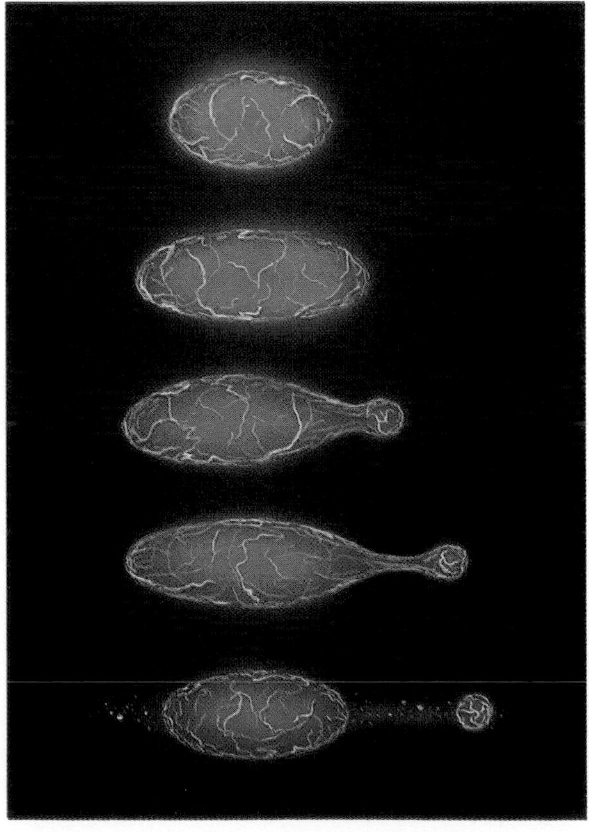

A molten Earth may have flattened before giving birth to the moon, according to a theory depicted at left. Clinging to Earth by a slender umbilical, the moon-to-be finally snaps the cord and flies into orbit. Such an origin could explain the low density of moon rock. A recently revived theory says that a body from afar may have struck our planet, gaining mass and bouncing back into orbit, at far left.

The question of the moon's origin also involves the gravitational history of the Earth-moon system. We all know about the tides that are raised in our oceans by the moon and, to a lesser extent, the sun.

Tides have two important effects on the system. First, the sloshing of water in the oceans dissipates energy, slowing down the rotation of the Earth and increasing the length of the day. Indeed, the record of the increasing length of the day can be read in the fossil remains of corals, tiny animals that added a small growth ring on their shells each day. These markings are analogous to the annual growth rings in trees. And by counting the number of daily rings contained within the larger annual rings, paleontologists can deduce the length of the day at the time the coral was alive. For example, 350 million years ago during the Devonian period, a day had only 22 hours.

In addition, the tides on Earth influence the moon's orbit. As they move around the globe, the tides create a considerable bulge in the planet's general profile. The moving tidal bulge exerts a small extra force on the moon, one that pumps energy into its motion. This, in turn, pushes the moon away from the Earth.

In a sense, we see a feedback mechanism at work here. The moon helps to raise a tidal bulge. In turn, the bulge affects the moon, causing it to recede from the Earth. The slowing down of the Earth's rotation and the recession of the moon, then, are intimately linked. Since the Apollo program, when astronauts planted laser reflectors on the lunar surface, it has been possible to measure the distance to the moon with high accuracy. Presently, our satellite recedes from us by three centimeters a year. The standard tidal theory holds that the moon was closer to the Earth in the past than it is now. Indeed it indicates that only two billion years ago the moon was touching the Earth.

Calculations like these are almost always tricky. We have a good idea that the rate of recession depends on the way the tides interact with the Earth's oceans, and that this, in turn, depends on the actual shape of the oceans. The theory of plate tectonics tells us that the oceans have not always been the way they are now, and hence casts considerable doubt on the standard tidal calculation. To further complicate the problem, recent research suggests that the solar wind and other periodical influences of the sun can alter the length of day and thus affect the rhythm of the Earth's waltz with the moon.

In 1982, Kirk Hansen of the University of Chicago carried out a calculation relevant to the question of the Earth-moon system. He put the changing length of day into his computer and concluded that the recession has never been faster than it is today and that the supposed collision two billion years ago may very well have been the result of an oversimplified assumption.

In the same vein, it should be pointed out that the fact of similar materials in the moon and in the Earth does not necessarily mean that they have a common origin, as assumed in fission theories. This point was brought home in a lighthearted way by scientists investigating lunar materials brought back by the Apollo astronauts. They discovered that seismic waves move through moon rock and various samples of cheese at about the same rate. They travel through rocks of the Earth's crust at quite a different rate.

The Solar Neutrino Problem

For well over a century, scientists have debated the question of the source of the sun's energy. With the discovery of atomic energy and the working out of the physics of the hydrogen-fusion reaction, scientists regarded this question as solved. The sun was powered by nuclear reactions at its core, and we knew just about everything there was to know about the way those reactions worked. By common consent, the subject dropped and everyone turned to newer and more exciting fields of research.

This may not have been such a good idea. In the early sixties, Raymond Davis, Jr., of the Brookhaven National Laboratory began to think about ways of looking into the center of the sun to see the fusion reactions directly. A nuclear chemist, he was well aware that many relativistic particles are produced within the sun. Among these is the neutrino. A highly energetic entity with little or no mass, it can pass through large amounts of material at the speed of light. Some ener-

Creating its own bull's-eye, an asteriod may have smashed into Earth, as envisioned by Adolf Schaller. Dinosaurs and other Mesozoic creatures could have perished in what might be called a "Fallout Winter." Dust clouds may have filled the air, cutting out the life-giving light. Phobos, below, may be a captured asteroid, now orbiting Mars as the innermost of its two moons.

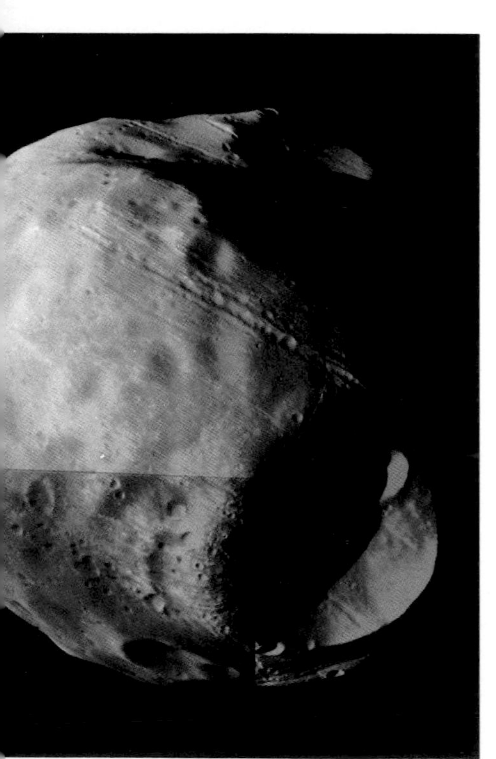

getic particles—including those of light—can remain inside the sun for hundreds of thousands of years as they work their way from the core to the surface. Though also generated through the sun's nuclear reactions, neutrinos can emerge in a mere 2.3 seconds.

By catching and counting these particular particles, we can have a window into the workings of the solar core. Davis reasoned that if we could design an experiment to detect them, then we could test the standard model of the sun—the particular theory that is most satisfying to the most scientists.

Of course, the very property that makes neutrinos so potentially useful as a probe of the sun's interior makes them very difficult to catch in any measuring apparatus. After all, if we are to know that a neutrino has come our way, we need to see some effect of its presence on other matter. But if a neutrino can escape from the sun without interacting with any of the materials there, it is unlikely to start leaving indications of its passage within a relatively minuscule experimental setup on the earth.

Consider, for example, the following: right now, as you read these words, neutrinos from the sun are passing through your body at the rate of trillions per second. This has been going on ever since you were born, and will continue for the rest of your life. It doesn't even matter if it's night, with the entire planet between you and the sun, because neutrinos can pass quite easily through the solid sphere! If you think of your body as a neutrino detector, you may ask how often one of them will actually interact with one of your atoms. The answer is about once every year. So the scientist is caught on the horns of a dilemma—on the one hand, any particle that interacts easily with matter (and is therefore easy to detect) will never escape the sun before it has been altered. On the other hand, the neutrino interacts so seldom that it can leave unscathed. For this same reason, it is very difficult to catch a neutrino when it reaches the earth. Neutrinos *can* be detected in the laboratory by sending billions of them down the beam of an accelerator in the hopes that one will hit a target—but one rarely does.

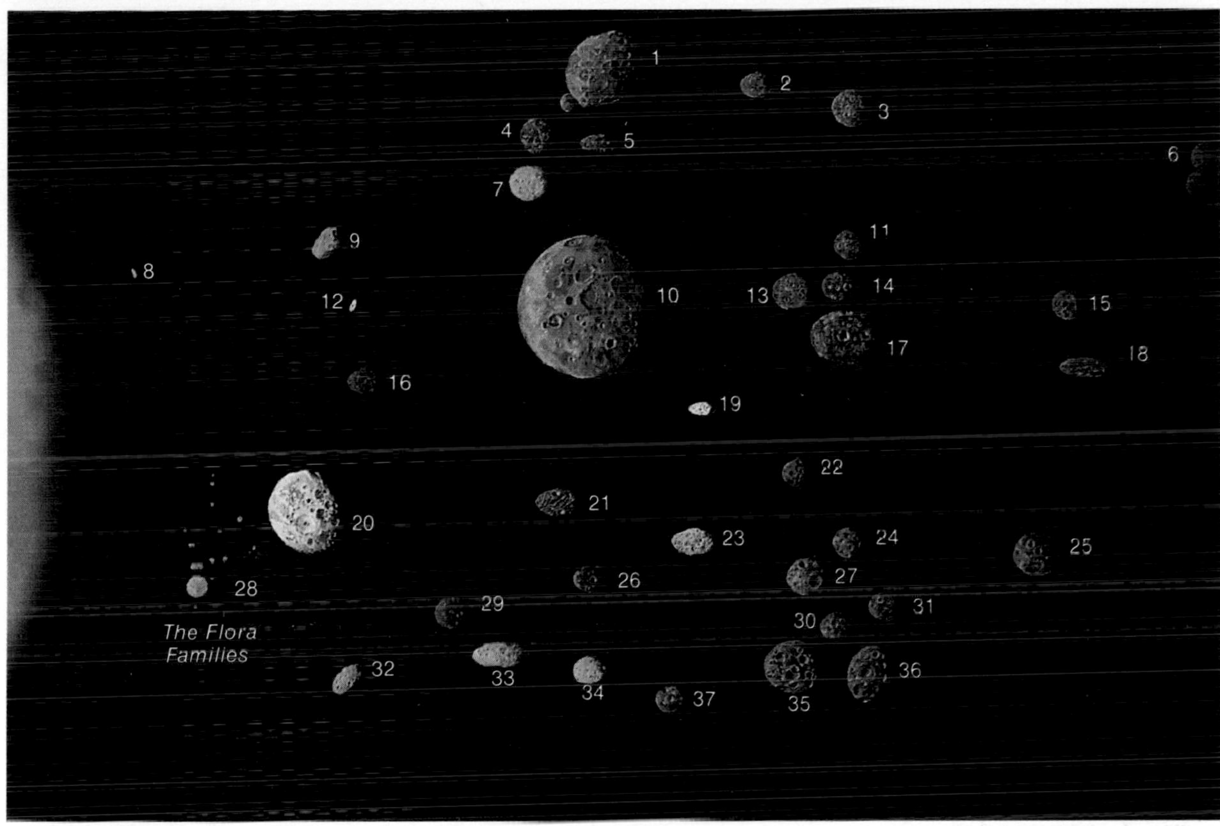

All 33 asteroids with diameters more than 200 kilometers appear in Andrew Chaikin's artwork at left. The Flores asteroids, with diameters greater than 15 kilometers, appear near the limb of Mars. The planet is shown to indicate scale.

1. Pallas
2. Winchester
3. Euphrosyne
4. Bamberga
5. Daphne
6. Hektor
7. Juno
8. Eros
9. Iris
10. Ceres
11. Bettina
12. Nysa
13. Patientia
14. Themis
15. Hermione
16. Fortuna
17. Hygiea
18. Camilla
19. Dembowska
20. Vesta
21. Eugenia
22. Diotima
23. Psyche
24. Loreley
25. Cybele
26. Thisbe
27. Europa
28. Flora
29. Egeria
30. Ursula
31. Alauda
32. Hebe
33. Eunomia
34. Herculina
35. Interamnia
36. Davida
37. Siegena

The heart of the experiment designed by Davis is a giant tank of perchloroethylene (ordinary dry-cleaning fluid) located 4,800 feet underground in the Homestake gold mine in Lead, South Dakota. He selected such a deep neutrino target to avoid the effects of especially energetic cosmic rays.

When a neutrino from the sun hits a chlorine atom in the cleaning fluid, the chlorine changes into an atom of argon. After a while, we would be able to "detect" the neutrinos by counting the atoms of argon they leave behind in the cleaning fluid. These atoms would be "visible" because the argon produced is a radioactive isotope. Thus its presence can be monitored in much the same way that radioactive tracers are detected in medical diagnosis. Even so, finding a needle in a haystack would be simple compared with detecting fewer than 100 argon atoms in 10 railroad cars full of cleaning fluid, the challenge Davis faced.

According to the theories of the solar interior prevalent in the mid-sixties, there should have been up to 10 atomic transformations a day in the tank. When the experiment was turned on in 1965, however, astronomers received a major shock—only one interaction every two days instead of the expected 20.

Some theoreticians began revising their predicted values downwards, while some experimentalists were giving Davis' apparatus a critical going over. In a display of the kind of cooperative spirit that is a hallmark of good science, Davis supplied unlimited access to his apparatus and analytical programs, even to critics who were trying to find flaws. After 15 years of work, the result is easy to summarize: only a fraction of the expected number of neutrinos was being detected, even using the lowest possible prediction of the revised theories.

Once the reality of the data was accepted, the attention of the scientific community turned toward explaining the effect. The general procedure has been for each group involved to try to pin the blame on someone else. The astronomers say the nuclear physicists are wrong about reaction rates, the nuclear physicists say the particle people don't really understand what happens to neutrinos

Near the scene of a Siberian cataclysm, Soviet scientist Leonid A. Kulik studies the locale of a stupendous blast from the summer of 1908. A huge meteorite may have disintegrated here, or perhaps the core of a comet. Millions of trees were blown down, their trunks pointing away from the explosion site. Heat was felt 40 miles away.

between the sun and the Earth, and the particle physicists say the astronomers don't understand the solar interior as well as they say they do. There have been so many nonsolutions to the problem proposed during the last decade that there is little point in listing them all. My sentimental favorite is the suggestion that a black hole occupies the center of the sun, quietly eating away at the solar interior. In this scheme, we see fewer neutrinos because a good part of the fusion region has disappeared.

At the moment, the most popular explanation of the solar neutrino problem has to do with the nature of the neutrinos themselves. Here we must evoke the so-called Grand Unification Theories, or GUTs, that revolutionized the physics of atomic and subatomic particles in the late seventies. We will learn more of this later. Suffice it to say that some versions of these theories predict that the neutrino has some mass. Earlier theories held that the neutrinos possessed zero mass.

Let us avoid the details of this prediction. If it is true that neutrinos have a bit of mass, then those that leave the sun will indeed be liable to change before they reach the Earth. By the time a group of neutrinos reaches us, according to the revised model, only one in three will be able to transmute a chlorine atom into an isotope of argon. Thus the puzzle would be solved.

There have been many equally plausible explanations in the past, and none has worked. And the evidence that the neutrino has a mass rests on a few data points in a Russian experiment whose interpretation is very much open to question. At this time it is surely prudent to adopt a wait-and-see attitude.

While Davis' tank of chlorine continues to monitor neutrinos a mile underground in the Black Hills, scientists around the world are busily planning the next generation of experiments in hopes of solving what has become known as the "solar neutrino problem." The main emphasis in this work is not to repeat the chlorine experiment; it is generally conceded that the results there are correct. Consequently, experimental thinking has turned toward measurements which

probe other parts of the fusion reaction.

The idea is this: because it takes a rather large amount of energy to convert chlorine into argon, only neutrinos from a relatively rare branch of the fusion reaction can be detected in a tank of cleaning fluid. Technically, atoms of gallium would make a much better target for a solar neutrino experiment. With up to 50 tons of the stuff, a few years' running time would tell us unequivocally if our ideas about the power source of our sun need to be revised.

This situation has turned neutrino physicists into experts on metallurgy. I remember a fascinating dinner during which Ray Davis spent hours explaining the difficulties of acquiring gallium to faculty members at the University of Virginia. It is expensive. Attempts to obtain a loan of gallium have been unsuccessful, even though, as one physicist pointed out, "We only want to use a few thousand atoms." The next generation of solar neutrino experiments, therefore, will probably not be carried out in the United States. Requisite amounts of gallium have already been assembled in the Soviet Union, and experiments have reached the advanced prototype stage in West Germany.

If from all these words you gain the impression that science progresses through questioning even the most reliable and popular theories, then you have penetrated rather close to the heart of science and the scientific method.

Extinctions

Paleontologists have long been aware of abrupt changes in the kinds of plants and animals found on the earth. The fossil record is full of species that lasted for a long time and then disappeared suddenly, to be replaced by entirely new species. The most spectacular as well as the most familiar of these were the dinosaurs, whose sudden disappearance some 65 million years ago signaled the end of what geologists call the Cretaceous period. For almost 200 million years these giant reptiles had been the dominant life form on earth, and then in the blink of an eye (geologically speaking) they vanished. Perhaps less well known is the fact that while the dinosaurs were disappearing,

Cloaked in mystery, the bright Tunguska blast rocks a remote corner of Asia. Don Davis' artwork captures the drama of an episode which continues to puzzle scientists. In recent years, tiny metallic spherules have been recovered from the site, further evidence of an extraterrestrial source for the great explosion.

Slanting rays tint the circular ramparts of Australia's Wolf Creek meteor crater. Johnny Hart's cartoon character, opposite, proposes a theory soon to be shattered.

fully 70 percent of all living species perished along with them. For some species, such as ocean plankton, the extinction rate exceeded 90 percent. A similar catastrophic extinction occurred at the end of the Permian period, 250 million years ago. What could cause these sudden, large-scale obliterations of living creatures?

Although there have been many attempts to explain these events, the first real breakthrough occurred in 1980 when a group of scientists at the University of California at Berkeley published a rather surprising study. The group was headed by the father-and-son team of Luis Alvarez, a particle physicist who had won the Nobel Prize in physics in 1968, and Walter Alvarez, professor of geology at Berkeley.

They noted that the constant rain of small meteorites on the earth could be expected to have deposited a steady stream of extraterrestrial material in the earth's atmosphere. This material would not have gone through the differentiation (sorting out or classifying according to density) that took place on earth, so it could be expected to contain relatively high levels of heavy elements compared with its earthly counterparts. Their thought was that by monitoring these heavy elements of interesting geological formations, they could decide how long it took the formations to be created.

For various technical reasons they chose to search for the element iridium, a heavy metal akin to platinum. Working at a site in Italy, they started well below the layer of clay that marked the boundary between Cretaceous and Tertiary periods. They took samples as they came up through (and past) the layer. The result was astonishing. The concentration of iridium in this geological horizon was 30 times greater than in the limestone stratum immediately above as well as in the one below it.

The only way to explain the Alvarez result and the studies that followed is to assume that just as the dinosaurs were meeting their doom, a great deal of extraterrestrial material entered earth's atmosphere. For example, we might have been hit by an errant asteroid or comet. The Berkeley group accepted this explanation, and suggested that the great extinction at the end of the Cretaceous was caused, in fact, by the impact on the earth of an asteroid measuring about six miles across.

In a version proposed in the early eighties, the extinction scenario goes like this: the asteroid comes streaking toward the Earth, creating a giant crater upon impact. It really doesn't matter if it lands in the ocean or on land, it's moving so fast that the few miles of water in the ocean won't slow it considerably. So great is the energy of the collision that huge amounts of dust and pulverized rock are thrown into the air. These particles are actually catapulted into ballistic trajectories—they leave the atmosphere and then fall back. In a matter of hours after the collision, then, the entire atmosphere is saturated with the dust cloud raised by the asteroid.

It is relatively easy for scientists who have studied the theory of cratering to estimate the length of time the skies would remain dark after a major asteroid collision—about three months. The scenario proposed by the Berkeley group, then, is quite simple: the asteroid hit, the lights went out, and living things on earth began to die. The first to go would have been the plants and ocean dwellers like plankton, followed by herbivores and then by carnivores. When the air cleared and the sunlight once again reached the surface, the dinosaurs (and many other types of plants and animals) were gone, leaving the way clear for the development of mammals and, eventually, for human beings.

The reception accorded the Berkeley proposal was mixed, to say the least. It is hard to argue against the reality of the asteroid impact. At last count, the iridium anomaly had been detected in more than 50 different places on the earth's surface, including both oceanic and continental sites. In addition, a number of other heavy metals similar to iridium have been seen in the boundary layer, strengthening the case for its extraterrestrial origin. The argument, instead, centered on whether the impact actually caused the extinction, or whether it just happened to occur at the same time.

A strong piece of evidence on this point came from an unexpected source. For over a decade, paleontologist J. John Sepkoski at the University of Chicago had been collecting a unique record of the appearance and disappearance of fossil marine organisms. Literally thousands of life forms, now extinct, found their way into his accounts. His colleague at Chicago, David Raup, had long been interested in the question of whether or not it was possible to discern long-term patterns in the history of life on earth. Together they analyzed the accumulated data and found a rather amazing fact. The great extinction at the end of the Cretaceous was not a unique event in history. Over the last 250 million years, massive extinctions have occurred a dozen times. Furthermore, waves of extinction seem to come regularly—every 26 million years.

Publication of these results rocked the scientific world. For almost a century the doctrine of gradualism had reigned in the fields of earth science and paleontology. Now a claim emerged that sudden, catastrophic incidents have been responsible for changing the patterns of terrestrial life, and like the seasons these changes were a regularly recurring feature of our past. As of the mid-eighties a storm raged over the question of whether the claim made by Raup and Sepkoski is really substantiated by the fossil records.

You can get some flavor of the debate by noting two points that are frequently raised. First, one may ask if the fossil record fairly represents all the organisms that were alive at a given time. Second, we might question the accuracy of the dates attached to each extinction.

On the first point, Sepkoski says, "The fossil record is a better sample of past life than the Nielsen TV survey, but it is far from a complete census." On the second point, there is no question that establishing the dates of the geological formations in which fossils are found is often a difficult task, and dates for a given formation can often differ by 10 percent (or much more). But 10 percent of 250 million years, the length of time covered by the data base used, is 25 million years—a period as long as the time between successive extinctions. It is difficult to establish the regularity of a sequence of events when the time at which each event occurs could vary by such an appreciable amount. Furthermore, British and American geological societies have established different time scales for the documentation of events in the fossil record. It will probably be some time before the Raup and Sepkoski conclusion is as firmly established as that of the asteroid impact.

Meanwhile, back in Berkeley, Walter Alvarez and astronomer Richard Muller were thinking very seriously about the idea of extinctions occurring every 26 million years. If, as they believed, the extinction at the end of the Cretaceous was caused by the collision of an object with the Earth, then it was reasonable to suppose that the other extinctions might have a similar cause.

To test this idea, they gathered data on known large craters on earth. Taking those craters whose dates had been well determined by geological means, they plotted the dates of the craters as a function of time. And much to their surprise, they found that the craters exhibited the same 26-million-

year cycle as the extinctions! The result, while suggestive, has to be taken with a grain of salt because of the small numbers of old craters available for study.

Assuming that the data are correct, one theoretical problem remains. This is to identify the astronomical processes that produce the impacts on such a regular basis. So far, two theories have been suggested, and I expect there will be more. In both theories, the material that collides with Earth comes from the Oort cloud, a region beyond Pluto suspected of harboring gases that freeze and condense into comets.

One group of astronomers builds on the idea that the sun passes through the galactic plane about every 26 million years. In their hypothesis, the solar system emerges from the crowded part of the Galaxy like a porpoise leaping out of the sea. We later return to and re-enter the galactic plane. The plane itself is full of dust and loose debris, and it is not too hard to imagine this material disturbing the Oort cloud and sending comets into the inner solar system.

In these theories the extraterrestrial material can be either loose fragments in our dusty galactic plane or bodies in the solar system whose orbits are perturbed by collisions. The latter is considered more likely, since detailed study of the material at the Cretaceous boundary indicates it originated in the solar system. One of the problems with this theory is that astronomers believe the sun last crossed the plane of our Milky Way five million years ago, while the last extinction occurred 11 million years ago. As of early 1985, this approach seemed to be falling out of favor.

An entirely different explanation involves the possible existence of a companion star to the sun. This star has been given a variety of names. The Berkeley astronomers who first published the hypothesis named it "Nemesis," and headline writers promptly labeled it the "Death Star," but Walter Alvarez prefers the more neutral "Companion Star." Whatever name we assign to it, the star itself is supposed to revolve around the sun in a markedly elliptical orbit, as do long-period comets. The theory requires that it encounter the Oort cloud every 26 million years. Furthermore, this small and dim sun could

perturb the orbits of comets in the cloud and send them into the solar system. Some could be expected to strike Earth, giving rise to the cratering and periodic extinctions we have discussed.

As soon as the Death Star hypothesis was published, a massive sky search began. Because the star has never been seen, we can deduce that it must be very faint. The usual way to detect such a hypothetical object is to compare photographs of star fields taken at different times and see if anything has moved. In this case, it is difficult to implement this procedure because the Death Star (assuming that it exists) would now be at its greatest distance from the sun and hence, by Kepler's laws, moving very slowly.

We should note that fully two thirds of the stars in the sky belong to double-star systems, so it would not be unusual for our sun to possess a companion.

At present, the whole question of species extinction is the subject of intense work in fields from astronomy to paleontology. Who knows what the next few years of search and research will bring?

Hinting at past and future catastrophes, an eerie pall cloaks the firmament as the moon masks the sun during an eclipse, opposite. Sun disk at left reveals its oscillations, as detected by the Fourier tachometer—a device for detecting tiny changes in speed of our star's moving surface. Polish stamp highlights the sun-Earth-moon system, a gravitational unit within the greater solar system.

Are We Alone?

Few things grip the mind as forcefully as the question of intelligent life elsewhere in the universe. And the implications of a positive response to the question are as stupendous—if not more so—as those of a negative answer. In September 1959 the first step was taken toward finding a realistic answer. The prestigious British journal *Nature* published an exchange between two well-known physicists, Giuseppe Cocconi and Philip Morrison. They speculated that the new window opened in the sky by radio astronomers would allow us not only to learn more about the physical objects in the universe, but to detect signals sent by other civilizations in our Galaxy as well. In other words, for the first time the human race had the technical expertise to listen for anyone out there broadcasting. At the same time a project was underway at the National Radio Astronomy Observatory in Green Bank, West Virginia, to search for such broadcasts. It was based on the same reasoning.

In response to such thoughts a small conference convened at Green Bank in November 1961. Eleven scientists laid the intellectual foundation for subsequent efforts in this field. Their work is generally expressed in a mathematical statement called the Drake equation, which allows us to make a reasonable estimate of the number of extraterrestrial civilizations that might try to communicate with each other at any given time. To do this, the equation lays out in logical form the various factors involved in the development of a civilization that would send the kind of signals we can receive. If we plug in the right numbers we will obtain a useful answer. The Drake equation and a key to its terms appear on page 171.

The first three terms have to do with the formation and evolution of stars and planets. These processes involve the laws of physics and chemistry, and we can apply our knowledge of these areas to determine the terms with fair accuracy. The next two terms involve the development of life and intelligence. Here, the laws of biology and evolution apply and, despite important gaps in our knowledge, we can still assign some of the probabilities with confidence.

The final two terms of the Drake equation involve the development of technology, the desire to communicate, and the length of time that a civilization will attempt to communicate. These take us onto very shaky ground indeed, and no one believes that we can predict these numbers with any degree of confidence.

Typically, investigators assign numbers to the various factors in the Drake equation and draw conclusions. But to what end? One "communication" from the stars would solve the problem once and for all, but we may have to wait an eternity to find one. For myself, I would suggest that we—humanity—are indeed alone, the product of very special circumstances. Our astronauts may be the only extraterrestrials.

Comments by Frank Drake:
The development of intelligent, technical civilizations in a multitude of places seems an expected process in the Galaxy's evolution. Everything we have learned about the evolution of stars, the formation of planetary systems, the origins of life, and the course of evolution has indicated that what took place in our solar system is the result of completely normal phenomena in the universe. Our existence, in other words, did not require any special, freak circumstances. [In the scientist's jargon, this idea is called the principle of mediocrity.] Recognizing this, we look at the striking pace at which technology, especially space technology, has been advancing, and wonder, is it now likely that soon we will embark on the coloniza-

Editor's Note: *The author has invited two distinguished colleagues to join him in a discussion of SETI (Search for Extra-Terrestrial Intelligence). Frank D. Drake is Dean of Natural Sciences and Professor of Astronomy and Astrophysics of the University of California at Santa Cruz. Robert T. Rood is Professor of Astronomy at the University of Virginia's campus in Charlottesville.*

Light is life and it glows from ages past in amber—here a termite's tomb. Nature's plastic, amber is a fossil resin. A laboratory carboy holds artificial DNA, at right. In life, this giant molecule transmits genetic traits. The presence of complex organic chemicals attests to ages of evolutionary development on earth.

tion of space? I refer not just to the colonization of our solar system, but of other stellar systems. If so, it is easily calculated that a civilization which lives on a time scale like ours could well colonize every star in our Galaxy in less than 100 million years, or in less than one percent of the age of the Milky Way.

If this is so, and there are also many other civilizations in space, why have no colonists from other worlds come to Earth long ago? Could it be that we are the first or most advanced technical society in the Milky Way? Perhaps this should give us a sense of superiority. But if true, our searches for other civilizations are bound to fail.

Now this lack of definitive evidence of

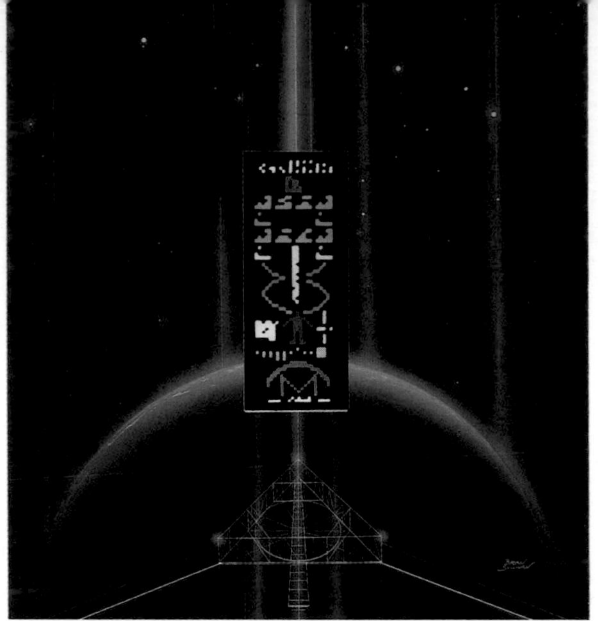

Great antenna-ear at Arecibo, Puerto Rico, most often listens for radio noise from the stars. But in 1974 it beamed a message, at left. Scientists intended the binary code to be cracked by an alien intelligence in the Great Cluster of Hercules, 21,000 light-years away. In 42,000 years, an answer may come.

extraterrestrial visitors provides us with an impressive and powerful argument. For it requires that only one civilization embark on massive interstellar colonization for *them* to have come to us by now. For there to be other civilizations in space to find through radio searches, for instance, it must be the case that *no* civilization in galactic history has set out to colonize all the habitable planets. To justify a large effort in searching for other stars as we are now doing, we would do well to discover a compelling reason why the colonization of the Milky Way has been avoided to date. I think there are some strong arguments as to why interstellar colonization has not been attempted by distant civilizations.

A host of reasons has been offered. Some suggest that hazards in interstellar space might make colonization missions just too dangerous. For example, even small meteoroids might collide at great speed with spaceships and cause massive damage. It has been suggested, also, that interstellar colonization may be occurring, but along a random walk rather than directed radially—ever outward from a center. If so, the colonists would not have arrived here yet, though we might expect them to come out of the sky any day now!

Still another idea: perhaps the Earth has somehow been declared a "zoo!" We are some kind of cosmic nature preserve, to be left untouched by advanced worlds so that their creatures may gain knowledge and enjoyment by observing us struggle along in our primitive ways. This implies that somewhere in the sky observers quietly watch us, as they rest peacefully in their equivalent of tourist buses!

Again, they may have visited our solar system, but have chosen to colonize our asteroids, rather than Earth. We sense, however, that if an advanced civilization were conducting a major technological project in the asteroids, we would have seen some signs of this activity by now; explosions, flashes of light, radio transmissions. There have been no such signs.

To me, the strongest argument against interstellar colonization is simply that it costs too much. If your resources are limited—and I submit that all creatures have limited resources—you can create far better living space in your own planetary system than you can by going to the stars. If you colonize space, you do it near home, and do not travel to even the closest stars. To see the power of this argument, look at the quantitative costs of interstellar travel. It is not what is possible that counts, but what things actually cost.

What, then, might be the very minimum expenditure required to launch the mission to a target 10 light-years away? In terms of energy consumption, such a one-way trip would need propulsive power equal to 10 years of the total present energy consumption of the United States! These figures would apply only for a fly-by of the objective. To slow down and stop (say from a speed equal to one-tenth that of light) would boost the price in energy to that required to sustain the present United States for 1,000 years! To express it another way, the energy required to transport the 100 colonists on a hazardous mission with an uncertain fate is the amount of energy which would provide a good life to some three billion people back on Earth! In contrast, the cost of placing the same 100 colonists somewhere in the solar system is 10 million times less.

This, then, seems to be a very strong argument against interstellar colonization by any civilization, no matter how advanced and powerful it might be. There are circumstances that might prevail, however, as was the case with Superman's parents on the doomed planet Krypton.

Considering the high costs of interstellar colonization, I do not think that even one civilization would have embarked upon such an adventure. And yet there should be many civilizations in space. Of these, perhaps most will proceed with the colonization of space; but it will take place in their own planetary systems.

We should not be surprised, therefore, that no colonists have come to Earth, even if many ancient and powerful civilizations exist throughout the Milky Way. Yet, as I see it, we should search for other civilizations, for without such investigation, we will never know the truth about the existence and destinies of other intelligent creatures.

The Drake Equation

$$N = Rf_p n_e f_l f_i f_c L$$

N = the number of extraterrestrial civilizations that are trying to communicate with each other at any given time.
R = rate at which stars form per year.
f_p = the probability that once a star has formed it will have planets.
n_e = the number of planets in each system on which the conditions are right for the development of life.
f_l = the probability that once conditions favoring the development of life are present, life will be created.
f_i = the probability that once life is present it will develop intelligence.
f_c = the probability that intelligent life will develop both the capability and the desire to communicate by radio waves.
L = the length of time that a communicating civilization will continue to broadcast once it starts.

N.B. Young people might attempt the quantification of these factors using their home computers.

Comments by Robert T. Rood:
To use the Drake equation to estimate the number of extraterrestrial civilizations which might be trying to communicate with each other, one must rely quite heavily on the principle of mediocrity, i.e. there is nothing particularly special about the Earth and solar system. Yet we should not be surprised when the application of the principle of mediocrity gives the wrong answer. Two decades ago it seemed quite reasonable, for instance, to conclude that both Mars and Venus were similar to the Earth. Earlier, around the turn of the century, Percival Lowell and others argued convincingly that life existed on both of Earth's neighboring planets.

The space program, however, has given us a picture of a frozen world for Mars and a hell with a perpetual rain of sulfuric acid for Venus. Factors such as the size of the planet and the distance of the planet from the sun have made *far* more difference than anyone would previously have thought.

And so we have learned that when applying the principle of mediocrity, one should be aware of any deviations from the Earth's local environment, whether they appear to be of importance or not. In every term of the Drake equation, the Earth, the sun, or the solar system might be in some way special to the successful establishment and continuance of life. Jim Trefil and I tend to worry about these special circumstances rather more than the SETI (Search for ExtraTerrestrial Intelligence) optimists. We arrive at estimates for N (the number of extraterrestrial civilizations trying to communicate) a factor of a thousand to a million smaller than Frank Drake's estimate. Indeed, in some ways the Earth might be unique in the Galaxy.

One key to our apparently special situation may involve the moon. Neither I nor anyone else can demonstrate that the moon was essential for the origin of life on the Earth, but it might well have been. Tides, for instance, may have acted as the cocktail shaker for mixing the ingredients needed for concocting life. So if the moon is essential, we could be the only life now in the Galaxy, and, beyond that, the only life which has ever been present, unless there are similar moons accompanying planets that resemble the Earth. Moreover, recent computer studies suggest the need for a star like our sun.

Supposing that there are extraterrestrial civilizations: what are they like? We already have direct evidence of an extraterrestrial civilization—namely, the footprints which Neil Armstrong and other astronauts left on the moon. Our society already has an extraterrestrial subculture which has a very good chance of becoming much larger.

Will we, then, be the colonizers of the Milky Way? Yes, this future is possible, and would be most interesting to another civilization. This destiny, of course, is not inevitable. Even with the most optimistic values for the first six terms of the Drake equation, there will be an abundance of civilizations to be found only if communicating civilizations continue to broadcast for a long time. This is factor L in the equation. Whether we are considering radio searches or something else, we are forced to speculate about the evolution of technological civilizations over millions of years. We must be futurists on a grand scale.

As such, the three contributors to this chapter agree that long-lived technological societies will leave the planets on which they first evolved. The business of a technological society basically comes down to manipulating energy and building things. The amount of energy a planet-bound society can use is limited, and at the current rate of growth in energy consumption, our society will reach this limit of terrestrial expansion in a few centuries.

Most of us Earthlings still consider the notion of life in space as strange and foreboding. The Earth, after all, is a place very hospitable to life, while space is hostile indeed. Earth, however, is very hostile to technology: gravity makes our structures fall; earthquakes shake them; winds blow them over; the atmosphere is corrosive. Space, then—like California—is a relatively benign environment for technology. My old Dodge Dart would be much less rusty if I lived in San Diego rather than Charlottesville. It would never rust in orbit.

It is likely, then, that in a few thousand years more people will live in space than on Earth. Space colonies will most likely be lo-

Dreams of space travel have entranced readers for centuries, but science-fiction hardware caught up with the future only in our century. During World War I, Hugo Gernsback's Space Flyer provided an exciting foretaste of a moon-landing space capsule. Frank Paul created the art. In the World War II era, futuristic writers inspired a generation of young people who became the scientists of the eighties.

cated near the most desirable objects in the solar system, such as the asteroids and moons of the Jovian planets.

Yes, I believe that the human race will eventually colonize space. But which space?

You have almost certainly heard or read some distinguished scientist arguing that interstellar travel is impossible. What they really mean is that round-trip travel with a duration less than a current human lifetime is impossible. Since few of us would embark on a trip that would not reach its destination before our deaths, interstellar travel does indeed seem improbable if not impossible. A society of space colonists, however, might view things very differently.

A few thousand years from now space colonies might be commonplace. Most people will have been born out there, along with several generations of their ancestors. Space will be their home and most people will probably never visit the Earth.

If this sounds strange, consider this: do you know where all of your great-grandparents lived? Your great-great-grandparents? Have you visited there? Along these lines, most space colonists might someday think of Earth as a terrible place. "Yeah, my great Uncle Max once visited Earth. He was bitten by insects constantly and everything he ate gave him diarrhea."

In a few centuries, ships of colonists much as in the TV program "Battlestar Galactica" could reach Vega, for instance, and move into its asteroid belt and build colonies. After a thousand years or so Vega might become so crowded that a few colonists would set out for another star. At this rate *only* 100 million years or so would be required to colonize every suitable star system in the Milky Way.

Only a hundred million years, you say? On the cosmic time scale, as difficult as it may be to imagine, this is a short time. To appreciate the point, compress the history of the universe into one year. The present is midnight on New Year's Eve, with the Big Bang occurring exactly one year earlier. On this calendar, the Earth and sun were formed on the first day of September. The dinosaurs were wiped out about 10 a.m. on the 30th of December; the pyramids were built about 10 seconds before midnight on New Year's Eve, and so on. What about the future? The champagne cork pops at midnight!

Before the first glass is poured more people will live in space colonies than on the Earth. Before the party is over a few nearby stars will have been colonized. About the time the Rose Bowl Game starts on New Year's Day, every suitable star in the Milky Way will have been colonized.

Now, if Professor Drake's estimates for the terms in his equation are correct, 40 million stars and worlds come into being each day. What about the 40 million stars that formed on the 30th of August of the previous year? They should have come to support 40 million technological civilizations that first had the ability to communicate by radio on the 30th of December. If *just one* of these civilizations had decided that interstellar colonization was a good idea, they should have started re-assembling our asteroids into space colonies before 6 p.m. on December 31st—or more than 10 million years ago, long before our species existed. If they have come, and perhaps gone, we should have seen—or soon will see—a sign.

Whether a long-lived technological society might try to communicate by radio, or involve itself in interstellar colonization, or follow yet some other path, is all very uncertain. Yet it is important for us to consider all of the possibilities. In other words, we should search.

Before searching for an extraterrestrial civilization, we would do well to realize that we will probably be searching for a society of space dwellers. To find them we must think like space dwellers. In the long run we may only find ourselves.

Joint Statement by the Contributors

We hold very different views about the probability that intelligent life exists elsewhere in the Galaxy. One of us (Frank Drake) believes that there is a reasonable number of civilizations trying to communicate by radio waves, one (Robert T. Rood) that there are at most a few other civilizations, and one (James S. Trefil) that the human race is completely alone in the Galaxy. Despite this wide disparity, however, we all agree with the following statements:

Possible solar system only 50 light-years away. The disk of star material circling the central star, Beta Pictoris, may resemble the solar nebula which shaped our own Earth and the planets. Scientists are unable to determine if Beta has planets.

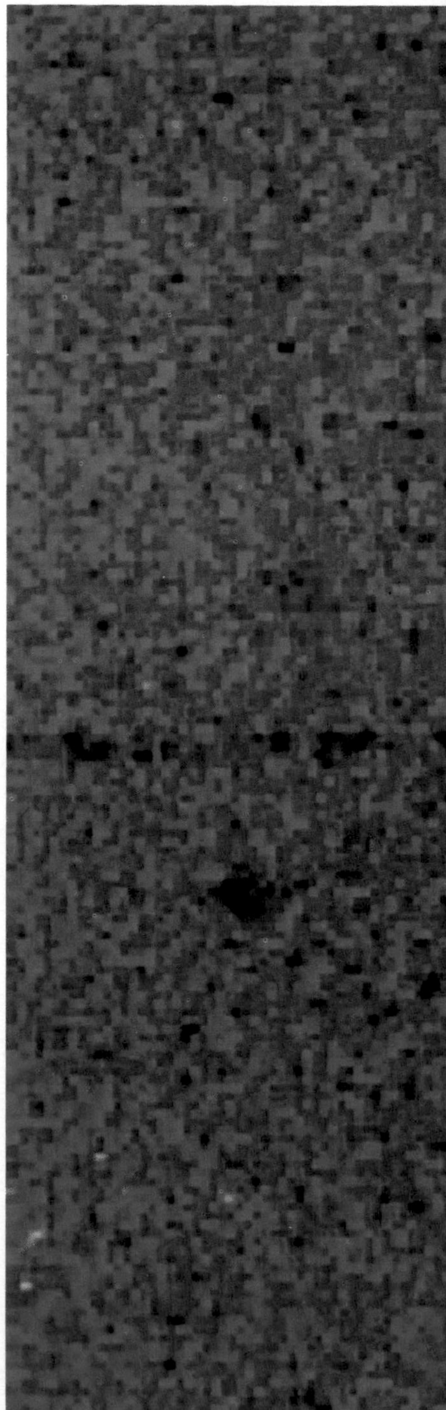

First, that there are probably fewer extraterrestrial civilizations than was believed 20 years ago.

Second, that although there is no evidence for the existence of such civilizations, the searches conducted to date have been of sufficiently small scope that we can in no way rule out the possibility that we will come into contact with them in the future.

Third, that the theoretical arguments against the existence of ETI (ExtraTerrestrial Intelligence) cannot rule out the existence of a number of other civilizations.

Fourth, that the SETI program is one of the few areas of science where a major effort is guaranteed to yield an important result, be it positive or negative.

Fifth, that initiating and maintaining an all-sky, all-frequency search for extraterrestrial radio signals should be an important goal of the scientific community.

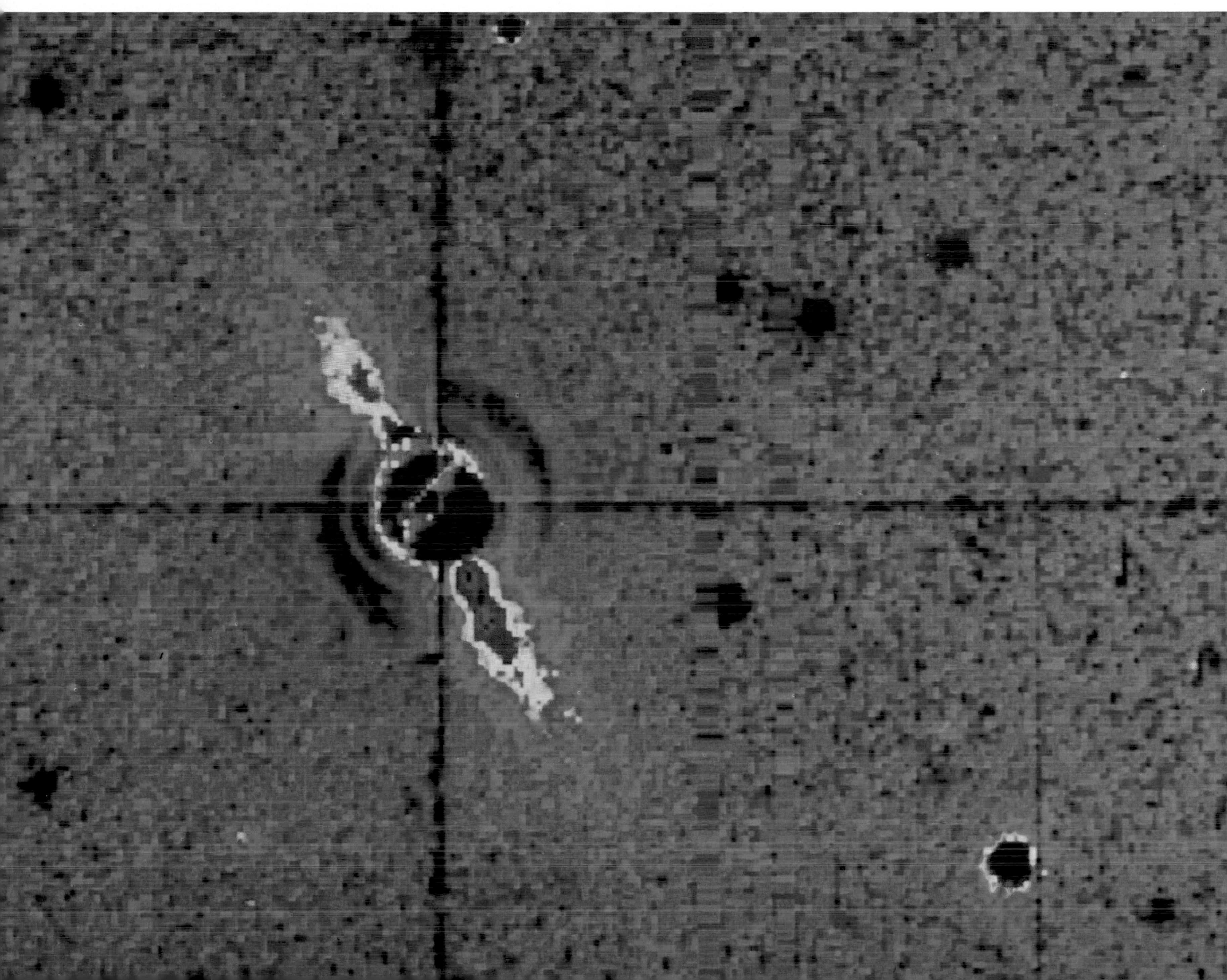

CHANNEL
PROFILE
DIG.
LUT
IFM
FLIP
CURSOR
HELP
ZOOM
LABEL
FREEZE
LINEAR
CHAN. C
XLINK
MENU
ROAM
GR.OFF
CIRCLE
LOG
CHAN. D
YLINK
IDLE

Part 4

Charting Space Through Time

Overleaf: *In the Image Processing Laboratory, Harvard-Smithsonian astronomer Rudolph Schild projects an optical image of a galaxy taken with a CCD or charge-coupled device. A graph is superimposed on the galactic image and displays the energy-output level of a puzzling source of radiation. Key to the interpretation of the skies, opposite, the "universe" according to Copernicus appears in an illustration from the* Harmonia Macrocosmica *of Cellarius (1660).*

In 1905, Albert Einstein had a very good year. He published some remarkable papers, including one on Brownian motion, that random walk of microscopic particles in a fluid; another on the influence of photons on metals, the so-called photoelectric effect; and he proposed the special theory of relativity. It has been called his miraculous year. He was ultimately awarded the Nobel Prize for his photoelectric work, which, incidentally, set the scene for quantum mechanics. (Einstein never really believed in quantum mechanics.)

In 1916, Einstein published his general theory of relativity. His equations went a long way toward proving that the universe must be expanding. No observations were available to confirm the idea. Indeed, there were few observations to establish that the universe was more than the starry system we could see as the Milky Way.

Some scientists thought, no doubt, that there was more than met the eye, but no one was absolutely sure. Thus swayed by facts—or the lack of them—Einstein modified his equations with a term called "the cosmological constant." It had the effect of holding the universe in a fixed state. The universe according to Einstein was static: he had saved the appearances.

Then, in the early 1920s, Hubble determined the distance to the Andromeda nebula. And at the Lowell Observatory in Flagstaff, Arizona, V.M. Slipher used the photographic form of the spectroscope—the spectrograph—to find that spiral nebulae seemed to be in rapid motion. The spectra of all these objects had their spectral lines shifted to longer wavelengths, toward the red end of the spectrum. Interpreted as a velocity through the Doppler effect, this meant that they were going away from us. Furthermore, the farther away one of these systems was, the faster it receded. The inescapable conclusion—the universe was expanding. Einstein's prediction had come true, though his cosmological constant had been unnecessary.

Although the idea was not new, the observations of a universe in expansion brought to the fore the concept of a universe that had once been very much smaller. In fact, if we turn the expansion numbers around, we can see the universe shrink. Playing this movie backwards we get the idea that some tremendous explosion started the whole thing off. George Gamow, a great scientist and popularizer, coined the name "The Big Bang," and it has stuck. The date at which this expansion began is related to Hubble's expansion law. Thus today's observations of velocities and distances, and their interpretations, give some indication of the age of the universe.

But the Big Bang concept was challenged by some British workers as long ago as 1948. Thomas Gold teased his colleague, Hermann Bondi, with a suggested alternative. Bondi embraced it and Fred Hoyle wrote widely about this Steady State universe. Thus, it is often called Hoyle's theory. Because it has philosophical implications that many people find appealing, it still has a few adherents.

In the Big Bang expansion concept, the mass of the universe remains constant. Thus, as the matter disperses into the distance, the volume occupied by matter grows larger, and the average density (mass per unit volume) of the universe grows smaller. In the Steady State concept, the expansion is real, but as the matter recedes, just enough matter is formed in space to keep the density constant. The matter is formed from "nothing." Hoyle has remarked that if some people can accept the idea of one single "miracle" to start up the universe, what is the problem with a continuous miracle?

Nor does Steady State help explain some important phenomena, including the origin of elements. In this pursuit we find another Nobel Prize, the one given to Hans Bethe of Cornell. When the conditions at the center of the sun and other stars became known, it was possible for Bethe to examine reactions of the atomic nuclei of possible chemical elements present in their centers.

According to Bethe, the final net reaction is the combination of four hydrogen nuclei (protons) into the single nucleus of a helium atom, called the alpha particle. Along the way, two electrons also enter the reaction. When all of the ingredients are added up and compared to the mass of the final product, some mass is missing. It has been converted into an amount of energy calculated from the famous expression $E = mc^2$.

This is another valuable concept we owe to Albert Einstein. In a short paper, he said that he wondered if a system was more massive if it possessed energy. He set up some equations and found that his hunch was correct. $E = mc^2$ is the result. This little equation is deceptively simple, but a bit of examination reveals vast implications.

On its face, it says that if one multiplies a given amount of mass by the square of the velocity of light, one learns the energy equivalent of that amount of matter. Now the square of the velocity of light is a very large number; a little mass goes a long way.

The mass not accounted for by the summation process, above, reappears as energy. This energy streams out through the star, heating the star as it goes. The hot surface glows with the light that streaks through space to our telescopes, and we see the star.

Now let's look more carefully at Einstein's equation. If we rearrange it by dividing through by c^2, we get $(E/c^2) = m$. The left side is all energy. E represents radiation—electromagnetic radiation. And c is the velocity at which that radiation travels through space. On this side we find all that pertains to electricity and magnetism; electronics, light, radio, television, computers, X rays, and so on. On the right side we find mass with its implications; gravity, inertia, our world, us, the stuff of space and space travel, ponderability.

Right in the middle of Einstein's equation an equal sign appears. The great theoretician had made a giant leap of faith with that sign; he could not prove equivalency. Yet the tiny mathematical notation speaks volumes. It says that not only are the two sides equivalent, but interchangeable.

When Einstein saw this he knew that something was hidden in this little equation: that electromagnetism and gravity were somehow intimately interrelated. He saw that his short cut to its derivation had bypassed the relatedness. If he could only unify these two fundamental natural forces. But such a unified field theory eluded him.

In recent years, workers have succeeded in bringing the electromagnetic forces together with the weak nuclear force, calling the new concept electro-weak. All four forces, including the strong nuclear force, are targets of searchers for the Grand Unified Theory. Several such GUTs have been proposed, and some look promising.

Someday we may know how the universe works. But learning why it works will take more than GUTs. K.L.F.

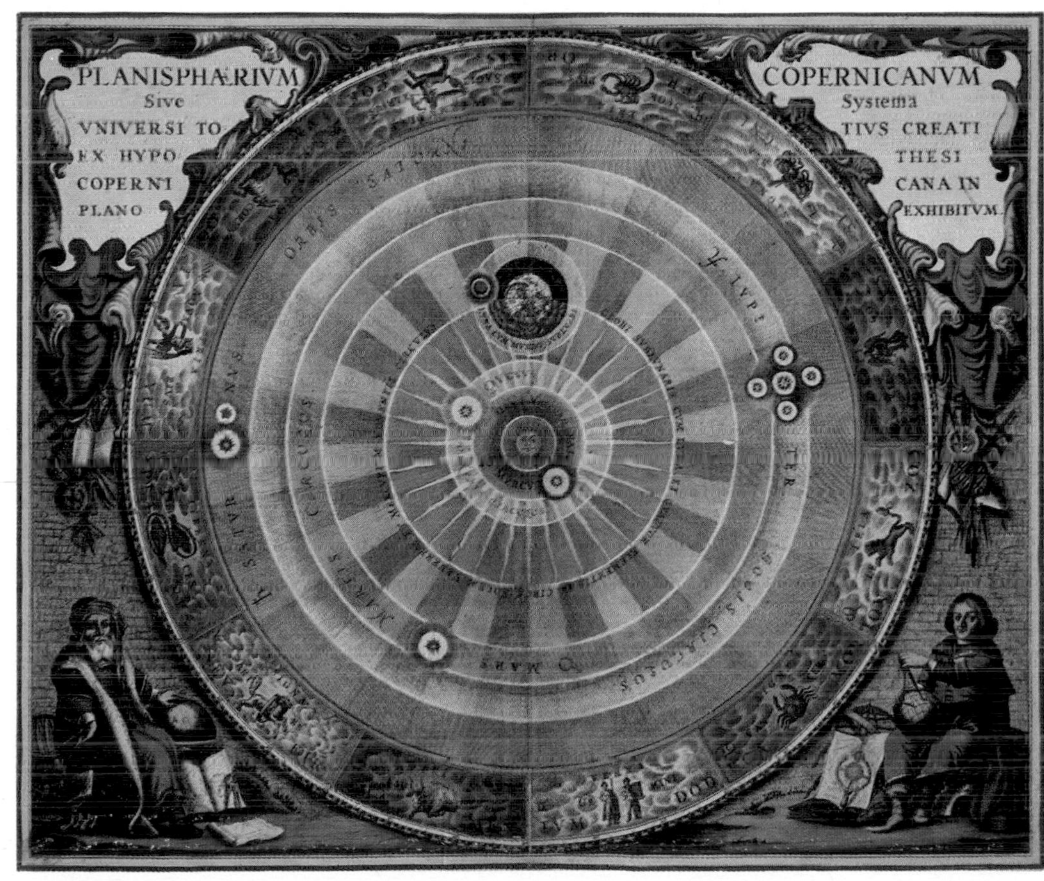

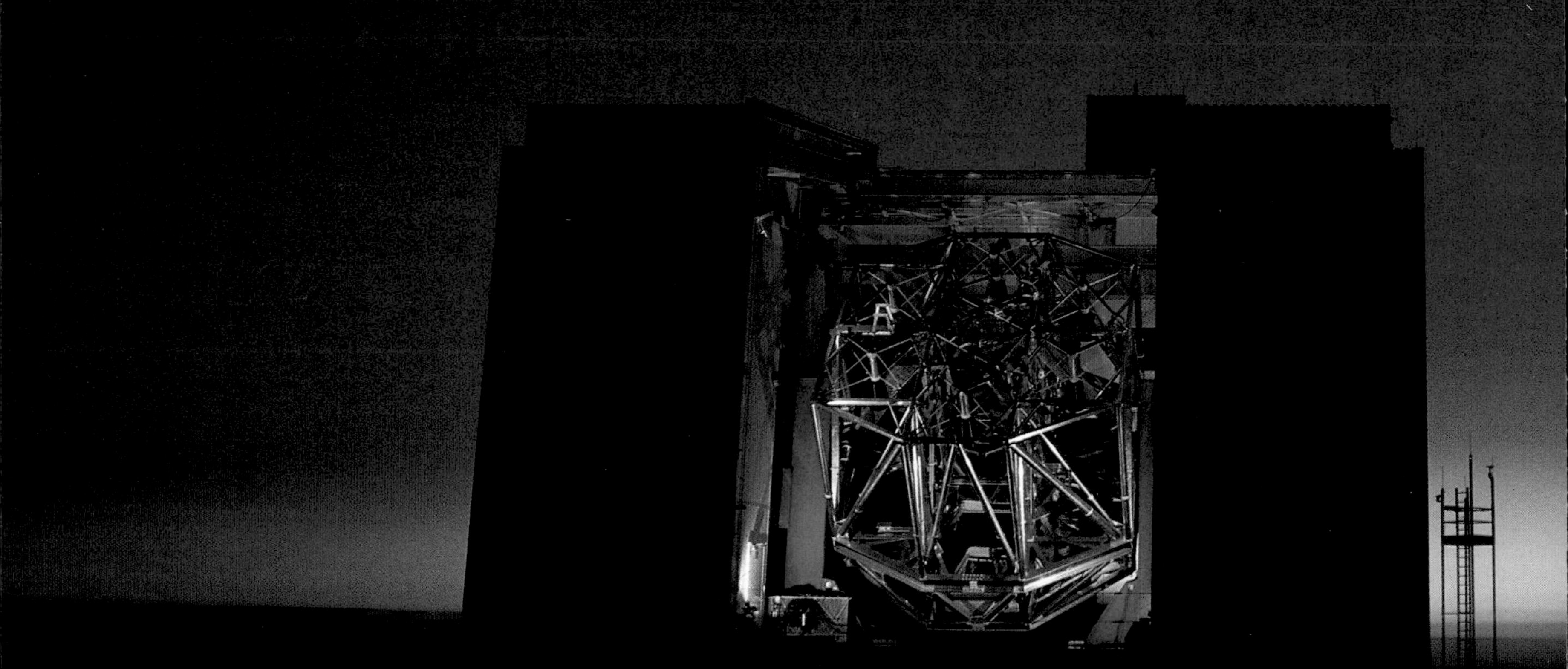

State of the Art

Pulling onto the exit ramp from Route 89, some 25 miles north of the Mexican border in southern Arizona, it was hard to believe I was near the site of one of the most advanced pieces of technology in the world. The road from Tucson, 35 miles away, had climbed slowly through a desert dotted with Saguaro cactus and retirement villages. The most striking feature of the town of Amado, the exit point, was the County Line Cafe, a ramshackle cowboy bar with an entrance in the shape of a huge longhorn skull (you enter through the mouth). As I drove down the dusty main street, I saw an adobe brick building on the left, looking like an old schoolhouse. In front was a large wooden sign saying "Smithsonian Institution—Fred Lawrence Whipple Observatory." I have to admit that seeing that sign out there in the desert, so far from the Mall in Washington, made me do a double-take.

Inside the crowded building I met Daniel Brocious, an information specialist for the observatory. Soon we would leave the desert floor to climb to the observatory proper, located 8,550 feet above sea level on Mt. Hopkins, the second highest peak in the Santa Rita mountains. Leaving our puny highway cars in the parking lot, we transferred to a rugged van for the trip. The paving ends when we leave the town—from here on up it will be a switchback, gravel, and don't-look-over-the-edge-if-you're-nervous mountain road.

The first obstacle is a washed-out concrete highway bridge—a legacy of the terrible flash floods that hit Arizona in the fall of 1982. The road climbs through the foothills as Dan, an amateur naturalist, points out key features of the desert ecology—blooming ocotillo cactus, mesquite, palo verde trees. A road runner scoots along the road. As we continue to climb, the desert gives

Longhorn skull opens into a cafe at Amado, Arizona, near the foot of Mt. Hopkins. A winding road links the dusty town to the top of the 8,000-foot peak, site of the Multiple Mirror Telescope (MMT). The mechanism itself, with six mirrors, emerges at sunset, opposite.

Buried electrical heaters melt treacherous snow and ice from the last quarter mile to the peak of Mt. Hopkins. Sturdy observatory vehicle hugs the rugged road.

way to small oak trees and eventually to pines. Dan's talk turns to the sheer task of maintaining this road to the top against the ravages of flash floods and washouts. Negotiating the sharp turns, I wonder how in the world the builders of the telescopes managed to haul their loads up the mountain.

At the top, spectacular vistas of the southwestern desert unfold in every direction. The place seems to be detached from reality—floating halfway between the earth and the heavens it was built to study. There are actually two observatories strung along the mountaintop. One, running along a ridge, is the Whipple Observatory proper. It is named after Fred Whipple, a distinguished American astronomer who has a long association with the Smithsonian Institution and who was director of the Harvard-Smithsonian Astrophysical Observatory from 1955 to 1973. It was he who located and developed Mt. Hopkins as the site for an astronomical observatory.

The other part of Mt. Hopkins—the part that makes it unique among the world's observatories—is the Multiple Mirror Telescope (MMT), built and operated jointly by the Smithsonian Institution and the University of Arizona. It is located in a box-shaped building at the very summit of the mountain. In between these two installations are some low wooden buildings that serve as dormitories and eating places for the astronomers who are using the telescopes. This arrangement is typical of large observatories. The cost of developing and maintaining a mountaintop requires that as many telescopes as possible be located at the top. At the neighboring Kitt Peak National Observatory, for example, there are no fewer than 14 separate telescopes.

Walking along observatory ridge is a familiar experience for anyone who has seen films about large telescopes. Two white domes house optical telescopes—reflectors whose mirrors are 150 and 61 centimeters (59 and 24 inches) respectively. At the edge of the ridge is an unusual instrument. It's a telescope made of 248 independently mounted hexagonal mirrors. Each mirror is about two feet across and the entire apparatus measures thirty feet in diameter. This is not the sort of telescope we're used to thinking about—it doesn't form images, for example. Each of the individual mirrors can be controlled independently as the telescope is aimed at the sky. The purpose of the instrument is to detect the faint bluish light emitted when high-energy cosmic rays enter the atmosphere. When not being used, it has to be stored facing away from the sun. Otherwise it will focus sunlight and start a fire. Char marks on wooden buildings near the telescope bear mute witness to what happens when the operator is careless.

A short, steep drive brings us to the peak itself. The last few hundred yards of the road are paved to keep the dust down and electrically heated to melt snow and ice. At the top, perched in lonely splendor, sits the MMT. My first impression was that the building just didn't look right. Like most of us, I'm used to thinking of telescopes in terms of great white domes projecting gracefully above mountaintops. As we'll see, however, the MMT's blocky building has turned out to be an enormous asset to the instrument. It is very likely that the MMT experience means that major telescopes in the future will be housed in such buildings. The domed observatory, at least for large telescopes, may be a thing of the past.

There are so many novel features about the telescope that it's hard to know where to begin describing them. Let's start with history. Fred Whipple, while installing the smaller telescopes along the ridge, was saving the summit of the mountain for "something special." A chance phone conversation with Azen Meinel at the University of Arizona revealed that the University had recently acquired six surplus telescope mirrors from the Air Force. Each had a diameter of six feet. A perfect partnership—the university had the mirrors, the Smithsonian had the mountaintop. Plans were made and, since the mirrors were already in hand, a radical new design for the telescope had to be devised. In the final design, the six mirrors were mounted on a single frame. Each of these primary mirrors focuses light onto its own single secondary mirror which, in turn, reflects the light onto a tertiary mirror. The six tertiary mirrors bring the six beams together at the beam combiner. Finally, light reaches the telescope's focus.

Moving the light around in this way sounds easy, but in practice a design like the MMT would not have been possible before the advent of fast computers. Electronic assistance is required because large telescopes like the MMT are designed to probe the sky for very faint, very distant objects. The telescope, therefore, has to bring six small images to a point at the focus and keep them there. Even a small misalignment of one mirror can ruin the observation.

But a telescope is not a static structure. The framework sags because of gravity, it shrinks and expands as the temperature changes, it vibrates slightly from the wind and the motion of the motors which allow it to track objects through the sky. Any one of these tiny perturbations could cause a misalignment. It is the job of the computers to keep constant track of the positions of the mirrors and to correct the alignment when necessary. It is this wedding of optics with modern electronics that make a telescope like the MMT possible.

The MMT building is also unusual. As you drive up to the summit, you notice a

At first, the MMT's mirrors appear mounted on a big Tinker-Toy frame. Such construction allows the entire device to cool quickly at night. Structural strains are minimized and the astronomer's long night's work can begin earlier.

ring of ordinary orange plastic cones in the parking lot—the sort of thing highway crews use to close off traffic lanes when they are working. The rings mark the area that will be swept out when the building moves. You read me right—the building itself moves with the telescope! Apparently there were quite a few dented fenders caused by the building hitting parked cars before the cones were put up. (Can you imagine trying to explain one of those accidents to your insurance agent?)

The moving building, as well as the square design, were dictated by cost. In this case, though, the observatory builders received more than they bargained for. It was a happy accident. It has to do with the doors that open when the telescope is used. In a conventional dome, the telescope looks at the sky through a slot in the roof. Essentially, the instrument is inside, looking out through a window. When the MMT doors are opened, however, the entire telescope is, in effect, outside.

This is a very important point, because one of the major sources of error in making precise astronomical observations is the response of the telescope to changes in temperature. Like any other materials, the glass and steel in the telescope change dimensions when the temperature changes. Among other things, this means that the mirror itself changes shape slightly as it cools off, blurring the observed image. This difficulty is usually minimized by keeping large telescopes cool during the day, so that they are close to nighttime temperature when the dome is opened. This is accomplished by insulating the domes and painting them white to reflect the daytime sun. The idea is to keep the inside as close to the cold nighttime temperature as possible. This is why it's always a good idea to take a sweater along when you visit a telescope, even if it's warm and sunny outside!

The MMT has several advantages in dealing with the temperature problem. For one thing, its open framework and light, small mirrors cool off quickly—there is little mass in the telescope to retain heat. Equilibrium with the temperature of the air is established quickly. The openess of the building, obviously, is valuable in this respect. Finally, the building is located on the very peak of a mountain, rather than along a ridge. In effect, the MMT sits on a tall tower, well above the bulk of Mt. Hopkins. After sunset the rock underneath it, exposed to the air on all sides, cools off quickly. This means that there are fewer currents of rock-warmed air to rise around the telescope and interfere with the observations.

As an amateur carpenter, I was fascinated with the idea of an entire building mounted and rotating with a telescope. The interior wasn't like anything I expected. It looks like an ordinary office building, except for the breathtaking view from the windows. There was a small kitchen with every home convenience—even a dishwasher. Crawling down

Housing divided upon itself splits, each half moving aside. The clamshell structure can also close, and in seconds, to prevent a collision between the telescope and a rain cloud. Once exposed, the MMT swivels up and down on its turntable base. Six mirrors are aimed at a single location in the sky as a computer coordinates the various movements of the base and the optical assembly.

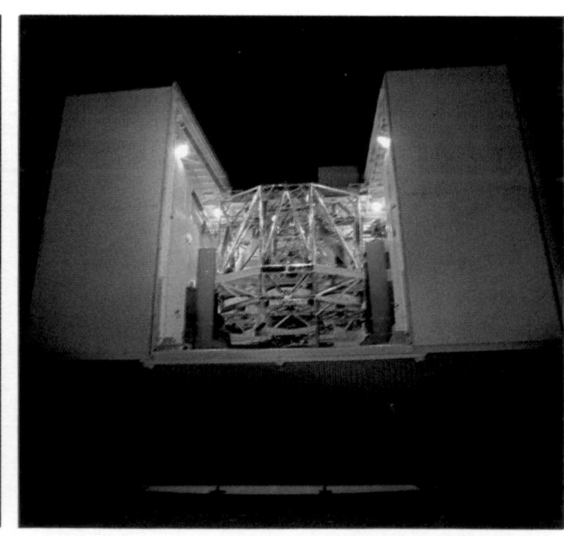

a ladder into the basement, I was shown the circular steel track on which the entire building rotates on a series of wheels. The whole thing is now turned by two electric motors of 15 horsepower, but Dan Brocious said that they once used an ordinary three-quarter horsepower hand drill to do the job. In a pinch, there are cranks which allow the entire apparatus to be rotated by a single graduate student.

The telescope itself is mounted on a central pier set into the ground. This footing is hollow and the electrical and plumbing lines enter the building through it. Inside, there is a maypole type of arrangement which allows the flexible lines to wrap and unwrap as the building turns. To keep from breaking the lines, the building can turn only 270° in either direction before it stops. That way, none of the utility lines can be twisted enough to cause damage. Sensors in the wall detect the motion of the telescope and move the building accordingly, keeping the parts synchronized.

Amid all of this high-tech virtuosity, it did my heart good to see some old-fashioned down-home ingenuity applied to practical problems. I particularly enjoyed the "just in case" snowshoes stacked under the stairs and the twenty gallon garbage pail sitting under the place where the plumbing drains come into the basement, for what Dan called the "Oh my God" emergency. It's all right to scan the skies and unlock the secrets of the universe, but the plumbing had better work while you're doing it!

The room that houses the telescope itself is surprisingly small. Unlike domes, which have to allow room for the movement of the telescope independently of the building, the MMT just needs enough room to be sheltered from the weather. The open "Tinker-Toy" construction gives the telescope an insubstantial air—there just doesn't seem to be enough there to make a major research tool. The tubing is wrapped in metallic tape to allow the metal to cool off more quickly when the roof is opened. This also keeps the telescope itself from interfering with infrared observations.

Perhaps the biggest surprise is what's located at the focus of the telescope. Most of us have a vision of astronomers peering at

MMT mirror rests within a spiderwork support. A backing of glass honeycomb reduces the weight of each mirror. At the University of Arizona in nearby Tucson, an optical technician cuts cores from (and thus lowers the weight of) a thick glass blank destined to become a telescope mirror.

the heavens through the eyepiece of a telescope, or at the very least taking pictures with a camera. It turns out that at the MMT no one has ever looked through the eyepiece except for alignment operations. What's more, the building doesn't have a darkroom. The reason for this isn't hard to understand. The human eye, for all its flexibility, is not a particularly good detector of faint objects. A photographic plate can pick up and also make a record of such things if it is exposed for a long time, but even good photographic emulsions will register only a few percent of the light that falls on them.

One way to understand the astronomer's concern with this inefficiency is to realize that light from extragalactic objects collected in our telescopes is a rare commodity indeed. In fact, all such light ever collected corresponds to a few minutes output of an ordinary flashlight. Once you've built a multimillion dollar instrument to collect these feeble beams, you want to use them as efficiently as possible. Just as modern electronics is revolutionizing the design of telescopes, it is revolutionizing the way that observations are made. Instead of ordinary photographic film, the light is recorded electronically with devices resembling television cameras. The best of these, the charge-coupled device (CCD) cameras, can record more than half of the light that strikes them. This sort of increase in efficiency is obviously important in dealing with the detection and recording of very faint and distant objects. The MMT is not alone in this trend, of course. All around the world the skies are probed with electronic eyes. It may take some time for the image of the astronomer in the popular mind to catch up to what astronomers actually do.

The MMT started operation in 1978 and cost about nine million dollars to build. This may sound like a large sum of money, but in terms of modern big-time science, it is quite modest. An ordinary particle accelerator, for example, costs several hundred million to build, and million dollar experiments are not at all uncommon at the research frontiers. On this scale, the cost of the MMT does not seem unusual at all.

A telescope is customarily rated in terms of its performance in two areas: resolution and light collecting. Resolution refers to the ability to see details in distant objects. The actual resolution obtainable at a telescope (as opposed to the theoretical limit) depends on a complex mixture of the instrument design, building design, the site, and the atmosphere—all of the things that astronomers lump into the word "seeing." You'll hear them say "The seeing was good last night," by which they mean that all of these factors combined to give their observations a high level of resolution. In southern Arizona, resolutions of two arc seconds or less are typical. The MMT, on the other hand, has achieved resolutions of half an arc second. A handy rule: the smaller the figure the better the resolution.

In terms of light-gathering ability, the MMT is equivalent to a single 176 inch mirror. In this category it is the third largest "light bucket" in the world, ranking behind the six meter Soviet telescope in the Caucasus and the 200 inch mirror (5.08 meters) at Mt. Palomar. However, as we have already noted, the Soviet telescope suffers from design and siting problems that limit its usefulness for research. Palomar, unfortunately, has been seriously compromised by light pollution from San Diego—a fate which threatens many major American telescopes. It may be, therefore, that the MMT will have to carry a major share of the burden of optical astronomy until the next generation of telescopes is built.

As I watched the sun sinking toward the Arizona mountains and felt the evening chill start to set in around the MMT, I was again struck by the appropriateness of the site to the kinds of things that were being done here. How better to emphasize the otherworldly quality of astronomy than to climb to the top of a mountain, the traditional place for the seeking of enlightenment? Across the Santa Rita valley, the sun glinted on a rough, pyramidal peak known as Baboquivari, "The Needle Between Earth and Sky." According to Papago Indian lore, this peak is the center of the universe. They may have been closer to the mark than they realized, for the mountains of Arizona seem to have become the place where mankind is seeking, if not the center of the universe, at least an understanding of its secrets.

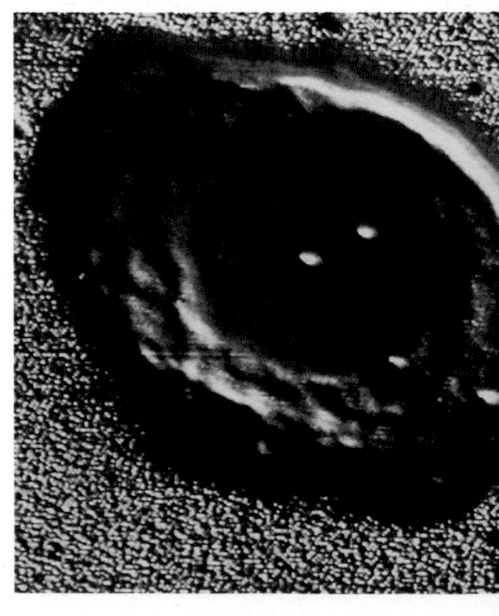

Scientist holds a solid-state sensor, the charge-coupled device (CCD). Such silicon chips, produced by several high-tech companies, can gather more light than photographic emulsions. Typical CCD installation replaces photographic film at the focus of a telescope at the Harvard-Smithsonian Center for Astrophysics, above. Images are stored on magnetic tape, recreated with the help of a computer, then displayed on a monitor, here operated by Rudolph Schild at the Whipple Observatory on Mt. Hopkins. He adds contrast and color to reveal details of the Ring nebula in Lyra.

A dark galaxy (at the center of the diagram above) exerts gravity and thus acts like a lens to bend and split light from a quasar. From Earth, at bottom, observers see two ghost images, A and B, of the single quasar. Left, more than a dozen telescopes cling to Arizona's Kitt Peak, a national observatory established near Tucson in 1957.

The Future of Ground-Based Astronomy

It seemed altogether fitting that I first encountered Dr. Frederic K. Chaffee, Jr., Resident Director of the Whipple Observatory, home of the MMT, on that impossible Mt. Hopkins' road. He was driving up in a pickup. I was on my way down with the dayshift crew. Through the open windows of our vehicles, we made arrangements to meet the next day, after he had spent the night on the ridge. Having been associated with Mt. Hopkins since the early seventies, he is the ideal person to tell us about the history and future of the MMT.

"When the MMT was being finished, we were all anxious to get started making measurements," he recalled. "We loaded the spectrograph from the 60 inch (on the ridge below the peak) and the computer on a pickup truck and drove up to the peak. The second night of observation, we made a critical observation on a gravitational lens. That was probably the main discovery so far at the MMT."

The discovery to which Chaffee referred had to do with a controversy of the late seventies. There are only about 1,500 quasars known, and they tend to be well separated. There was, however, a "twin quasar"—two that seemed to be very similar and located close together. MMT measurements showed that the velocities of these two objects differed by no more than 15 kilometers per second. Since the red shift indicated recession velocities on the order of 70 percent of the speed of light, it became very difficult to argue that the twins were not related to each other but were simply images that happened to overlap on a particular line of sight. Ultimately, observations showed that the "twins" were a single quasar whose image was split by an intervening galaxy, a phenomenon related to the way light rays can be bent by a gravitational field. Such a system is called a gravitational lens. As of 1984, four (eight quasar images) had been identified.

Fred Chaffee's eyes lit up when I asked him about future uses of the MMT. This was obviously something he liked to talk about. One project involves the use of the MMT for interferometry. The multiple mirror design is perfect since the mirrors can be used in pairs. In this mode, the telescope would have the equivalent resolving power of a single mirror 273 inches across. In the longer term, high speed electronics in the telescope might be used to overcome one of the oldest problems in the annals of astronomy—the twinkling of the stars. It is caused by motions of the air, and amounts to a shift in a stellar image about ten times a second. "The image formed by each of the MMT mirrors will flicker, of course," explains Chaffee, "but it may be possible to combine those images so that the total image doesn't." So the MMT, in addition to being the first of the modern electronic telescopes, may be the first to un-flicker the stars.

How about the future of optical telescopes in America? "The breakthrough at the MMT is in the electronics," says Chaffee. "Every large telescope built from now on will involve some sort of active control of the mirrors." But this doesn't mean that future telescopes will be of the multiple mirror type. Remember that the design of the MMT was largely dictated by the availability of the mirrors. The next large telescopes may use MMT-style electronics and a single, though segmented, mirror. Such a reflector would resemble a honeycomb, with each piece separately controlled to give the desired image at the focus.

Toward the mid-eighties, there were three groups in the United States planning to build large telescopes. One of these was designed by the National Observatory at Kitt Peak, though for reasons which will become obvious in a moment, the telescope will not be built there. By 1984 University of Texas also had a telescope in the design stage (one with the MMT-style square building), as did a University of California Caltech group. The latter recently received a $70 million gift, making construction possible. Each of these telescopes incorporates light-gathering power equivalent to a 10 meter single dish mirror—twice the diameter of Palomar.

All three telescope designs could be realized. With construction and development costs generally exceeding the $50 million mark, they are big projects, but not so big that they couldn't be managed by some combination of public and private money. As one scientist pointed out to me, ever since the construction of Palomar there has been a rule of thumb governing the cost of telescopes—the world's best telescope always costs about as much as a major freeway interchange. It was true in the thirties, it's true now, and, given skyrocketing highway costs, it will probably remain true in the future.

Light Pollution

The question of where the next telescope will be placed touches on a very sore point for modern astronomers—the problem they call light pollution. As we probe farther out into the universe and further back into the past, we see fainter and fainter objects. Their dim light can be swamped by city lights. To understand what astronomers mean by the term light pollution, imagine that you are driving along a country road at night. Your windshield is dirty. Ahead, you can just barely make out a traffic sign. Just then, another car comes around a curve, shining a bright light onto your windshield. There would be no chance of seeing the road sign in such a situation—it's message would be completely lost in the glare.

In just the same way the faint objects in the sky get lost when man-made illumination introduces light into the night sky near a telescope. Mercury vapor street lamps are particularly bad in this regard because mercury emits light in lines throughout the light spectrum. Low pressure sodium lamps, on the other hand, emit light at only a few frequencies, so that astronomers taking spectra of distant objects can work around the unwanted light.

"Tucson is unique in the country in its concern for astronomy" Fred Chaffee points out. "The city and surrounding counties have already adopted strict lighting ordinances to protect the telescopes." These include a ban on mercury vapor lamps and a requirement that large nighttime lighting installations, such as parking lots and tennis courts, place shields over the lamps to direct the light downward. "Nevertheless," says Chaffee, "this sort of thing just postpones the inevitable. The MMT has already lost a third of the sky. Population growth has seriously compromised southern Arizona as a site for observatories."

This means that the new telescope simply

Skies glow over the Santa Clara Valley, California, in this view from Lick Observatory. Such light pollution threatens astronomical viewing at Lick and other western sites. High above the island of Hawaii, Mauna Kea rises nearly 14,000 feet, at far right. This major site, with some of the world's best astronomical seeing, attracts observers—and new telescopes—from Japan, Great Britain, and the United States.

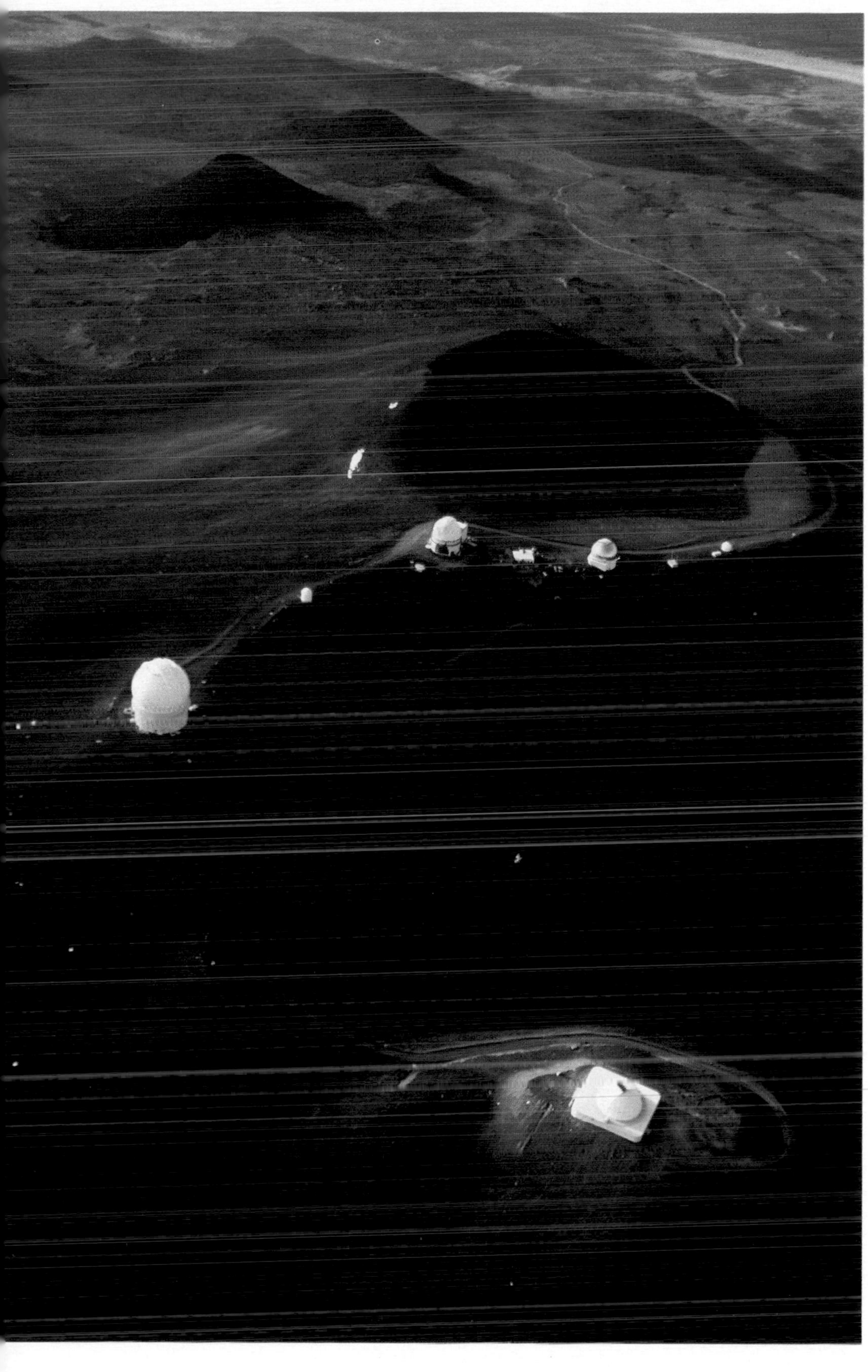

can't be put down at Kitt Peak or Hopkins, even though those sites are well surveyed and have support facilities already in place. The two places being considered right now are Mauna Kea in Hawaii, a place which is already a major international astronomical center, and Mt. Graham near Safford, Arizona, 85 miles northeast of Tucson. A team from the Smithsonian is already testing this peak for suitability.

Ground-Based Astronomy in the Future

I have to admit that I was a little surprised to find ground-based optical astronomy in such vigorous health. I had thought that since the advent of astronomy in space, and with light pollution affecting so many major observatories, astronomers would have their eyes firmly fixed on orbiting telescopes. But here are several large groups engaged in designing new ground-based telescopes—telescopes that will, in all probability, be built. I asked Fred Chaffee why.

For one thing, he pointed out, traditional telescopes are much cheaper than telescopes in orbit. The space telescope bears a price tag of more than a billion dollars, a hundred times that of the MMT and ten times the cost of the next generation of instruments. This means that if there are observations that can be made from the ground, ground-based instruments will be used. "Besides, if you want to look faint, you just have to collect the light," Dr. Chaffee continued. "At some point, a telescope with a large area will win, despite the atmosphere."

"Besides," and here the working astronomer emerged, "in an observatory, there's a certain amount of hands-on work necessary. If one instrument doesn't do the job, you pull it off and fiddle with it until it works. It's hard to do that sort of thing in space."

There is, of course, no doubt that the future of astronomy in space is assured. In fact, there are some types of astronomy that must be done in space. What I heard from Fred Chaffee and the other astronomers in Arizona, however, was that the process of collecting light in large mirrors and analyzing it with state of the art electronic equipment at mountaintop sites around the world will still be important well into the foreseeable future.

Astronomy of the Future

Māshā' allāh, a Jewish astronomer of the eighth century, measures a girdled globe with calipers. Etching by Albrecht Dürer (1471–1528). Opposite, garbed for work in the clean room at the Harvard-Smithsonian Center for Astrophysics, physicist Heinz Weiser at far right and engineering associate Frank Rivera assemble the Spartan-2 Ultraviolet Coronal Spectrometer. To obtain data, Spartan will be released over the side of the space shuttle where it will be left to operate independently, then later retrieved.

By the year 2000, astronomy will move into space in a way that could have been imagined only by the wildest dreamers a decade ago. It is the astronomers, of course, who have led the way in exploring these new regions and in showing that there is exciting new science to be done above the atmosphere. Companies of the aerospace industry helped to develop the hardware that has turned the astronomers' dreams into reality, and even now they are deeply involved in planning the next steps to be taken. In this chapter we will look at some of the projects in development, and others still on the drawing boards. From such examples, we can see what astronomy will bring us in the future.

Hubble Space Telescope

We have frequently mentioned the problems of making our astronomical observations from the bottom of the atmosphere. So it should come as no surprise that putting a telescope into orbit has long been a major goal of the scientific community. The idea first appeared (officially, at least) in 1962, when the development of an orbiting telescope was mentioned as a long-range goal in a NASA study. The idea continued to be proposed by astronomers, and in 1973 NASA assembled a blue-ribbon study group to set out the basic design that such an instrument would require. Money for the project was authorized in 1977, appropriated in 1978, and a major construction effort has been under way ever since.

The instrument is named for astronomer Edwin Hubble (1889–1953). As is the custom with large development contracts like this, more than one corporation has been involved. The telescope contract was awarded to The Perkin-Elmer Corporation, while responsibility for the spacecraft and integration of the system went to the Lock-

heed Missiles and Space Company, Inc. The entire system fits in the space shuttle's cargo bay. Target date for launch: late 1986.

The telescope will be carried to a point 300 miles above the Earth and placed in orbit by the shuttle's remote arm. After launch, the astronauts will assemble the detectors at the back of the space telescope (ST). This system allows for changes in the instrument package from time to time. In any case, the plans call for bringing the entire instrument back to Earth every five years for refurbishing and major maintenance. Experience gained during initial deployment will aid in the design of new systems.

Overall, the ST is a cylinder 43 feet long and 14 feet across. The heart of the instrument, the main mirror, measures 94 inches across and is capable of focusing radiation from the infrared to the ultraviolet (waves from 1,000 times to a third the length of waves of visible light).

Unlike the telescope itself, which was developed by large corporations, the instruments were developed by individual research groups at universities. I attended a meeting on the project during the mid-seventies and remember being absolutely amazed that the scientists in these groups were willing to spend the better part of a decade—a quarter of their professional lives—developing instruments in return for the first month of observing time. This should give you some idea of how important this project has become to astronomers and how certain they are that the space telescope will make important new discoveries.

We should note that all of the cameras, spectrometers, and other instruments on board will use electronic (rather than photographic) cameras. They do not take pictures on film, but allow the light to fall on sensitive solid-state devices that turn the light into electrical impulses which, in turn, are stored in the on-board computers until they can be relayed back home through the satellite's communication link.

The potential information to be gained from ST is enormous. For instance, quasars have been considered a transitory phase in the evolution of galactic nuclei. One bit of supporting evidence for this conjecture

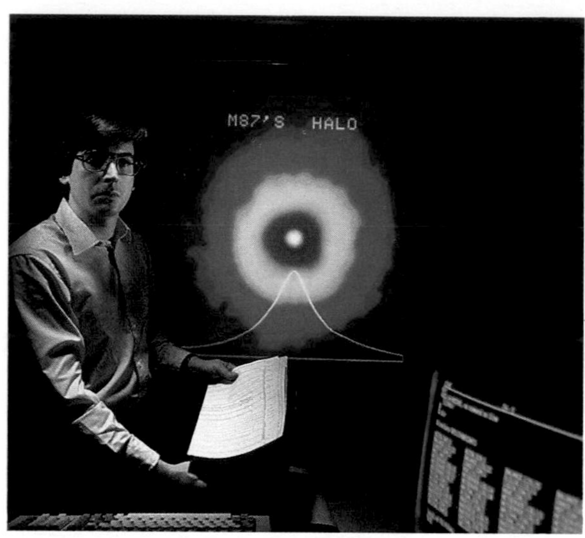

Harvard-Smithsonian astrophysicist Daniel Fabricant projects a false-color image of X-ray emission from M 87. The curve indicates the level of emissions from the hot gases surrounding the galaxy. Astronomer Margrethe DeFaccio, at right, selects a magnetic tape filled with data from the Einstein satellite's survey of the X-ray sky. In the foreground, we see a glass photographic plate from the Harvard Observatory's collection of more than 400,000. The research collection dates from 1885. Both the tapes and the plates represent massive and irreplaceable "benchmark" collections, frequently consulted by researchers seeking changes in the skies.

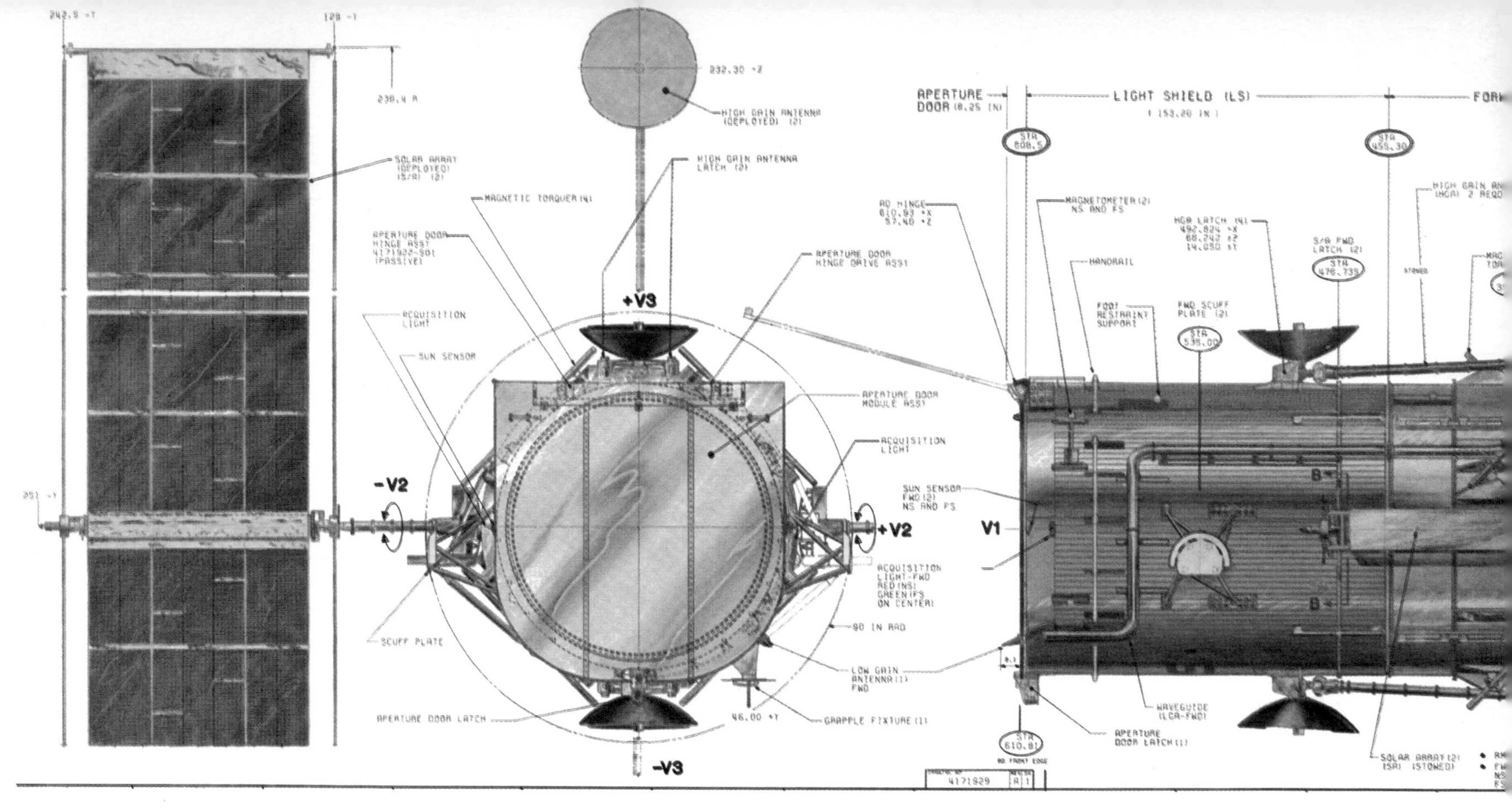

Two solar-cell arrays provide power for the Hubble Space Telescope and make it largely self-sufficient. The telescope itself is self-contained, but power arrays and antennas will be deployed soon after the payload reaches orbital altitude as the shuttle's cargo. The space telescope (ST) represents the shuttle's maximum load. The unmanned observatory will be serviced periodically, and returned to Earth as needed for overhaul.

would be galactic disks around distant quasars. Some nearby ones have such disks. If observations were to reveal few others, we'd be back to square one in our understanding of the nature of quasars.

ST may allow us to see distant galaxies so clearly that we can extend the Cepheid variable scale tenfold, and perhaps settle the debate about the true age of the universe. Seeing the end of all-that-exists should be very useful. And we may be able to if our theories are correct.

Another possible impact of ST on the distance scale will be a by-product of the guidance system. This system will of necessity make extremely accurate measurements of the positions of many stars, an important step in pinpointing absolute distances.

All in all, the ST will represent a major advance in world astronomical capabilities, so it is appropriate that it has something of an international character. The European Space Agency (ESA) has contributed 15 percent of the cost of the ST, supplying the solar panels and part of the instrument package. Consequently, European astronomers have access to 15 percent of the viewing time. The ST organization runs like any other major scientific facility. Astronomers from around the world send proposals to the Space Telescope Institute, located at the Johns Hopkins University in Baltimore. There, committees of working scientists judge the proposals on their scientific merit and parcel out time on the telescope. The way such decisions are made is often complex but, on the whole, the system seems to work well. For all their contentiousness, scientists are usually able to recognize a good idea when they see one.

But if the majority of astronomers are eagerly awaiting the new data that will flow from ST, a small group of intrepid pioneers has already begun work designing its successor, which goes by the name of Large Deployable Reflector (LDR). Bill Alff, senior staff engineer in Lockheed's Electro-Optics Laboratory, has been involved both with the ST and the LDR. Just how does a gigantic project like a new space telescope get started? "About four years ago, Lockheed went to NASA and gave a presenta-

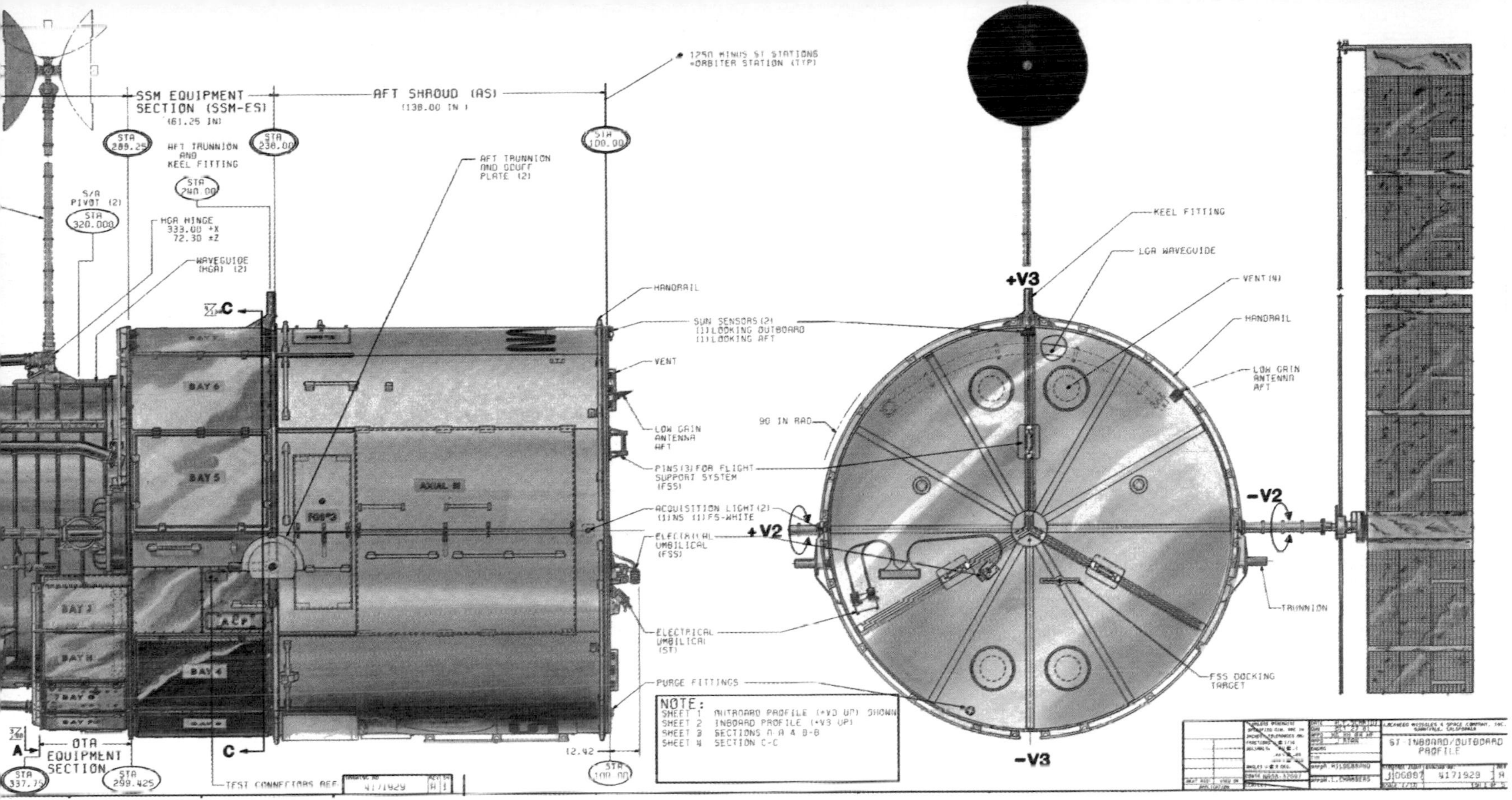

tion," he explains. "We told them about new developments in the field of lightweight telescopes. Basically, we said 'Here's what we can do—is it any use to you?' "

NASA responded by asking Lockheed to study the idea further, and eventually called a meeting at which astronomers, industry representatives, and government officials got together to draft a list of requirements for the successor to the ST. What they came up with was an optical and ultraviolet telescope 20 meters (65 feet) across.

What has to be done before such a telescope can be built?

"The first thing," Bill explains, "is the development of a lightweight telescope. The ST mirror weighs 36 pounds per square foot. We'll have to do a lot better than that with the advanced telescope. Other technical problems need to be examined. For example, it would take two shuttle loads to put this telescope in orbit. Do we have the technology to assemble something this complex in space?" Examining such questions may take Lockheed, working under contract to NASA, five years or more. Eventually, the question of whether LDR will be a free flyer like the ST or tethered to a space station must be settled. "It may be that this telescope will be the major justification for building the station," Bill points out.

SIRTF and AXAF

There's no way around it—when you get into an area where the government and the aerospace companies are involved, both the professional and the interested layman will run into a lot of the alphabet; space research abounds with acronyms. SIRTF stands for Satellite InfraRed Telescope Facility. This will be the follow up to the infrared surveys made by IRAS. It was originally conceived as an infrared telescope that would fly with the shuttle, but this proved to be impractical. Because an infrared telescope would pick up heat generated by other experiments in the shuttle bay, the telescope would require an entire shuttle mission to itself —a very expensive prospect.

Besides, as Lockheed's SIRTF program manager Robert Pelzmann pointed out, an infrared telescope is extremely sensitive to

Inside a gigantic clean room at Sunnyvale, California, NASA's Hubble Space Telescope nears completion. Before ST can be launched into space, it must travel from the Pacific coast to the Atlantic. Too large to be flown, the main tube in its air-conditioned pod is designed for barge travel by way of the Panama Canal to Cape Canaveral, Florida.

After deployment, the ST will operate according to instructions transmitted from the ground. To avoid damage, though, the ST will remain closed until well after the shuttle's departure. Also, it will change position to avoid even the slightest glimpse of the sun, moon, or Earth. These bodies are far too bright, and might burn the sensing instruments in the rear compartment. These are designed to record images of very faint objects at great distances. Art by Rick Sternbach and Don Dixon. Technicians at The Perkin-Elmer Corporation in Danbury, Connecticut, inspect ST's primary mirror at right. Measuring 94 inches in diameter, it is widely regarded as the most perfect large telescope mirror ever created.

A science-fiction device come true, Exosat (European X-ray Observatory Satellite) went into orbit in May 1983. Belonging to a group of advanced payloads, it will help lead the way to observatories associated with a space station or a base on the moon.

Transparent domes shelter astronomers at a lunar outpost. The futuristic scene, depicted here by Chesley Bonestell, may well be realized when mankind returns to the moon, a trip envisioned for the turn of the century.

dust. It cannot distinguish between dust motes floating around the telescope and the interstellar dust it is supposed to be measuring. An infrared telescope needs what are called class 100 conditions—fewer than 100 dust particles per cubic foot in its environment. To achieve these sorts of conditions in clean rooms on earth, the air is filtered. Then someone in a special suit picks out the individual particles with a small vacuum device. Such conditions would be hard to maintain in the shuttle. "Consequently," says Pelzmann, "the choice for SIRTF now is between a free flyer and something attached to a space station."

All sorts of problems face those studying an instrument like SIRTF. For example, it is necessary to cool the telescope down to keep it operating. The picture I had in mind was something like this: the telemetry from the satellite indicates that it's running low on liquid helium. On its next flight the shuttle pulls alongside, an astronaut gets out and refills the tanks with liquid that has been carried in the shuttle bay, and the shuttle departs, leaving SIRTF functioning as usual. What could be simpler than that?

"The problem," explains Pelzmann, "is that in space you may know that a container is half empty, but you have no way of knowing where in the container the liquid is." The problem is a little like trying to find the soap in your bathtub when your eyes are shut—you know it's there somewhere, but putting your hands on it when you want it is another matter. This is just one small problem involved in long-term cryogenic (low-temperature) operations in space—a technology which, in the language of aerospace people, has yet to be "proved."

Another problem with cryogenic systems, both on the ground and in space, is that they are difficult to repair and modify. Changing an instrument packet on SIRTF

Physicist specializing in high-resolution spectroscopy, Kouichi Yoshino appears with a vacuum spectograph with a scanning device used for studying molecules and atoms in the upper atmosphere and interstellar media. A member of the United States-Japan Cooperative Science Program, he conducts research at the Harvard-Smithsonian Center for Astrophysics. Sensor-carrying satellites at right observe a single phenomenon, the effect on the Earth of a major solar flare. This deployment of satellites is part of NASA's proposal for the International Solar-Terrestrial Physics Program.

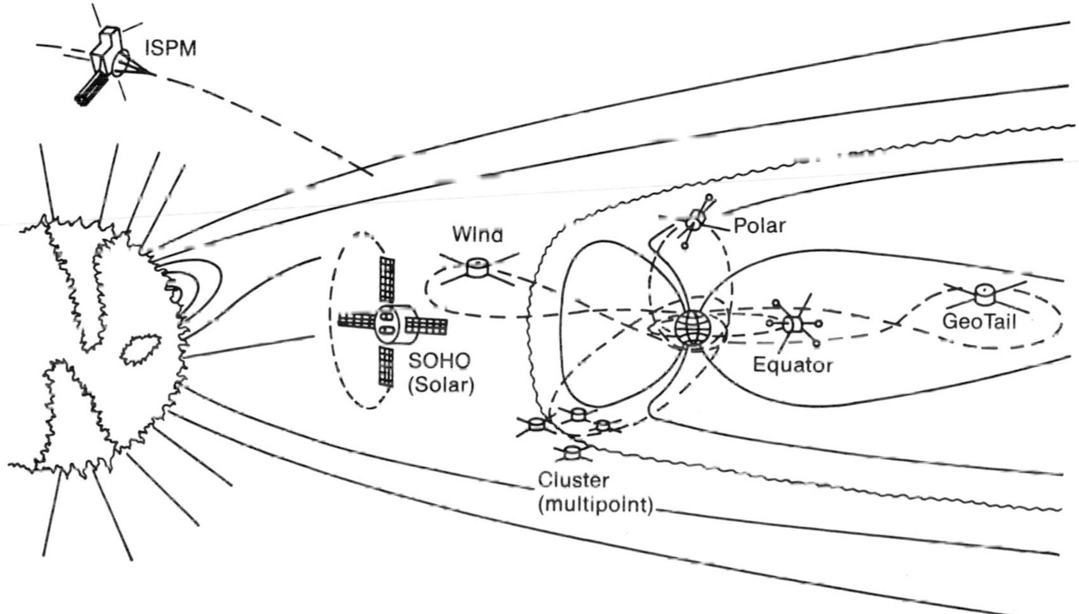

Model for the proposed McDonald telescope gleams against a starry backdrop. Planned for the University of Texas, the completed device would feature a 300-inch mirror, half again as large as the Palomar reflector.

would not just be a matter of bolting on a new module. The telescope first has to be warmed up, then worked on, then brought back to low temperatures. In laboratories on the surface this kind of process can easily take weeks. How will it be done in space?

The only way to show that you know how to solve this sort of problem, of course, is to carry equipment into space and work on it. This explains why astronauts in orbit spend so much of their time doing seemingly inconsequential experiments. It doesn't seem that an astronaut trying to get liquid helium from one tank to another is doing anything to resolve the mysteries surrounding the birth of stars, but unless we learn how to do such mundane tasks, we'll never have long-lived infrared observatories in orbit and the riddle may remain unsolved. This is a good thing to keep in mind the next time you watch a shuttle crew at work.

Another major project of this type now under intensive development is AXAF, for Advanced X-Ray Astrophysics Facility. In the report on astronomy in the eighties prepared by the National Academy of Sciences, this particular project was given the highest priority among astronomy-in-space programs. Like SIRTF, AXAF will be in permanent orbit.

AXAF will be about four feet across—twice the size of the Einstein Observatory, and will have 10 times the resolving power. This means that it will be able to study X-ray emissions from thousands of nearby stars as well as radiation emitted from extragalactic sources. It should be able to give good photographs of distant quasars (most of which are X-ray emitters). These studies should shed more light on basic questions. What are quasars? How do they produce so much energy?

A project of the mid-to-late eighties, going forward even as you read these words,

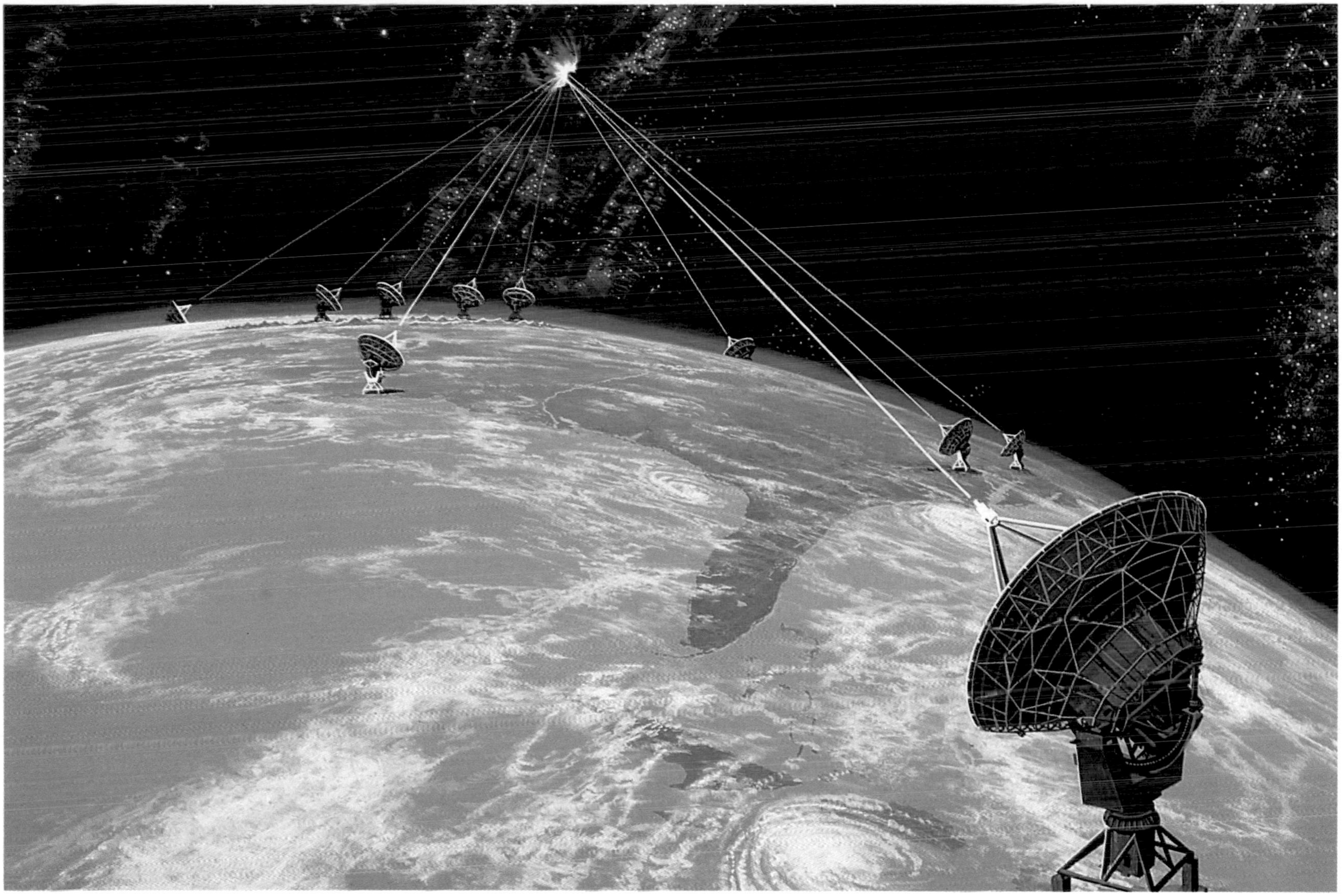

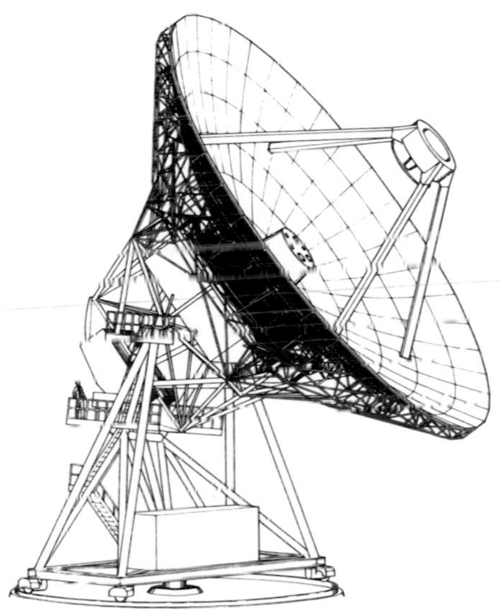

Teamed-up telescopes may soon transform North America and parts of the Caribbean into one colossal radio dish. In the version shown above, dishes of the VLBA or Very Long Baseline Array would be able to combine their readings to yield very detailed "images" of some active stars and galaxies. Conventional "light buckets"—the big telescopes—can seldom resolve these radio sources as anything more than points of light. In radio frequencies, however, their "invisible" matter is clearly seen. The long-baseline idea may result in radio dishes in Europe or even on the moon.

Companion suns shine in a distant planetary system. Without an artist's help, no one on Earth today could behold such an alien vista. Illustration by the distinguished artist of intergalactic horizons, Chesley Bonestell.

involves construction of the VLBA (Very Long Baseline Array). This collection of 10 radio telescopes, each about 75 feet across, is to be scattered throughout the United States. Their purpose will be to do long-baseline interferometry, a technique employing widely-scattered radio telescopes to produce extremely precise high-resolution pictures of radio sources.

What's Next in Space?

In addition, the astronomical community has a number of long-range plans that are still at the gleam-in-the-eye stage. One of the most interesting of these goes by the acronym OPEN (Origins of Plasma in the Earth's Neighborhood). This project marks an attempt to go beyond single-purpose observatories, to monitor an astronomical phenomenon in all its complexity.

With increased experience in mechanical and electronic miniaturization, many diminutive probes could be placed in separate orbits around the Earth or other planets. With the eruption of a suitable solar flare, for instance, each cocoon-like sensing package could emerge (with wings of solar cells and electronic antennae) into a resplendent "space butterfly," in the words of Princeton professor Freeman Dyson.

Whatever form the future of space astronomy takes, however, one thing is certain. Astronomers and aerospace scientists today are preparing to exploit (and with a vengeance) the new windows in space—from cosmic rays through the entire radio-wavelength spectrum.

Splendid example of scientific illustration, Rob Wood's painting shows the launch of an artificial comet in an investigation of effects of the solar wind in the Van Allen radiation belts.

Members of the International Association of Space Artists convene an annual meeting—this year in Death Valley, California. They study the geology, explore, and paint. Such illustrators help to shape our ideas and images of the cosmos.

©Chesley Bonestell

Big Bang and Beyond

Innermost and outermost territories of the universe appear at left and below. Tracks that curl in upon themselves mark the frantic flight of relativistic particles, refugees from the tiny and highly-structured realm of the atom. The quasar,

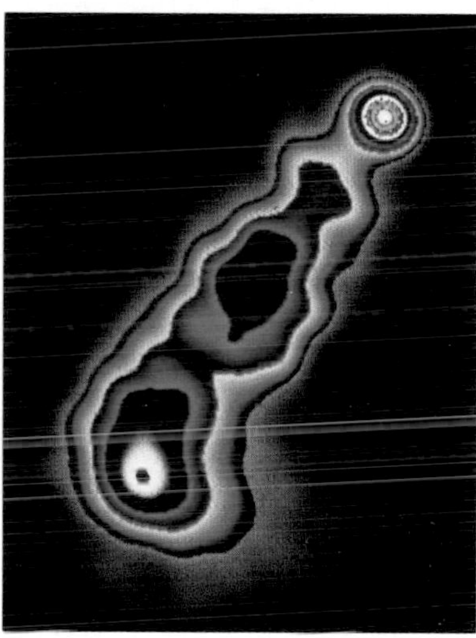

above, shines at our outermost horizon, the present limit of observability. Some quasar light has been traveling toward us for billions of years, so the quasars themselves may have disappeared or changed long ago.

Hubble gave us the picture of the expanding universe, with galaxies receding from each other like raisins in a rising bread dough. One interpretation of this result, as we have seen, is a view in which the creation of the universe began as a single, infinitely-dense collection of matter that has been expanding ever since. We have called this picture the Big Bang. It is not, however, the only possible interpretation of Edwin Hubble's data.

A rival theory, championed by British astronomer Fred Hoyle, postulated that as the galaxies separate, matter is created in the void, so that new galaxies are formed in the spaces vacated by the old. In such a picture, there would be perpetual recession, but no Big Bang. Some humorists suggested that Hoyle invented this theory so that there would always be an England, but if the only data we had was the Hubble red shift, we would have a hard time ruling out Hoyle.

In fact, there are two other important pieces of data that have come to hand since Hubble's time, both of which provide strong confirmation of the Big Bang picture. These are the discovery of the cosmic-microwave background and the abundance of helium in the universe.

We have frequently alluded to the connection between the temperature of an object and the kind of radiation it emits. Burning coal first glows red hot, for example, then white, then blue, and then (if heated enough) ultraviolet. The higher the temperature, the shorter the wavelength. This is why extremely violent (and therefore high-temperature) regions of the universe emit X rays. But this proposition works in reverse as well: as objects cool, the wavelength of

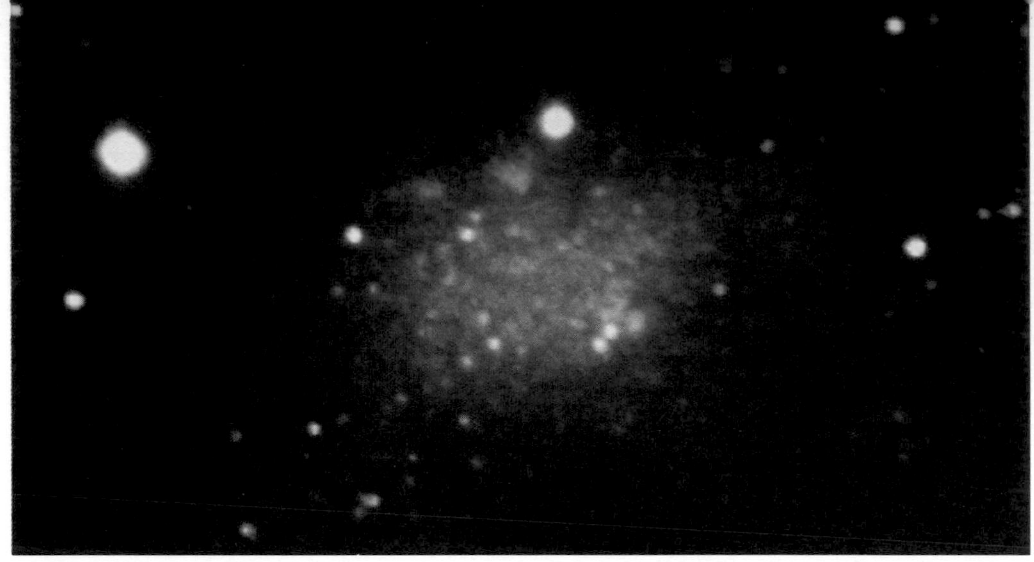

Seen through a screen of bright stars within the Milky Way, a neighbor galaxy resides within our Local Group. This is a collection of 30 galactic bodies influenced strongly by the gravitational attraction of our Milky Way and Andromeda, the other large spiral in the Local Group. In addition to the more highly evolved entities, primitive star groups called globular clusters accompany our Milky Way. These probably contain very ancient stars, and may be relics from a far earlier time when quasars were evolving into the galaxies we see today.

the radiation they emit gets longer. For example, if you come into a room and want to know if there has been a fire in the fireplace, you can look at the coals. If they are glowing brightly, you know the fire was active very recently. If they are barely glowing, you know there has been a fire, but that it ended a while ago. If the coals aren't glowing, you still may be able to detect infrared radiation by holding out your hand to see if you feel heat. If you do, you know that the fire has not been burning for at least half an hour.

Coals emit radiation that steadily progresses down through the electromagnetic spectrum from short visible wavelengths to longer visible wavelengths into infrared as the coals cool off. If you feel no heat, it doesn't mean the coals are no longer radiating, but only that the wavelength has changed. Its energy level has dropped so much that your hand is not stimulated. With the proper equipment, you could trace the radiation until the coals reached the temperature of their surroundings.

Going back to the Big Bang, we see the analogy with the fireplace clearly. If the universe was very hot a long time ago, then we ought to be able to feel the "coals" of that first great fire. Of course, it's been a long time since the universe was hot, so we expect the radiation to be well down the scale—in the microwave region, in fact. In the early sixties, two scientists at Bell Telephone Laboratories were making measurements of radio and microwave sources in the sky. The motivation for this program, and the equipment being used, arose from the early attempts to use satellites for communications. (We tend to forget how recent our globe-girdling communications net is. I can remember when live TV from Europe was so unusual that a caption "Live via Satellite" was shown at the bottom of the screen.)

If we want to receive radio communications from satellites, then finding sources of noise in the sky is very important.

Arno Penzias and Robert Wilson had taken over a large moveable antenna at Bell Labs to do such a study. What they found was totally unexpected. There was a noise in their receiver that didn't seem to vary at all from day to night and didn't seem to change when they pointed the telescope in different directions. It was very disturbing because this sort of result usually means that there's something wrong with the apparatus. The experimenters were aware of at least one persistent possible source of error in their system—a pair of pigeons had taken up residence in the antenna, coating parts of it with a "white dielectric substance." This insulating substance could be removed, of course, but were there other problems?

Their puzzling results soon got out on the grapevine, and the experimenters eventually made contact with P.J. Peebles, a young theoretical astrophysicist at Princeton. Peebles had just finished working out the problem of radiation in an expanding universe, and when everybody got together the nature of the "noise" became clear. Penzias and Wilson had detected the radiation from the "coals" of the Big Bang, just as surely as you feel the heat of coals with your hand.

The radiation they found would correspond to that emitted by a body just three degrees above absolute zero, a temperature physicists call three degrees on the Kelvin scale (or 3 K). This radiation pervaded the entire universe, and its discovery marked the death knell of alternate theories to the Big Bang. The existence of the 3 K background radiation remains one of the strongest pieces of evidence for the accepted picture of an evolutionary universe. For their discovery, Penzias and Wilson received the 1978 Nobel Prize in physics.

The second piece of evidence, less direct than the 3 K background, concerns the relative abundance of the light elements in the universe. We know that carbon and elements of a greater atomic weight are made in stars, and that light elements like lithium, beryllium, and boron appear when heavier elements collide with cosmic rays in the interstellar void. In the early stages of the Big Bang, as we shall see shortly, only deuterium (an atom whose nucleus consists of a proton and neutron), helium, and an isotope of lithium can be formed. If we know the conditions that prevailed during the early stages of the Big Bang (and we believe we do) then we can look at nuclear reactions in our laboratories and calculate how much of the primordial hydrogen would have been turned into deuterium and helium at that time. These calculations can then be compared to the abundance of these elements we actually see in the universe.

For example, the standard Big Bang model predicts that the universe should be roughly 24 percent helium. This is an extremely precise prediction—if the percentage of primordial helium were lower than 23 percent or higher than 27 percent, we would have to rethink the entire Big Bang picture. Fortunately, the observed fact and the theory fit each other.

The standard Big Bang model also predicts how many hydrogen atoms in the universe should actually contain deuterium nuclei. Since these atoms also occur on earth, we have the opportunity to do "astronomy with a shovel," as Arno Penzias says. The amount of "heavy water" (that is, water in which one of the hydrogen atoms is replaced by deuterium) involved in the formation of our planet should be the same as it is everywhere else. Again, we find general agreement between the Big Bang and the experiment, although many researchers are working out the details.

We have come to see that almost from the beginning our universe has evolved through simultaneous expansion and cooling, a picture well-supported by experiment. It makes sense, then, for us to look a little more closely at the consequences of this picture.

The Multiple Freezings

The best analogue for the universe is a collection of very hot steam confined in a small volume. If you release the steam, it will expand and cool off. When it has cooled off to a special temperature—212°F—an important process will take place. The steam will condense into water. If that water continues to expand and cool off, eventually another singular event will occur: the water will freeze into ice. An expansion, in other words, necessarily implies a drop in the temperature, and lower temperatures may involve changes in the state of matter—in this example, from steam to water and then from water to ice. I will refer to these changes by the generic term "freezing." This is a somewhat unfamiliar use of the term, because it implies that hot things can freeze as well as cold ones. But this shouldn't be too surprising. Molten iron, for example, "freezes" (solidifies) at temperatures below 2,800°F, which is hot by normal standards. In our analogy, steam "freezes" (condenses) into water at 212°F, then freezes into ice at 32°F.

The expanding universe can be expected to go through freezings, too. In fact, our modern picture of the Big Bang is one in which long periods of relative quiet are interspersed with short periods of rapid change. There are five such events (six eras) in the standard Big Bang scenario, and understanding all of them is one of the great tasks of modern science.

The most recent freezing took place about 500,000 years after the Big Bang. This means that the past 14,999,500,000 years of the 15-billion-year history of the universe have taken place in a setting that is much like what we see now—matter existing in the form of atoms, stars forming and dying, and elements being manufactured. If we were to go backward in time, the only things we'd notice would be a general warming, a trend evidenced by a shortening in the wavelength of the background radiation that fills the universe. At the 500,000 year mark the temperature would have climbed to the point where the collisions between atoms were so energetic that electrons would start to be torn off their nuclei. We have a situation in which atoms, a familiar form of matter, could not have existed before the universe was 500,000 years old, but could have existed afterwards.

If an electron happened to attach itself to a nucleus to form an atom before 500,000

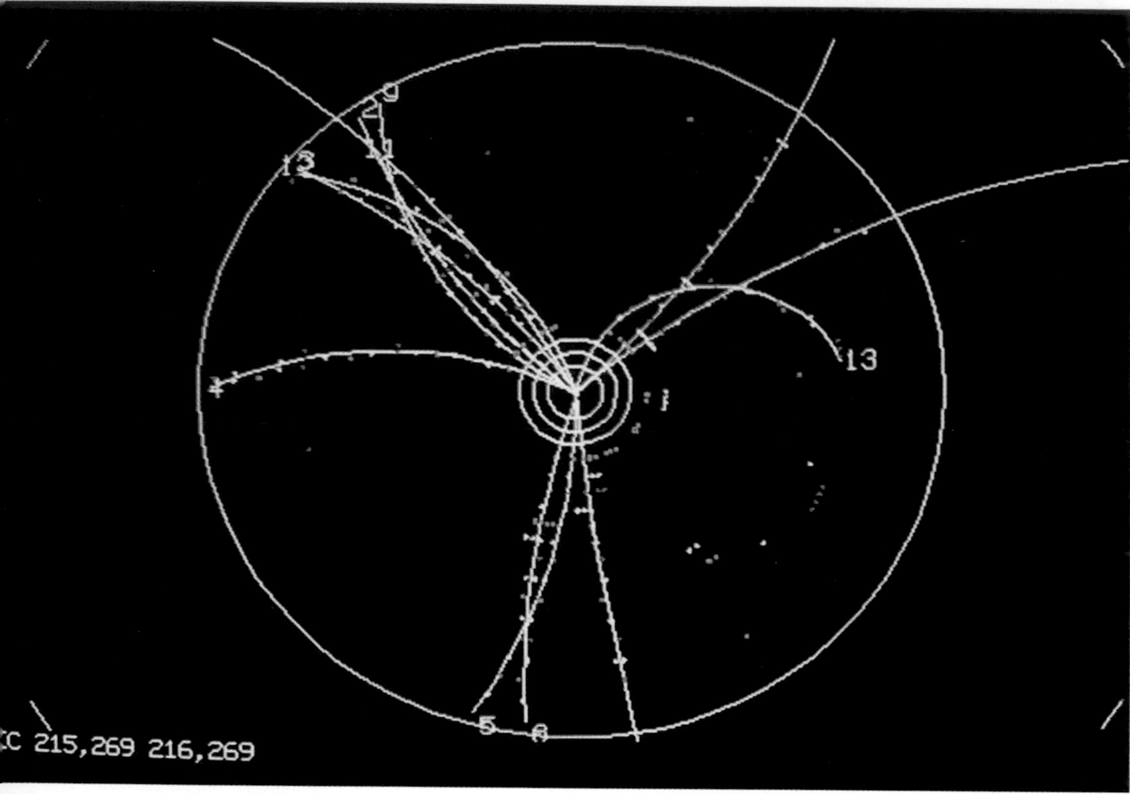

Computerized display reveals a nuclear signature, above. Known as a three-jet event, the pattern confirms the existence of a state of matter probably occurring in the collapsing cores of large stars. Opposite, at Chicago's Fermi National Accelerator Laboratory, Director Leon Lederman and a student discuss experimental techniques employed in high-energy physics. Key to such investigations are the tracks left when smashed atoms spew particles into space. Trails often diverge in a V-shaped pattern from the site of an atom's disintegration. Curlicues occur when particles are caught in strong magnetic fields, as seen opposite.

year mark, a collision would have quickly knocked it off again. After this time, however, the temperature had dropped to the point where such collisions would be sufficiently mild to allow the electron to stay attached. We say, then, that atoms "froze" out of a collection of nuclei and electrons (a system which physicists call a plasma).

This final freezing eventually resulted in our own familiar universe. It should be pointed out, however, that unlike some of the transitions which occurred earlier, and unlike the water and ice in our analogy, the freezing of atoms did not occur at a single, well-defined temperature. It's much better to think of this as a gradual process, where a few atoms are present as early as 100,000 years after the Big Bang, and with most electrons accounted for by the millionth birthday of the universe.

This freezing did more than just provide us with the building blocks for living systems. So energetic was the environment before the formation of atoms that stars and galaxies stood no chance of developing. When the freezing occurred—with the creation of atoms—the universe literally became transparent and the energy it contained could escape easier. With the heat turned down in nature's pressure cooker, atoms could clump together. Matter originates as single atoms, which form masses as gravity's influence increases.

High levels of energy could no longer keep the new form of matter from coalescing into protogalaxies. The detailed process by which galaxies took shape remains one of the major problems in modern cosmology. We feel certain, however, that no matter could have collected into galaxy-sized pieces until after atoms had formed, thus enabling the universe to become transparent.

For a simple but effective analogy, watch your iced tea next time you stir in a spoonful of granulated sugar. At first, the tea appears cloudy. Light interacts with the individual grains of sugar and is scattered—in effect, it exerts a small pressure. As the sugar goes into solution, however, the tea becomes transparent again, for molecules do not interact strongly with light. The clearing of the tea resembles what happened to the expanding universe during its most recent episode of freezing.

Before the freezing of the atoms, the universe was characterized by electrons and nuclei floating around independently of each other. Physicists refer to this energetic situation as matter in the plasma state. It was the norm almost from the beginning, starting about three minutes after the Big Bang. Earlier, collisions between the constituents of the universe were so violent that nuclei of atoms could not stay together. We must venture into this bizarre period before three minutes, however, if we are to learn as much as we can about the origins of matter.

Particles and Quarks

If we want to know what happened during the first three minutes, we should first enter the recently discovered world of elementary particle physics—a world that bears little resemblance to the one we are used to.

We learn that the nuclei of atoms are not made up of just protons and neutrons, but of hundreds of different kinds of particles. These particles are born, live out their brief existence, and die within the nucleus of a single atom. Since they are not as visible as the building blocks of nuclei, they are not as well known as protons and neutrons.

The first of these elementary particles was discovered in the debris of cosmic-ray collisions in the 1930s, and sorting out their behavior has been the task of specialists in high-energy physics ever since. For our purposes, we need to know only three things about these particles. First, they were all present in the universe during the first three minutes. Second, they are almost all unstable. And finally, most aren't really elementary in the usual sense of the word. They are made up of other, still more elementary species, collectively known as quarks.

We know that energy and matter are interchangeable—this is what Einstein taught us in his famous equation $E = mc^2$. In the very early stages of the universe, this remarkable property meant that the energy involved in collisions between fast-moving particles could be converted into the mass necessary to make any of the hundreds of other kinds of particles.

With the temperature high, the universe was a giant vat of soup in which particles appeared during collisions, decayed into other particles, and collided again to produce still other particles. This was an era of extraordinary complexity, one whose mysteries we've been able to unravel only because we can reproduce some of these collisions in high-energy particle accelerators.

The particle era itself began about 10 microseconds after the Big Bang and lasted until the particles froze together into nuclei at three minutes. During this period all of the elementary particles now produced only in our laboratories were present, some familiar (such as the proton and neutron), and many not so familiar.

We usually imagine elementary particles as being something like bricks—stable building blocks of larger structures. In fact, an elementary particle left to its own devices will usually decay (that is, break down into other particles of smaller mass). If you watched something as familiar as a free neutron, for example, you would see that after a space of 10 minutes or so it would disappear, leaving behind a proton, an electron, and a neutrino.

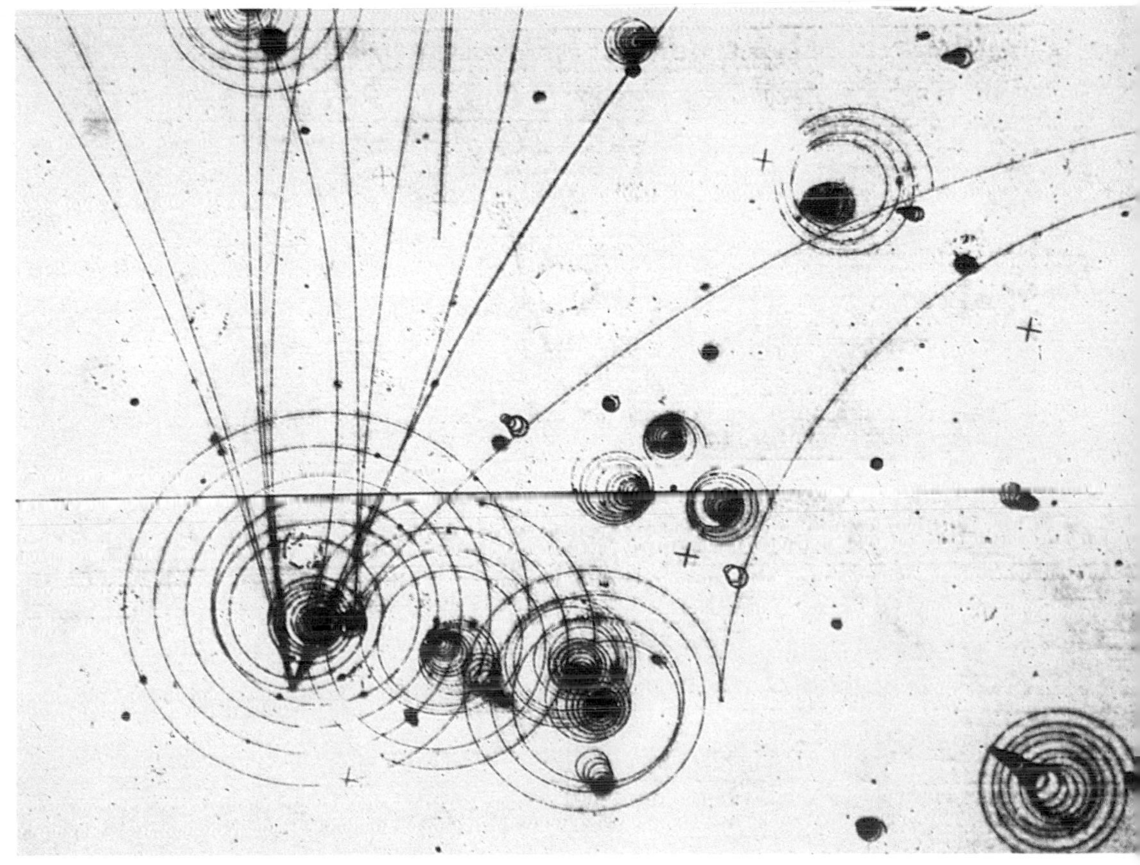

New computer program creates signatures of events involving subatomic particles, providing scientists with an idea of what might appear in their atomic accelerators.

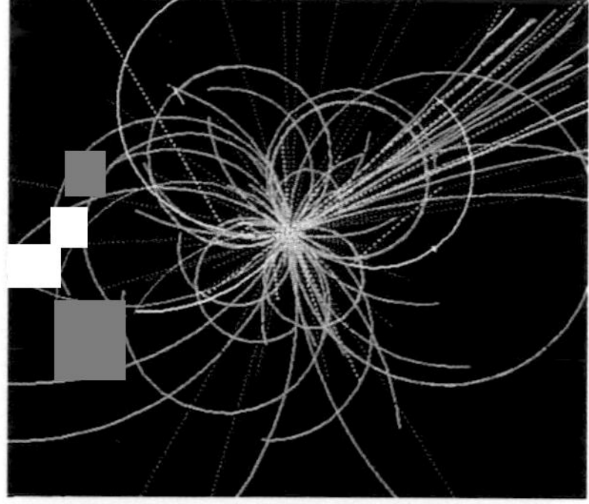

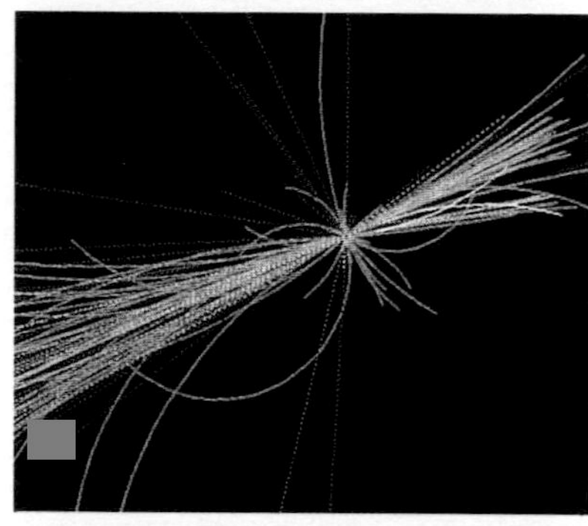

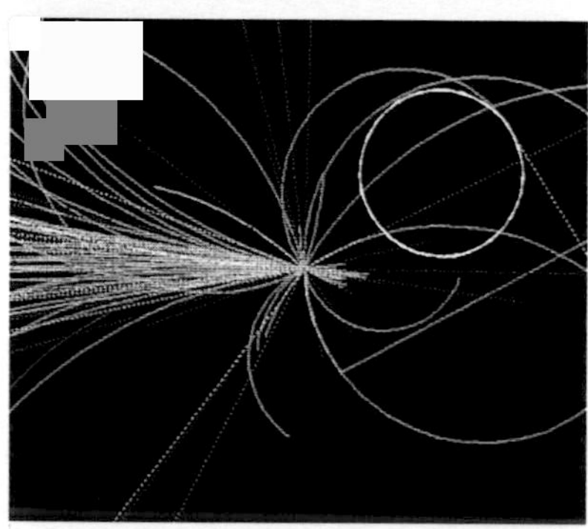

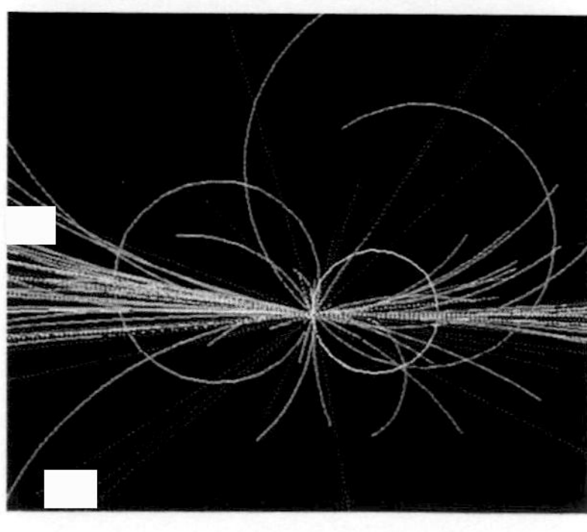

This last particle may play an important role in cosmology, so we'll review a few of its properties here. It has no electrical charge, thus its name which means "little neutral one." Its mass is either zero or very small (we don't know for sure since no one has been able to measure it). According to the conventional wisdom, it has a mass that is exactly zero and travels at the speed of light. It is like the electron in that it is not part of that maelstrom of particles we call the nucleus. Particles like the electron and neutrino, which do not participate in the nuclear interactions, are called leptons which mean "weakly interacting ones."

Given enough time, almost all of the elementary particles decay into lighter particles. Exceptions include the electron, neutrino, and possibly the proton. There are two consequences of this fact for cosmology. First, if we start with a single massive particle, it will decay into other particles, which will in turn decay, and so on. Thus, all species of particles can be expected to make an appearance in the sea of hot matter that was the universe during the Big Bang era. Furthermore, any remaining particle soon disappears as the temperature of the universe drops below the point where there is energy enough to support its mass. The surviving members will decay and no new ones will be created. The species will simply die out. This is why most particles are seen today only in unusual circumstances.

Finally, scientists realized during the sixties that all of the hundreds of "elementary" particles that had been discovered couldn't really be elementary. Nor could the nucleus of each different chemical element be a unique building block of matter, unrelated to others. The theoretical problem of the proliferation of species was resolved by the discovery that each nucleus was just a different arrangement of two basic ingredients, protons and neutrons.

Similarly, the proliferation of elementary particles was recognized to be nothing more than a consequence of the fact that these particles (leptons excluded) were made up of quarks—things still more elementary. They come together in different arrangements to make the elementary particles, and then these particles join together in the nuclei of atoms. The family name for the basic building blocks that form atoms comes from a line in James Joyce's *Finnegan's Wake*—"Three quarks for Muster Mark." When the quark theory was first proposed, there were supposed to be three kinds of quarks, which explains the use of Joyce's word. Today, we know of at least six different species—up, down, charm, strange, top-truth, and bottom-beauty.

Thus, as it turns out when we look closely at the structure of matter, we find only two kinds of building blocks—quarks and leptons. In a sense, simplicity triumphs, however complex the subatomic world may appear. The quarks are the building blocks from which the nuclei are made, the electrons (which are one kind of lepton) then circle the nuclei to make atoms, and atoms combine to make the chemical compounds we see everywhere in the universe—in the earth as in the sky.

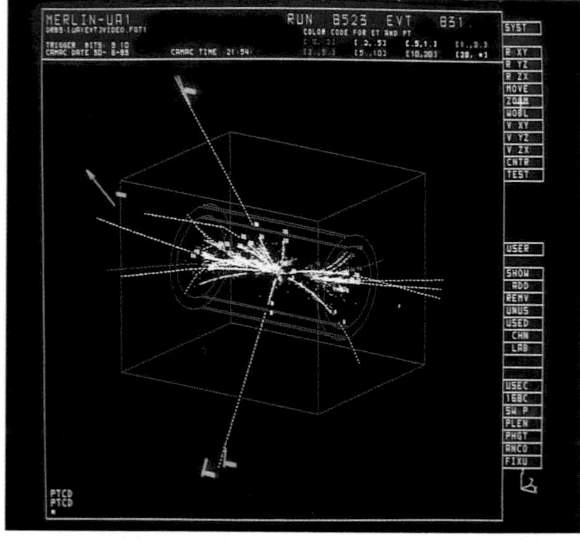

With this knowledge in hand, we can resume our trek toward the moment of creation. The freezing that preceded the formation of nuclei at three minutes was the joining of the quarks into elementary particles. Before this episode, the quarks were floating about freely in the universe. According to our present theories, once the quarks had become confined—frozen in—they ceased to possess a separate identity. Then, during a complex cooling process, species of particles disappeared as the temperature fell. Eventually, cooling progressed far enough for nuclei of atoms to form.

Our understanding of the basic structure of matter, then, allows us to work our way backwards into the Big Bang until the universe was just 10 microseconds old. We could not span this great distance before the marriage of cosmology to the science of elementary particles. The first concerns itself with the largest thing we know of (the universe), the second with the smallest (the elementary particles). That these two fields should come together in this way is not surprising in retrospect, but it certainly wasn't foreseen by people in either discipline.

This interdisciplinary fertilization has had many consequences. Perhaps the most significant, science and scientists have become organized in such a way that theoretical and experimental advances in one area will probably mean important gains for the other.

Unification of Forces

During the late seventies, physicists and astronomers began to apply new theories about the behavior of elementary particles to the processes that went on before the first microsecond. These new theories concerned themselves not so much with the constituents of matter, but with the ways that bits of matter interact with each other—the phenomena we call "force."

Physicists recognize four distinct forces in nature. Two of these—gravitation and elec-

To create samples for research, scientists bombard atoms to smash loose subatomic particles, as with those below at the University of California's Riverside campus. Experimental confirmation of the Weinberg-Salam electroweak theory came in the form of the computer image of the W particle, at center. The important discovery was made near Geneva in the early eighties at CERN, a remarkably successful European scientific consortium.

Members of the "Smithsonian World" TV team visit a Morton salt mine near Lake Erie. Here, experimenters have created a subterranean reservoir in which to test theories about the longevity of atoms and their subatomic particles. When atoms disintegrate spontaneously, flashes of light may occur. Sensors in the pool of unusually pure water catch hints of such events, which may provide evidence of the predicted decay of protons.

tromagnetism—are familiar in everyday experience. The other two were discovered in the twentieth century and concern elementary particles. They are called the strong and the weak forces. The strong force acts between particles to hold the nucleus together against the repulsive electrical forces trying to push individual protons away from each other. The most common manifestation of the weak force is in some of the slow radioactive decay we see in nuclei and elementary particles. Everything that happens in the universe happens because of one or more of these four forces.

On the one hand, being able to reduce every observed change to a manifestation of one of only four forces may seem like a tremendous simplification. To a physicist this multiplicity is suspicious. Four forces imply four separate and disjointed theories which, in turn, implies that the marvelous interconnectedness of nature is lost. Put another way, physicists believe—as did Einstein—that when we find the correct theory of the universe we will see that it is beautiful and elegant. Having four separate forces is definitely not up to standard.

We see a historical precedent for reducing the number of forces in nature. We saw how Newton managed to unify the seemingly different forces of heavenly and earthly gravity, showing that there was only one force responsible for both the fall of the apple and the orbit of the moon. Many great scientists, Albert Einstein among them, believed that the present multiplicity of forces could be resolved by the development of a so-called unified field theory, a theory in which all of the forces are seen as identical at some level. In this case, the apparent differences we see are due to our inability to look beyond the surface of things.

The first step toward a modern realization of this old dream of unity was taken in 1967 by Steven Weinberg (then at MIT) and, independently, six months later by Abdus Salam in London. Their work was ignored for a period of about five years, and it wasn't until the early seventies that people began paying attention to it. In essence, they had produced a theory in which the electromagnetic and the weak forces were seen as basically identical. The differences between the forces was a result of observing them in a relatively frigid era. If the temperature were high enough, the underlying identity would be manifest.

Consider an analogy in which two skaters approach each other at high speed on the ice. They come closer and closer and just as they pass, one throws a bucket of water at the other. The act of throwing causes the first skater to recoil, while being splashed causes the second to do the same. The net result of the exchange, then, is that the direction of motion of both skaters has been altered. From Newton's first law, this sort of change is what we expect to see when a force acts. In this situation, we notice that the force is associated with the exchange of

"Oh my ears and whiskers, how late it's getting!" exclaims the White Rabbit from Lewis Carroll's Alice's Adventures in Wonderland. *Illustration by John Tenniel, London, 1866.*

Scientists at left watch preparations for something of a Carrollesque experiment. They wait for atoms to spontaneously disintegrate. Such events in this watery "rabbit-hole" could substantiate features of the so-called Grand Unified Theories. If experiment confirms theory, we may have reason to suspect that in the distant future the stuff of earth, sky, and even time itself might literally come unglued.

material between the skaters—water, in this case. In modern physics, we think of all of the fundamental forces as being generated when something is exchanged between elementary particles.

Now suppose we had two sets of skaters in the rink. The first set is identical to the ones in our first example, with a force being generated by an exchange of water. In the second set, a bucket of liquid is exchanged, but this time the liquid is alcohol instead of water. Most of us would have little difficulty in accepting the statement that the forces associated with each of these two situations were fundamentally identical—the difference between water and alcohol would not strike us as being crucial.

But now suppose we began lowering the temperature in which these two sets of skaters operate. When we reach a crucial level—32°F—we would see the water freeze while the alcohol would remain a liquid. Now one skater would be hit with a liquid, the other with a solid block of ice. Obviously, the nature of the materials and of the forces, metaphorically speaking, is no longer the same. The freezing of the water has changed the identity of one of the two forces, but if we raised the temperature the ice would melt and the forces would again be the same. Thus, the forces appear different only when viewed at a low temperature, but at a high temperature they seem to be fundamentally the same.

Diver installs light sensors to catch hints of proton decay in a 2.5 million-gallon tank. The IMB project shares support from the University of California at Irvine, the University of Michigan, and the Brookhaven National Laboratory.

This is exactly what happens with the electromagnetic and weak forces in the Weinberg-Salam theory. They appear different now because we are operating in a cold universe. If, however, we travel back far enough in the Big Bang, the temperature would climb and the true identity of the forces would become manifest. In effect, the ice would melt. Before the universe had cooled to this temperature, there would be only three fundamental forces acting in nature—the unified electroweak, the strong, and gravitational.

Before the quarks froze into particles at 10 microseconds, the universe consisted of quarks, leptons, and radiation interacting through the same four fundamental forces we see operating around us today. Proceeding backwards in time, we would have seen this same state of affairs until we reached a point about 100-trillionths of a second after the moment of creation. At this crucial instant, the underlying identity of the weak and electromagnetic forces would become evident. Before there were only three basic forces, afterward there were four.

Before going on, it would probably be a good idea to say a few words about the experimental confirmations of the Weinberg-Salam theory. The theory makes a number of predictions that can be checked in the laboratory. For one thing, this particular model predicts the existence of an interaction between neutrinos and nuclei of a type that had never been seen before. When these rare interactions were detected at the Fermi National Accelerator Laboratory near Chicago in 1973, people began to take the new theory very seriously. For their work in developing the unified theory, Weinberg, Salam, and Sheldon Glashow of Harvard were awarded the Nobel Prize in 1979. The theory also predicted that it would be possible to produce the particles whose exchange is responsible for the weak interactions, the particles corresponding to the ice in our analogy. In 1983, the W and Z particles were discovered at the European Center for Nuclear Research (CERN) near Geneva, Switzerland. They appeared just where the theory said they should.

We are getting into an area of time spans so short that we are going to run out of convenient ways to designate them. From now on, therefore, we will use the scientific notation. The basic idea is that instead of writing 10 microseconds as 0.00001 seconds, we write it as 10^{-5} second. We understand a negative number in the exponent of the 10 to mean "move the decimal point this many places to the left." Thus the weak force freezes out 10^{-10} second after the moment of creation.

Once we realize that the freezings in the early universe can involve forces as well as particles, new possibilities for transitions become obvious. Once we have reduced the number of fundamental interactions from four to three, what is to prevent us from going further? In fact, physicists took this step in the late seventies, when they began to apply what are called the Grand Unified Theories (or GUTs) to the early universe. In these theories, the strong force becomes unified with the electroweak force, leaving only two forces in nature—gravity and the new unified force. According to this body of theory, the universe would have reached the temperature at which this particular unification could occur at 10^{-35} second.

This particular freezing was a crucial one because many of the critical features of our present universe were decided then. This is also the time at which "inflation" occurred. Determining the course of such events challenges scientists at the frontiers of cosmological knowledge. In the next chapters we will describe some of the problems that have been solved and some whose solutions are still being sought.

Like the Weinberg-Salam theory, the GUTs make certain assertions about the early universe, but some of these assertions can be verified in the laboratory. The most striking of these concerns the stability of the proton, a particle that had always been considered absolutely stable—that is, it had been assumed that the proton did not decay. The GUTs predicted that experimenters would find that this was not quite true. The proton would decay, but so slowly that no previous experiment would have detected it. The lifetime of the proton was originally predicted to be about 10^{30} years (that's a one with 30 zeroes after it). This is much longer than the age of the universe, so the chance that an individual proton will decay while we're watching it is pretty small.

Experimenters decided on a simple strategy (at least in principle). If one proton decays every 10^{30} years, then in a collection of 10^{30} protons we'll see one decay a year. For reference, 10^{30} protons is about 50 times the number in a human body. A team of scientists from the University of Michigan, the University of California at Irvine, and the Brookhaven National Laboratory, working in a salt mine near Lake Erie, are watching protons in a tank of water the size of a five story building. Other of their colleagues monitor large collections of protons in a dozen places around the world.

But finding an instance of proton decay is somewhat difficult. Events have been seen that could be the signature of decaying protons, but the experimenters can't prove that they *must* arise from that source. It turns out that neutrinos in cosmic rays could occasionally trigger an event that could easily masquerade as a proton decay. No one knows how this debate will turn out, but we do know that the proton lifetime predicted by the simplest versions of the GUTs—the ones that motivated the experiments in the first place—were wrong. The proton lifetime must be at least 100 times longer than originally expected. This means that more complicated versions of the theories should be explored, and many physicists have now turned their attention to this task.

The Planck Time—End of the Line

Even though the freezing out of the strong force at 10^{-35} second represents the frontier of our present knowledge of the Big Bang, enough people have thought about what must come next for us to have a pretty good idea of what to expect. The era in which a sea of hot matter and radiation interact through two fundamental forces began

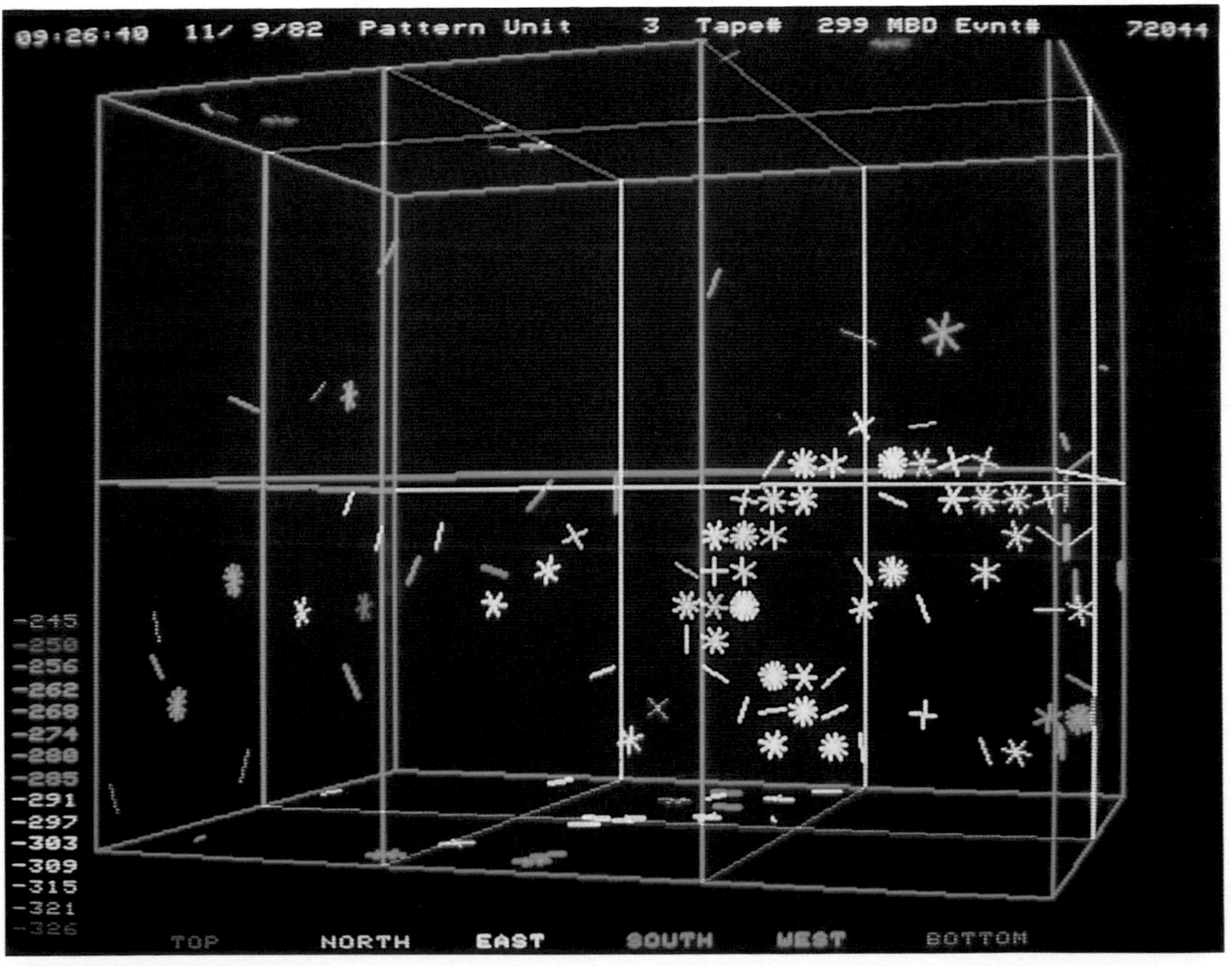

Computer imagery shows an array of subatomic particles from a candidate for proton decay at the Lake Erie site. Curiously, the IMB tank shows a variety of exotic atomic episodes, some associated with especially energetic radiation from deep space. Such serendipitous observations increase the sense of excitement surrounding experiments probing the frontiers of astrophysics.

10^{-43} second after creation (a figure referred to as the Planck time) and ended at 10^{-35} second. The name for 10^{-43} second comes from Max Planck, the renowned German physicist (1858–1947) who helped originate quantum mechanics. At the Planck time, the temperature of the universe was so high that the underlying identity of all the forces should have been manifest. I say "should" for a special reason. In order to unify gravity with the other forces, we would need a description of gravity in which it—like the other forces—was seen as arising from an exchange of some sort of particle. In the language of theoretical physics, we would need a quantum theory of gravity. No such theory exists. Some of the best minds of our generation are trying to develop one. It is probably only a matter of time before such a theory is written down.

So as far as gaining a complete mastery of the Big Bang is concerned, the Planck time represents a barrier we cannot, for the moment, penetrate. We can, however, look at some of the theories now being explored and make an educated guess about what might lie on the other side of the barrier. During its first 10^{-43} second of existence, the universe would have a single unified force operating on matter. In addition, all the kinds of particles we have talked about—quarks, leptons, various particles whose exchanges generated forces—would all be able to transform themselves into one another, so that there would be, in effect, only one kind of particle present. This universe, with a single force acting between particles of only one kind, represents the ultimate in simplicity and elegance.

A Summing Up

We cannot yet describe the actual moment of creation, so we are forced to begin our story at the Planck time. The first freezing of the universe resulted in the splitting off of gravity from the other three "unified" forces. Then there were two fundamental forces in operation. In the next freezing, at 10^{-35} second, the strong force split away, leaving a universe with three fundamental forces. At this freezing, many of the features of our present universe were decided. At 10^{-10} second the final freezing of the forces occurred, leaving us with our present complement of four—strong, electromagnetic, weak, and gravitational.

As the universe continued its expansion and cooling, a new kind of freezing entered the picture, one that involves the basic constituents of matter. At 10^{-5} second the quarks condensed into the elementary particles, and at three minutes protons and neutrons came together to form the nuclei of lightweight atoms. Finally, when the universe was about 500,000 years old, electrons were able to stay in orbit around these nuclei and atoms were formed. Then, radiation ceased exerting pressure on matter. The force of gravity initiated the slow collapse of matter into galaxies and stars.

The most recent events—the formation of nuclei and atoms—occurred at energies low enough for us to create in our laboratories. Only then can we study these episodes directly. The same can be said of the events that took place after the freezing of the quarks. After about 10^{-5} second, then, we have both experimental and theoretical verifications of the Big Bang scenario. Theories that describe the freezings at 10^{-5} and 10^{-10} second are well-worked out and have met many experimental tests. Thus, although we cannot reproduce the conditions of the universe at those times, we can have some confidence of what actually happened.

The GUTs and the freezing at 10^{-35} second are not on equally firm foundations. To date, the major prediction of the GUTs, the decay of the proton, has not been verified. In effect, the GUTs mark the outer limits of modern physics, and it is on this frontier that the present generation of scientists is working. The events at the Planck time remain a subject for theoretical speculation. There have been no experimental tests of any current theory. Such work might give us information applicable to the very first freezing. About the moment of creation itself, we can only wonder.

An understanding of our limitations in no way detracts from perhaps the most startling aspect of this recently discovered story. It actually took the real universe less time to go through the aforementioned stages of its development than it has taken you to read about them in this chapter!

Best Knowledge

The modern picture of the evolutionary universe given in the previous chapter is a beautiful and compelling one, but it would be wrong of us to ignore its flaws. It solves some long-standing problems in cosmology, but that does not mean that the standard model has succeeded in solving them all. It's important to keep in mind that theories are still evolving. This is exactly what you'd expect in a vital field of science. If we knew everything there was to know and there were no more problems to solve, science would be a dusty warehouse of facts instead of what it is. More to the point, it just wouldn't be fun.

So there are always unsolved problems. Some are basic, some are not. For example, the question of whether the universe is 10 or 20 billion years old is not a basic problem in Big Bang cosmology. We feel quite comfortable leaving it to the experts to thrash this sort of thing out, and nothing essential in the Big Bang scenario depends on the answer they come up with. It's a problem, even an important one, but not a question upon which our entire understanding of reality hinges. And we must turn to other tasks.

Five questions reveal basic problems concerning the Big Bang. They are not necessarily listed in order of importance.

The antimatter problem—Why is the universe composed almost exclusively of matter, when matter and antimatter seem to be on an equal footing in the world of elementary particles?

The horizon problem—Why is the microwave background radiation much the same regardless of the direction of our observation, even though the regions emitting that radiation couldn't have been in contact in the past?

The flatness problem—Why is the amount of matter in the universe so close to the critical amount needed to reverse the presently observed expansion?

The galaxy problem—Why is matter clumped into galaxies and clusters of galaxies, and is there a large-scale structure in the universe?

The universe problem—Why is there a universe at all? Why, in other words, is there something instead of nothing?

Computer symbols paint an electronic image of the passage of cosmic rays from deep space. This high-energy episode happened in an experimental setup in a salt mine in Ohio. Far left, Albert Einstein and J. Robert Oppenheimer confer at Princeton University's Institute for Advanced Studies in 1947. Einstein provided relativistic theory and Oppenheimer translated it into the first plutonium weapon. Wizards of an earlier age, at left, medieval scholars calculate star positions.

Coppery glow emanates from the first linear accelerator of protons, created at the University of California at Berkeley in 1947. A neon tube marks the path taken by the speeding particles used to smash atoms. This early accelerator gleams in the "Atom Smashers" exhibit at the Smithsonian's National Museum of American History.

All of these problems have one thing in common. They can be "explained" by the assumption that the universe just started out that way. For example, we can "explain" the absence of antimatter by assuming that none was present at the creation, or "explain" the amount of mass by assuming that everything we see was in the initial Big Bang, and so on. But these aren't real answers; they beg the question, as so often is the case with assumptions.

When we say that we want to solve these problems, we mean that we need to explain the universe without resorting to special assumptions about the initial conditions. In the best of all possible outcomes, we will find that the laws of physics guarantee the universe must be the way we find it, regardless of the conditions existing when it began. Obviously, finding these laws is a formidable task. It should come as no surprise to learn that it has been only partially completed.

In this chapter and the next, we review the progress that scientists have made in dealing with these basic problems during the past few years. Recent developments, particularly the Grand Unified Theories and the Inflationary Theories of the universe, have brought us much closer to understanding them than we have ever been before.

The Antimatter Problem

One of the discoveries made during the decades of research in high-energy physics is that for every particle we find, it is possible to create an antiparticle. The antiparticle will have the same mass as the particle, but will be opposite in every other respect—sort of a mirror image. For example, the antiparticle of the electron is called the positron. Discovered in a cosmic-ray experiment in 1932, it is the same as the electron except that it has a positive charge. Similarly, the antiproton, first produced in the laboratory in 1955, has the same mass as the proton but a negative electrical charge, and so on. When a particle and an antiparticle come together, they undergo a process called annihilation; their mass is converted either into radiation, lighter particles, or some combination of the two. This depends on the nature of the particle-antiparticle pair.

At the level of particles, there seems to be an almost perfect symmetry between matter and antimatter. In a reaction involving antiparticles, then, the analogous reaction involving particles will proceed at exactly the same rate. Whenever a particle is created in a reaction, the corresponding antiparticle is created as well; annihilation removes the particle and the antiparticle from the scene simultaneously. Thus, the net particle-antiparticle balance cannot be changed by reactions which we now create and observe in the laboratory.

We know beyond any doubt that our solar system is made up exclusively of matter (i.e., not antimatter). Otherwise our space probes and landers might well have disappeared in flashes of energy. During the seventies this state of affairs led physicists to assume that there must be enough antimatter in some corner of the Galaxy to compensate for the matter we see around us. The idea that there might be "antigalaxies" somewhere is an intriguing one. But if such galaxies existed there would be an antimatter-matter boundary between the realm of matter and that of antimatter, probably in the intergalactic void. Annihilation taking place at this interface would appear as an extended patch of brightness in the X-ray or gamma-ray sky. Since no such patch is seen, we can presume that at least the nearby galactic clusters are free of large collections of antimatter, and we can guess it will be true everywhere. So, we ask, why only matter?

Until the advent of the GUTs, cosmologists could only assume that, for some unknown reason, the universe had been created from matter alone. But with these theories it is possible to connect a laboratory oddity, as we shall see, to the behavior of the universe in the period immediately following the freezing of the strong force at 10^{-35} second. The strong force holds together the nuclei of atoms. It turns out that there is one situation in which the seemingly universal symmetry between matter and antimatter doesn't hold. There is a particle known as the K°_L (pronounced K-zero-long) which is its own antiparticle and which decays more often into a positron than into an electron. This is the only reaction we know of which violates the matter-antimatter symmetry. As such it appears vital to our understanding. If we adjust the Grand Unified Theories to reproduce this laboratory result, they tell us that even if the universe started out with equal complements of matter and antimatter, the asymmetry built into the laws of physics (and displayed in the decay of the K°_L) would guarantee that after 10^{-35} second had passed, matter would dominate the universe.

The scenario runs like this: because of the high energies present before 10^{-35} second, very massive particles were created, particles that we do not see in our own frigid, low-energy universe. After the strong forces froze out, these particles could no longer be created in collisions, and their population began to drop as they started to decay. Ordinarily, we would expect that if there were equal numbers of heavy particles and antiparticles, there would be equal amounts of matter and antimatter in the decay products. However, because we have had to match the observed asymmetry in the K°_L, this doesn't happen. It turns out that we can arrange things so that for every ten billion antiquarks, which are produced as the heavy particles decay, there are ten billion and one quarks—the basic building blocks of the nuclear cores of atoms.

Because the universe was very dense at this early time, the quarks and antiquarks began running into and annihilating each other. In a very short time the 10 billion quarks and the 10 billion antiquarks had participated in their mutual extinction, leaving one lone bit of matter—the leftover

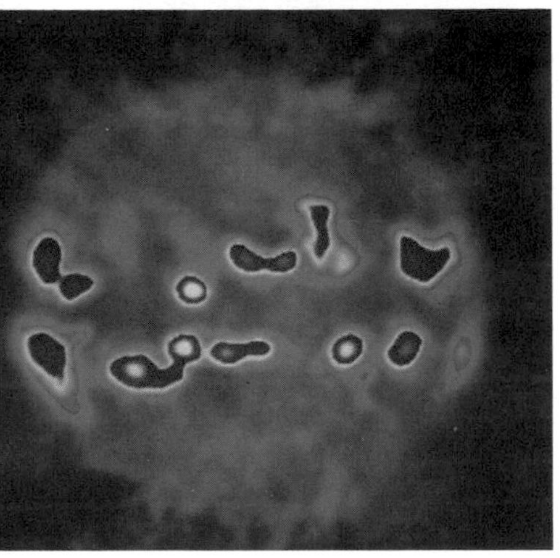

"Tandem mirror," huge electric coils shaped in a yin-yang configuration, provides power for attempts at triggering thermonuclear fusion. Plasma particles are confined, then fiercely squeezed in a magnetic force field. Rings of bright solar spots, above, are associated with both thermonuclear fusion and magnetic fields. Opposite, a smith forges new iron, an illustration from William Gilbert's work on magnetism in 1600. His experimental work with the Earth's magnetic fields helped prepare the way for modern astrophysics.

quark. At 10^{-5} second a good many quarks had accumulated, and these combined to form the elementary particles that make up the nuclei of atoms. There were no antiatoms formed because all of the antiquarks which would have gone into them were demolished early on, along with their opposite numbers. Only the tiny excess of matter remained to help make up the visible universe.

This explanation of an old problem in cosmology was the first (and greatest) success of the GUTs as applied to the early universe. It's what made physicists and astronomers sit up and take notice. Even if the universe were initially in a state with equal parts of matter and antimatter, the laws of physics would guarantee that eventually only matter would be left. And we would expect just such a state if the early universe arose from a conversion of energy to matter. The dominance of matter in the early universe no longer has to be postulated; it follows from laws of nature that we can see operating in our laboratories right here and now.

The Inflationary Universe

Many of the other basic problems with the Big Bang are solved in a natural way by a new version of the cosmology known as the inflationary universe. We have touched on this approach earlier.

First proposed in 1980 by Alan Guth (of the Massachusetts Institute of Technology), this scenario is identical to the ordinary Big Bang from about 10^{-35} second on, so nothing we have said so far has to be changed to accommodate it. Using a combination of the GUTs and general relativity, however, Guth was able to show that the freezing out of the strong force was accompanied by some rather remarkable behavior. In effect, at around 10^{-35} second the rate of expansion of the early universe underwent a brief period of discontinuous change, fueled by energy released in the freezing. During this episode the relatively sedate expansion we now observe was replaced by a much more rapid one. This anomaly was dubbed "inflation," and it went on to provide a name for a body of theory.

In essence, the inflationary period took the universe from a "space" with a radius of curvature smaller than an individual proton to a space the size of a grapefruit. If you recall our raisin-bread analogy, the inflationary period represented an era when the cosmic dough was rising much more rapidly than it did before or has since. Since inflation represents an expansion *of* space, rather than movement *in* space, the usual strictures against faster-than-light travel from the relativity theory are not violated.

Since Guth's original papers, inflationary universe theory has gone through many revisions, and each new incarnation appears technically better than the last. The currently fashionable version is called the "new inflationary scenario," although whether or not it is the final theory is very much a subject of debate. Whatever the outcome, the general features of the universe according to Guth are pretty clear.

The freezing out of the strong force is a process very similar to the more familiar freezing of water. In normal circumstances, water will freeze at 32°F. It is possible, however, to cool water below this temperature without having it solidify. The ice crystallization needs a nucleus—a starter. But if we deal with very pure water, in which there are no such centers, or seeds, water can stay liquid even while the temperature is 20 degrees below the freezing point. We say the water is supercooled. Sometimes, you can get supercooled water to freeze just by tapping the container it's in. When it finally freezes, of course, it gives up heat to the environment. It is this latent heat that your refrigerator removes when you make ice cubes.

According to the inflationary scenario, the universe supercooled to well below the temperature at which we would expect the strong force to freeze out. It turns out that the forces acting on the universe in this supercooled state are such as to cause the rapid expansion we call inflation. The process is parallel to that which causes water to expand when it turns into ice. When the "freezing" finally occurs, the latent energy is not dumped in the form of heat, as with water, but is converted into mass. For the first time we have a theory which is capable of predicting the amount of matter in the universe. To get on with our problem, we no longer need assume that the total is whatever our measurements happen to show.

With this picture of the behavior of the early universe in mind, we turn to some of the other basic cosmological problems on our list.

The Horizon Problem

If you set up a microwave detector and point it north, you see the background radiation corresponding to a body with a temperature of three degrees Kelvin. If you then take the detector and turn it 180°, so that it's pointing south, you will obtain the same reading. In fact, no matter which way you look with your detector, you will find that the background radiation is the same to within an accuracy of one-hundredth of a percent. Why?

In other words, why should the universe look so uniform? When you point your telescope in opposite directions you are looking at the opposite ends of the universe. Why should they have emitted radiation characteristic of bodies at the same temperature? When the universe became half a million years old and turned transparent, the radiation which we now perceive as the cosmic microwave background was emitted from opposite regions of the universe. The fact that the radiation is the same when we look in both directions tells us these two regions had to be at the same temperature when the radiation was emitted. In the conventional Big Bang scenario, however, these two regions could never have been in contact, so why are their temperatures equal? As before, we can simply assume that the universe started off with the same temperature everywhere, but this is profoundly unsatisfying.

An analogy here is helpful. Suppose you filled a bathtub with water—hot at one end and cold at the other. You know that eventually the temperature of the water would even out, but that it would take a certain amount of time (perhaps half an hour). The reason time must elapse for things to reach equilibrium is that the fast-moving molecules on the hot side have to diffuse through the water, sharing their extra energy through collisions. Working out the actual time it would take to achieve equilibrium would be complicated, but we can make one statement unequivocally. The temperature in the water could not become uniform in less time than it would take a single molecule to move from one side of the tub to the other. It may take longer, but the fact that the heat is transferred through molecular motion tells us that there is a lower time limit.

If we wanted to be excessively pedantic, we could note that the theory of relativity tells us that nothing can move faster than the speed of light, so that the shortest possible time it could take to establish equilibrium in the tub would be the time it would take light to get from one side to the other. In actual fact, the time it takes a molecule to cross the tub will be much longer than this, just as the time required for molecules to share their energy is much longer than the time it takes a molecule to make

Astronomy and Astrophysics

During the nineteenth century, a major change occurred in the way that the heavens were studied. From the time of the Babylonians, the main emphasis had been in understanding *where* the lights in the sky would appear. From Ptolemy to Kepler and Newton the question asked was "How does this particular object move?"

In the mid-nineteenth century, however, the development of the art of spectroscopy changed all that. For the first time it became possible for astronomers to study not only where a star or planet was, but *what* it was. By observing the light emitted by distant stars, or seeing what was absorbed when light passed through dust clouds in the Galaxy, we could find out what sorts of atoms there were in those stars and clouds. The connection between light and atoms allowed us, for the first time, to study the structure and composition of distant objects—a pursuit which has now been in full cry for over a century. Since the emphasis is on the physics of the things being studied, the new field of study acquired the name of astrophysics—the physics of the stars. And it was no fluke that in 1890 the Institution's Secretary, Samuel P. Langley, named a new research facility the Smithsonian Astrophysical Observatory.

Today, almost all astronomy is concerned with astrophysics: the traditional study of positions is called astrometry and is important mainly in the development of navigational systems for satellites.

the transit unimpeded. It is clear, however, that the light-transmission time is a lower limit on the time it takes to establish equilibrium. We would certainly be at a loss if we found equilibrium established in the tub during a shorter period.

Now let's return to the problem of the microwave background radiation of the universe. The two regions which we mentioned are too far apart for light to have traveled from one to the other. Furthermore, in the conventional Big Bang scenario they were always too far apart for communication to have been established at any time before the 500,000 year mark. They were independent or, in the jargon of cosmologists, outside of each other's *event horizons* (a term which explains how this particular problem got its name). Finding that they are at the same temperature, then, is equivalent to filling a tub with hot water at one end and cold water at the other, and then finding all the water at the same temperature in less time than it would take light to cross the tub.

The solution of the horizon problem is quite straightforward in any version of the inflationary universe. Before the time of the onset of inflation, the universe was very small—so small that there was ample time for whatever temperature irregularities were present to be smoothed out. Light would have had time to crisscross the universe many times during this stage. Later, when inflation occurred, the universe suddenly expanded to a much larger size. By this time, however, everything possessed the same temperature. There was nothing in any subsequent changes of form—we've called them "freezings"—to alter this uniformity. Indeed the uniformity of the microwave background is an expression of it.

Consequently, the horizon "problem" isn't really a problem with physics. It arose because we insisted on making a straight-line projection backward in time that ignored the very real changes in the rate of expansion associated with the inflationary period. This led us to conclude that by the old model the universe could never have established equilibrium during its early stages. Once we account for inflation, however, we can see that our previous extrapolation is wrong, and the "problem" disappears.

The Flatness Problem

The central feature of the universe as we know it is the universal expansion discovered by Hubble. Once we know this, it is natural to ask whether expansion will go on forever or whether, at some time in the distant future, it will stop and turn into a universal contraction. In our earlier raisin-bread analogy, this question corresponds to asking whether the dough will rise forever.

To approach this question, we ask what natural forces exist that might slow down galaxies receding from us at a good fraction of the speed of light. The only such force is gravity. Perhaps an analogy will make this point clear. If you throw a baseball into the air from the surface of the earth, it will eventually turn around and fall back down. The reason is that a very massive object—our planet—pulls on it. If you were to repeat the experiment on a small asteroid, the baseball might just sail off into space.

Now substitute the farthest galaxy for the baseball. The galaxy is moving outward, but it feels the gravitational attraction of the rest of the universe pulling it back. The question is this: how strong is that attraction? Or, to pose the question another way, how much matter exists in the universe to do the pulling? Do we have a situation similar to the baseball thrown on Earth, or to the one pitched off of the asteroid?

As it turns out, the answer to this question is not as simple as you might think. It won't do to count up the mass of the stars in the various galaxies we see, because the stars represent only the stuff that shines. There is no particular reason to believe that this bright matter is all there is.

Cosmologists customarily describe the total amount of matter in the universe by a ratio of the actual observed mass to the mass that would be just enough to bring the observed expansion to a halt. (In the jargon of astronomers, this amount of matter would "close" the universe.) This ratio is denoted by the Greek letter omega, Ω. If we count only the luminous matter—stars and illuminated dust clouds—we would find $\Omega = 0.001$. In other words, the amount of luminous matter in the universe comes to only about a tenth of a percent of the amount needed to close the universe.

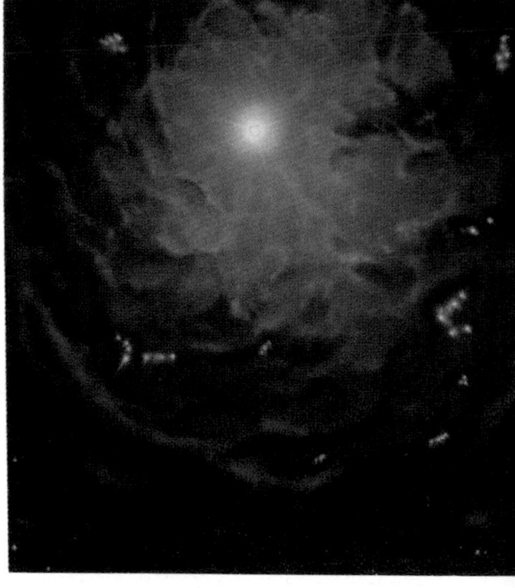

Microwave radiation as from a maser—a research tool analogous to a laser—bursts from a cloud of dust cloaking a newborn star. Before light itself can penetrate the curtain of nebulosity, stimulated dust molecules emit their invisible microwaves. Visualizations like this one, whether from a computer or the human mind, aid cosmologists in their search for clues to the intimate workings of the universe. Artwork by Kim Poor.

At the other extreme, if there were significantly more mass in the universe than the critical amount, the expansion would have slowed down long ago. From the fact that expansion continues today, some 15 billion years after the moment of creation, we can conclude that Ω can't be much bigger than one, and is certainly less than 10.

These two arguments, then, tell us that of all the possible amounts of matter that could have been incorporated into the universe at the beginning, the actual amount was within a factor of 100 of the critical amount needed to close the universe. Again, we seem confronted with a question that can be answered only in terms of our arbitrary assumption—"that's just the way things are." This is called the flatness problem.

Perhaps it would be worthwhile to make a short digression to explain the origin of that name. In general relativity, the action of gravity is explained in terms of the distortion of space by the presence of mass. Imagine a large rubber sheet marked out in a grid. If you dropped a heavy ball bearing on the sheet, the weight would sink down, distorting the sheet as it went. Another mass (a marble, for example) in the vicinity would tend to be pulled down into the hole thus created, and observers would say that the marble had been attracted to the ball bearing by the force of gravity.

In this way, cosmologists imagine the mass of the galaxies distorting the space-time grid around them. If the mass is large enough, this distortion is so large that the grid simply folds over on itself, in effect closing the mass off from any contact with whatever might be "outside." This is a closed universe and would exist if Ω were greater than one. The opposite case is one where objects are free to move to infinity, and the transition case is one in which the net effect of the mass is to make the grid flat. In the language of general relativity, then, we live in a universe where the amount of matter is near to that needed to produce flatness—hence the name of the problem. If you don't like to think in these geometrical terms, simply consider this as the amount of matter needed to just barely bring the outward flying galaxies to a slow, gradual stop at infinity. There would not be enough force left over to turn the expansion around and begin a general contraction.

Solutions to the flatness problem proved elusive until inflationary scenarios came along. You will recall that a crucial step in the picture—the one that ended the period of rapid expansion—was the release of energy following the supercooling. As we mentioned, this energy was released in the form of mass. In fact, it seems that virtually all the matter we now see in the universe was created at this time. The important point is that since we have a theory that describes the process by which the strong force freezes out, we can calculate how much energy should have been released when that particular freezing occurred.

The inflationary scenarios make a rather remarkable prediction. When the calculation of the energy release is carried out, it is found that the mass of the universe should be exactly the critical value. The prediction is that Ω equals one to an accuracy of over 50 decimal places!

We can understand how such a prediction could arise if we think of flatness in terms of the kind of grid discussed above. Imagine this grid marked out on a balloon, and then imagine the balloon crumpled up and left in a heap. In general, the grid would be a complex three-dimensional shape, with one part being quite different from another. Suppose now that we pay attention to one small part of the grid and start to blow the balloon up. As the balloon expands, the individual bumps and wiggles in the grid would get stretched out until finally, if the balloon were large enough, the grid would appear perfectly flat.

This feature of the inflationary scenario has two important consequences. First, the mass from the freezing must correspond to the final configuration of the grid. Since a flat grid corresponds to the critical amount of matter, this means that Ω must be precisely equal to one. Secondly, it tells us that no matter what the configuration of the grid was in the era previous to 10^{-35} second, the process of inflation will always produce the same flat universe. This is very encouraging, because it tells us that inflation is a physical process guaranteeing that the final state of the universe will correspond to our observations. Moreover, this is true regardless of what we assume about the way the universe was created. A large element of arbitrariness is thus removed from cosmology.

Whither Inflation?

The success of the inflationary picture in solving the horizon and flatness problems is impressive. I find its ability to "clear the slate" even more impressive. In other words, the inflationary picture makes the properties of the present universe independent of the pre-inflationary situation. The idea clearly shows that the universe underwent a period of very rapid expansion followed by a mass conversion, a dumping of energy into mass. And this will be a part of any future cosmology. Nevertheless, many problems with the inflationary models need to be cleared up before we can claim a real understanding of this crucial period in the early universe.

Perhaps the best way to introduce these difficulties is to notice that the success of the inflationary scenario depends primarily on the general properties of inflation, not so much on the details of the theory. When it comes to making detailed predictions with specific versions of the model, however, the situation is not so rosy.

As we shall see in the next chapter, theorists have encountered some difficulty in explaining the formation of galaxies in terms of the model. Obviously, if the theory is to evolve, various transitions from one model to the next must be made. These changes have to do with interactions of the particles in the universe at 10^{-35} second. Since these particles cannot be produced in our laboratories, we have to deduce their properties from very scanty evidence. A good many assumptions are involved. This means that there's still lots of room to maneuver in the inflationary theories.

For example, the currently fashionable "new inflationary scenario" predicts that the observable universe (that 10-billion-light-year sphere we can probe from earth) is just a tiny piece of a huge region of essentially similar composition. A few years ago, however, some older versions of the model talked of "parallel universes" and predicted that our own universe was just one of a large number of bubbles created during the inflationary period. The only difference between these two models, however, was a modification in the assumptions about the way certain particles interacted at temperatures characteristic of 10^{-35} second. Both of these pictures created excitement in the science press. It's probably a good idea to keep this example in mind when you run into yet another headline about the predictions of the next version of the model.

Things haven't settled down in this field yet, and it'll be a while before they do.

Stephen Hawking, in wheelchair, opposite, develops mathematical formulas to crack the mysteries of black holes, objects invisible to our telescopes. He teaches at England's Cambridge University. The world-renowned mathematician calculated that black holes emit quantum energy, now known as Hawking radiation. Artist Don Dixon captures the energy of a galactic maelstrom, at right, the rapidly revolving disk of cosmic matter being drawn into a black hole.

Unsolved Problems

During its early life, we believe that the universe was a smeared-out blob of dense matter. Today we observe the concentrations and collections of stars and dust that we call galaxies. These, in turn, are grouped together in clusters, which form superclusters. And there is strong evidence for a large-scale filamentary structure throughout the universe. The overall problem is this: how did the universe move from a state of uniform density to its present lumpy structure? At first, this may seem a simple problem. We will see, however, that it is composed of problems within problems.

A single thread becomes a mystic mandala in this drawing attributed to the school of Leonardo da Vinci around 1510. When unraveled, the knot leads to the heart of nature itself, not unlike the quest of modern scientists in search of a single unifying force. Shadowy, primordial shapes lurk in a computer simulation of the early universe, opposite. Not long after the Big Bang, these pieces of matter and radiation began to coalesce, eventually influencing the formation of galaxies.

The Galaxy Problem

We have already suggested that the galaxies, like the sun, formed in the aftermath of the collapse of a gas cloud. Scientists even have an overall notion of the sequence of events; at some point the cloud contained, purely by chance, a spot with more than the average concentration of matter. Even a few atoms grouped together will exert a greater-than-average gravitational attraction on matter of less density. Neighboring particles move in closer, adding their gravitational attraction to that of the group, and so on. The force of gravity acting on a cloud of gas would tend to segregate the gas into discrete clumps. We believe that such a process led to the formation of the solar system from interstellar dust.

While gravity undoubtedly played a role in the formation of galaxies, its action alone fails to explain the structure of the universe as we observe it. The reason: unlike the solar system, galaxies took shape in rapidly expanding gas clouds. It turns out that if galaxies formed by the process outlined above, the Hubble expansion would have swept most material out of reach long before the galactic nuclei could have collected. Gravity acts too slowly to attract primordial matter and to cause it to clump in the manner required both by theory and astronomical observation.

An attractive and straightforward solution—to let the gravitational attraction start to work earlier—simply isn't available to the cosmologist. Our standard model of the Big Bang precludes this alternative. Until the time when atoms formed from nuclei and electrons—500,000 years after the Big Bang—the expansive pressure of radiation was high enough to counteract the attractive force of gravity, a situation that had to change before the formation of galaxies could begin. A particular transformation—a freezing or condensation in the assembly of matter—was required so that atoms could emerge and the universe could receive its initial allotment of matter. Gravity would have its chance to draw the early material into

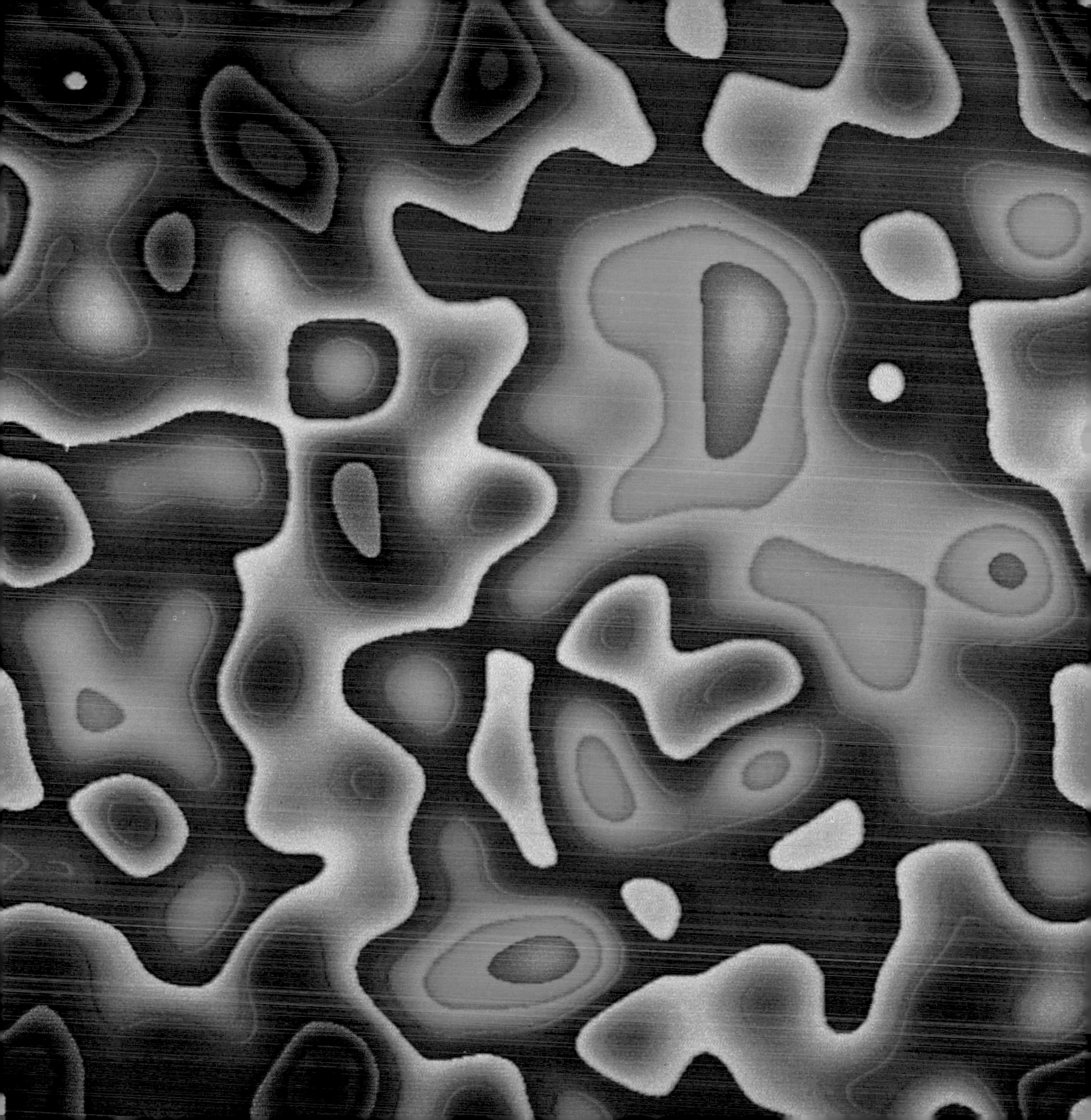

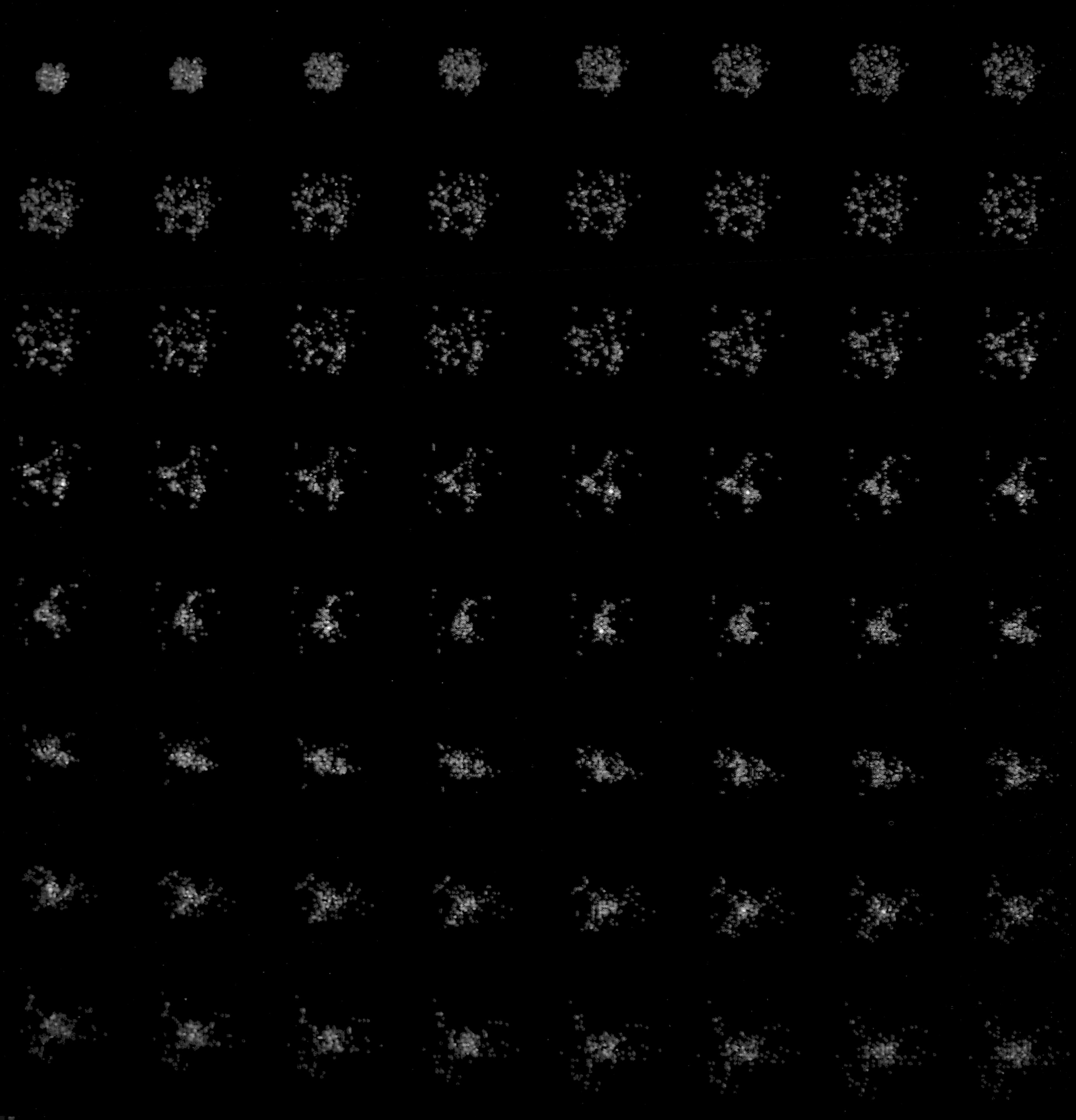

Computer simulation helps scientists understand the dynamic evolution of a cluster of galaxies. Sixty-four frames mathematically trace a dense piece of the early universe from shortly after the Big Bang when it expands with the "Hubble Flow" through 10 billion years as it collapses from its own gravity.

clouds at the same time that further expansion and cooling occurred. This gravitational ingathering had to take place before atoms could be swept so far apart that there would not have been enough material around the various condensation points for galaxies to develop. Thus, theoretically speaking, we see a very tight fit, a very brief opportunity for galaxies to form.

The only way to meet these rigorous constraints is to have the galaxies "preformed" in the universe before the atoms are made. Protogalaxies need not spring full-blown from the pre-atomic turmoil, but some sort of nuclei are required almost from the beginning if galactic coalescence is to move with sufficient speed to outpace the Hubble expansion.

In effect, something must happen in the first 500,000 years that "seeds" the universe with nuclei around which galaxies will later condense. This mechanism would play a role analogous to that of rainmakers who seed clouds with tiny crystals around which water droplets can condense to form rain. If such a mechanism existed, galaxies could form in the short span of time allotted for this stage by theoreticians.

At first, it might not seem difficult to provide nuclei for the galaxies. After all, any process as violent as the formation of the early universe is bound to be highly turbulent, and the ripples and vortices that were sure to form could easily provide small concentrations of mass here and there. Unfortunately, the problem isn't that easy to solve.

We believe that the early universe was what physicists call a dissipative system. In such systems, irregularities arising from turbulence smooth out quickly—in this case, too quickly to be around when they are needed to make the galaxies. Think of a rock sticking up out of a large river. The obstacle creates a disturbance but, farther downstream, the strong flow of the river overcomes the ripples and turbulence. In the same way, the Hubble expansion tends to smooth out rough spots in the early universe so that by the time the crucial period for galaxy formation is reached, these irregularities can no longer play their role in the formation of nuclei for condensation. Paradoxically, the galaxy problem appears not in the creation of wrinkles in space and time, but in preserving such "galactic seeds" until they are needed.

Before the Grand Unified Theories (GUTs) started revolutionizing our ideas about the early universe, the galaxy problem was simply that—a problem that no one knew how to solve. In the time-honored tradition of science, there was a tacit agreement to ignore it, to string it along until someone could find a new approach. As it happens, the inflationary theories provide that new approach, although it is fair to say that working out the details of the process will remain a major challenge for theorists in this field.

The general idea is this: during the freezing of the strong force, some sort of stable structure is formed. Unlike the whirls and eddies associated with turbulence, these stable structures do not dissipate, but float along unchanged through all the subsequent freezings. They bide their time, so to speak, until called upon to serve as the condensation points for future galaxies. In the various versions of the inflationary theories, these structures are formed by various physical processes and thus have quite different forms. Any one of them is capable of solving the galaxy problem, at least in principle. Which, if any, of these versions will pass the test remains a matter of debate among cosmologists. While the inflationary scenarios probably can account for the process by which the condensation nuclei are formed, no one has yet produced a version of the theory that spells out this process in detail.

Let's approach two versions of the inflationary theory to see how different processes can lead to possible solutions of the galaxy problem. In an older version of the theory, the freezing of the strong force took place by a process very similar to that seen when ice forms on a pond. The pond doesn't become covered with ice all at once, but begins freezing in separate isolated spots. Various domains (discrete centers of ice crystallization) spread out over the surface of the pond, eventually joining up to make a smooth covering. In each domain, the ice crystals are oriented in one direction, but there is a discontinuity in crystal orientation at the points where domains join.

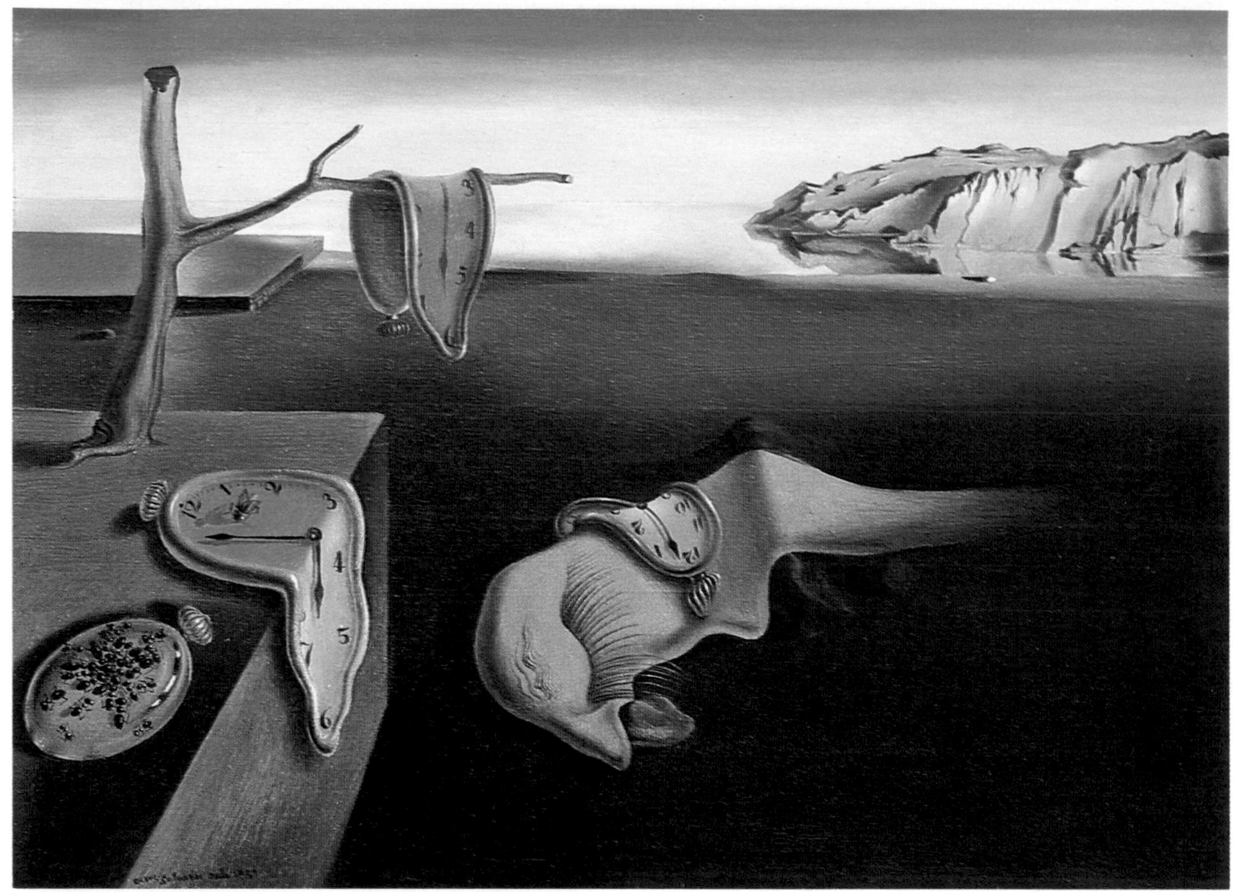

Salvador Dali's droopy clocks in The Persistence of Memory *(1931) suggest the often peculiar kinship of time to space—a relation, some scientists contend, made up of 11 dimensions. Sitting like a Mont-Saint-Michel in space,* Tetrahedral Planetoid *(1954) is M.C. Escher's fanciful interpretation of a space colony.*

A similar process occurs in the freezings described by the GUTs 10^{-35} second after the Big Bang. We are really dealing with the universe very, very early on. One form assumed by the discontinuities at the domain boundaries is that of very massive one-dimensional objects called "strings." Certain defects in natural crystals exhibit this sort of structure. Once created, the strings cannot be destroyed by the turbulence of the subsequent expansion. From their development after 10^{-35} second, the strings stay in the background, but eventually become the centers around which galaxies form.

In the new inflationary scenario, however, the entire observable universe is tucked well inside a single domain, so we do not expect large numbers of strings to be visible to us. In this scenario, the necessary inhomogeneities can be generated by processes quite different from those leading to strings. As we have described it, the inflation process is smooth. If we were to look at it in sufficiently fine detail—the kind we'd need if we were describing the behavior of elementary particles—we'd find that it wasn't really all that smooth but incorporated many random fluctuations. These are the same sort of movements that occur among atoms in the air that surrounds you. Such motion existed in the early universe as well, but the process of inflation tended to magnify these fluctuations. The mass concentrations that started out as tiny, particle-sized irregularities wound up, after inflation, as precisely the sort of inhomogeneities needed to start off the galaxies.

Unfortunately, this prediction derived from the inflationary models is very sensitive to small variations in the terms of the theory used to describe the interaction of particles at the time of the freezing according to the Grand Unified Theories. The simplest GUTs model, for example, gives a set of inhomogeneities which has the right proportions but is about a factor of 100,000 too large to explain the presently observed universe.

Some supersymmetric versions of the inflationary universe can produce the correct nuclei for galactic condensation, but—to put it mildly—these theories are highly speculative. To sum up; the inflationary scenarios would appear to have the potential for solving the problems associated with the formation of galaxies. We have no firm evidence, though, that they actually do.

But even if we knew how the condensation nuclei for galaxies were formed, we would still not be sure of the process by which galaxies took shape once the condensation process started. In fact there are two alternate pictures of what may have happened. In one picture, the atoms that made up the universe after the freezing at 500,000 years condensed first into large clouds of gas—clouds which correspond to the presently observed galactic clusters. In this picture, the clusters formed first, to be followed by the formation of individual galaxies as each large original cloud broke up. In the other picture, the individual galaxies coalesced first and then collected into clusters. The resolution of this debate is likely to take some time, if for no other reason than that the collapse of a cloud of atoms into protogalaxies under the influence of gravity must be simulated by computer. This extremely complex process taxes the best machines available today.

Large-Scale Structure Problem

One area of research related to the problem of galaxy formation concerns the question of whether or not an overall structure exists in the universe. To find an answer, someone must plot out the distribution of galaxies and clusters and see if a pattern emerges. Unfortunately, this process isn't as simple as it sounds. The human eye is quite capable of perceiving order and pattern in dots that are totally random—the basis of the famous Rorschach tests in psychology. Consequently, there will always be a good deal of skepticism among astronomers over the reported discovery of such patterns.

During the last few years, however, the scientific community has begun to come around. Mathematical studies have established that galaxies are not spread randomly in space. A galaxy is much more likely to have near neighbors in space than to be isolated. Furthermore, there are large volumes of space (called voids) in which almost no galaxies exist at all. Our universe most definitely exhibits a filamentary structure, with galaxies spread out in stringlike patterns through space.

While we are sure that the universe has structure, we are not sure why this structure should be there. Obviously, any theory that purports to explain the formation of galaxies will have to explain their distribution in space as well. This is another aspect to the already difficult galaxy problem.

Dark Matter Problem

When we look out into the universe, the most obvious structures that meet our eyes are stars and galaxies—the collection of things we have called luminous matter. We have already mentioned the strong suspicion among many scientists that the shiny and the shined-upon materials are in the minority. The bulk of the mass of the universe could involve matter that does not shine. We call this non-luminous stuff dark matter, and ask three questions about it: how much is there; where is it; and what is it?

We can uncover frequent references to

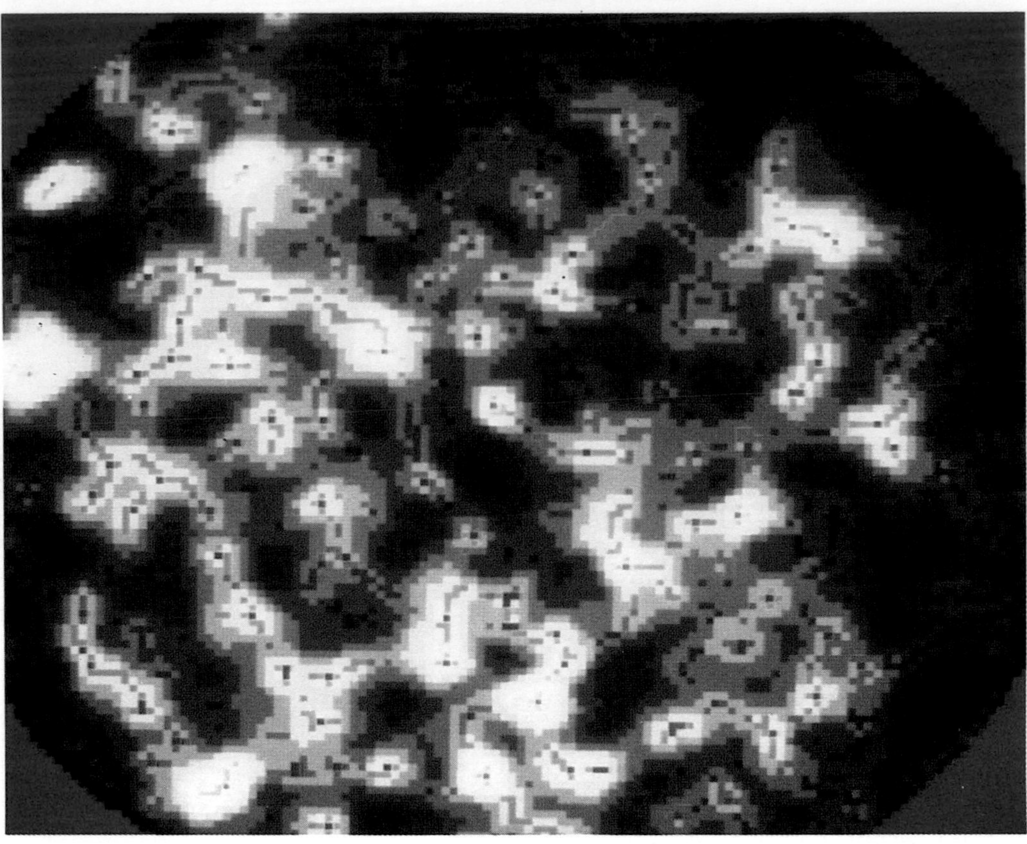

Celestial mosaic of 400,000 galaxies sweeps across the sky, highlighting filamentary patterns. Dark areas indicate voids while brighter colors reveal an increasing number of galaxies. Green symbolizes superclusters of galaxies perhaps spanning a distance of 100 million light-years. Astronomers carefully analyze such distribution of matter throughout the cosmos for clues about the evolution of the universe.

the "missing mass" of the universe in the traditional literature. This terminology arose because some astronomers felt that the expanding universe had to close back in upon itself. They were well aware that the amount of luminous matter was less than the amount needed for closure. They felt dark matter had to exist, even though it had been largely undetected. Hence the use of "missing mass." This name is, however, singularly inappropriate. It implies that there *must* be enough mass to close the universe. But this is a question that is best decided by observation, not by assumption. Consequently, I find the current trend toward the term "dark matter" very welcome indeed. Use of this term implies that there is some matter (such as that in stars) which is hot enough to shine, and other matter which is not, but it does not imply how much matter of each type there ought to be.

The first intimation that what we see might not be all that there is to see came with the discoveries of galactic haloes—the tenuous circular clouds that surround many spiral galaxies. The key concept in dealing with these haloes is something astronomers call a rotation curve. This graph tells us that the speed of bits of matter in a galaxy varies as a function of their distance from the galactic center. There are many shapes such a curve could have. For example, if everything in a galaxy were locked together like pieces of a solid wheel, then the farther from the center something was, the faster it would move. In another possible situation, one like that of our solar system, we find almost all the mass concentrated at the center. Here we expect that the farther away from the center the slower things would move, just as the outer planets move more slowly than the inner ones. Orbits which have this property are said to be "Keplerian," after Johannes Kepler, who first worked out the orbits of the planets.

If nothing existed beyond the luminous part of the galaxy, then atoms and molecules of the spiral arms should have Keplerian orbits. In fact they do not, but instead act as if they were surrounded by matter—as if in fact they were wagon wheels.

Something special may be happening. A bit of matter circling far from the visible galaxy does not resemble a planet circling a star, but instead acts as if it were still surrounded by the central mass. This means that the galaxy must be encased in a halo of dark matter extending out beyond the bounds of the luminous material. We can't say exactly how far out, but most estimates of the spatial extent for a galaxy put it at around five times that of the central disk. For binary galaxies—those that orbit a common center of gravity under the influence of their mutual attraction—as well as for the Milky Way, we estimate the total mass of the unseen material at up to 100 times that of the luminous material.

Other evidence for the presence of unseen matter can be found in studies of clusters of galaxies—concentrations that may contain a thousand or more galaxies. In the Coma cluster of galaxies, for instance, we find the paradoxical situation in which a group of galaxies is stable even though the cluster does not seem to contain enough visible mass to hold everything together. Adding mass for galactic haloes and diffuse background light does not solve this problem (although it makes the discrepancy less acute). Conclusion: there is additional unseen mass in the Coma cluster of galaxies. The actual mass of the system could be 10 or 20 times that of the matter we observe in the individual galaxies.

Adding this intergalactic material to our stock of dark matter, we find that the value of Ω (the Greek letter omega) has increased to something in the range of 10 to 30 percent. We still have not closed the universe, but we are now so close that many astronomers are starting to take the prediction of the inflationary models (Ω = 1) very seriously. In the words of Stephen Hawking, one of the leaders of British theoretical astrophysics, "Twenty years ago omega was one-tenth of a percent, now it's near 20 percent. Maybe the future will bring it all the way up to 100 percent." The closer the observations come to Ω = 1, of course, the more confident will be the predictions of the theorists that if their observational colleagues would just look a little harder, they'd find the rest.

For the third question about dark matter—what is it?—the answers are not so clear-cut. I talked to David Schramm, Chairman of the Department of Astronomy at the University of Chicago and a member of the Center for Theoretical Astrophysics at the Fermi National Accelerator Laboratory near Chicago. Schramm was involved in setting up this Center, an oasis of astronomical research within a major laboratory devoted to the study of elementary particles. The Center is an institutional embodiment of the coming together of these two fields—the first such attempt made anywhere.

"As far as galactic haloes go, we could just be seeing dark, Jupiter-sized objects," he pointed out in answer to my question about dark matter. Such objects would be made up of familiar types of matter—atoms whose nuclei are protons and neutrons. This sort of stuff is called "baryons" or "baryonic matter" in the jargon of particle physicists (from the Greek *barys*, meaning heavy).

"From our calculations of the synthesis of nuclei in the early universe," Dr. Shramm continued, "we surmise that the total mass of baryons in the universe will not be less than 15 percent of the critical mass, nor more than 30 percent. These calculations show that while baryons cannot close the universe, their mass must be greater than that of luminous matter alone."

This is a useful example of the way that the new cosmology works. Once we have sorted out one process (in this case, nucleosynthesis), we can use the results to put tight constraints on other processes (in this case, the creation of dark matter). We are satisfied that we know how much helium was created three minutes after the Big Bang. If there had been more baryons, they would have interacted more frequently, and more helium would have been produced than is observed. Had the number of baryons been too small, the interactions would have been too infrequent to produce the helium we see. This sort of reasoning led to the above limits. A similar agreement (with similar conclusions) can be worked out for deuterium (an atom whose nucleus is composed of one neutron and one proton) and its concentration in nature.

"The limits on baryon mass and the present observational values of Ω are consistent with each other," Schramm points out. "Right now," he says, "we aren't forced to assume that there are any other contributors to dark matter in the universe."

But suppose we wanted to believe the predictions of the inflationary theories. Where could the rest of the matter needed to close the universe come from?

"There are many possibilities," says Schramm. "They range from massive neutrinos to the new particles predicted by supersymmetry. The main point to realize is that this matter may be more uniformly distributed than the galaxies."

In other words, if we seek evidence for the ultimate closure of the universe, we will need to discover new particles or new properties of familiar particles. Perhaps the most popular candidate at the moment is the massive neutrino. The mass of the neutrino is ordinarily taken to be zero. In 1980, however, a group of Russian physicists reported an experiment that contradicted this conventional wisdom. They reported finding a small mass for the neutrino.

Through the early eighties, however, one careful experiment after another pushed the bounds on the neutrino mass downward. As of 1985, only this one report provides any comfort to cosmologists. The group in Moscow maintains its claim of a non-zero neutrino mass, but its interpretation of the data remains open to debate. Scientists could surely make good use of a clear-cut answer to the question of the mass of the neutrino, or the lack thereof.

Should the Soviet experiment be sustained, the community of cosmologists would have a lot to think about. Hitherto, neutrinos were ignored when people spoke of dark matter. If these exceedingly numerous entities were to possess mass, they might provide enough mass to close the universe.

Once we leave the relatively familiar neutrino behind, the candidates for dark matter become progressively more exotic. Particles with names like axion, photino, gravitino, and heavy lepton all have been evoked to close the universe. The black hole is also a candidate for the job.

Most of these particles (whose existence is predicted by some theories) have never been seen in the laboratory. This lack of verification gives the theorist ample elbow room to adjust a particle's properties to produce a universe like the one we see around us, but it certainly takes away from the faith one can put in the final results.

One interesting point about the hypothetical particles is that some (such as heavy neutrinos) tend to form large clusters, while others (such as gravitinos) tend to make small clusters. This introduces the interesting idea that all of the dark matter in the universe may not be the same stuff. The galactic haloes, for example, might be made at least partly of gravitinos, while the extra mass in clusters of galaxies might consist of neutrinos. Before we accept either of these ideas, however, we need to know for sure whether neutrinos have a mass and if gravitinos even exist.

Before the Bang—The Universe Problem

We've come so far in our attempt to solve the riddle of the universe that it would seem a shame to stop at 10^{-43} second from our goal. Known as the Planck time, this is the

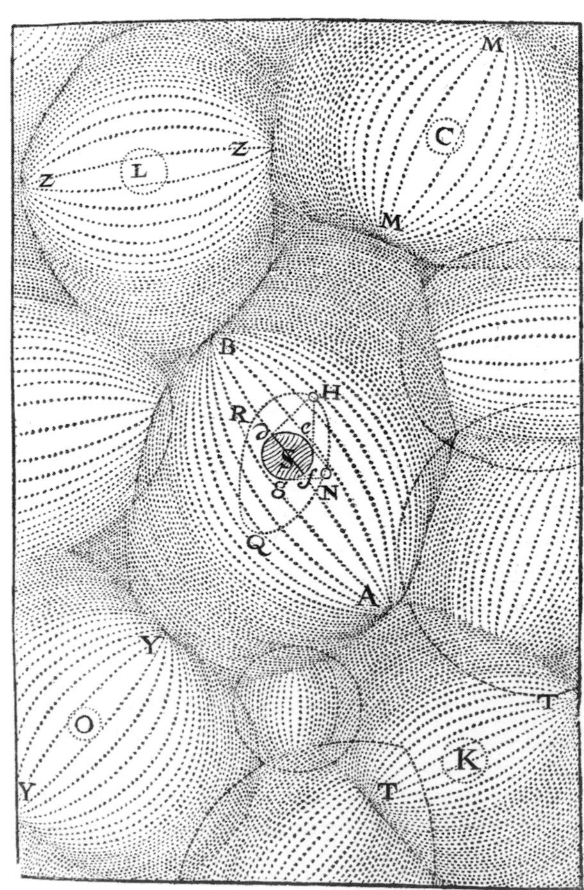

Frogs eggs, right, and René Descartes' model for the movement of celestial objects, far right, bear testimony to patterns reoccurring throughout the natural world. Not limited by size, these forms appear also in recent models of gravity and cosmic neutrinos. In particular, the "unseen" matter about a central and easily visible core suggests the proportion of bright to dark matter in galaxies. Far more than one million galaxies appear in these computerized sky charts of the northern and southern hemispheres, opposite. In terms of area covered, these images are perhaps the largest and most comprehensive graphic representations ever seen.

earliest instant that present theories can address. It is fascinating to speculate about what we will find when we penetrate this ultimate barrier. One possibility—accepted as conventional until quite recently—is that the density of the universe was infinitely great at what we might call "time zero," just before 10^{-43} second. In this case, the universe would have started with what mathematicians call a singularity—something our mathematics can't describe. And we would have reached, then, the end of the road in our quest for understanding.

The idea that there might be a singularity in our past, however, is based on a gross simplification, a projection in a direction opposite to the present universal expansion. Such viewing-in-reverse is not required by any law of physics or logic. It's merely the simplest thing to do and it may—or may not—lead us to the correct answer.

Must we choose blindly between sheer simplification or something more complicated? To understand our quandary, and to see how current speculation offers the possibility of dodging the singularity, we can consider a homey example of rising bread dough. During the period when the dough is rising, the chemical reactions in the yeast produce carbon dioxide and the dough expands, often to many times its original size. If someone came into the kitchen while this was going on, it would be a relatively simple matter for him to measure the expansion rate of the dough and extrapolate the expansion backwards in time. Through this procedure, he could find the time when the extrapolation would put all of the material in the dough into a single, infinitely dense point—another singularity, in fact. He would probably call this "time zero." We know, however, that this conclusion is not reasonable in the case of the bread. The observed expansion of the bread goes back only a finite period in time, at which point a completely different process (the mixing together of the ingredients) has taken place. We do not believe that the expanding dough originated in a singularity because we have seen too many loaves of bread rise. In cosmology, however, we have only one universe to observe, so the situation is not nearly as simple. Nevertheless, as this analogy shows,

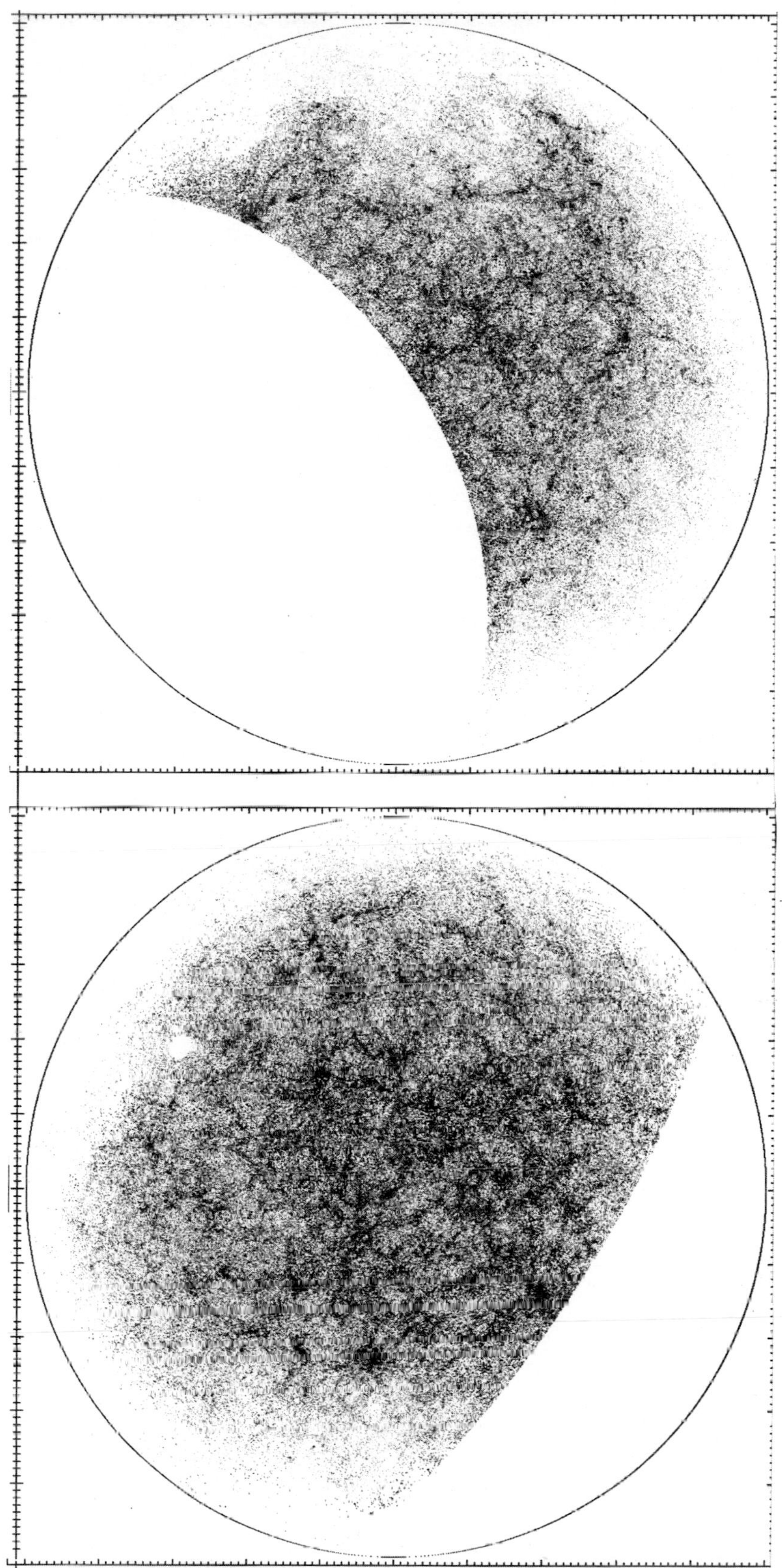

At right, the transition of liquid crystal into its spherical solid phase suggests the process by which nebulosities form brilliant stars. Dramatic phase transitions or "freezings" abound at every step of astronomical study. At the sub-atomic level, astrophysicists study how atoms group to form molecules while cosmologists ponder the way galactic clusters form superclusters.

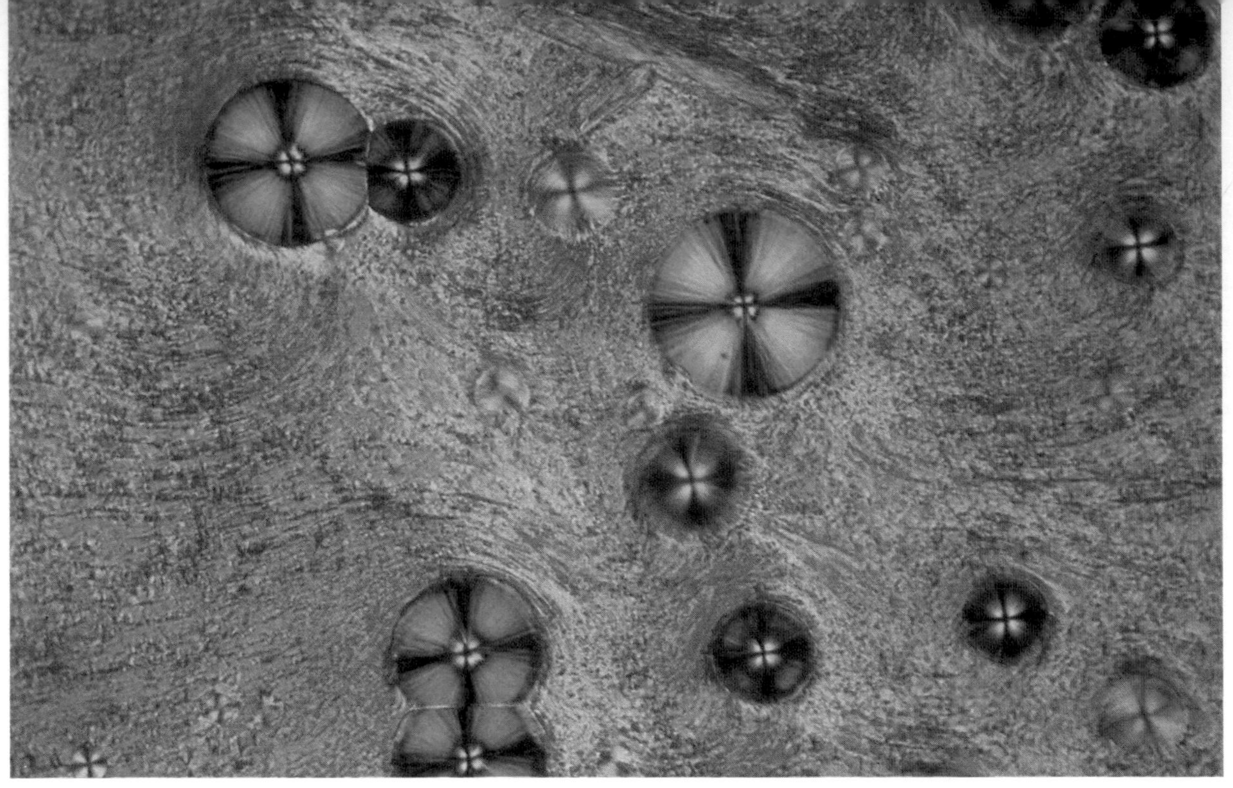

it is not inevitable (and perhaps even not likely) that the current expansion implies that the universe actually originated in a singularity.

Most of the current speculations about the ultimate origin of the universe have one thing in common: they all agree that somewhere around the Planck time something radically different happened, and that the concept of time zero has no more meaning for the universe than it had for the loaf of bread. And, although there are about as many speculations as there are authors, we can divide these theoretical approaches to the origin of the universe into three major categories; geometrical, multi-dimensional, and dynamical.

The geometrical scenarios tend to be favored by those cosmologists who come to the question with a background in general relativity. For the most part, they postulate the existence of conditions that lead to the universe's arrival at the Planck time with just the right characteristics to start the ordinary Big Bang. They do not, however, explain how those conditions can arise from the known laws of particle interactions.

One example of such a scenario, and one easy to visualize, was proposed a few years ago by Francois Englert and Raoul Brout at the Free University of Brussels. They developed a picture in which the universe was an ordinary vacuum at a time long before the occurrence of what we perceive to have been the start of the Big Bang. They begin, however, with a universe in which the vacuum is inherently unstable. You can picture this instability by imagining the vacuum to be a flat grid marked out in space. If a small bit of matter should appear in the Brout-Englert universe, its effect would be to make the grid expand slightly.

The positive energy needed to create the bit of intrusive matter is balanced by the negative energy stored in the expanding grid, so there's no violation of the conservation of energy involved in this sort of event. This model of the universe is constructed in such a way that once the grid starts to expand at any point, more matter is created. This matter, in turn, causes more expansion, which creates more matter, and so on. In this picture, the universe is very much like a piece of cloth held under high tension. Everything is fine so long as there is no tear anywhere in the fabric, but the second a small rip starts, it spreads quickly across the entire cloth.

In just the same way, this model universe can remain as a perfect vacuum until a small bit of matter appears. Once it does, the "rip" will grow until the universe reaches the proportions it had at the Planck time. From then on, it evolves as we have already described. In this example of a geometrical beginning, a vista reached off to infinity before the Planck time, and the instability of the vacuum slowly grew until it reached the critical size needed to start the Big Bang. What we have called time zero has no special significance in the picture. Think back just a moment to our analogy of dough rising for bread. Before the Big Bang a "mixing" was going on, a mixing unlike anything seen in the universe since.

As is the case in most of the other theories we'll discuss, the geometrical case regards the initial bit of mass as the product of a random fluctuation of the type often seen in subatomic systems. It triggers the instability in the grid. The important point: once a bit of matter appears, however small

it may be, it will grow into the present universe. The potential for growth is inherent in the dynamics of the vacuum.

The multi-dimensional scenarios are somewhat more difficult to visualize than the geometrical. Instead of the familiar three-dimensional world of everyday life or the more esoteric four-dimensional world of relativity, they deal with a world of 10 or 11 dimensions. (Don't bother trying to picture such a world—it is not a job for your imagination. You need to rely on mathematics.) To approach a multi-dimensional universe, think of a garden hose. From a distance the hose looks like a long, thin line—a one-dimensional system. As you draw closer, you notice the hose that appeared one-dimensional from far away actually has another dimension, one represented by its hollow cylindrical shape. In just the same way, a world which appears in four dimensions when viewed in the ordinary course of affairs may actually sprout extra dimensions when viewed more closely.

We find in this approach that the extra-dimensional character of the physical world is apparent only when the radius of the universe is very small. In practical terms, this means that the extra dimensions have almost no effect after the Planck time, but will be very important before that instant.

In our present world, the extra dimensions are still there, of course, but they may be thought of as separated into tiny spheres much smaller than elementary particles. These relics have played no important role since the early moments of the universe and lie beyond our present capabilities to detect.

"The idea," says Edward Kolb, Co-Director of the Center for Theoretical Astrophysics at the Fermi National Accelerator Laboratory, "is that what looks like a singularity in four dimensions may not be singular at all when viewed in eleven."

Now we turn to the final category of speculations—the dynamical theories. They include my own favorites. The approach: take the known properties of elementary particles and try to guess how they might behave under conditions prevailing before the Planck time. For example, some of the first speculations about the origins of the universe were based on some differences between classical and quantum-mechanics "pictures" of the original vacuum. Classically, a vacuum is simply the absence of matter. In quantum mechanics, however, the existence of the uncertainty principle leads us to view the vacuum as a very complex system. (The uncertainty principle says that we can neither detect nor measure fundamental particles without altering them.) A particle-

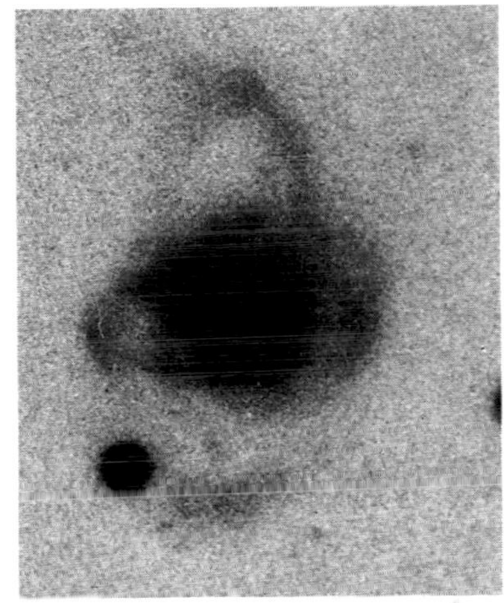

Eerie limbs exert strange pressures in M.C. Escher's Gravity *(1952), left. Next to nothing has been learned about this pervasive yet mysterious force since Newton's first description in 1665. Mystery of deep space, ESO 474–G 26, above, may have cannibalized a passing galaxy to form a puzzling polar ring.*

antiparticle pair can pop into existence in empty space, provided that the opposing particles annihilate each other in a time so short that the violation of energy conservation implicit in this process cannot be detected. The vacuum, then, is a bit more like a hot pan of rather exotic popcorn kernels than a featureless, empty sea. Particle-antiparticle pairs pop into existence here and there, but disappear quickly.

A number of scientists, beginning with Edward Tryon of the City University of New York, have speculated that the universe itself is one of these fleeting bubbles in a universal vacuum. Given the right conditions, the 15-billion-year lifetime of the universe could be "short" in the quantum mechanical sense, and our new knowledge of elementary particles tells us that a universe that started out as a mixture of matter and antimatter would quickly evolve into one composed of matter only. Consequently, as bizarre as this idea of a fast shuffle may seem, it is completely consistent with the known laws of physics. In this picture, the universe came into existence as a fluctuation in the quantum mechanics vacuum—a notion that leads to a view of creation in which the entire universe is simply an accident.

Borrowing from chemistry, astronomers have found striking correlations between waves of chemical change, right, and computer-generated, galaxy-like spiral patterns. By modeling dynamic processes, cosmologists have come closer to understanding galactic evolution. Below, galactic engine fuels gigantic, wispy lobes of the sky's second most powerful radio source, Cygnus A. Only a pinpoint between lobes, the galaxy is so energetic, some scientists believe that it contains a black hole. Shrouded in great mystery, galactic jets may be the key to star formation.

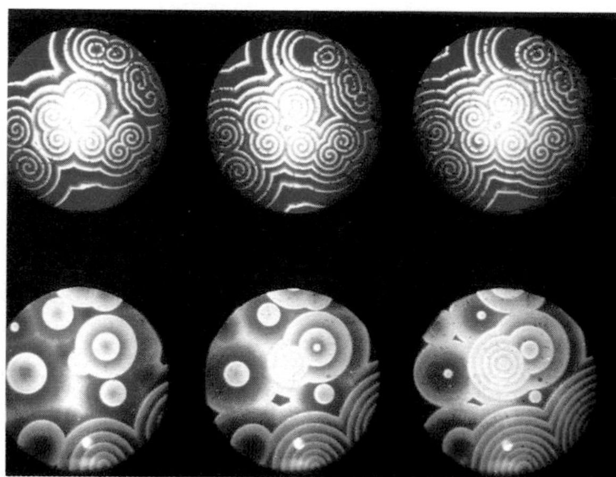

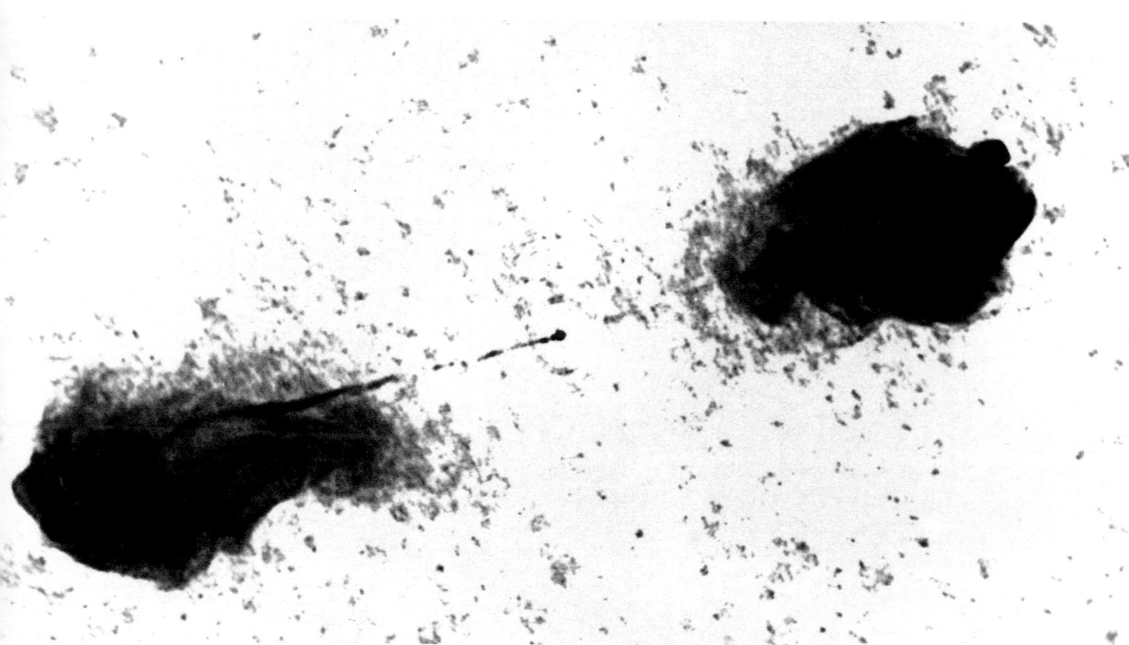

A more modern version of this sort of speculation was described to me by David Schramm. "We know that at the Planck time the energy of every particle is so high, and its mass so great, that each particle would have to be a black hole." (This follows from the fact that as a particle's energy increases, its mass increases also.) According to the laws of quantum mechanics, he pointed out, this sort of black hole will be unstable. It will emit energy in the form of radiation, eventually radiating itself out of existence. Schramm also noted that the universe in the period before the Planck time might be "a foam of black holes." The black holes would appear, radiate their energy away, and disappear in a process analogous to the appearance and disappearance of bubbles in an ordinary foam.

In this scheme of things, if we could see the universe before the Planck time, we would find the elemental foam extending back into the infinite past. As in the vacuum fluctuation picture, the universe began when enough "bubbles" happened, by chance, to come together. Unlike the fluctuation picture, however, in this scheme the Big Bang actually started at the Planck time. There is no time zero and hence no singularity.

The idea of the universe-as-fluctuation can be an intriguing one, and many scientists have been taken with the notion. My own favorite quote is from Edward Tryon who, after proposing the theory, commented, "It may be that the universe is just one of those things that happens from time to time."

A Final Word

These speculations about the creation of the universe are heady stuff indeed. As we work our way back from three minutes into the Big Bang to 10^{-43} second, we can only admire the ingenuity of the human minds that have conceived these new theories.

Above all, we admire the beauty and elegance of the laws of nature. Operating at unimaginable temperatures and pressures, these laws governed each successive freezing from early times, and make the universe what it is today.

Implicit in all of our discussion of what may have happened before the Planck time is a very singular idea. It holds that the laws we can discover in our laboratories here and now have governed not only the universe since the beginning, but governed the moment of creation as well. This is a profound way of looking at a very old philosophical problem. We are saying that the very existence of the universe is an inevitable result of the laws of physics. The study of the early universe does indeed become the study of the mind of God, as William Herschel argued two centuries ago. And when we look at the beauty and elegance of the theories that are unfolding before us, we can only agree with Nobel Laureate Arno Penzias when he said, "It's comforting to have a God who knew how to do the job right."

Spiral shapes are created by turbulence in a study of fluid mechanics, below. The ubiquitous spiral reveals a history of dispersion over time, making spiral galaxies important documents to astronomers studying galactic evolution.

Epilogue

In a dance of cosmic creation, the Indian deity Shiva overcomes the ever-present forces of destruction. An allied Hindu god Vishnu—entered the folklore of the Atomic Age through the creator of the first atomic bomb, J. Robert Oppenheimer. After Trinity, the first detonation, on July 16, 1945, Oppenheimer quoted Vishnu from the Bhagavad Gita, "I am become death, the destroyer of worlds."

Now that we have witnessed the creation of the universe and have followed its evolution, we know that it is a dynamic, changing system. Now that we have seen its transformation from a collection of unimaginably dense, hot matter to the stars and galaxies of today, it is only natural to ask how this evolution will proceed in the future. To find a reasonable answer to this ultimate question we would do well to break it into several parts.

One question I'm often asked: since the history of the universe is a series of freezings, is it possible that there will be another freezing at some time? To answer this question, it must be remembered that each freezing occurs when the temperature of the universe falls below a certain critical value. Today this temperature is about three degrees above absolute zero. We see no evidence for further freezings when we test the behavior of materials at temperatures lower than that of interstellar space. So it is reasonable to conclude that there will be no freezings in our future.

The prediction of the fate of the universe, then, does not depend on our ability to understand the properties of matter under conditions that we cannot reproduce in our laboratories. As the universe cools slowly from its present state, we can make a pretty reliable picture of what it will be like. The missing ingredient is not to be found in the realm of theory, but in that of observation.

We have discussed the existence of dark matter in some detail. Perhaps soon we shall know if the universe contains enough matter to reverse the universal expansion: but today our ignorance of the amount of dark matter leads to enormous differences in the predicted fate of the universe. For example, if the dark matter is only 20 to 30 percent of the critical value, the Hubble expansion will continue forever in an eternally cooling universe. If, on the other hand, the amount of dark matter exceeds the critical value, even by the smallest amount, the expansion will ultimately reverse and the universe will collapse back in upon itself, heating up as it does so. The dark-matter problem, then, leads to this question about the future of the universe: will it end in emptiness? Or, indeed, will it end in fire or in ice?

Perhaps the best way to picture our dilemma is to imagine a train coming into a switchyard. All of the switches are set before the train arrives, so that its path is completely predetermined. Some switches we can see, others we cannot. There is no ambiguity if we can see the setting of the switch: we can say with confidence that some possible futures will not materialize and others will. At the unseen switches, however, there is no such certainty. We know the train will take one of the tracks leading out, but we have no idea which one. The unseen switches are true decision points in the future, and what happens when we arrive at them will determine the subsequent course of events.

When we think about the future of the universe, we can see our "track" many billions of years into the future. After that, however, there are decision points to be dealt with and possible fates to consider. One goal of modern astronomy is to reduce the ambiguity at the decision points and find the true road that will be followed.

We have a pretty good idea about the short-term fate of the universe. We expect that the galaxies will continue to separate and stars will continue to form and evolve for many billions of years. The universe is now about 15 billion years old, the Earth and sun a little less than five billion. In another five billion years the sun will have used up all the hydrogen it can. The sun will then swell into a red giant, and life upon the earth will be extinguished.

Ten billion years is a typical lifetime for a star the size of the sun; smaller stars, which are more numerous, live longer. Whatever the lifetime, each star uses up a certain amount of raw material. In 40 or 50 billion years, then, we expect that star formation will have slowed down considerably. Stars will continue to go out: first the bright ones, then the more sedate ones. Our own Galaxy would be dull, mostly a sprinkling of stars of lesser caliber than our sun. The sky from the region of the Earth (or, more correctly, from the region where the Earth *was*) would contain only a few stars. Perhaps it would resemble a darker version of the night sky seen from a major city, with only a few widely separated lights to break the gloom.

Early Italian tarot card represents a union of the forces of earth and sky. Since Babylonian times, or before, people have sought to align their lives with the celestial realm.

The Closed Universe

Let us assume that nature has chosen to hide 99 percent or more of the mass and that the universe is actually closed. In this case we are in for a spectacular future. For another 40 or 50 billion years the universe will continue to expand, but ever more slowly. Then, like a ball falling back to earth, the expansion will reverse at some point—50 billion years is a reasonable guess—and a great contraction will begin. Instead of a universe where light from distant galaxies is shifted toward the red (indicating that the source is receding from us), we will find such light is blue-shifted.

Eighty to a hundred billion years from now the Earth and the sun will be long dead. The galaxies will be decidedly less luminous, with populations of white dwarfs, neutron stars and other faint objects. As the contraction progresses, galaxies move closer together and the cosmic background radiation begins to shift toward the visible part of the spectrum. The sky will eventually blaze with light. By this time, the universe will have contracted to a thousandth or less of its present size. The stars and planets themselves will dissolve into a universal sea of hot material, and atoms and molecules will dissociate into their constituent nuclei and electrons. From this point on, the stages of the Big Bang will simply play backwards—nuclei dissociating into quarks and so on—until we are back to the state in which it is thought the Big Bang occurred.

This scenario leads inevitably to the most fascinating question of all. Will the universal contraction (which cosmologists half-jokingly call the Big Crunch) be followed by another expansion (the Big Bounce)? In other words, will the universe arise as a phoenix from its ashes and repeat the entire cycle? The picture of a universe which is reborn every 100 billion years or so is very attractive to some people. The principal advantage of an eternally oscillating universe is that certain basic questions—Why did it all start? Where did it all come from?—simply do not need to be asked. The universe always was and always will be. A hundred billion years from now the universe may again consist of a large collection of separating galaxies. And perhaps there will be another version of you reading another version of this book.

It is a fascinating thought, but before we go too far into speculation, I should warn you that there are some serious problems with this picture. At least a few theorists argue that unless some of the basic laws of physics change during part of the cycle, the average disorder of the universe might have to increase during each bounce, so that eventually the system would run down.

The Open Universe

Scientists used to think that the universal tendency of every system to run down would eventually result in what has been called the "heat death" of the universe. This cannot happen in an eternally expanding system as the components eventually become too isolated to interact. Let us, then, consider what might actually take place. Freeman J. Dyson, one of the most inventive minds in the fraternity of theoretical physicists, has explored this possible course of the universe. He did so not only because of the intrinsic interest of the problem, but because, as he says, a closed universe gives him a feeling of claustrophobia.

Because the expected lifetime of an open universe is infinite, we will have to think about very long times indeed if we are to follow the twists and turns of this possible future. Once again we will find it convenient to use scientific notation. In this scheme the number 10^3 should be interpreted as a one followed by three zeroes, or 1,000. The universe is now roughly 10 billion years old, a number with 10 zeroes, and we would render it as 10^{10} years. The life cycle of a closed universe is often taken to be around 100 billion, or 10^{11}, years. Each time the power of 10 is increased by one unit, the number increases tenfold.

When we think about the future, it is tempting to imagine that we are watching a film being run at a uniform speed. But another way to think about it—one that will give a better feeling for the immense time scales involved—is to imagine that the film speed is multiplied by 10 when the power of 10 goes up one digit. Thus, if we imagine that we are watching such a film being run at the rate of 10 billion years every minute, then right now we are a little less than two minutes into the story following the Big Bang. Eight minutes from now we will be seeing the universe when it is 100 billion (or 10^{11}) years old. The power of 10 has gone up one digit, so at that point the film speed increases by 10. The next 10 minutes will take us to a trillion (10^{12}) years, at which point the speed again increases by 10, so that time is going by at the rate of a trillion years a minute, and so on. Adopting this method of looking at things is the only way we can even begin to imagine the immense time scales involved in working out the death of the universe.

If the universe is open, the only change in its expansion will be a gradual slowing down. The process of star formation will begin to wind down in the next billion years or so, as we have already seen. The burning-out process would go on for a long time. Small, slow-burning stars could last as long as 10^{14} years, giving a pale illumination to the sky. As these stars cool off, other kinds of dissipation begin to become important. Some stars will evaporate from the outer regions of the Galaxy in a time scale of 10^{19} years, while the densely packed stars in the galactic center may collapse together into a large black hole.

When the universe is a billion times older, corresponding to nine changes in film speed, we will see an ever thinner sea of background radiation in which an occasional black hole is embedded. Scattered among these landmarks in nothingness will be the solid remains of the evaporated stars and some debris. The universe will keep its composure through 13 more increases in film speed, until about 10^{32} years.

We must ask about the fate of the remaining solid matter. According to theory, the protons that make up all matter are unstable, and have a lifetime of roughly 10^{32} years. If the proton is indeed unstable, matter will be disintegrating fast enough for us to notice its disappearance on our film.

If, on the other hand, protons are stable, nothing of this sort will have happened at 10^{32} years. Universal expansion and cooling will continue. Now and then, miscellaneous solid material will fall into a black hole and produce flashes of radiation. As this state of affairs would persist until 10^{65} years had passed, a hypothetical astronomer observing the universe would be getting very bored.

With the film running at about 10^{65} years per minute, an important process is starting to take place among the black holes the size of our sun. We think of black holes as bodies so dense that nothing can ever escape their gravitational pull, yet on long time scales it turns out that this is not quite accurate. Black holes will lose appreciable energy through thermal radiation. In a sense, the black hole resembles an ember, giving off heat to its surroundings.

With the film running at 10^{65} years per minute, a black hole will start radiating substantial energy, getting brighter and brighter as it does so. In one minute of film time, the black hole will brighten the sky and then disappear, its only monument an addition to the expanding sea of radiation. As the film runs on, speeding up every 10 minutes, larger and larger black holes will undergo the same process and evaporate themselves away. For the next 35 changes in film speed we would see occasional fireworks as a black hole dies in an expanding universe. By the time all the black holes are gone the film will be running at 10^{100} years a minute.

If the protons have decayed, this is the end of our story, because there is nothing left in the universe to produce any real change. If the proton does not decay, the disappearance of the black holes still leaves us with some solid matter to watch. The film now runs for 10 days, until each minute corresponds to 10^{1500} years. Just writing the zeroes in this number would require a full typewritten page! On this scale matter turns to iron, the most stable nucleus.

On still longer time scales—scales so long that we might have to watch our film for longer than the lifetime of the Earth—these iron spheres would become black holes, which would eventually evaporate.

This means that at some distant time in the future, the universe will be a cold, thin sea of radiation, with perhaps a few forlorn particles mixed in. It was perhaps this bleak prospect that caused Nobel Laureate Steven Weinberg to remark, "The more the universe seems comprehensible, the more it also seems pointless."

Following pages: Helmut Wimmer's depiction of the future of the universe. The great spiral of creation begins to wind down in a manner outlined in the text of this epilogue. Main features include the swelling and death of our sun and the progression of galaxies toward quiescence. The Hubble Space Telescope has been chosen as a symbol of humanity's cosmic curiosity and of the array of new tools developed by astronomers and physicists. These help us to see as far as we can and to know all we can of our origins and ultimate fate. Scientists have discovered such secrets only in this century.

H. k. WIMMER

Index

The following are abbreviations used to identify Smithsonian Institution museums and other organizations in the index, acknowledgements, and picture credits.

SI	Smithsonian Institution
SAO	Smithsonian Astrophysical Observatory
CFA	Center for Astrophysics
NASM	National Air and Space Museum
NMAH	National Museum of American History
NMNH	National Museum of Natural History
NGA	National Gallery of Art
SIL	Smithsonian Institution Libraries
AIP	American Institute of Physics
AURA	Association of Universities for Research in Astronomy
CIT	California Institute of Technology
ESA	European Space Agency
JPL	Jet Propulsion Laboratory
JSC	Lyndon B. Johnson Space Center
MOMA	Museum of Modern Art
NASA	National Aeronautics and Space Administration
NRAO	National Radio Astronomy Observatory
NOAO	National Optical Astronomy Observatories

Numbers in italic signify picture references.

Picture Credits

Legend

B bottom

C center

L left

R right

T top

Front Jacket: JPL/NASA
Back Jacket: NRAO
Flap: Judith Peatross

Front Matter: p. 1 David F. Malin/Anglo-Australian Telescope Board; 2–3 Rudolph Schild/SAO-CFA; 4–5 Ronald E. Royer and Steve Padilla/courtesy of Astro Media Corp.; 7 Hartmann Schedel, *Nuremberg Chronicle of 1493,* Nuremberg, Dibner Room, SI Libraries/Ed Castle; 8–9 art by Helmut Wimmer/photo by Ed Castle; 11 Dr. Kris Davidson/Photo Researchers, Inc.

Part 1: pp 12–13 British Library; 15 Ray A. Williamson; 16–17 Pieter Bruegel the Elder, 1563, Kunsthistorisches Museum, Vienna; 17 courtesy of the Trustees of the British Museum/Michael Holford Picture Libraries; 18 Edinburgh University Library; 19 *Description de l'Egypte,* Vol. 4, France, 1809–18, Dibner Room, SI Libraries/Ed Castle; 20–21T The National Museum, Copenhagen/Lennart Larsen; 20–21B art by Barbara Page; 22 James Sugar/Black Star; 23L, 23R Universitatsbibliothek, Tübingen; 24T Museum of the American Indian, Heye Foundation, N.Y.; 24B Christy Collection, British Museum/Lee Boltin Picture Library; 25T *Bodley Codex,* Bodleian Library, Oxford; 25B Ron Church/Photo Researchers, Inc.; 26–27 Erich Lessing/Magnum; 27 courtesy of Editions Houvet, Chartres/Owen Gingerich; 28 The Granger Collection, N.Y.; 29 Gregor Reisch, *Margarita Philosophica,* Basle, 1508/Ann Ronan Picture Library, Somerset; 30 British Library; 31 The Granger Collection, N.Y.; 32 British Library; 33 art by Barbara Page; 34L Scala/Art Resource, N.Y.; 34R Bibliothèque Nationale, Paris; 35 Malcolm S. Kirk; 36 Bibliothèque Nationale, Paris; 37 Gianni Tortoli/Photo Researchers, Inc.; 38 Erich Lessing/Magnum; 39L Cellarius, *Harmonia Macrocosmica,* Rare Book Division, Library of Congress; 39R Copernicus, *De Revolutionibus Orbium Coelestrium,* The Granger Collection, N.Y.; 40 Thomas Digges, supplement to 1576 edition of Leonard Digges' *Prognostication Everlasting,* The Granger Collection, N.Y.; 41 Copernicus, "Commentariolus," Stockholm University Library and Royal Swedish Academy of Sciences/Owen Gingerich; 42 art by Henrich Hansen, The National History Museum, Frederiksborg, Denmark; 44L *Epistolarium Astronomicarium Libri,* Uraniborg, 1596, Dibner Room, SI Libraries/Charles H. Phillips; 44T NMAH/Ed Castle; 44B Joan Blaeu, *Atlas Maior,* Amsterdam, 1662, Dibner Room, SI Libraries/Ed Castle; 45L Dibner Room, SI Libraries/Ed Castle; 45R Joan Blaeu, *Atlas Maior,* Amsterdam, 1662, Dibner Room, SI Libraries/Ed Castle; 46 Le Comte, *Voyage to China,* 1698/Bettmann Archive; 47T Mary Evans Picture Library, London; 47B The Granger Collection, N.Y.; 48 courtesy of Colchester Borough Council, Colchester and Essex Museum; 49 art by Barbara Page; 50TL Foundation St. Thomas, Strasbourg; 50TR Johannes Kepler, *Epitome Astronomiae Copernicanae,* 1618/Ann Ronan Picture Library, Somerset; 50C BL BR, 51T, BR Johannes Kepler, *Harmonices Mundi,* 1619, Dibner Room, SI Libraries/Charles H. Phillips; 51BL Owen Gingerich; 52 Biblioteca Nazionale, Florence, Scala/Art Resources, N.Y.; 53 Robert Fleury, "Galileo Before the Holy Office," 1847, Cliché des Musées Nationaux; 54T Erich Lessing/Magnum; 54B NMAH/Ed Castle; 55T Ed Castle; 55B Ufano, *Artillerie,* Zutphen, 1621, Rare Book Division, New York Public Library; 57 Joseph Wright, "Philosopher Lecturing on the Orrery," 1766, Derby Museums and Art Gallery.

Part 2: pp. 58–59 Harald Sund/Image Bank; 61 NRAO; 62 René Descartes, *Opera Philosphica,* Amsterdam, 1650, Dibner Room, SI Libraries/Charles H. Phillips; 63 Allegheny Observatory, University of Pittsburgh/Ed Castle; 64T Science Museum Library, London; 64B Julia Margaret Cameron, 1867, NMAH/SI; 65 photo by John Adams Whipple, 1852, Harvard College Observatory; 66T National Research Council, Canada; 66B art by Barbara Page; 67 1917, Harvard College Library, courtesy AIP Niels Bohr Library; 68 NMAH, SI Libraries/Ed Castle; 69 art by Helmut Wimmer, from *Skyguide,* © 1982, Western Publishing Co., Inc.; 70T Palomar Observatory; 70B © CIT; 71 Palomar Observatory; 72 James Sugar/Black Star; 72–73, 74 Royal Observatory, Edinburgh; 75 James Sugar/Black Star; 76L Paul Gorenstein and Steven Kahn/SAO-CFA; 76R High Energy Astrophysics Division, SAO-CFA; 77 art by Helmut Wimmer, *Fire of Life,* SI, © 1981/Ed Castle; 78L NRAO; 78R Lick Observatory; 79L Steve Mandel; 79R S. Djorgovski, University of California, Berkeley; 80 Royal Observatory, Edinburgh; 81 *Sky & Telescope,* © 1983 Sky Publishing Corp.; 82L Fred Espenak; 82R Erich Lessing/Magnum; 83 AIP, Niels Bohr Library; 84 CIT; 85 Mary Lea Shane Archives, Lick Observatory; 86–87 Anglo-Australian Telescope Board © 1980/David F. Malin; 87 Ed Castle; 88L © CIT; 88R Rudolph Schild/SAO-CFA; 89 Dr. Jean Lorre/Photo Researchers, Inc.; 90L Starlink, Appleton/Photo Researchers, Inc.; 90R © R.J. Dufour, Rice University; 91 Etan Schreier and Eric Feigelson, SAO-CFA/Dane Penland/SI; 92L Dr. S. Gull/Photo Researchers Inc.; 92R Rudolph Schild/SAO-CFA; 93L Dr Jean Lorre/Photo Researchers, Inc.; 93R Rudolph Schild/SAO-CFA; 94, 95 Dr. Halton C. Arp, (from slide set) The Astronomical Society of the Pacific; 96L NRAO, 96C Harvard College Observatory, courtesy AIP, Niels Bohr Library; 96R © LIFE Magazine, courtesy AIP, Niels Bohr Library; 97 R. Walterbos, Leiden Observatory, Netherlands; 98 CIT, © 1984; 99 NOAO; 100 CIT, © 1984; 101 Dr. Halton C. Arp/Palomar Observatory; 102 James Sugar/Black Star; 103 Claude Michaelides; 104 art by Jackie Leatherbury Douglass, from *Fire of Life,* SI, © 1981/Charles H. Phillips; 105 Department of the History of Science and Technology, NMAH/Ed Castle; 106 Rudolph Schild/SAO-CFA; 107 Tom Stephenson and Rudolph Schild/SAO-CFA; 108–109T Lund Observatory, Sweden; 109B European Southern Observatory, Munich, 110 ESA; 111 Los Alamos National Laboratory; 112 James Sugar/Black Star; 113L Anglo-Australian Telescope Board; 113R NRAO; 114 JPL/NASA; 115 Fred Espenak.

Part 3: pp. 116–117 JPL/NASA; 119 Giotto di Bondone, *Adoration of the Magi,* 1303–4,

Padua, Scala/Art Resource, N.Y.; 120 JPL/NASA; 121 Naval Research Laboratory; 122 art by Don Davis; 123 JPL/NASA; 124T NASM; 124BL Ross Chapple; 124BR JSC/NASA, courtesy of USSR Academy of Sciences; 125L JPL/NASA; 125R art by Andrei Sokolov/Space Art International, "Soviet Venera 9 Spacecraft on Venus," from *Life Among the Stars,* U.S.S.R., 1980; 126T JPL/NASA; 126B United States Geological Survey; 127 JPL/NASA; 128 art by Kurt Wenner, JPL/NASA; 129, 130TL TR JPL/NASA; 130BL art by Maralyn E. Vicary, "Vapor Eruption on Europa"; 130BR, 131T JPL/NASA; 131B Dan McCoy/Rainbow; 132TB, 133, 134TL JPL/NASA; 134TR J. Weston and Son, Eastbourne, England, courtesy of Mrs. Maxwell Phair/Ed Castle; 134B art by Kim Poor; 135L U.S. Naval Observatory/James W. Christy; 135R art by James Hervat; 136, 137 JPL/NASA; 138 art by Rick Sternbach, NASM/Ed Castle; 139 Naval Research Laboratory; 140 Ira Wyman; 141T Fred Espenak/Photo Researchers, Inc.; 141B Robert Hooke, *Collection of Lectures: Physical, Mechanical, Geographical and Astronomical,* Dibner Room, SI Libraries/Charles H. Phillips; 142T Donald E. Brownlee, University of Washington; 142B © 1985 Roger Ressmeyer; 143 art by Helmut Wimmer, from *Skyguide,* © 1982 by Western Publishing Co., Inc.; 145T Jack Dykinga/Bruce Coleman Inc.; 145B Griffith Observatory Archives; 146 ESA; 147 *Les Très Riches Heures du Duc de Berry,* c. 1411, Chantilly, Musee Conde, H. Josse/Art Resource, N.Y.; 148 JSC/NASA; 149 art by Andrei Sokolov/Space Art International, "Apollo Soyuz Over the Caspian Sea" U.S.S.R., 1975, NASM/Ed Castle; 150 Dr. William Haxby, Lamont-Doherty Geological Observatory, Columbia University; 151L,R Sovfoto; 152 art by Don Davis; 153 Victor Krantz/NMNH; 154 Vincent van Gogh, *The Starry Night,* 1889, oil on canvas, 29 × 36¼″ (73.7 × 92.1 cm), The Museum of Modern Art, N.Y., acquired through the Lillie P. Bliss Bequest; 156 Royal Greenwich Observatory; 157 NASA; 158T art by Don Dixon, "Moonrise: Four Billion B.C."; 158BL art by William K. Hartmann; 158BR art by Steven Simpson, courtesy of *Sky & Telescope;* 160T art by Adolf Schaller, © 1975 *Astronomy* Magazine; 160B JPL/NASA; 161T art by Andrew Chaikin, "Whole Asteroid Catalog"; 162 courtesy of *Sky & Telescope;* 163 art by Don Davis; 164 Georg Gerster/Photo Researchers, Inc.; 165 by permission of Johnny Hart and News Group Chicago, Inc.; 166 Roger Ressmeyer; 167T National Center for Atmospheric Research; 167B courtesy of John Arnosti; 168 J. Koivula/Photo Researchers, Inc.; 169 Erich Hartmann/Magnum; 170T "The Message," art, photo by Brian Sullivan/Hayden Planetarium, American Museum of Natural History; 170B Barrett Gallagher; 173 art by Frank Paul, "Gravity Flyer," NASM, gift of M. Harvey Gernsback; 174–175 JPL/NASA.

Part 4: pp. 176–177 Ross Chapple; 179 Doug Munson, courtesy of the Department of Special Collections, University of Chicago Libraries; 180–181 Dane Penland/SI; 182T Gary Ladd; 182B Dane Penland/SI; 183T James Sugar/Black Star; 183B Gary Ladd; 184LCR Charles H. Phillips; 185TB Dane Penland/SI; 186T Ross Chapple; 186B Rudolph Schild and Tom Stephenson/SAO-CFA; 187T Ross Chapple; 187B Patrick P. Murphy; 188 James Sugar/Black Star; 189 art by Rob Wood/Stansbury, Ronsaville, Wood Inc.; 190 Carol A. Foote; 191 James Sugar/Black Star; 192 Albrecht Dürer, *De Scientia Motus Orbis,* Nuremberg, 1504 Dibner Room, SI Libraries/Charles H. Phillips; 193, 194, 195 Ross Chapple; 196–197 Lockheed Missiles & Space Co., Inc.; 198L JPL/NASA; 198R art by Rick Sternbach and Don Dixon; 199 The Perkin-Elmer Corporation; 200T ESA; 200B art by Chesley Bonestell/Bonestell Space Art, "Observatory on the Moon," 1961, from *Rocket to the Moon,* Columbia Records, 1962; 201T Ross Chapple; 201B International Solar-Terrestrial Physics Program/NASA; 202 Roger Ressmeyer; 203T art by Dean Ellis/Ed Castle; 203B NRAO; 204T art by Rob Wood/Stansbury, Ronsaville, Wood Inc.; 204B William K. Hartmann; 205 art by Chesley Bonestell/Bonestell Space Art, "Beta Lyrae," 1963, from *Beyond the Solar System,* Viking, 1964; 206–207 P. Loiez/Photo Researchers, Inc.; 207 Steve Northup/Black Star; 208 Rudolph Schild/SAO-CFA; 210 David Parker/Photo Researchers, Inc.; 211T Hank Morgan/Photo Researchers, Inc.; 211B © Omikron, Science Source/Photo Researchers, Inc.; 212 courtesy of *Scientific American*/James Kilkelly; 212R David Parker/Photo Researchers, Inc.; 213 Heavy Ion Group, University of California, Riverside; 214L,R, 215L Kenneth Garrett; 215R art by John Tenniel, Lewis Carroll, *Alice's Adventures in Wonderland,* London, 1866; 216 Nick Caloyianis; 218 David Parker/Photo Researchers, Inc.; 220 Photo Researchers, Inc.; 221L LIFE Magazine © 1947, Time Inc., Alfred Eisenstaedt; 221R Petrus Apianus, *Instrument Buch,* Switzerland, 1533, Dibner Room, SI Libraries/Charles H. Phillips; 222 Ross Chapple; 224T University of California, Lawrence Livermore National Laboratory/Department of Energy; 224B NRAO; 225 William Gilbert, *De Magnete Magneticisque Corporibus et de Magno Magnete Tellure,* 1600, Dibner Room, SI Libraries/Charles H. Phillips; 226 art by Kim Poor, "Cosmic Masers" © 1981; 228 art by Don Dixon, "Maelstrom"; 229 David Montgomery/N.Y. Times Syndication Sales Corp.; 230 courtesy of the Trustees of the British Museum; 231 S. Djorgovski, University of California, Berkeley; 232 Christine J. Jones and William R. Forman, SAO-CFA/John J. Lupo; 234T Salvador Dali, "The Persistance of Memory," 1931, oil on canvas, 9½ × 13″, The Museum of Modern Art, N.Y.; 234B M.C. Escher, "Tetrahedral Planetoid," 1954, two-color woodcut, 19⅞ × 19⅜″, Cornelius Van S. Roosevelt Collection, National Gallery of Art, Washington, D.C.; 236 John E. Moody, Edwin L. Turner, J. Richard Gott III, Princeton University; 238L Hans Pfletschinger/Peter Arnold Inc.; 238R René Descartes, *Opera Philosophica,* 1650, 2nd ed., Amsterdam, Dibner Room, SI Libraries/Charles H. Phillips; 239 M. Seldner, B. Siebers, Edward Groth, P.J.E. Peebles; 240 James Bell/Photo Researchers, Inc.; 241L M.C. Escher, "Gravity," 1952, lithograph, 15½ × 15½″, Cornelius Van S. Roosevelt Collection, National Gallery of Art, Washington, D.C.; 241R François Schweizer, Carnegie Institute of Washington, D.C.; 242T Professor A. Winfree/Photo Researchers, Inc.; 242B NRAO; 243 Milton Van Dyke, *An Album of Fluid Motion,* 1982/Sadatoshi Taneda; 244 The Granger Collection, N.Y.; 246 Bergamo/Galleria dell' Accademia Carrara, Scala/Art Resource, N.Y.; 247–248 art by Helmut Wimmer/photo by Ed Castle; 256 NRAO.

Acknowledgements

Kenneth L. Franklin, Astronomer Emeritus of the Hayden Planetarium, provided introductory essays for the volume's section openers. Helmut Wimmer, also of the Hayden, contributed special illustrations. Both also took part in *Fire of Life: The Smithsonian Book of the Sun*, companion volume to *Space, Time, Infinity.* The Hayden Planetarium is associated with the American Museum of Natural History of New York City. Dr. Franklin also contributes to the "Sky Watch" feature of the Sunday *New York Times.*

First, we would like to extend our thanks to Irwin I. Shapiro, Director of the Harvard-Smithsonian Center for Astrophysics at Cambridge, Massachusetts. Without the aid of scientists and others at Cambridge, this volume would not have been possible. In particular, James C. Cornell, Jr., Publications Manager, Smithsonian Astrophysical Observatory, guided staff members of Smithsonian Books and the author at Cambridge and in planning for visits to the astronomical facilities in Arizona. Owen Gingerich, an astrophysicist at SAO and Professor of Astronomy and History of Science at Harvard University, advised on historical chapters. Many astrophysicists and others in Massachusetts and in Arizona assisted during research for the manuscript, and for photography.

Other Advisers: Von Del Chamberlain, Director of the Hansen Planetarium, Salt Lake City, Utah; David Devorkin, Chairman of the Space Science and Exploration Department, NASM; and Ray A. Williamson, Project Director, Office of Technology Assessment, U.S. Congress.

Special Thanks

We were also fortunate to work again with Silvio A. Bedini who provided information and insight on the early days of astronomy in Europe and America. Mr. Bedini is Special Assistant to the Director of the Smithsonian Institution Libraries. Our thanks go to Jurrie J. van der Woude, Public Information Officer, Jet Propulsion Laboratory, Pasadena, California. He also assisted in *Fire of Life.* In addition, our special thanks go to the following: Halton Arp, CIT; Shirley A. Ballard, Program Plans Coordinator, Space Telescope, Lockheed Missiles and Space Company, Inc., Sunnyvale, California; Bert Bulkin, Program Manager, Space Telescope, Lockheed; Jack Carr, Director of the Charles Hayden Planetarium, Museum of Science, Boston; Andrew Chaikin, Assistant Editor, *Sky & Telescope;* David Clark, Producer, *Smithsonian World;* Roy S. Clarke, Jr., Curator, Department of Mineral Sciences, NMAH; Elvira Clain-Stefanelli, National Numismatic Collection, NMAH; Edward Collins, The Perkin-Elmer Corporation; Dennis di Cicco, Associate Editor, *Sky & Telescope;* Roberta Diemer, SI/OPPS; Freeman J. Dyson, Princeton University; Russell Elwell, Indiantown, Florida; Anne L. Goodwin, Indexer, Kensington, Maryland; Paul Hanle, Associate Director for the Department of Research, Space Science and Exploration Department, NASM; Brian Hadley, Royal Observatory, Edinburgh; Francis Hueber, NMNH; Sandra Kitt, Librarian, American Museum of Natural History-Hayden Planetarium; Michael J. Klein, Manager, Jet Propulsion Laboratory, SETI Project, Pasadena, California; Monica Knudsen, NASM; Victor Krantz, SI/OPPS, NMNH; E.C. Krupp, Director of the Griffith Observatory, Los Angeles, CA; William C. Livingston, Senior Scientist, Kitt Peak National Observatory; David Malin, Anglo-Australian Observatory; Jack F. Marquardt, Senior Reference Librarian, Main Library, Smithsonian Institution Libraries; George M. Mulhern, Director of Public Relations, Lockheed; Agnes Paulsen, Kitt Peak National Observatory; Dane Penland, SI/OPPS; Mark de Solla Price, New York City; Ian Pryke, European Space Agency, Washington, D.C.; Philip Ross, National Academy of Sciences; Glenn Sandlin, Naval Research Laboratory; Janette Saquet, SIL; Robert Schulman, NASA; William Shawcross, Managing Editor, *Sky & Telescope;* Priscilla Strain, NASM; Daryl Stroud, Ames Research Center, NASA; Joseph Tatarewicz, NASM; Mary Valdivia, Curator of Art, NASM; Lisa Vazquez, Media Services Corporation, JSC; Arlene Walsh, SAO, Margaret Weems, National Radio Astronomy Observatory; Ellen B. Wells, Chief of Special Collections, SIL; Ray White, University of Arizona, Tucson. Others are mentioned in text and captions.

Overleaf:
Two extragalactic, twin jet radio sources in false color as seen by the Very Large Array.

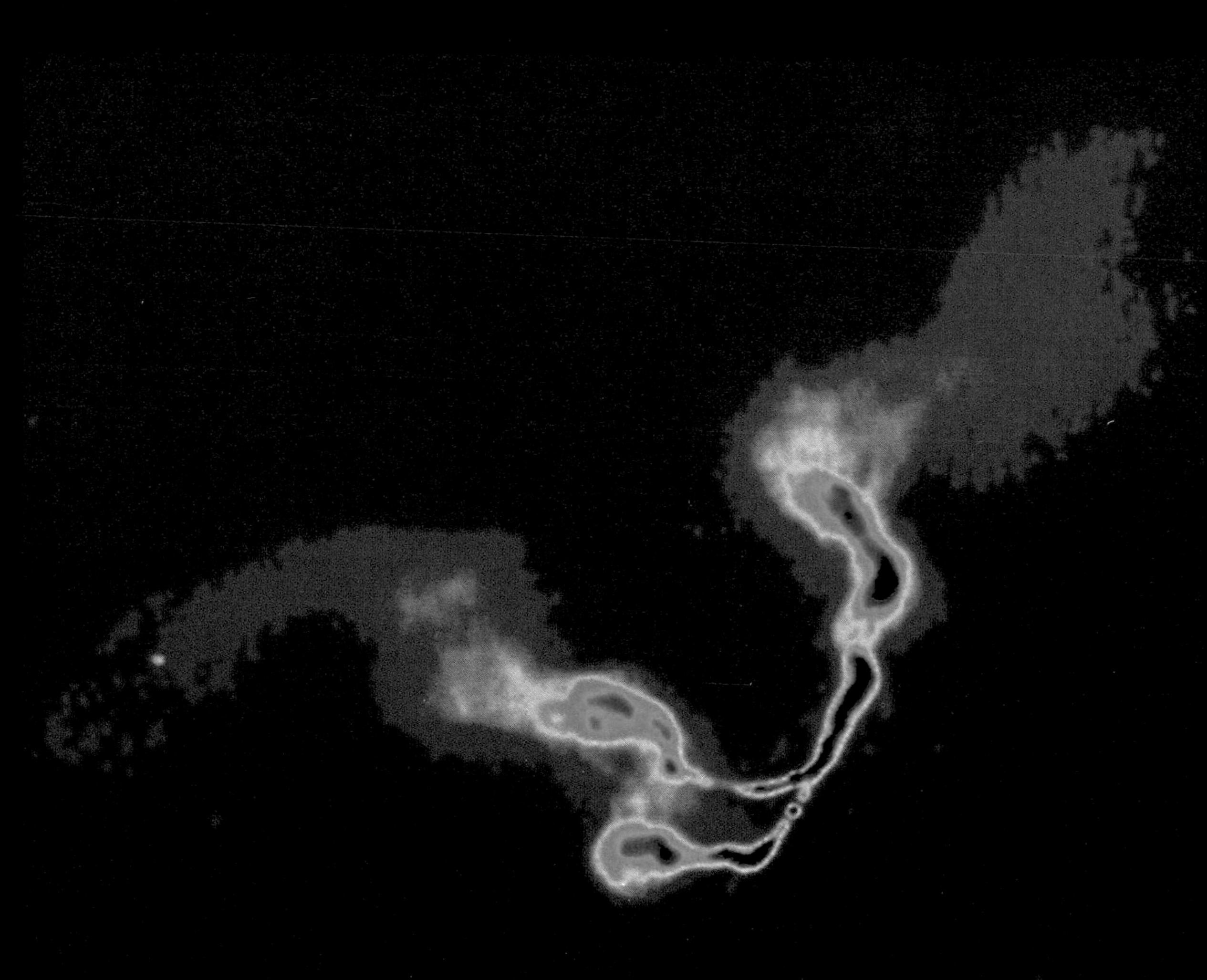